This book provides a clear, well-written and stimulating guide to key debates and issues in contemporary US foreign policy. It will both inform and provoke debate about this hugely important, and equally controversial, subject.

Professor Mark Phythian, University of Leicester, UK

This book delivers on its promise of being lively and opinionated. In addition it is thoughtful and well-informed. These esteemed academics tackle the key issues of the day with aplomb.

Brendon O'Connor, Associate Professor in American Politics, United States Studies Centre, University of Sydney, Australia

New Directions in US Foreign Policy

New Directions in US Foreign Policy is a state of the art overview of US foreign policy, providing a comprehensive account of the latest theoretical perspectives, the key actors and issues, and new policy directions. Offering a detailed and systematic outline of the field, this text:

- Explains how international relations theories such as Realism, Liberalism and Constructivism can help us to interpret US foreign policy.
- Examines the key influential actors shaping foreign policy, from political parties and think tanks to religious groups and public opinion.
- Explores the most important new policy directions from the 'war on terror' and relations with the UN to democracy promotion and American 'imperialism'.
- Supplies succinct presentation of relevant case material, and provides recommendations for further reading and web sources for pursuing future research.

Written by a distinguished line-up of contributors actively engaged in original research on the topics covered, this text provides a unique platform for rigorous debate over the contentious issues that surround US foreign policy. This wide-ranging text is essential reading for all students and scholars of US foreign policy.

Inderjeet Parmar is Professor of Government and Head of the Department of Politics, University of Manchester, UK. He has published several monographs and is the co-editor of the *Routledge Studies in US Foreign Policy* series.

Linda B. Miller is Professor of Political Science, Emerita, at Wellesley College, MA, USA. An international relations specialist, she has also taught at Barnard, Harvard, and Brown and held research appointments at Princeton, Harvard, Columbia, and Brown, where she is currently Adjunct Professor (Research) at the Watson Institute.

Mark Ledwidge is an Honorary Research Fellow and Visiting Lecturer in American Politics at the University of Warwick and in the Department of Politics, University of Manchester, UK.

Contributors: Donald E. Abelson, Christopher Candland, Mick Cox, Stuart Croft, David Hastings Dunn, Aggie Hirst, Steven Hurst, Richard Jackson, Thomas M. Kane, Nicholas Kitchen, Mark Ledwidge, Timothy J. Lynch, Jim McCormick, Matt McDonald, Linda B. Miller, Martyn Mos, Craig N. Murphy, Inderjeet Parmar, Giles Scott-Smith, Robert Singh and Doug Stokes.

Routledge Studies in US Foreign Policy

Edited by Inderjeet Parmar, University of Manchester and John Dumbrell, University of Durham

This new series sets out to publish high quality works by leading and emerging scholars critically engaging with US foreign policy. The series welcomes a variety of approaches to the subject and draws on scholarship from international relations, security studies, international political economy, foreign policy analysis and contemporary international history.

Subjects covered include the role of administrations and institutions, the media, think tanks, ideologues and intellectuals, elites, transnational corporations, public opinion, and pressure groups in shaping foreign policy, US relations with individual nations, with global regions and global institutions and America's evolving strategic and military policies.

The series aims to provide a range of books – from individual research monographs and edited collections to textbooks and supplemental reading for scholars, researchers, policy analysts, and students.

United States Foreign Policy and National Identity in the Twenty-first Century
Edited by Kenneth Christie

New Directions in US Foreign Policy
Edited by Inderjeet Parmar, Linda B. Miller and Mark Ledwidge

New Directions in US Foreign Policy

Edited by
Inderjeet Parmar, Linda B. Miller and
Mark Ledwidge

Routledge
Taylor & Francis Group

LONDON AND NEW YORK

First published 2009 by Routledge
2 Park Square, Milton Park, Abingdon, Oxon OX14 4RN

Simultaneously published in the USA and Canada
by Routledge
270 Madison Avenue, New York, NY 10016

Reprinted 2009

Routledge is an imprint of the Taylor & Francis Group, an informa business

Typeset in Times New Roman by
Taylor & Francis Books
Printed and bound in Great Britain by
TJ International Ltd, Padstow, Cornwall

British Library Cataloguing in Publication Data
A catalogue record for this book is available from the British Library

Library of Congress Cataloging in Publication Data
New directions in US foreign policy / edited by Inderjeet Parmar, Linda B. Miller and
Mark Ledwidge.
　　p. cm. – (Routledge studies in US foreign policy)
　　1. United States–Foreign relations–2001– I. Parmar, Inderjeet. II. Miller, Linda B.
III. Ledwidge, Mark.
　JZ1480.N48 2009
　327.73–dc22
　　　　　　　　　　　　2008045131

ISBN13: 978-0-415-77748-3 (hbk)
ISBN13: 978-0-415-77749-0 (pbk)
ISBN13: 978-0-203-87881-1 (ebk)

Contents

Illustrations

Figures

Tables

Contributors

Donald E. Abelson is Professor, Chair of the Department of Political Science, and Director, Centre for American Studies, at the University of Western Ontario. His publications on think tanks include: *Do Think Tanks Matter? Assessing the Impact of Public Policy Institutes* which was translated into Arabic by the Emirates Center for Strategic Studies and Research, 2007; and *A Capitol Idea: Think Tanks and US Foreign Policy* (Montreal and Kingston: McGill-Queen's University Press, 2006).

Christopher Candland is an Assistant Professor of Political Science at Wellesley College, USA.

Michael Cox is Professor of International Relations at the London School of Economics and Political Science. The author of numerous books and journal articles, Michael is currently editing the leading journal, *International Politics*.

Stuart Croft is Professor of International Security at Warwick University. He is currently Director of the ESRC/AHRC Foreign and Commonwealth Office funded programme in *New Security Challenges*, and from 2009, Chair of the British International Studies Association. His most recent book was *Culture, Crisis and America's War on Terror* (Cambridge: Cambridge University Press, 2006). He was guest editor of special issues of *International Relations* in December 2006 (vol. 20 no. 4), and of *Government and Opposition* in the summer of 2007 (vol. 42, no. 3), and has recently published articles in *International Affairs, International Politics, Defence Studies* and *The Journal of Homeland Security*.

David Hastings Dunn is Reader in International Relations at the University of Birmingham.

Aggie Hirst is a doctoral candidate in the Department of Politics at the University of Manchester.

Steven Hurst has a PhD from the University of Lancaster and is Senior Lecturer in the Department of Politics and Philosophy, Manchester Metropolitan University. He is the author of *Cold War US Foreign Policy* and *The United States and Iraq since 1979* (forthcoming 2009).

Richard Jackson is Reader in the Department of International Politics, Aberystwyth University, where he is also the Deputy Director of the Centre for the Study of Radicalisation and Contemporary Political Violence. He is the founding editor of the journal, *Critical Studies on Terrorism*, and the author of *Writing the War on*

Terrorism: Language, Politics and Counterterrorism (Manchester: Manchester University Press, 2005). He is co-editor and co-author of three forthcoming volumes, including: *Critical Terrorism Studies: A New Research Agenda*, co-edited with Marie Breen Smyth and Jeroen Gunning (Routledge, forthcoming 2009), *Contemporary State Terrorism: Theory and Cases*, co-edited with Eamon Murphy and Scott Poynting (Routledge, forthcoming 2009), and *Conflict Resolution in the Twenty-first Century: Principles, Methods and Approaches*, co-authored with Jacob Bercovitch (Michigan University Press, forthcoming 2009).

Thomas M. Kane is a Lecturer in International Politics and Strategic Studies at the University of Hull. His recent publications include: *Emerging Conflicts of Principle: International Relations and the Clash between Cosmopolitanism and Republicanism* (Aldershot: Ashgate, 2008); *Ancient China on Postmodern War* (Abingdon: Routledge, 2007) and *Theoretical Roots of US Foreign Policy* (Abingdon: Routledge, 2006).

Nicholas Kitchen is a PhD candidate in the Department of International Relations, London School of Economics. He has a MRes in International Relations from Keele University and a BA in Philosophy, Politics and Economics from Oxford University. He is currently working on US grand strategy debates in the 1990s with Professor Michael Cox, and is co-managing editor of the journal *Cold War History*. Nick is responsible for the IDEAS website and IDEAS research publications.

Mark Ledwidge is currently Visiting Lecturer in American Politics at the University of Warwick and Honorary Research Fellow in the Department of Politics at the University of Manchester. Achieving his doctorate at Manchester, he is currently writing a number of journal articles. His research monograph on the African-American Foreign Affairs Network is to be published by Routledge in 2010.

Timothy J. Lynch has a BA from East Anglia, an MA from London and received his PhD from Boston College. He is a Senior Lecturer in US Foreign Policy at the Institute for the Study of the Americas, School of Advanced Study, University of London. He is the author of *Turf War: The Clinton Administration and Northern Ireland* (Aldershot: Ashgate, 2004) and, with Robert Singh, *After Bush: The Case for Continuity in American Foreign Policy* (Cambridge: Cambridge University Press, 2008). He is currently writing a history of US foreign policy after the Cold War for the CUP Essential Histories Series.

James M. McCormick is Professor and Chair of the Department of Political Science at Iowa State University. He received his PhD from Michigan State University in 1973. He is also a former American Political Science Association Congressional Fellow (1986–87), and was co-editor of *International Studies Quarterly* (1999–2003). Professor McCormick has authored or edited nine books, including the fifth edition of *American Foreign Policy and Process* (Cengage/Wadsworth, 2009) and the fifth edition of *The Domestic Sources of American Foreign Policy: Insights and Evidence,* co-edited with Eugene R. Wittkopf (Lanham, MD: Rowman & Littlefield, 2008). In addition, he has published more than fifty book chapters and articles in such journals as *World Politics, American Political Science Review, American Journal of Political Science, The Journal of Politics, International Studies Quarterly*, and *Legislative Studies Quarterly*. He was a recipient of the Iowa State University Foundation Award for Outstanding Research at Mid-Career in 1990, a Fulbright Senior

Scholar Award to New Zealand in 1993, the Fulbright-SyCip Distinguished Lecturer Award to the Philippines in 2003, and the 2004 Iowa State University College of Liberal Arts and Sciences Award for Outstanding Achievement in Departmental Leadership. He is currently vice-president of the Foreign Policy Analysis Section of the International Studies Association.

Matt McDonald is Associate Professor in International Security in the Department of Politics and International Studies at the University of Warwick. His central research interests are in the area of critical theoretical approaches to security, and their application to environmental change; Australian foreign and security policy; and the 'war on terror'. He has published articles on these themes in journals such as *European Journal of International Relations, Review of International Studies, International Relations, Global Society*, and *Australian Journal of Political Science*. He is co-author (with Anthony Burke) of *Critical Security in the Asia-Pacific* (Manchester: Manchester University Press, 2007), and is completing an ESRC-funded project (with Richard Jackson) on the coalition of the willing and the construction of the 'War on Terror'.

Linda B. Miller is Professor of Political Science, Emerita, at Wellesley College, USA, and Adjunct Professor of International Studies (Research) at Brown University, USA, where she teaches and writes about American foreign policy. She is also the American Editor of *Argentia*, the electronic newsletter of BISA's US Foreign Policy Working Group. Widely published in US, British and Israeli journals, she is also the author of *World Order and Local Disorder: The United Nations and Civil Strife* (1967), and *Ideas and Ideals: Essay on Politics in Honor of Stanley Hoffmann* (1993).

Martijn Mos graduated summa cum laude in Liberal Arts and Sciences from Roosevelt Academy, Utrecht University, The Netherlands. He is currently enrolled in an Erasmus Mundus graduate programme on Global Studies at the Universities of Vienna and Leipzig, specialising in global history and globalisation from a European perspective. Upon completion of this programme, he envisions continuing his academic career in the field of European Studies.

Craig N. Murphy is M. Margaret Ball Professor of International Relations at Wellesley College, USA, where he teaches courses in comparative politics, international relations, North–South relations and peace studies. He also works for the United Nations Development Programme as its historian. Professor Murphy's research focuses on international institutions and the political economy of inequality across lines of gender, class, ethnicity, race, and geography. His book *The United Nations Development Programme: A Better Way?* (Cambridge: Cambridge University Press, 2006) is a critical history of the UN's efforts in the developing world. His articles have appeared in many policy and scholarly journals, including *Contemporary Security Policy, The Democratic Leaders of the Asia-Pacific Forum, International Affairs, International Interactions, International Organization, International Political Science Review, International Studies Quarterly, Millennium, New Political Economy, Polity*, and *TransAfrica Forum*.

Inderjeet Parmar is Professor of Government and Head of Politics at the University of Manchester. He is vice chair of the British International Studies Association (BISA), and is currently co-convenor of the BISA Working Group on US Foreign Policy. He is currently writing a research monograph, *Foundations of the American Century: Rockefeller, Carnegie and Ford Foundations and US Foreign Affairs, 1917–2005* (New York: Columbia University Press).

Giles Scott-Smith is Senior Researcher at the Roosevelt Study Centre and Associate Professor in International Relations at the Roosevelt Academy, both in Middelburg, the Netherlands. In 2009, he will occupy the Ernst van der Beugel Chair in the History of Transatlantic Diplomatic Relations at Leiden University. His research interests cover the theory and practice of public diplomacy and the role of private organisations in international relations. He has published *The Politics of Apolitical Culture: The Congress for Cultural Freedom, the CIA and Postwar American Hegemony* (London: Routledge 2002), *Networks of Empire: The US State Department's Foreign Leader Program in the Netherlands, France and Britain 1950–1970* (New York: Peter Lang, 2008), and numerous articles in such journals as *Cold War History, Journal of American Studies, Journal of European Integration History, Foundations of Science, British Journal of Politics and International Relations*, and the *Annals of the American Academy of Political and Social Science*.

Robert Singh is Professor of Politics in the School of Politics and Sociology at Birkbeck College, University of London. He is co-editor of *The Bush Doctrine and the War on Terrorism: Global Responses, Global Consequences* (London: Routledge, 2006) and co-author of *After Bush: The Case For Continuity in American Foreign Policy* (New York: Cambridge University Press, 2008).

Doug Stokes is a Senior Lecturer at the University of Kent, Canterbury. He has published widely in the area of US foreign policy. His latest book, *Imperial Logics: Global Energy Security and US Intervention* (Baltimore, MD: Johns Hopkins University Press, 2009) examines the human rights implications of the increased use of US counter-insurgency warfare to stabilise oil-rich non-Middle Eastern states in Africa, South America and Central Asia, and the increased rivalry for diminishing energy supplies among the industrialised nations.

Introduction

*Inderjeet Parmar, Linda B. Miller
and Mark Ledwidge*

This is a textbook with a difference: one written by scholars who are actively engaged in original research on the topics covered in this volume, who have their own particular standpoints that they are willing openly to debate, and who frequently disagree. And that is surely what American foreign policy has recently been, and is, (and if the authors are to be believed, will continue to be) characterised by: vigorous, contentious – if not violent – debate the world over. Indeed, the scholars gathered here are symptomatic of the worldwide interest in the character and deployment of American power and of its foreign and national security policy responses. The terrorist attacks on New York and Washington, DC, on 11 September, 2001, and the subsequent 'global war on terror', have generated iconic images that will long remain imprinted on the world's consciousness: smoking twin towers, Osama bin Laden, prisoners in orange jumpsuits at Guantánamo Bay detention centres, and the deadly promise of 'shock and awe'. The post-9/11 period has also brought forth further terrorist attacks – in London, Madrid, across India, Bali, etc. – as well as the Anglo-American wars on Afghanistan and Iraq, with no end in sight. Inside the United States, the Bush administration's policies have led to political division and rancorous debate: Bush, at below 30 per cent, had the lowest approval rating of any president, including Richard Nixon after the Watergate scandal. Civil liberties have been eroded as the 'Homeland defense' bureaucracy has grown in size and scope. The election of Senator Barack Obama to the US presidency was, arguably, at least in part, due to his early 'opposition' to the Iraq War – in the autumn of 2002. In (most of) the rest of the world, 'anti-Americanism' has risen to levels that disturb even the most complacent of Americans and their allies, leading to renewed calls for more effective use of America's 'soft power' to limit the damage to America's global moral authority and image (Chapter 4 on this below makes the point most clearly). American power, it may without exaggeration, be said, is on trial. The rest of the world has already made its desires known: they want change, and with Barack Obama in the White House since January 2009, they hope and pray that such an outcome will transpire. The jury, however, was entirely American and split down the middle in an historic election, the racial contours of which are explored below.

The presidency of George W. Bush is not the first to have generated such intense interest, of course, but it certainly matches the post-Vietnam era for the quantity of analysis, debate and controversy that it has ignited. It is fitting that attempts be made to assess the character and deployment of US power and foreign and national security policy across a wide range of areas, and to consider the extent to which the Bush administration has inaugurated a 'revolution' in foreign affairs likely to outlive his administration. Chapters on the war on terror and America's grand strategy, attitudes towards its transatlantic allies and international organisations, and towards the Middle East, provide a solid basis for considering where US policies came from and where they may be headed. Consideration is also given to whether America is an empire or, once again, is even in decline. This book provides scholars and students with a systematic engagement with the whole host of ways in which US foreign and national security policy has changed and may be thought about.

The rise of the non-state actor in international politics has been noted by numerous observers and policy-makers. Consequently, there are chapters on the roles of non-state actors in American foreign affairs, including political parties, racial minorities, think tanks, neoconservative intellectuals and the Christian Right. Given its democratic character, the role of public opinion is explored for its stability and structure, as a guide to what kind of foreign policies – towards Iran, North Korea, and so on – that it might sustain.

It is also clear, however, that the analysis of American foreign policy depends on our concepts and theories: the very intellectual apparatus with which we try to make sense of the world. It is an assumption of the editors of this volume that our ideas, concepts, prejudices and values matter when we think about and make sense of the world. Facts do not speak for themselves; common sense is normally made up of hardened residues of thought long past their usefulness. Consequently, the book devotes several chapters at the very beginning to the task of teasing out the principal features and critical insights provided by key schools of thought: there are offerings on realism, constructivism, liberalism, neo-conservatism and, most unusually, Marxism. Each author makes a trenchant – even opinionated – case for the efficacy of their theoretical approach, writing in a manner unusual for a textbook. But they have earned, through years of engagement with their chosen field and ideas, the right to make the claims they do. They have made the most persuasive case they can for their viewpoint: it is up to readers, in the end, to decide for themselves what to make of the ideas presented.

New Directions in US Foreign Policy therefore performs a number of functions that serve the common interests of academics and advanced students. The book is designed to consider new developments in several senses:

- *new ways of conceptualising* US foreign policy, or aspects of US foreign policy, that examine how international relations and political science theory can illuminate our understandings of those policies;
- *new empirical areas* of scholarly research and study of US foreign policy;
- *new policy directions* in regard to actual US foreign policy.

What makes this collection stand out is that it consists of research-based chapters that provide in one volume a fairly systematic overview of the field – a state-of-the-art snapshot with regard to new research, new policies and new conceptualisations. Additionally, each chapter features succinct presentation of relevant case material sufficient to illustrate its specific theme, and provides recommendations for further reading and web sources for scholars who wish to pursue additional research.

Part I

Theorising contemporary US foreign policy

1 Realism

Thomas M. Kane

> For all realists, calculations about power lie at the heart of how states think about the world around them. Power is the currency of great-power politics, and states compete for it among themselves. What money is to economics, power is to international relations.
>
> (Mearsheimer 2001: 12)

The Realist school of thought in international relations studies is notoriously diverse, but practically all Realists are likely to agree with Mearsheimer on this point. If any particular doctrine distinguishes Realism from other schools of thought, it is probably this emphasis on power (Morgenthau 1948: 5; Pangle and Ahrensdorf 1999: 13). Therefore, the contemporary United States of America offers an instructive case study for Realists of all descriptions. At the dawn of the twenty-first century, the United States of America possesses staggering quantities of power by any index one can reasonably apply.

This case study is provocative, because contemporary Realists have not been particularly effective at anticipating America's policies or their consequences. Perhaps increasing the irony, America's leaders have used their power more energetically than leading Realists considered wise. Nevertheless, Americans may be grateful to note that, as of 2008, the United States has also proven more successful at preserving its power than those influential Realist thinkers considered likely. Readers may decide for themselves whether America has remained a superpower because of its leaders' policies or in spite of them. This chapter reviews contemporary Realist writings on America's position in international politics and draws on the works of one of their intellectual ancestors, Niccolò Machiavelli, to offer an alternative explanation of recent US policy.

Although contemporary Realists have a mixed record of accounting for America's experience with supremacy, the classic works that inspired the Realist tradition remain insightful. The proto-Realist Niccolò Machiavelli lived approximately five hundred years ago in Florence, but he stands out for his success at anticipating the issues the United States and its leaders have faced in the twenty-first century. Machiavelli succeeded in large part because he was willing to think about politics in ways that contemporary Realists have rejected for their alleged lack of methodological rigour. Machiavelli sympathized with people's will to shape their political environment, he remained acutely conscious of the fact that people exercise this will in the context of specific historical circumstances and he was willing to consider the ways in which this exercise relates to all other aspects of human thought and experience. The Florentine's method is a poor technique for formulating general theories, but it appears to be an effective approach to understanding human affairs.

America's experiences also remind us how Machiavelli earned his sinister reputation. The Florentine advocated policies of preventative war much like the one the G.W. Bush administration has implemented in practice. Machiavelli was also content to accept the consequences of such policies – but many Americans, for compelling reasons of prudence and principle, are not. The Florentine is a penetrating analyst but a dangerous advisor.

This chapter demonstrates the fact that Machiavelli's insights remain at least as accurate as those of contemporary Realist writers and explores the reasons why this is so. The next section outlines the contemporary Realist response to America's rise. The third section summarizes America's actual policy under G.W. Bush. The fourth section details Machiavelli's success at anticipating this policy, and the fifth section notes the reasons why, despite the Florentine's insight, he remains a treacherous guide for Americans. Finally, the concluding section reflects on the strengths and dangers of Machiavelli's approach.

As simple as possible

> Make everything as simple as possible – but not simpler.
>
> (Albert Einstein, quoted in 2008)

Few Realists of the 1970s or 1980s anticipated America's rise to supremacy (Gaddis 1992–3: 5–58; Gaddis and Hopf 1993: 202–10). The very fact that America had held superpower status since 1945 inclined many followers of this school of thought to predict its imminent decline. As scholar Michael Cox generalises, most Realists subscribe to the idea that there are 'certain basic laws governing the international system, the most important of which [is] that all empires [have] a finite lifespan' (Cox 2007: 645). Cox identifies statesman and self-described Realist Henry Kissinger as an influential advocate of this position (ibid.: 645). Kenneth Waltz, founder of the prominent Neorealist branch of Realist theory, espouses it as well (Waltz 2000: 37).

Thus, in 1981, Robert Gilpin could note that expectation of America's imminent decline was the 'prevalent view' within the international relations discipline (Gilpin 1981: 49). Gilpin himself suggested no reason to challenge this common wisdom, at least on that occasion. There were, in fact, numerous scholars who wrote about the trends that ultimately led to the dissolution of the Soviet Union and the subsequent rise of America – but the Realist-dominated mainstream of the international relations discipline largely ignored them.

Adam Roberts, in his valedictory lecture at Oxford University, provided an impressive list of such scholars (Roberts 2008: 338–42). Roberts notes that the commentators who analysed the trends that had taken America to its current position in world politics most perceptively were the ones who rejected tenets shared by most contemporary versions of Realism. Those who failed to understand the later years of the Cold War, Roberts argues:

> were those who have made the boldest claims to being capable of foreseeing and influencing the future, and whose supposedly scientific methodologies have tended to be parsimonious, seeking to explain outcomes in terms of a limited range of considerations. With their emphasis on states and international systems, they have

often played down the domestic and human dimension of decision-making. They have tended to place more reliance on abstract reasoning and hard facts than on understanding foreign languages and cultures. They have often missed the uniqueness of particular individuals, situations and moments.

(ibid.: 338–9)

The founders of contemporary Realism have explicitly embraced this parsimonious emphasis on states, systems of states, generalities and abstractions. Morgenthau, for instance, wrote his seminal *Politics among Nations* to 'detect and understand the forces that determine political relations among nations' (Morgenthau 1948: 18). These forces, he writes elsewhere, are 'inherent in human nature' and thus independent of culture, ideology, domestic constitutions, individual personalities, and other particularities (ibid.: 3–4). Twenty-first-century Realist thinkers have confirmed their commitment to this reductionist, state-centric approach even more explicitly and in even more absolute terms. (Mearsheimer 2001: 17–18).

This parsimonious Realism has influenced political studies throughout the world, but it has been particularly popular in American universities, where, indeed, it often overshadows all other approaches to the study of international politics (Smith 2002: 67–85). Roberts suggests that this explains why relatively few of the scholars who anticipated America's rise to temporarily unchallenged supremacy were themselves Americans (Roberts 2008: 338–9). Roberts goes on to note that 'the end of the Cold War caused particularly deep soul-searching' among many scholars, Americans in particular. This soul-searching, Roberts suggests, prompted many international relations theorists to turn to the school of thought known as constructivism (ibid.: 339). Perhaps ironically, Alexander Wendt's influential constructivist work *Social Theory of International Politics* also takes an abstract approach focusing on states and systems of states (Wendt 1999: 11).

Meanwhile, having acknowledged the end of the Cold War, committed Realists have explored the implications of America's newfound dominance. Unsurprisingly, different branches of Realist thought suggested different responses to US hegemony. Michael Mastanduno, for instance, drew on Realist thinker Stephen Walt's so-called balance-of-threat theory to propose a scenario in which Washington might prolong its period of hegemony by convincing potential competitors that its intentions were benign, and by using its power to defend a world order that other capable nations recognised as desirable (Mastanduno 1997: 59–61). Mastanduno examined actual US behaviour circa 1997 and found that America followed this approach in its security policies, but fell back on the more aggressive approaches predicted by other branches of Realism when dealing with economic issues (ibid.: 49–88). (One can only speculate about whether Mastanduno might have come to different conclusions if he had continued his study to include G.W. Bush's presidency.)

Other Realists of the 1990s proposed similar ideas to those of Stephen Walt. In a 1995 article entitled 'Realists as Optimists', Charles Glaser develops the idea that strong states can maintain peace and, in fact, preserve their own position of supremacy by reassuring potential competitors that they will use their power in a commonly approved fashion (Glaser 1994–5: 50–90). Although William Wohlforth did not explicitly base his 1999 article 'The Stability of a Unipolar World' on any particular work of Realist theory, he found that the United States was successfully behaving much as Walt and Glaser might have suggested (Wohlforth 1999: 5–41). The main threat to

America's continued hegemony, Wohlforth warned, was that Americans might balk at the various costs of preserving it (ibid.: 40).

In offering this warning, Wohlforth repeated a point Mastanduno made in his 1997 article. Mastanduno also offered Americans several other pieces of advice, incorporating insights from the relatively benign interpretations of Realism. Having found that Washington tended to behave more aggressively in its economic dealings than in security issues, Mastanduno reminded US leaders not to let their competitive trade policies undermine their attempts to sustain cooperative security relationships (Mastanduno 1997: 86–7). Mastanduno went on to argue that:

> U.S. officials must manage what might be called the arrogance of power. The dominant state in any international order faces strong temptations to go it alone, to dictate rather than to consult, to preach its virtues and to impose its values.
>
> (ibid.: 88)

When dominant powers succumb to such arrogance, Mastanduno warned, they turn supporters into competitors, destroying the consensus that allowed them to maintain their position in world politics. After that, the bitter international competition associated with gloomier versions of Realism is likely to return. As a relative optimist, Mastanduno believed that American leaders could restrain the impulse to 'go it alone' for a time, so that, in his words, the 'transition to a new international order' might be 'prolonged' (ibid.: 88). Realist thinker Kenneth Waltz has made similar points about the inevitable lure of unilateralism and the equally inevitable consequences of yielding to it, but he doubted that Americans could resist either the temptation or the result even for the briefest of periods (Waltz 2000: 36–8).

Optimistic Realists were, moreover, always a minority. Mastanduno and Wohlforth themselves acknowledged this point (Mastanduno 1997: 52; Wohlforth 1999: 6). In 1993, Christopher Layne asserted the more traditional Realist view in his article 'The Unipolar Illusion: Why New Great Powers Will Rise' (Layne 1993: 5–51). Layne based his argument on the version of Realist thought known as Structural Realism. Most particularly, he based his ideas on arch-Structuralist Kenneth Waltz's contention that the very fact that one state has become excessively powerful drives other states to 'balance' its power by joining forces against it. (ibid.: 7). Layne continued to develop this theme throughout the 1990s (Layne 1997: 86–124). Waltz himself reiterated it in 2000, identifying Russia and China as the states most likely to take the lead in curbing American power (Waltz 2000: 36–8).

In Waltz's and Layne's view, there is only one feasible way for America to proceed. America must accept the fact of its decline, refrain from wasting its diminishing political capital on attempts to retain hegemony and use the resources it can still muster to 'balance' against whatever new powers bid for its place (Layne 1993: 47). Layne claimed that this was a controversial view among Realists. In 1997, he wrote that both so-called Defensive Realists and so-called Offensive Realists were urging America to hold onto 'preponderance' (Layne 1997: 92). Layne identified the previously mentioned optimist Stephen Walt as a primary example of a Defensive Realist, along with Barry Posen, Jack Snyder and Stephen van Evera (ibid.: 92).

As for Offensive Realism, Layne named John J. Mearsheimer as its 'leading academic proponent' (ibid.: 92). Therefore, it is noteworthy that when Mearsheimer articulated the principles of Offensive Realism in *The Tragedy of Great Power Politics,* he gave American policy-makers much the same advice as Layne himself. Layne was correct to note that Mearsheimer assumed that America's overall goal would be that of maintaining its preponderance. In Mearsheimer's own words, '[t]he United States does not want a peer competitor' (Mearsheimer 2001: 387). Mearsheimer added his belief that Americans would be particularly unwise to permit the People's Republic of China to assume that role. (ibid.: 401–2).

Nevertheless, despite the fact that Mearsheimer disagrees with Layne over the issue of what America aims to achieve in the abstract, he shares the other Realist's views about the actual policies America should adopt in practice. Like Layne, Mearsheimer believes that the twenty-first-century world will be multipolar (ibid.: 362). Like Layne, Mearsheimer urges the USA to withdraw its troops from overseas bases, despite the fact that America will inevitably lose some control over international events as a consequence (ibid.: 386–9). Like Layne, Mearsheimer justifies these arguments on the grounds that this policy will insulate the United States from conflict and 'maximize its relative power position' (ibid.: 389).

Mearsheimer writes:

> It would be best for the United States either not to become involved in the fighting or, if it had to join the war, to do so later rather than earlier. That way the United States would pay a much smaller price than would the states that fought from start to finish, and it would be well-positioned at the war's end to win the peace and shape the postwar world to its advantage.
>
> (ibid.: 389)

Thus, by the early twenty-first century, many of the most influential Realist thinkers believed that the world was inevitably becoming multipolar. Those theorists believed that America's most promising response would be to adopt a restrained policy of what contemporary Realists refer to as 'offshore balancing' (Layne 1997: 86–124; Mearsheimer 2001: 392). Many had specifically identified Russia and China as America's most likely antagonists. Mearsheimer, at least, urged Americans to view the latter as the greatest threat (Mearsheimer 2001: 401–2). Such ideas followed logically from Realism's most widely-held premises. By 2000, such opinions had become, to borrow Gilpin's phrase, the prevalent view.

Theory and practice

When George W. Bush took office as president of the United States, his early rhetoric suggested that he might follow the prevailing Realist advice. From the terrorist attacks of 11 September 2001 onward, he has done almost the opposite. Where mainstream Realists advised America to withdraw its armed forces from overseas deployments, the G.W. Bush administration has sought new bases in Poland, Hungary, Romania, Bulgaria, Azerbaijan, Uzbekistan, Tajikistan, Kyrgyzstan, Morocco, Algeria, Tunisia, Senegal, Ghana, Mali and Kenya. Where mainstream Realists advised America to commit its armed forces to overseas wars 'later rather than earlier' the G.W. Bush administration adopted a national security strategy of preventing 'hostile acts by our adversaries' by striking first (The White House 2002: 15). The G.W. Bush administration has since implemented that strategy, not against states that had the potential to challenge its dominant position within the international system, but against the relatively non-threatening (in structural Realist terms) governments of Afghanistan and Iraq. Optimistic Realists must be dismayed to see how flagrantly the G.W. Bush administration has chosen to proceed unilaterally, cooperating only with allies that accept its lead.

Rather than 'balancing' America, Russia initially supported the G.W. Bush Administration's policies. On 24 September 2001, Russian President Vladimir Putin announced a five-point programme of assistance to US-backed operations in Afghanistan. This programme included a successful diplomatic campaign to pressure Uzbekistan, Kyrgyzstan and Tajikistan into providing bases for US forces (*East Asian Strategic Review 2007* 2007: 40–1). Russia later turned against the Bush administration's policies. Chinese representatives have been more consistent in opposing US actions, although even China supported invading Afghanistan in principle (ibid.: 42).

Mainstream Realists may take satisfaction from the fact that many Americans, including prominent G.W. Bush administration supporters, have come to rue invading Afghanistan and Iraq. Nevertheless, before such Realists say 'we told you so', they must note that America's regrets have little to do with the dangers they warned about. Russian and Chinese leaders commonly express their desire to 'balance' US power, but they have taken little overt action to interfere with American policies, even diplomatically. In 2003, for instance, it was French Foreign Minister Dominique de Villepin who rallied international opposition to America's plans to invade Iraq in an impromptu press conference G.W. Bush administration insiders dubbed the 'Day of Diplomatic Ambush', and de Villepin again who spoke first in opposing a United Nations Security Council resolution that would have effectively authorised the United States to put its plans into effect (Burrough *et al.*: 2004: 177, 179). Up until that point, Russian representatives had at least suggested that they might yield to America's wishes (ibid.: 179). Mearsheimer, one might note, dismisses all the Western European nations, including France, as insignificant (Mearsheimer 2001: 382).

Since 2003, America's most damaging antagonists in Iraq have not been states of any sort, but the loosely organised movement of gangsters, semi-independent militia organisations and religiously inspired militants commonly known as the insurgency. This insurgency recruits its fighters from many nations, including America's allies. State governments undoubtedly use elements of this insurgency as proxies, but even Mearsheimer might find it difficult to represent the relationships involved meaningfully in terms of mechanical interactions among featureless billiard balls.

The events of the early twenty-first century have not contradicted mainstream Realist predictions as straightforwardly as the events of 1989–91 contradicted the dominant Realist views of that time. Nevertheless, contemporary Realists must concede that America has not adopted the policies they presented as effective. Russia and China have come closer to following the Realists' model, but even their dealings have been subtler and more varied than writers such as Waltz and Mearsheimer seemed to predict. Moreover, the immediate consequences of America's policies have not been the consequences Realist thinkers wrote about most extensively. Although this section has focused on comparing the events of 2001–8 with the influential versions of Structural Realism articulated by Waltz, Layne and Mearshehimer, one may note that dissenters such as Glaser and Walt were little more – or less – successful at accounting for the history of the first decade of the twenty-first century.

Realists are entitled to counter these points with a variety of observations. Such thinkers might, for instance, argue that G.W. Bush has behaved foolishly.

Contemporary Realists must, however, exercise caution when attributing historical events to the stupidity of decision-makers. As earlier sections have noted, most twentieth- and twenty-first-century Realists seek to explain state behaviour in abstract terms, without reference to domestic politics or individual personalities.

More significantly, most branches of contemporary Realism conflate prescription and prediction. Most contemporary Realists seek to understand international politics in terms of what Morgenthau called objective laws (Morgenthau 1948: 4). The more freedom state leaders have to disregard those laws, the less Realist theory is good for. Most Realists acknowledge that leaders do violate Realist principles in practice. Nevertheless, Realists from Morgenthau onward have also maintained that such violations are irrational (ibid.: 7). Since those who persist in irrational behaviour are unlikely to succeed – or to survive – for long, this implies that lawbreaking will be short-lived, and that Realist behaviour will govern international relations most of the time.

Thus, Realists are free to argue that America's policies under G.W. Bush were a momentary folly, and that, one way or another, the objective laws of international politics will re-assert themselves. This raises the question of how much time those laws will require. In 1993, Layne predicted that American hegemony would give way to multipolarity between 2000 and 2010 (Layne 1993: 7). In 2001, Mearshehimer predicted that 'existing power structures in Europe and Northeast Asia' would revert to multipolarity and bloody interstate competition by 2020 (Mearsheimer 2001: 385). As of 2007, M.J. Williams could make a persuasive case that America's economic and, presumably military, capabilities rested on stronger foundations than any of its possible rivals, and that America was likely to 'play a principal role in world politics for at least the next fifty years' (Williams 2007: 945).

At the time of this writing, in 2008, American political leaders show no more interest in adopting a policy of offshore balancing than they have showed since 2001. To the contrary, the presidential nominees of both major parties have emphasised their willingness to wage a third preventative war against Iran (Bohan 2008; Haberman 2008). The presidential candidates presumably believe that this is what their constituents expect of them, but this only begs the question of why so many voters should remain loyal to costly policies that Realist theory portrays as irrational. Some may be content to take this as further evidence that the United States is a nation of lunatics. Those who believe that people, including Americans, have at least a qualified capacity for reason may wonder whether G.W. Bush's approach to foreign policy might fulfil some sort of rational purpose that contemporary Realists have neglected.

The method to the madness?

Niccolò Machiavelli would have found America's policy of preventative war perfectly logical. One fundamental reason why he would have understood America's twenty-first-century course of action more accurately than most contemporary Realists is that he took a different view of human agency. Like contemporary Realists, he assumed that knowable principles – Morgenthau might say objective laws – govern political relationships. Like contemporary Realists, he believed that certain of those principles cause states which were once successful to become corrupt and collapse (Machiavelli 1940: 111–14). Machiavelli, however, urged readers to do something about it.

Most contemporary Realists would view such advice as misguided. Morgenthau spoke for his intellectual successors when he intoned that Realism 'believes that the world, imperfect as it is … is the result of forces inherent in human nature. To improve the world, one must work with those forces, not against them' (Morgenthau 1948: 3). Those inspired by Waltz's structural version of Realism might prefer to talk about forces inherent within the international system, but the advice would remain similar.

Machiavelli did not overlook Morgenthau's points. 'It is not unknown to me', the Florentine wrote, 'how many have been and are of opinion that worldly events are so governed by fortune and by God, that men cannot by their prudence change them' (Machiavelli 1940: 91). Ceasing to mention the Christian divinity, Machiavelli personifies the forces beyond human control as the Roman goddess Fortuna, and writes:

> I would compare her to an impetuous river that, when turbulent, inundates the plains, casts down trees and buildings, removes earth from this side and places it on the other; everyone flees before it, and everything yields to its fury without being able to oppose it; and yet, although it is of such a kind, still when it is quiet, men can make provision against it by dykes and banks, so that when it rises it will either go into a canal or its rush will not be so wild and dangerous.
>
> (ibid.: 91)

One notes that Machiavelli's concept of Fortuna includes more than random chance. The timing and potency of the floods seem random. They are, at least, unpredictable. The presence of the river, by contrast, is certain, albeit beyond anyone's control. Other natural properties of the river will be both known and unknown, both fixed and malleable, in varying degrees and in myriad combinations. All of this is within Fortuna's realm.

The basic logic and psychology of political relationships appear to be within Fortuna's realm as well. There may be – as Machiavelli believes that there is – a natural process that causes powerful states to fall. People cannot wish that process away, any more than the valley dwellers can wish away the river. Nevertheless, people can find – and, perhaps, create – opportunities to modify the way in which that process affects their own community at any particular time.

Furthermore, unlike many contemporary Realists, Machiavelli distinguished between different types of states with different types of governments. The Florentine was particularly interested in republics. A republic, influential Machiavellian scholar J.G.A. Pocock tells us, is a community specifically organised to take control of its own destiny (Pocock 1975: viii). The United States of America is formally constituted as a republic and has been committed to this particular goal ever since its founders pledged their lives, fortunes and sacred honor to establishing the thirteen colonies' ability to do all the 'acts and things which independent states may of right do' (Maier 1997: 241). Thus, Machiavelli's advice on overcoming Fortuna should be especially relevant to the United States.

As it happens, the individuals who developed the G.W. Bush administration's foreign policy explicitly agreed with Machiavelli on the importance of mastering Fortuna. Such senior administration figures as Secretary of Defense, Donald Rumsfeld, and Special Assistant to the President, Elliott Abrams, expressed their collective views on international affairs by signing the Project for a New American Century (PNAC)'s 1997 *Statement of Principles* (*Project for the New American Century Statement of Principles* 1997). This statement featured the question 'does the United States have the resolve to shape a new century favorable to American principles and interests?' (ibid.). Signatories presumably hoped that the answer would prove to be yes.

Elsewhere, the *Statement* affirms that 'the history of the twentieth century should have taught us that it is important to shape circumstances before crises emerge, and to meet threats before they become dire' (ibid.). One notes that the *Statement*, like Machiavelli, presents this issue in terms of actively one's shaping circumstances, not in terms of passively adapting to them. Although Rumsfeld and his colleagues signed the *Statement* as private citizens, the G.W. Bush administration adopted a striking number of its proposals into its 2002 and 2006 National Security Strategies (White House 2002; 2006). In short, those responsible for America's foreign policy in the first decade of the twenty-first century perceived this fundamental aspect of their task much as Machiavelli depicted it.

Many contemporary Realists would respond that this does not matter. 'To search for the clue to foreign policy exclusively in the motives of statesmen', Morgenthau argued:

> is both futile and deceptive. It is futile because motives are the most illusive of psychological data, distorted as they are, frequently beyond recognition, by the interests and emotions of actor and observer alike. Do we really know what our own motives are? And what do we know of the motives of others?
>
> (Morgenthau 1948: 5–6)

Morgenthau went on to argue that, even if 'we had access to the real motives of statesmen, that knowledge would help us little in understanding foreign policies' (ibid.: 6). In his view, there is little connection between what people aspire to achieve and what they actually accomplish. There is undoubtedly a great deal of worldly wisdom in Morgenthau's view. Nevertheless, the history of American foreign policy in the first decade of the twenty-first century stands out as an example of an incident in which understanding the motives of state leaders actually does appear to explain critical elements of their policies. American political leaders understood their role in Machiavellian terms, not those of contemporary Realists. Those leaders went on, as the next paragraphs will show, to approach that task in ways that Machiavelli – if not contemporary Realists – would have found sensible.

Machiavelli often appears to have assumed that powerful states have more to fear from internal corruption than from external enemies (in this regard, he may differ from members of the G.W. Bush administration, many of whom emphasise threats from without.) Nevertheless, Machiavelli also believed that war and other foreign entanglements could spur class conflict within a community (Machiavelli 1950: 226). Handled correctly, he suggested, this conflict could actually strengthen the state. Handled incorrectly, it would precipitate the corruption that brings on catastrophe. Therefore, in Machiavelli's view, such conflict requires firm management.

Since external disputes often drive internal ones, Machiavelli reasoned that a government which wishes to manage conflict within its own territory must maximise its control over its foreign relations as well. Where most contemporary Realists attempt to separate foreign policy from domestic affairs, the Florentine saw them as linked. In this spirit, Machiavelli urged republics to emulate Rome. Rome, like America since 2001, waged a continual series of preventative wars (Machiavelli 1940: 279–81).

Because Rome started these wars, Machiavelli notes, it could do so at moments its leaders found 'advantageous' (ibid.: 279). Machiavelli's Romans attacked enemies only when they were vulnerable, and, most crucially of all, timed these campaigns to minimise the chance that they would have to contend with more than one competent opponent at a time (ibid.: 279). From a Machiavellian perspective, the fact that America overthrew the Taliban regime in Afghanistan and prepared to attack the Baathist regime in Iraq during a period when Russia and, to a lesser extent, China temporarily found it expedient to support the concept of a so-called Global War on Terrorism was more than coincidence. Machiavelli might suggest that Fortuna presented the G.W. Bush administration with the chance to destroy two persistent antagonists at relatively low risk, and that the American president took this opportunity. As for France's diplomatic ambush, Machiavelli noted that Rome was no stranger to revolts from querulous 'associates', adding that that the Romans took measures to prevent such stings from interrupting their plans (ibid.: 293).

Machiavelli also discusses the way in which Rome managed relations with its allies. The Florentine emphasises that Rome would not have been able to achieve its position if it had not succeeded at getting other states to support it. Nevertheless, Machiavelli's Romans were wary of committing themselves to 'leagues' with powerful states (Machiavelli 1950: 368). Since the members of such leagues all expect a voice in alliance decisions, organisations of this nature are poor tools for a state determined to retain control over its foreign relations. To Optimistic Realists who warn that powerful states must listen to weaker partners in order to retain their support, Machiavelli would likely have responded that such supporters turn out to be liabilities as often as they turn out to be assets (ibid.: 382). Accordingly, Rome preferred alliances – some might say coalitions of the willing – with states that would defer to its leadership.

Nor did Machiavelli overlook the consequences that normally ensue when one conquers a foreign state, whether preventatively or for any other reason. Chapters 4–7 of *The Prince* discuss the problems that can arise when one tries to establish control over a conquered opponent. Machiavelli notes that it is particularly hard to maintain control over territories which contain 'a large number of ancient nobles, recognised as such by their subjects'. The parallels between such states and Iraq, with its ethnic and religious factions and their local leaders, are strong.

Machiavelli warns that territories of this type are relatively easy to invade. Nevertheless, he notes, 'if you wish to keep possession, infinite difficulties arise' (Machiavelli 1940: 17). Rome, Machiavelli tells us, dealt with these 'difficulties' by crushing resistors so brutally that none were left even to remember who the rebels were or what they had fought for (ibid.: 17). Even for Rome, this process took generations.

The ungrateful Americans

From a Machiavellian perspective, the G.W. Bush administration's policies have succeeded. Baathist Iraq will never attack America's oil-producing allies again. More significantly, Saddam Hussein will never join forces with any of America's more capable rivals to unseat Washington as the dominant power in the Persian Gulf. Perhaps of equal importance, American society will never have to respond to the threat that such a thing might occur. The fact that America managed to eliminate Iraq's Baathist regime at a moment when that regime's stockpile of so-called weapons of mass destruction amounted to little more than the remnants of its once-extensive chemical arsenal would probably strike the Florentine as yet another example of the advantages inherent in striking first.

That insurgencies persist after seven years for Afghanistan and a mere five for Iraq would hardly have fazed the Florentine. Even the financial cost of the war to the

United States would have been unlikely to disturb him. 'Money is not the sinews of war', he opined, 'although it is commonly so considered (ibid.: 308–11). Those familiar with the intimate relationship between wealth and military capability throughout history may feel that Machiavelli is excessively glib about this subject.

Nevertheless, although Machiavelli underestimates the importance of economics in general, his points remain valid in connection to twenty-first-century America. The G.W. Bush administration spends approximately 6.2 per cent of America's gross domestic product on its armed forces (Teslik 2008). American military expenditures in the 1950s and 1960s routinely amounted to 8–10 per cent of gross national product (Sakamoto 1987). The Korean War forced the US government to spent over 13 per cent (ibid.).

These figures show that America's economy is capable of sustaining a considerably more expensive military policy than the G.W. Bush administration has pursued. A Machiavellian might add that they further illustrate the argument in favour of pre-ventative war. In the Korean War, America's superpower rivals used the smaller but militarily capable state of North Korea as a proxy. The fact that North Korea was acting in concert with stronger states played a significant role in making this war peril-ous and costly for the West. In 2003, America put off the day when America's future rivals will be able to contemplate using Iraq in a similar role. If the G.W. Bush administration needed to spend 6.2 per cent of its GDP in a time of relative economic prosperity to forestall a situation in which later American governments might have to spend twice that amount under unknowable economic conditions, a Machiavellian might view the investment as worthwhile even in purely financial terms.

Machiavelli would have been unlikely to sympathise with Americans who – rightly or wrongly – blame G.W. Bush's expenditures for inflation, the collapse of the housing market, and other threats to their personal standard of living. To the contrary, he welcomed privation as a way of stopping citizens from pursuing individual satisfactions and thus of forcing them to devote their energies to the state (Machiavelli 1940: 118). The Florentine might well have made a similar response to those who point out that G.W. Bush's policies do not appear to have been particularly successful at pro-tecting US citizens from terrorism. Machiavelli believed that one of the most important steps in preventing citizens from lapsing into selfish individualism was to keep them in a state of fear (ibid.: 397–402).

US citizens have the right to object to being deprived and bullied into collectivist behaviour. Few have ever found Machiavelli's ideas palatable. Moreover, American patriots have formal reasons to reject Machiavelli's teachings about the proper rela-tionship between citizens and their government. America's Declaration of Indepen-dence – the document that purportedly justifies the existence of the USA as a republic – states that all men, for which one may read all individual human beings, enjoy the right to pursue happiness. Human beings receive this right directly from God, whether governments – however nobly republican in their aims – find it convenient or not.

Conclusion

Machiavelli offers considerable insight into America's twenty-first-century situation. Nevertheless, those who blindly apply his methods risk producing a more Machia-vellian outcome than they might wish. The document that established the United States as a republic rejects fundamental elements of the Florentine's teaching, and although few US citizens refer to the Declaration of Independence when forming their opinions on current events, public opinion research suggests that increasing numbers are becoming increasingly disenchanted with the consequences of George W. Bush's policies (Pew Research Center 2007).

International relations scholars may find Machiavelli a dangerous teacher for intellectual reasons as well. Where contemporary Realists labour to achieve scientific detachment, Machiavelli addresses his works to specific audiences and identifies with specific causes. Machiavelli permits himself the luxury of writing in poetic language. Like the Renaissance man he literally was, he pursues his interests across whatever disciplinary boundaries they happen to cross, freely mixing what contemporary scholars call levels of analysis. From the perspective of a contemporary Realist, his writings are biased, imprecise, unmanageably dense in detail and riddled with unwarranted assumptions.

Nevertheless, Machiavelli succeeds not only at anticipating important aspects of America's foreign policy in the twenty-first century, but at explaining them. This suggests that those who wish to understand world politics in the twenty-first century do well to study his works. Moreover, the fact that the Florentine remains at least as insightful as his more methodologically puritanical successors suggests that Machiavelli's approach accounts for critical aspects of political relations in ways that approaches based purely on social scientists' interpretations of natural scientists' methods do not. We must consider Machiavelli's methods critically, in scholarship as in the practice of statecraft, but we would be foolish to dismiss him.

References

Bohan, Caren (2008) 'Obama Toughens Iran Stance, Backs Israel on Jerusalem', *Reuters*. Online. Available at: http://www.reuters.com/article/latestCrisis/idUSN04444172 (accessed 26 June 2008).

Burrough, Bryan, Peretz, Eugenia, Rose, David and Wise, David (2004) 'The Path to War', *Vanity Fair*, 102–16, 169–82.

Cox, Michael (2007) 'Is the United States in Decline – Again?', *International Affairs*, 83(4): 643–53.

East Asian Strategic Review 2007 (2007), Tokyo: National Institute for Defence Studies.

Einstein, Albert (2008) Quoted online. Available at: http://www.quotedb.com/quotes/1360 (accessed 26 June 2008).

Gaddis, John L. (1992–3) 'International Relations Theory and the End of the Cold War', *International Security*, 17(3): 5–58.

Gaddis, John L. and Hopf, Ted (1993) 'Getting the End of the Cold War Wrong', *International Security*, 18(2): 202–10.

Gilpin, Robert (1981) *War and Change in World Politics*, Cambridge: Cambridge University Press.

Glaser, Charles L. (1994–5) 'Realists as Optimists: Cooperation as Self-Help', *International Security*, 19(3): 50–90.

Haberman, Maggie (2008) 'McCain Warns of Iran in City Visit', *New York Post*. Online. Available at: http://www.nypost.com/seven/12112006/news/nationalnews/johnny_apple_nationalnews_maggie_haberman.htmable (accessed 26 June 2008).

Layne, Christopher (1993) 'The Unipolar Illusion: Why New Great Powers Will Rise', *International Security*, 17(4): 5–51.

—— (1997) 'From Preponderance to Offshore Balancing: America's Future Grand Strategy', *International Security*, 22(1): 86–124.

Machiavelli, Niccolò (1940) *The Prince and the Discourses*, trans. Luigi Ricci and Christian E. Detmold, New York: The Modern Library.

—— (1950) *The Discourses of Niccolò Machiavelli*, trans. Leslie J. Walker, London: Routledge & Kegan Paul.

Maier, Pauline (1997) *American Scripture: Making the Declaration of Independence*, New York: Alfred A. Knopf.

Mastanduno, Michael (1997) 'Preserving the Unipolar Moment: Realist Theories and U.S. Grand Strategy after the Cold War', *International Security*, 21(4): 49–88.

Mearsheimer, John J. (2001) *The Tragedy of Great Power Politics*, New York: Norton.

Morgenthau, Hans J. (1948) *Politics Among Nations: The Struggle for Power and Peace*, New York: Alfred A. Knopf.

Pangle, Thomas L. and Ahrensdorf, Peter J. (1999) *Justice Among Nations: On the Moral Basis of Power and Peace*, Lawrence, KS: University Press of Kansas.

Pew Research Center (2007) 'War Support Slips, Fewer Expect a Successful Outcome', Online. Available at: http://pewresearch.org/pubs/412/war-support-slips-fewer-see-positive-outcome (accessed 26 June 2008).

Pocock, J.G.A (1975) *The Machiavellian Moment: Florentine Political Thought and the Atlantic Republican Tradition*, Princeton, NJ: Princeton University Press.

Project for the New American Century Statement of Principles (1997) Online. Available at: http://newamericancentury.org/statementofprinciples.htm (accessed 11 September 2003).

Roberts, Adam (2008) 'International Relations after the Cold War', *International Affairs*, 84(2): 335–50.

Sakamoto, Masahiro (1987) 'Pax Americana's Twin Deficits', *New Perspectives Quarterly*, 4(3). Online. Available at: http://www.digitalnpq.org/archive/1987_fall/pax.html (accessed 24 November 2003).

Smith, Steve (2002) 'The United States and the Discipline of International Relations: "Hegemonic Country, Hegemonic Discipline"', *International Studies Review,* 4(2): 67–85.

Teslik, Lee Hudson (2008) 'Iraq, Afghanistan and the US Economy', Council on Foreign Relations. Online. Available at: http://www.cfr.org/publication/15404/iraq_afghanistan_and_the_us_economy.html?breadcrumb=%2Fbios%2F12286%2Flee_hudson_teslik%3Fgroupby%3D0%26hide%3D1%26id%3D12286%26filter%3D255 (accessed 26 June 2008).

Waltz, Kenneth N. (2000) 'Structural Realism after the Cold War', *International Security*, 25(1): 5–41.

Wendt, Alexander (1999) *Social Theory of International Politics*, Cambridge: Cambridge University Press.

The White House (2002) *The National Security Strategy of the United States of America* Washington, DC: The White House.

—— (2006) *The National Security Strategy of the United States of America*, Washington, DC: The White House.

Williams, M.J (2007) 'The Empire Writes Back (to Michael Cox)', *International Affairs*, 83(5): 945–50.

Wohlforth, W.C. (1999) 'The Stability of a Unipolar World', *International Security*, 24(1): 5–41.

2 Constructivism, US foreign policy and the 'war on terror'

Richard Jackson and Matt McDonald

There is no doubt that the decision to launch a global 'war on terror' was a historic moment in US foreign policy which was to have profound consequences both internationally and domestically. To date, the 'war on terror' has entailed two major wars in Iraq and Afghanistan, significant military operations in Pakistan, Somalia, the Philippines, Georgia and elsewhere, a global intelligence and rendition programme, the expansion of US military bases to new regions, increased military assistance to new and old client regimes, an extensive international public diplomacy programme, the articulation of new national security doctrines and priorities, and a major domestic reorganisation of and increased investment in the military, domestic security agencies, policing, the legal system and numerous other agencies – among a great many other important developments. It is no exaggeration to suggest that the 'war on terror' is now comparable to the Cold War in terms of overall expenditure and its impact on all aspects of US foreign policy, external relations and domestic politics.

And yet, understanding or explaining these developments is not a straightforward task. It is not obvious that attacks by a small group of dissidents aggrieved by the US military presence in the Arabian Peninsula on 11 September 2001, as devastating as they were, should have generated such an expansive and far-reaching response from the world's only superpower, or that the response should have involved all of the specific elements we have thus far witnessed. In the first place, as ongoing contestations over the meaning and significance of the Pearl Harbor attack (Rosenberg 2003) or the Kennedy assassination clearly demonstrate, acts of political violence do not necessarily 'speak for themselves'; they have to be narrated and interpreted in meaningful ways within a particular social, cultural and historical context. The attacks on New York and Washington were potentially open to a number of different interpretations, only one of which was as an 'act of war' necessitating a military response. The choice to launch a potentially unlimited and global war is all the more puzzling given the relatively limited extent of the terrorist threat to human life (certainly compared to climate change, disease or poverty, for example) and the ultimately foreseeable consequences of specific actions such as intervention in Iraq, the Guantánamo Bay detentions, extraordinary rendition, the announcement of the Bush Doctrine, and so on. And it is certainly far from clear that the elimination or even significant reduction of the terrorist threat has been achieved through the means the Bush administration and its allies have employed in the 'war on terror'.

A key puzzle therefore, lies in understanding why the 'war on terror' was chosen over other foreign policy or counter-terror frameworks by key foreign policy decision-makers, and why it took the form that it did. Traditional accounts of international relations and security (most notably Realism) would provide at best a partial and at worst a misleading account of the US government's foreign policy choices and practices in this context, emphasising as they do the central role of material distributions of power and the rational calculation of the national interest.[1] In this chapter, we argue that a Constructivist perspective provides a productive and informative analytical lens through which to understand how the 'war on terror' emerged as the dominant US foreign policy discourse after the events of 11 September 2001, taking on the particular form/s that it did. We suggest that a focus on ideational factors characteristic of a Constructivist approach to international relations – narrative, framing, identity, norms, contestation and negotiation, among others – provides particularly important insights into the emergence and institutionalisation of the 'war on terror' in the US context.

The chapter begins with a necessarily brief overview of Constructivism, outlining its origins, variants, shared assumptions and ontology. The second section examines the application of Constructivist insights to US foreign policy in the 'war on terror', focusing in particular on the inter-subjective social construction of the 'war on terror' itself. In the conclusion, we reflect on the utility of the Constructivist approach.

Constructivism

Constructivism is a broad social theory rather than a substantive theory of international politics. In essence, Constructivists working in international relations are concerned with the (social) constitution of world politics. Based on the view that world politics is a social realm characterised by a dynamic and mutually constitutive relationship between agents (principally states) and structures (principally the nature of the international system or society), Constructivists are concerned with the processes through which the world has come to be as it is: the dynamics of interaction between actors, the meanings that actors give their actions, and the frameworks and patterns of interaction between those actors. In this process they are concerned with offering a more sociological account of global politics in which ideational factors (norms, rules, identities, and forms of representation) play a central role. As such, they offer the possibility of a more holistic, multidimensional understanding of political processes, dynamics and actions.

Constructivism has emerged relatively recently as a distinct approach to international relations, linked to a series of academic and practical developments. While building on insights in disciplines such as sociology, early Constructivist authors such as Alexander Wendt (1987), Nicholas Onuf (1989) and Friedrich Kratochwil (1989) drew also upon the more radical critiques aimed at orthodox approaches to international relations by theorists working within the critical theoretical and post-structural traditions, such as Richard Ashley (1984) and R.B.J. Walker (1988). In the process, they were more readily accepted within mainstream academic circles than these radical alternatives, at least in part because they were perceived as less alien and threatening to the canon of international relations.[2]

The 'Constructivist turn' in international relations was given further impetus by the collapse of the Soviet Union and the end of the Cold War, occurring as it did without any significant shift in the distribution of capabilities in the international system and largely through domestic political transformation enabled by strategic actors (see Fierke 1997). This seriously undermined the explanatory power of traditional approaches which had failed to predict, and had no real basis for understanding, such revolutionary transformations in the international system (Kratochwil 1993). In this way, international change provided a catalyst for theoretical change. It is important to reiterate here that despite occupying a prominent theoretical position in international relations thought today, Constructivism's entry to the discipline was relatively recent, certainly in comparison to more established variants of international relations thought associated with realism and liberalism.

Since its emergence, Constructivism has developed in a number of different directions, depending upon the specific theoretical traditions drawn upon, the central focus of the research and the main methodological approaches employed by the researcher. As a consequence of these fault lines, there is now an increasing variety of labels for Constructivist scholarship, including: critical, conventional, modernist, post-modern, thick, thin, narrative, strong, systemic and holistic – among others (Adler 1997: 335–6; Barnett 2005: 258). Perhaps the most important distinction is the broad division between conventional and critical approaches (see Hopf 1998: 181–5). Conventional Constructivists tend to employ the epistemology of traditional approaches and focus on examining relationships of causality in asking 'why' questions (Katzenstein 1996; Wendt 1999), while critical approaches are closer in approach and scope to more radical theoretical alternatives and examine relationships of constitution through asking 'how possible' questions (Doty 1993; Barnett 1999). In approaching international participation in the 'war on terror', for example, a conventional approach might focus on examining *why* different states were active participants or not (see Katzenstein 2003), while a critical approach might focus on how political actors within different states were able to render possible their preferred responses through strategic forms of representation to national audiences (see McDonald and Jackson 2008). The role of identity is central to both, although in conventional accounts it is usually viewed as relatively sedimented (to the point of compelling state action), while, in the latter, identity is the focal point of competition over action: attempts to justify or contest particular policy preferences.

Despite this distinction, however, Constructivists share a number of core assumptions about international relations. First, Constructivists view the world (and reality generally) as socially constructed. Rooted in sociological theory, this notion has a number of related elements, including the claim that the perceptions, identities and interests of individuals and groups are socially and culturally constructed, rather than existing outside of or prior to society. Related to this, Constructivists point to the existence of *social* facts which are dependent on human agreement. The existence of social facts draws attention to the inter-subjective nature of reality: even apparently natural institutions, actors and norms (such as states, anarchy and sovereignty) are the products of processes of social construction between different actors, and only ever appear natural or inevitable because they are presented and accepted as such. Critically, recognising the inter-subjective and socially constructed nature of reality – produced through processes of negotiation and contestation – allows us to recognise possibilities for (even structural) change.

Second, Constructivists hold that agents and structures in world politics are mutually constitutive (Wendt 1987). That is, agents constitute structures through their beliefs, actions and interactions, while structures constitute agents by helping to shape their identities and interests. Such a conception is particularly important in bringing human agency back into international political analysis, a contrasting position to the structural determinism of approaches such as neo-realism.

Third, Constructivists view ideational factors – representation, identities, beliefs, perceptions and norms – as central to the dynamics and processes of world politics. As the world is socially constructed between actors, forms and processes of communication become crucial. Constructivists suggest – following post-structuralists – that it is only through representation that we are able to give meaning to material 'reality' and to events like acts of political violence. In the process of representing, narrating or framing reality, actors go about constituting that reality as well as contesting and potentially marginalising alternative accounts and enabling particular forms of policy or actions (Laffey and Weldes 1997; Weldes *et al.* 1999; Hansen 2000). For critical Constructivists, what is crucial is the extent to which policy can be defined or justified in such a way as to resonate with a domestic constituency, though 'hailing' core identity narratives or providing compelling historical parallels for action (Barnett 1999; Weldes 1996). This is particularly applicable to the question of how particular forms and frameworks of policy – such as the 'war on terror' – become possible.

The central role of representation is clearly applicable to the role of norms: standards of legitimate behaviour in an international society. For Constructivists, these norms are central to world politics, constituting that society as well as conditioning the interests and realms of possible action for states within it. As Michael Barnett (2005: 255) has argued, the norm of sovereignty not only regulates state interactions but also makes possible the very idea of the sovereign state and helps to construct its interests. While norms can become sedimented and serve to define the limits of feasible political action, they are also susceptible to change, not least through the strategic action of 'norm entrepreneurs' (Keck and Sikkink 1998) or norm revisionists. As will be noted, attempts under the Bush administration to revise norms of pre-emptive self-defence and torture within the 'war on terror' should be viewed in this context.

Constructivist research has to date examined a range of subjects relevant to the broader understanding of foreign policy, including, among others: national security and the decision to use force (Katzenstein 1996; Williams 1998); the construction of national security threats (Weldes 1996; Howard 2004); national security cultures (Gusterson 1998); military doctrine and military strategy (Johnson 1995; Kier 1997); US counter-insurgency policy (Doty 1993); and culture and war (Mertus 1999; Alkopher 2005). There are also a growing number of Constructivist analyses of the war on terror which we draw upon in this chapter (see, for example, Katzenstein 2003; Murphy 2003; Jackson 2005; Croft 2006; Thrall 2007; Cramer 2007; Krebs and Lobasz 2007).

Constructivism and the 'war on terror'

The above account of Constructivism suggests a range of possible avenues for exploring US foreign policy in the context of the war on terror. The following discussion is therefore necessarily brief and selective. Its main aim is to provide a window into how Constructivist analyses might illuminate key dimensions and dynamics of US foreign policy in the war on terror. We focus here on a number of key concepts associated with Constructivism, namely: norms; identity and narratives; and change.

Norms

Constructivists pay significant attention to norms and normative frameworks in their accounts of world politics generally and the interests and actions of states specifically. Norms can be defined as shared expectations about appropriate or legitimate behaviour by actors with a particular identity. For Constructivists, these socially constructed expectations can constitute the interests – and constrain the room to move – of even the most powerful actors in the international system: states. While Realists dismiss the disciplining effect of norms altogether – suggesting either their total irrelevance or their role exclusively as a source of justification for action (Krasner 1999) – Constructivists point to the ways in which actors have adjusted their actions to adhere to norms associated with colonialism (Crawford 2003a) and the use of nuclear weapons (Tannenwald 2007). For theorists working in this tradition, norms (like other ideational factors) can come to be incorporated into a state's conception of its national interests (Finnemore 1996).

Such accounts of the disciplining effects of norms might intuitively seem to have little purchase in accounting for US foreign policy in the war on terror, given the extent of US power and the invocation of an exceptionalist rhetoric that suggests America alone will decide upon the legitimacy and limits of its actions. Yet even here a Constructivist account of norms has some explanatory power. Indeed, for many the failure to recognise the importance of international perceptions of the legitimacy of the war on terror and the Bush administration's prosecution of it has been central to the problems encountered by the United States in Iraq, for example (Nye 2004; Reus-Smit 2004). And even while employing an exceptionalist rhetoric, the US has nonetheless attempted to locate its actions in international normative frameworks, in some cases attempting to redefine existing norms so as to justify its own behaviour in the war on terror.[3] In this context the US has acted as a 'norm revisionist', a role particularly applicable to its position on the role of preventive war and torture.

While the invasion of Afghanistan was broadly accepted internationally as a form of self-defence, the US invasion of Iraq (also defined as part of the war on terror) was far more controversial. In the case of Iraq, the US was faced with both the absence of a significant attack on the United States linked to Saddam's regime that may have mobilised international support, as well as the lack of convincing evidence to point to the crucial dimension of pre-emptive self-defence: the existence of an *imminent* threat (Erskine and O'Driscoll 2007). In response, and as part of the so-called Bush Doctrine (elaborated in the 2002 *National Security Strategy*), the Bush administration argued that 'we must adapt the concept of imminent threat to the capabilities and objectives of today's adversaries' (Bush 2002: Chapter V). In this context, the US acted as a norm revisionist, suggesting the problems of relying on antiquated notions of 'imminence' as the standard of legitimacy for the use of anticipatory self-defensive force in the light of new terrorist threats. Indeed, Bush declared that we need to 'deal with those threats before they become imminent' (in Kaufmann 2004: 23). This was a central legal-normative claim for intervention in Iraq, one linked rhetorically to suggested links between Saddam Hussein and terrorists and to his alleged WMD programme. And while in the UN Security Council and elsewhere this justification failed to convince a host of other states, the Australian Prime Minister and Japanese Defence Minister both subsequently elaborated their own definitions of preventive war in the context of concerns about the threat of fundamentalist Islamic terrorism in Southeast Asia and North Korea's WMD programme respectively (McDonald 2007a). For Constructivists, such developments need to be viewed in the context of (even partial) changes in the normative context allowed by the US justification of preventative war.

Norms surrounding torture – the intentional infliction of 'severe pain or suffering, whether physical or mental' particularly on prisoners and detainees (UNHCR)[4] – became an important focal point of criticism for the US in the war on terror, given revelations of coercive interrogation and humiliation of detainees at Camp X-Ray at Guantánamo Bay and Abu Ghraib in Iraq. A significant component of the government's response to abuses in Abu Ghraib was that while the US government sought to distance itself from the actions of its military personnel, Defense Secretary Donald Rumsfeld argued that 'what has been charged [in Abu Ghraib] thus far is abuse, which I believe is technically different from torture' (in Blumenthal 2004). Erskine and O'Driscoll (2007) note that this position followed an earlier memorandum prepared for Bush's legal counsel, Alberto Gonzales, which suggested narrowing the definition of torture to include only those 'extreme acts' entailing physical pain 'equivalent in intensity to the pain accompanying serious injury'. The attempt to justify the infliction of pain or inhumane treatment was not wholly consistent (at different points the administration implicitly endorsed existing definitions of torture but suggested they didn't apply to unlawful combatants, for example), but an important dimension of this justification was the narrowing of the definition of torture to enable the use of coercion and violence against detainees.

While some might suggest here that the US attempt to redefine the norms of preventive war and torture constitutes little more than an instrumental attempt to justify preferred actions, Constructivists would rightly suggest that these attempts are important for several reasons. First, such attempts can serve to redefine the normative context of world politics, particularly if undertaken by a state with the material and social power of the US. The invocation of US definitions of prevention elsewhere (in Australia and Japan, for example), suggests at least a partial shift in the parameters of what constitutes appropriate behaviour regarding the use of force, reminding us that as social constructions, norms are liable to change. Second, in locating actions within (again even altered) norms and rules of international society, the US potentially strengthens this international society and its constituent components through positioning them as legitimate standards of appropriate behaviour. This can also serve to provide a basis for critique, particularly if the government is seen to be falling short of standards it set for itself (Krebs and Lobasz 2007). Finally, and perhaps most importantly, Constructivists would suggest that the failure to convince international audiences of the legitimacy of these redefinitions and the war on terror more broadly is not simply a speed-bump on the road to the realisation of the national interest. Rather, the failure to act in such a way as to be seen as a legitimate actor carrying out a legitimate set of practices is central to the failings in Iraq and the steady erosion of the international support for the war on terror generally (Reus-Smit 2004). It is here that Constructivists would retort to Realists' suggestion that they ignore the role of power in international politics by suggesting that theirs is a fuller, more realistic and more convincing account of power that takes account of the central role of normative and social power and the central importance of international legitimacy (Barnett and Finnemore 2004; Barnett and Duvall 2005).

Identity and narrative

As noted, Constructivists view identity as central to the dynamics and practices of global politics. For Constructivists, we cannot know 'what we want' unless we know 'who we are'. Put another way, the way in which the core values of a particular political community are defined will underpin the (foreign policy) goals of that community and potentially also the way in which it will go about attempting to realise or advance them.[5] This view stands in opposition to traditional assumptions of national interests determined by the structure of the international system and actions determined by varying levels of material capacity.

The notion of mutual constitution is particularly important for Constructivist views of identity, not least as it applies to security policy and practice. Some (more conventional) Constructivists tend to focus on the role of sedimented discourses of identity almost compelling actors to engage in particular types of action (see Katzenstein 1996), while other (more critical) Constructivists tend to focus on the role of strategic actors in enabling policy through instrumentally locating that policy in particular narratives of identity and marginalising others (see Barnett 1999). However, as sophisticated variants of these approaches argue (see Fierke 1997; McSweeney 1999; Williams 2007), any sharp distinction between agents (political leaders, for example) and structures (discourses of identity, for example) is imperfect. The reality is of course that some identity narratives might be more powerful and resonant than others, providing both an immediate limit to alternative stories of a group's core values and mitigating against the emergence of a strategic actor not already implicated by such narratives or discourses.[6] But even in these contexts there are possibilities for variation, both in terms of the possibilities for privileging alternative narratives or linking the same narrative to different policy priorities and action.

In the case of the war on terror, the key agents constructing the global counter-terrorism campaign – the Bush administration and its allies – did not have complete and unfettered freedom in its construction. Relatively sedimented and powerful historical and identity discourses certainly predisposed key political actors, media and the broader populace to particular interpretations of 11 September 2001, and particular political responses to it. In an immediate sense, analyses inspired by post-structuralist approaches to the role of discourse suggest a common pattern in the elaboration of discourses of threat over the course of the twentieth century. The positioning of terrorism as a fundamental and existential threat to America's core values (principally of freedom and democracy) certainly had powerful historical precedent, as analyses of the Cold War (Campbell 1992) and Ronald Reagan's first 'war on terrorism' (Jackson 2006) suggest. Importantly, Cramer (2007) suggests that over time such designations and responses to threat helped established a militarized political culture that in turn might be linked to the nature of the response to the threat of terrorism. And the sedimentation of freedom and democracy as core American values can also be viewed as a powerful narrative of identity, linked to the notion of the United States as the 'Chosen Nation' or 'light on the hill' (Hughes 2003). The power of these stories of identity and history certainly predisposed the US administration to a particular type of political response to the attacks of 11 September 2001, and perhaps even the promulgation of the war on terror.

Notwithstanding the power of these understandings, most Constructivist analysts would suggest that there remained room for choice and strategic action in both advancing particular understandings of identity or history and linking them to the war on terror. Narratives are central in this regard, understood here as particular stories about who we are that are linked – through framing – to particular policy action (see Barnett 1999). For Constructivists, myths, historical parallels, symbols and ideas can be deployed instrumentally by elites as a kind of 'symbolic technology' (Laffey and Weldes 1997) to enable action and the actors who undertake them. The political choice to represent the counter-terror campaign as a 'war' and 11 September 2001 as an 'act of war'; to link the event itself to Pearl Harbor and the threat posed to that of communists or

Nazis; to invoke the language of 'good' and 'evil'; to define intervention in Iraq as consistent with the goals of 'freedom' and 'democracy'; and to link the narrative of the 'Chosen Nation' to the administration's broader position on multilateralism, among a range of other identity narratives (on these points, see Jackson 2005) must be recognised as just that: a choice. These were choices arguably defined in such a way as to speak to a particular set of audiences and marginalise alternative accounts of US identity and foreign policy (see Cramer 2007; Krebs and Lobasz 2007). They were certainly neither inevitable nor rooted in rational assessment or investigation, a point applicable also to assessments of the extent of the terror threat (Kaufmann 2004).

It is important to reiterate here, as Constructivists argue, that foreign and security policy is a site of inter-subjective contestation and negotiation about the nature of a particular political community's core values, the threats to those values and the means that might be employed to advance or preserve those values. This contestation and negotiation take place in the context of significant power discrepancies, but is ultimately one in which a range of actors seek to develop accounts of political action that resonate with who a particular political community considers itself to be. In this sense identity is central to interests and to the dynamics of world politics, and recognising its role gives us a richer understanding of US foreign policy in the war on terror.

Change

The above account of the relationship between identity, narratives and resonance suggests an almost permanent state of instability in global politics and in the levels of legitimacy the US might enjoy in its prosecution of the war on terror, for example. If contestation and negotiation are relatively permanent features of the processes through which foreign policy is constructed, then constantly shifting policies and practices might be expected in response to interpretations of new events and dynamics. But Constructivists are generally eager to point out that such an image of flux and instability potentially overstates the case for possibilities for change. In the context of the war on terror, the constant reiteration of its central principles and the institutionalisation of practices tied to it mean that the war on terror has become a powerful discourse, providing a lens through which a range of policies is viewed across all sectors of society. It is significant to note here that numerous American opponents of the occupation of Iraq have suggested that the amount of resources committed to the invasion and long-term occupation of Iraq served to undermine the real goals of fighting Al Qaeda in the war on terror (BBC 2004). While criticising the linkage between Iraq and the war on terror, such a criticism not only fails to fundamentally contest the war on terror, it reinforces its position of dominance by using it as a standard against which foreign policy is judged and a lens through which foreign policy generally is viewed. The dominance of this discourse has become possible through its institutionalisation within and constant reiteration across American society.

In the first instance, the core narratives, assumptions and approaches of the discourse have been institutionalised in, among other things: new government departments like the Department of Homeland Security; new legislation such as the PATRIOT Acts; new security doctrines, action plans, strategic plans, surveillance and reporting programmes; the reorganisation and reforms of the security services, policing, the military, the justice system, immigration, banking regulations; political debate and speech-making; lobby groups and think tanks; and many other related activities and actors.

Importantly, the discourse has also been institutionalised in counter-terrorism activities and programmes at the international level in the United Nations, the European Union, the Organisation of SCE and NATO, suggesting a normative spread of the war on terror beyond the United States. A range of analysts also point to the ways in which the war on terror and its central assumptions are consistently communicated through government, the media, academia and in popular culture and have become a part of contemporary American life (see, for example, Silberstein 2004; Croft 2006). These analysts point to the role of a range of actors in promulgating elements of the war on terror discourse, from public bodies' information campaigns (e.g. FEMA's *Are You Ready?* booklet) to retailers' marketing of terror-related products (e.g. the sale of home WMD decontamination kits) and representations of the 'ubiquitous' terror threat in media and popular culture (see Croft 2006). Across American politics and society, the war on terror has become a living discourse which creates a shared understanding of the new 'reality', and which creates a 'grid of intelligibility' through which to interpret events and make decisions. This shared understanding also provides a cultural resource which political elites can draw upon when trying to legitimise or 'sell' new policies and programmes.

But while Constructivists have acknowledged that foreign policy discourses can become sedimented or dominant, the focus on negotiation and contestation enables some recognition of the possibility for change. Certainly, and as noted, Constructivists have long argued that normative change is possible through strategic actors acting as norm entrepreneurs or revisionists, altering the normative structure of international society over a period of time. Constructivists have suggested that even *structural* change in global politics and the most important dynamics of global interaction is possible through effective strategic action. Karin Fierke (1997), for example, argued in her analysis of the end of the Cold War that Gorbachev was able to act as a crucial agent of change through acting 'as if' another set of rules for the Cold War game (associated with a zero-sum security logic, suspicion and militarism) were in place. More specifically, a range of contemporary analyses of the war on terror have pointed to possibilities for change through successful contestation in the form of the failure of political leaders to meet words with deeds. Drawing on critical theoretical insights of immanent critique, these approaches suggest that the fissures, inconsistencies and tensions in the war on terror discourse and justifications for policy provide resources for realising change (Fierke 2007: 167–85; Krebs and Lobasz 2007; McDonald 2007b; McDonald and Jackson 2008).

A range of tensions suggest themselves here as bases for successful contestation. On the specific prosecution of the war in Iraq, critics have employed the 'support our troops' mantra of the government (arguably directed towards marginalising dissent) to contest the long-term occupation of Iraq. Pointing to ever-increasing casualty rates and widespread mental health problems among troops, these critics of policy have rallied behind the phrase 'support our troops: bring them home' (see www. bringthemhomenow.org). Here, the administration's rhetorical commitment to its military personnel is that which is used against the government itself. On the broader war on terror, the suggestion of a commitment to 'freedom and democracy' has been criticised on the basis of the erosion of civil liberties through anti-terror legislation; the willingness of the US administration to diplomatically support allies in the war on terror despite their human rights abuses; and the rising civilian death tolls in those countries being 'liberated' through militarised intervention. And of course a range of critics (and increasingly, branches of government) have suggested that the means employed in the war on terror are counter-productive. Here, critics suggest that military responses are likely to breed alienation, marginalisation and resentment that provide fertile ground for terrorists; that they are likely to make participant states targets of terrorism; and even that they undermine real security through diverting significant resources to invasion and occupation that might be spent on other 'security' programmes, from intelligence-gathering to healthcare or responses to environmental disasters (on these points, see McDonald 2007b; McDonald and Jackson 2008).

These criticisms constitute potentially promising avenues for successful contestation even of a discourse as sedimented and institutionalised as the war on terror. And while the tools of immanent critique are more readily associated with critical theory than Constructivism, Constructivism's focus on the role of contestation and negotiation align themselves well with the specific suggestions for (emancipatory) change found in critical theory. Constructivists suggest that large-scale public discourses such as the war on terror or the Cold War discourse before it are never entirely stable or hegemonic. Rather, they are inherently unstable, contradictory, vulnerable to destabilisation and prone to contestation; they contain within themselves the seeds of their own destruction; and in order to persist they must be continuously reproduced socially and forcefully defended by their supporters. Change is not always easy, but Constructivists are right to acknowledge its possibility and identify processes through which it might be realised.

Conclusion

As noted at the outset of this chapter, Constructivism is less a theory of international relations than a broader social theory that informs how we might approach the study of world politics. Indeed, this point has been noted by critics, who suggest that the breadth of Constructivism is such that it mitigates against discrete forms of political analysis. Anything, for critics, might be explained or understood through Constructivist analysis, although little predicted (Booth 2007: 153). At times, especially on questions of normative commitments and epistemology, the gap between conventional and more critical variants of Constructivism appears large indeed. Critics from more radical perspectives suggest that (conventional) Constructivist approaches give too much ground to traditional approaches on questions of epistemology and have problematic assumptions of the possibility for strategic action by political agents (Zehfuss 2002), while more traditional analysts suggest that the focus on ideational approaches risks downplaying the central role of material factors and hard power in the dynamics of world politics (Mearsheimer 1995).

It is beyond the scope of this chapter to engage with these criticisms systematically, although some raise important questions about future directions in Constructivist research. Constructivist approaches are certainly strong in theory on the question of the mutual constitution of agents and structures, but their analyses at times suggest either independent instrumental actors dissociated from society or 'cultural dupes' compelled to adhere to pre-existing identity discourses. Similarly, while Constructivists have responded convincingly to the suggestion that they ignore material factors (pointing out that it is through the ideational that the material is given meaning), the overwhelming focus of analysis on incremental progressive normative change (regarding slavery, colonisation, environmental change, human rights, and so on) does little to dispel the myth that Constructivists are unable to account systematically for power politics. The increasing prevalence of Constructivist analyses in international relations literature suggests it will become more rather than less prominent as a framework for the study of world politics in the foreseeable future. In this context, the nature of responses to criticisms or tensions in the theory could feasibly have implications for the broader study of international politics: the gaps and silences of the field and the central axes of debate between scholars.

We have argued here that Constructivism provides a powerful lens through which to understand US foreign policy. In drawing attention to the mutual constitution of structures and agents; the inter-subjective social construction of world politics; and the role of ideational factors such as norms, identity and narratives, Constructivism is able to offer rich insights into US foreign policy in the war on terror, particularly in illuminating the core question of how the war on terror itself became possible. And while helping us understand the constitution of the present, Constructivism also has an often overlooked capacity to provide a framework for understanding and imagining change.

Acknowledgements

The authors would like to acknowledge the support of the ESRC (RES 000-222-2126) which provided funding for research in this chapter. Our thanks also go to Cian O'Driscoll for his insightful comments on an earlier draft of this chapter.

Notes

1 Indeed, this is suggested by prominent Realists' criticism of intervention in Iraq as an abdication of national responsibility. See Mearsheimer and Walt (2003).
2 See Adler (1997). This is especially true of Alexander Wendt (1999), who sought to position his work as a middle ground between positivist and post-positivist approaches through employing an epistemology consistent with the former and an ontology of the latter.
3 This point echoes Quentin Skinner's argument that even those determined to work outside existing norms must engage with the existing normative context in order to do so, a point captured in his oft-quoted observation that revolutionaries 'are obliged to march backwards into battle'. See Tully (1988). We thank Cian O'Driscoll for drawing this to our attention.
4 The full definition of torture under Article 1 of the 1984 Convention against Torture is available at: http://www.unhchr.ch/html/menu3/b/h_cat39.htm.
5 For an application of this insight to US foreign policy in the 'war on terror', see, for example, Neta Crawford (2003b).
6 On the latter, Michael Williams (2007: 25–31) employs Bourdieu's conception of habitus in examining the security–identity relationship to suggest the importance of recognising that even strategically-minded political actors do not stand outside a community in deploying narratives to enable preferred outcomes, but are a product of (or at least implicated in) the social and cultural context in which they act.

References

Adler, Emanuel (1997) 'Seizing the Middle Ground: Constructivism in World Politics', *European Journal of International Relations*, 3(3): 319–63.
Alkopher, Tal Dingott (2005) 'The Social (and Religious) Meanings that Constitute War: The Crusades as Realpolitik vs. Socialpolitik', *International Studies Quarterly*, 49: 715–37.
Ashley, Richard (1984) 'The Poverty of Neo-Realism', *International Organization*, 38(2): 225–86.

Barnett, Michael (1999) 'Culture, Strategy and Foreign Policy Change', *European Journal of International Relations*, 5(1): 5–36.

—— (2005) 'Social Constructivism', in John Baylis and Steve Smith (eds) *The Globalization of World Politics: An Introduction to International Relations*, Oxford: Oxford University Press.

Barnett, Michael and Duvall, Robert (eds) (2005) *Power in Global Governance*, Cambridge: Cambridge University Press.

Barnett, Michael and Finnemore, Martha (2004) *Rules for the World: International Organizations in Global Politics*, Ithaca, NY: Cornell University Press.

BBC (2004) 'US War in Iraq "Strategic Error"', *BBC Online*, 13 January. Available at: http://news.bbc.co.uk/1/hi/world/americas/3391583.stm.

Blumenthal, Sidney (2004) 'This Is the New Gulag', *The Guardian*, 6 May. Available at: http://www.guardian.co.uk/world/2004/may/06/usa.iraq4.

Booth, Ken (2007) *Theory of World Security*, Cambridge: Cambridge University Press.

Bush, George (2002) *The National Security Strategy of the United States of America*. Available at: http://www.whitehouse.gov/nsc/nss/2002/index.html.

Campbell, David (1992) *Writing Security: United States Foreign Policy and the Politics of Identity*, Minneapolis: University of Minnesota Press.

Cramer, Jane (2007) 'Militarized Patriotism: Why the U.S. Marketplace of Ideas Failed Before the Iraq War', *Security Studies*, 16(3): 489–524.

Crawford, Neta C. (2003a) *Argument and Change in World Politics*, Cambridge: Cambridge University Press.

—— (2003b) 'The Best Defense: The Problem with Bush's Preemptive War Doctrine', *Boston Review*, 28(1): 20–3.

Croft, Stuart (2006) *Culture, Crisis and America's War on Terror*, Cambridge: Cambridge University Press.

Doty, Roxanne (1993) 'Foreign Policy as Social Construction', *International Studies Quarterly*, 37: 297–320.

Erskine, Toni and O'Driscoll, Cian (2007) 'Slouching Towards Torture and Preventive War: Norms, Names and Rhetorical Manoeuvre in the "War on Terror"', paper presented at British International Studies Association Conference, Cambridge, 17–19 December.

FEMA (US Federal Emergency Management Agency) (2004) *Are You Ready?: An In-depth Guide to Citizen Preparedness*. Online. Available at: http://www.fema.gov/pdf/areyouready/areyouready_full.pdf

Fierke, Karin M. (1997) 'Changing Worlds of Security', in Keith Krause and Michael Williams (eds) *Critical Security Studies*, London: UCL Press.

—— (2007) *Critical Approaches to International Security*, London: Polity.

Finnemore, Martha (1996) *National Interests in International Society*, Ithaca, NY: Cornell University Press.

Gusterson, Hugh (1998) *Nuclear Rites: A Weapons Laboratory at the End of the Cold War*, Berkeley, CA: University of California Press.

Hansen, Lene (2000) 'The Little Mermaid's Silent Security Dilemma and the Absence of Gender in the Copenhagen School', *Millennium*, 29(2): 289–306.

Hopf, Ted (1998) 'The Promise of Constructivism in International Relations Theory', *International Security*, 23(1): 171–200.

Howard, Peter (2004) 'Why Not Invade North Korea? Threats, Language Games, and U.S. Foreign Policy', *International Studies Quarterly*, 48(4): 805–28.

Hughes, R. (2003) *Myths America Lives by*, Urbana, IL: University of Illinois Press.

Jackson, Richard (2005) *Writing the War on Terrorism: Language, Politics and Counterterrorism*, Manchester: Manchester University Press.

—— (2006) 'Genealogy, Ideology, and Counter-Terrorism: Writing Wars on Terrorism from Ronald Reagan to George W. Bush Jr', *Studies in Language & Capitalism*, 1: 163–93.

Johnson, Alastair (1995) *Cultural Realism: Strategic Culture and Grand Strategy in Chinese History*, Princeton, NJ: Princeton University Press.

Katzenstein, Peter J. (ed.) (1996) *The Culture of National Security: Norms and Identity in World Politics*, New York: Columbia University Press.

—— (2003) 'Same War – Different Views: Germany, Japan and Counter-Terrorism', *International Organization*, 57(4): 731–60.

Kaufmann, Chaim (2004) 'Threat Inflation and the Failure of the Marketplace of Ideas', *International Security*, 29(1): 5–48.

Keck, Margaret E. and Sikkink, Katherine(1998) *Activists Beyond Borders*, Ithaca, NY: Columbia University Press.

Kier, Elizabeth (1997) *Imagining War: French and British Military Doctrine Between the Wars*, Princeton, NJ: Princeton University Press.

Krasner, Stephen (1999) *Sovereignty: Organised Hypocrisy*, Princeton, NJ: Princeton University Press.

Kratochwil, Friedrich (1989) *Rules, Norms, and Decisions*, Cambridge: Cambridge University Press.

—— (1993) 'The Embarrassment of Changes: Neo-Realism as the Science of *Realpolitik* without Politics', *Review of International Studies*, 19(1): 63–80.

Krebs, Ronald and Lobasz, Jennifer (2007) 'Fixing the Meaning of 9/11: Hegemony, Coercion, and the Road to War in Iraq', *Security Studies*, 16(3): 409–51.

Laffey, Mark and Weldes, Jutta (1997) 'Beyond Belief: Ideas and Symbolic Technologies in the Study of International Relations', *European Journal of International Relations*, 3(2): 193–237.

McDonald, Matt (2007a) 'US Hegemony, the "War on Terror" and the Asia-Pacific', in Anthony Burke and Matt McDonald (eds) *Critical Security in the Asia-Pacific*, Manchester: Manchester University Press.

—— (2007b) 'Emancipation and Critical Terrorism Studies', *European Political Science*, 6(3): 252–9.

McDonald, Matt and Jackson, Richard (2008) 'Selling War: The Coalition of the Willing and the "War on Terror"', paper presented at International Studies Association Convention, San Francisco, 26–29 March.

McSweeney, Bill (1999) *Security, Identity, Interests*, Cambridge: Cambridge University Press.

Mearsheimer, John J. (1995) 'The False Promise of International Institutions', *International Security*, 19(3): 5–49.

Mearsheimer, John J. and Walt, Stephen (2003) 'An Unnecessary War', *Foreign Policy*, 134 (Jan.–Feb.): 50–9.

Mertus, Julie (1999) *Kosovo: How Myths and Truths Started a War*, Berkeley, CA: University of California Press.

Murphy, J. (2003) '"Our Mission and Our Moment": George W. Bush and September 11', *Rhetoric and Public Affairs*, 6(4): 607–32.

Nye, Joseph Jr (2004) *Soft Power: The Means to Success in World Politics*, New York: Public Affairs.

Onuf, Nicholas (1989) *A World of our Making: Rules and Rule in Social Theory and International Relations*, Columbia, SC: University of South Carolina Press.

Reus-Smit, Christian (2004) *American Power and World Order*, London: Polity

Rosenberg, Emily (2003) *A Date Which Will Live: Pearl Harbor in American Memory*, Durham, NC: Duke University Press.

Silberstein, Sandra (2004) *War of Words: Language, Politics and 9/11*, London: Routledge.

Tannenwald, Nina (2007) *The Nuclear Taboo*, Cambridge: Cambridge University Press.

Thrall, A. Trevor (2007) 'A Bear in the Woods? Threat Framing and the Marketplace of Values', *Security Studies*, 16(3): 452–88.

Tully, James (ed.) (1988) *Meanings and Context: Quentin Skinner and His Critics*, Princeton, NJ: Princeton University Press.

Walker, R.B.J. (1988) *One World, Many Worlds: Struggles for a Just World Peace*, Boulder, CO: Lynne Rienner.

Weldes, Jutta (1996) 'Constructing National Interests', *European Journal of International Relations*, 2(3): 275–318.

Weldes, Jutta, Laffey, Mark, Gusterson, Hugh and Duvall, Raymond (eds) (1999) *Cultures of Insecurity: States, Communities and the Production of Danger*, London: University of Minneapolis Press.

Wendt, Alexander (1987) 'The Agent-Structure Problem in International Relations', *International Organization*, 41(3): 335–70.

—— (1999) *A Social Theory of World Politics*, Cambridge: Cambridge University Press.

Williams, Michael C. (1998) 'Identity and the Politics of Security', *European Journal of International Relations*, 4(2): 204–25.

—— (2007) *Culture and Security: Symbolic Power and the Culture of International Security*, London: Routledge.

Zehfuss, Maya (2002) *Constructivism in International Relations*, Cambridge: Cambridge University Press.

3 Neo-conservatism
Theory and practice

Robert Singh

Introduction

In the annals of international relations, it remains rare for an abstract school of grand strategy to feature in popular music. Yet the Rolling Stones' 2005 album entitled – perhaps appropriately enough – *A Bigger Bang* accorded neo-conservatism the full Jagger and Richards treatment. Two years after the US-led Iraq invasion, 'Sweet Neo-Con' echoed the sentiments of many in castigating US foreign policy: 'You call yourself a Christian/I think that you're a hypocrite/You say you are a patriot/I think that you're a crock of shit ... It's liberty for all/Democracy's our style/Unless you are against us/ Then it's prison without trial.' If its geo-political insights were neither especially elegant, precise nor profound, the track nonetheless added yet another indictment against the supposed philosophical underpinnings of the 'Bush Doctrine'.

No term has become more ubiquitous during the George W. Bush years than neo-conservatism and no group more politically controversial than neo-conservatives: 'hard-line', 'new fundamentalists' (Ikenberry 2004: 7, 9), 'deceitful', 'scare-mongering' and 'war-mongering' (Scheuer 2008: 122, 165, 208). The most common depiction suggests that a distinctly minority strand within the Republican Party and American conservatism, one markedly Jewish in composition, hijacked US foreign policy after 11 September 2001 in the interests of the state of Israel. This hawkish cabal exploited widespread public fear to lure a gullible nation into an unnecessary 'war of choice' in Iraq in a futile and utopian bid to transform the Middle East. The unintended but catastrophic consequence was not only an Iraqi quagmire, a weakened US and an emboldened Iran but also a more vulnerable Israel and a region more ripe for regional war than democratic peace. More generally, the neo-conservatives' self-consciously imperial project saw crucial US alliances frayed, state and sub-state enemies empowered, the United Nations weakened and American interests retarded on a global basis.

Rarely has so much malign international influence been attributed by so many to so few. This is ironic in three respects. First, the vast majority of those decision-makers most intimately involved in the formulation and implementation of Bush's foreign policy were anything but neo-conservatives. Moreover, many critics appeared confused as to what, and who, could be accurately labelled 'neo-con'. Almost one month into the Iraq War, for example, Alastair Campbell (Campbell and Stott 2008: 687), press secretary to British Prime Minister Tony Blair, asked Bush aide Dan Bartlett what 'neo-con' meant as Blair lamented the growing obsession with neo-conservatism as 'crazy'. (When Bartlett described 'neo-con' as 'the belief that government had a moral purpose', Campbell enquired if moral purpose could only be 'right-wing'.) One of the most oft-touted examples of neo-conservatives, former US Ambassador to the UN John Bolton, does not even include the term in his memoirs (Bolton 2007). Who qualifies as a neo-conservative therefore often appears more a matter of art than science.

Second, the very ubiquity of the terms as shorthand for 'right-wing', 'hawkish', 'Jewish', and 'pro-war' has rendered them more pejorative epithets than analytically revealing categories. 'Neo-conservative' and 'neo-conservatism' have become so widespread in the popular usage since 2001 as to lose any critical precision or coherent meaning. As David Brooks (2004: 42) observed, 'If you ever read a sentence that starts "Neo-cons believe", there is a 99.44 per cent chance everything else in that sentence will be untrue.' Nor are 'experts' free of such carelessness. In two recent accounts, even Iran's president, Mahmoud Ahmadinejad, was described as an 'Iranian neo-con' (Ehteshami and Zweiri 2007) while certain assertive Chinese foreign policy wonks were pithily labelled 'neo-comms' (Leonard 2008: 133).

Such difficulties are exacerbated, third, by the contested legacy of the Bush years for neo-conservatism. In particular, rival prognoses of neo-conservatism's relative health differ sharply in the light of its purported influence on foreign policy under the forty-third president. Some see neo-conservatism as a thankfully spent force. For Ikenberry (2004: 8):

> the intellectual high-water mark of the new fundamentalism was probably the October 2002 National Security Strategy report. Its political high tide was probably the moment President George W. Bush landed in a flight suit on the USS *Abraham Lincoln* to pronounce the 'end' of major hostilities in Iraq.

Others, though disdaining the development, view neo-conservatism as having now conquered the Republican Party (Gottfried 2007). In one volume deeply hostile to 'the new conservatism', neo-conservatives are viewed as having even the Clinton administration (1993–2001) and the Democratic Party establishment 'in their thrall' (Thompson 2007: 69).

This chapter assesses the analytic meaning and influence of neo-conservatism. First, the central tenets of neo-conservatism as they apply to US foreign policy are examined (neo-conservative thought has had much to say on domestic policy but contrasting interpretations of its influential contributions there can be assessed in Stelzer (2004) and Thompson (2007)). Second, the evolving relationship between these tenets, the personnel of the federal government (especially the executive branch), and foreign policy results are considered in the light of the Bush years (2001–9). Third, the extent to which the post-9/11 Bush foreign policy can be described as neo-conservative is evaluated. Finally, the prospects for neo-conservatism as an influence on foreign policy after Bush are assessed.

The central argument advanced here is three-fold. First, neo-conservatism represents a distinctly American (albeit an exportable) and coherent view of the world – a variant of realism that combines insights from the realist and idealist traditions of international relations. Second, while neo-conservative ideas informed some of the Bush grand strategy after 9/11, its practical embrace by Bush was conditional, limited and, ultimately, more rhetorical than substantive. If Bush's foreign policy was dominated by any one 'philosophical' influence, it was not the essentially internationalist-oriented neo-conservatism but a more nativist brand of nationalist realism far more powerfully represented within the post-Reagan Republican Party and the broader conservative movement. Partly as a result, neo-conservatives are well represented among those within and outside America to whom Bush proved a deep disappointment as president. Third, as the Bush years demonstrated, whatever its theoretical attractions, neo-conservatism's policy influence is conditioned less by the presence or otherwise of a 'cabal' of practitioners within the federal government than on its evolving relationship with broader tendencies in US foreign policy-making, government and politics. That is, as a distinctly minority strand in strategic thinking concentrated among a small network of think tanks, journalists and public intellectuals, neo-conservatives depend heavily on the success of their arguments to forge minimal winning policy coalitions. As such, and despite the hopes of critics such as Zbigniew Brzezinski (2007: 157) that Iraq represents 'the cemetery of neo-con dreams', neo-conservatism remains a potentially important and enduring influence on US foreign policy. Declarations of neo-conservatism's demise are decidedly premature.

The neo-conservative persuasion: when Hobbes met Kant

Evaluating what neo-conservatism is, and who may reasonably be considered a neo-conservative, is complicated by history, coalitional politics and the complex relationship between political philosophy and policy.

One of the few features of neo-conservatism on which its supporters and critics concur is its historical provenance. The original neo-conservatives were 'recovering Marxists' and Democrats who rejected the pacific and welfarist turn of the Democratic Party during the later 1960s and 1970s. Liberals who had been 'mugged by reality' at home and seen US power humiliated abroad in Vietnam, they rejected both the liberal idealism of the Democratic Left and Nixon/Kissinger-style Realism on the right. Some, such as Irving Kristol and Norman Podhoretz, were public intellectuals associated with influential journals such as *The Public Interest* and *Commentary*. Others were congressional staffers, such as Richard Perle and Elliot Abrams, aides to Senator Henry 'Scoop' Jackson (D-WA). In attaching the prefix 'neo' to conservatism, they acknowledged that their avowed principles departed from the conservatism of European and American tradition.

The historical specificity to neo-conservatism's origins gives rise to the problem of how to characterise those second- and third-generation individuals who were neither on the left nor Democrats. This in turn links to the second problematic element, the coalitional nature of American politics. Although some neo-conservatives remained formally registered as Democrats throughout their evolving political trajectories, such as Perle, the Reagan years consolidated the Republican Party as neo-conservatives' natural home. As nationalist Realists, Christian conservatives, social conservatives, supply-siders and deficit hawks allied in the GOP base, the exact philosophical differences between distinct conservative tendencies often became blurred. For figures such as William Kristol, editor of the *Weekly Standard*, Robert Kagan and Charles Krauthammer, one can argue that there is nothing 'neo' about their conservatism precisely because of the success of first generation neo-conservatives in influencing conservative thought.

Finally, how best to characterise a group that had no central organisational focus or philosophical unity provides a third problem. To describe neo-conservatism as a 'movement', as some critics are wont to do, exaggerates both the numbers and theoretical coherence of neo-conservative advocates, homogenising distinct currents. In terms of the former, remarkably few members of the appointed ranks of the executive branch – much less the permanent bureaucracy – under Bush were avowed neo-conservatives. Moreover, it remains virtually impossible to identify a single self-consciously neo-conservative member of the US Congress. On the latter concern, although some think tanks – the American Enterprise, the Hudson, the Manhattan and the Hoover Institutes – are widely seen as neo-conservative ideas factories, their Fellows encompass a broader range of conservative interests and viewpoints. More generally, while the principal historical and contemporary figures of neo-conservatism agree on shared principles, they differ on non-trivial points of policy, prize their individualism, and have mostly resisted rather than emulated self-styled political 'movements', such as the 'peace' and 'environmental' movements.

One of the foremost neo-conservative thinkers, Irving Kristol, therefore argues that 'persuasion' is a better characterisation of the neo-conservative approach. Another, Norman Podhoretz, has offered 'tendency' while Joshua Muravchik has described a neo-conservative 'sensibility'. Each highlights a general view of the world rather than a classical 'ideology' as such.

If one can identify certain shared tenets among this persuasion, what might they comprise? Kristol, widely regarded as neo-conservatism's 'godfather', has identified its historical task and political purpose as being 'to convert the Republican Party, and American conservatism in general, against their respective wills, into a new kind of conservative politics suitable to governing a modern democracy'. 'Distinctly American beyond doubt', neo-conservatism is:

> hopeful, not lugubrious; forward-looking, not nostalgic; and its general tone is cheerful, not grim or dyspeptic. Its twentieth century heroes tend to be TR [Theodore Roosevelt], FDR [Franklin Delano Roosevelt], and Ronald Reagan. Such Republican and conservative worthies as Calvin Coolidge, Herbert Hoover, Dwight Eisenhower, and Barry Goldwater are politely overlooked.
>
> (Kristol 2004: 33–4)

Distilled more specifically into foreign policy, neo-conservatism challenges idealism and realism alike, drawing on each while rejecting elements from both. Neo-conservatives tend to adopt the Hobbesian view of the international order shared by Realists. The world is a dangerous place, power matters, and states compete in an anarchic system. While there exists an important role for multinational institutions, multilateral action and international law, none of these can or should fully substitute for power. But neo-conservatives reject the notion that the only thing that matters in terms of states' external behaviour is the relative distribution of power in the international system. The domestic character of regimes has a major effect on their external activities, whether in terms of aggressive behaviour towards other states (Saddam's Iraq, post-1979 Iran) or repression of their own people (China, Burma, Sudan, Zimbabwe). Ideas, values and cultures matter because intentions matter as well as capabilities. If liberal inter-nationalists overestimate the importance of institutions such as the UN, realists underestimate the significance of values such as democracy, human rights and indivi-dual liberty in shaping states' international relations. In marrying idealist ends with realist means in a 'distinctly American internationalism' (Kaplan and Kristol 2003), neo-conservatives have been dubbed 'wolfish Wilsonians' (Lieven 2004) and 'hard Wilsonians'.

Analysts differ on the exact typologies by which neo-conservatives can be identified. Halper and Clarke (2004) identify three 'common themes' uniting neo-conservatives:

(1) a dualistic worldview; (2) a focus on the utility of military power; and (3) the threat posed the West by non-Western cultures (particularly Islam). The apostate neo-conservative, Francis Fukuyama (2006), identifies four strands to the neo-conservative tradition: (1) the transformation of pre-World War II Trotskyists into post-war anti-communists; (2) opposition to LBJ's 'Great Society' and the New Left's welfare statism; (3) the political philosopher Leo Strauss; and (4) the military thinking of nuclear strategist Albert Wohlstetter. But the problem with such typologies is that they can as easily encompass conservative/nationalist realists as any distinctively neo-conservative mindset for many politically active conservatives.

More useful analytic distinctions are offered by, respectively, two leading American critics, one British analyst, and one American neo-conservative. Ivo Daalder and James Lindsay usefully distinguish between 'assertive nationalists' and 'democratic imperialists'. Most of the Bush administration's foreign policy principals and advisers, including Vice-president Dick Cheney and Defence Secretary Donald Rumsfeld:

> were not neo-cons. Nor for that matter was Bush. They were instead assertive nationalists – traditional hard-line conservatives willing to use American military power to defeat threats to US security but reluctant as a general rule to use American primacy to remake the world in its image.
>
> (Daalder and Lindsay 2003: 15)

By contrast, neo-conservatives/democratic imperialists were mostly outside the administration, inside the pages of the *Weekly Standard* and the television studios of *Fox News*. What both groups shared was a deep scepticism of traditional Wilsonianism's commitment to international law and institutions and its privileging diplomacy and treaties over power and resolve. Such agreement allowed them to cooperate even as they disagreed over 'what kind of commitment the US should make to rebuilding Iraq and remaking the rest of the world' (ibid.: 16).

Refining this, Steven Hurst (2005: 83) argues that 'Despite a consensual core of key beliefs, therefore, conservative nationalists and neo-conservatives are clearly two distinct groups with important intellectual disagreements on fundamental issues.' Four elements unite neo-conservatives with conservative nationalists but two provoke disagreement. Both approaches concur that the US should preserve its primary leadership role, exercise unilateral action if necessary, increase defence spending substantially and develop a national missile defence system. They depart, however, on the importance of ideas, values and democracy and on humanitarian intervention, peace-keeping and nation-building. Conservative nationalists are deeply sceptical that Washington should, or can, effectively promote democracy and nation-building or end ethnic cleansing whereas neo-conservatives see these as part of the US national interest, not a distraction from it.

As Hurst notes, differences exist not only between the two groups but also within them. In this regard, Charles Krauthammer (2005) makes an important distinction within neo-conservative ranks between 'democratic globalists' and 'democratic realists'. While democratic globalists represent an improvement on traditional Realists, since the former appreciate that democracies typically provide the most secure allies and stable relationships, they embrace an excessively idealistic and ambitious agenda. A universalist commitment to human freedom and democracy everywhere is unrealistic, leading to overstretched resources, exhaustion of morale and diversion from the world's most urgent challenges. Idealistic universalism must be tempered by the realist consideration of strategic necessity. Democratic realism's central axiom is that while democracy promotion should be supported everywhere, American blood and treasure will only be committed where a strategic necessity exists. Democratic realism advances a targeted, focused and limited grand strategy that:

> intervenes not everywhere that freedom is threatened but only where it counts – in those regions where the defence or advancement of freedom is critical to success in the larger war against the existential enemy. That is how we fought the Cold War. The existential enemy then was Soviet communism. Today, it is Arab/Islamic radicalism. Therefore 'where it really counts today is in that Islamic crescent stretching from North Africa to Afghanistan'.
>
> (ibid.: 188)

Thus, where Kagan and Kristol supported NATO's intervention in Kosovo, Krauthammer opposed it. While Krauthammer arguably has the more acute definition of neo-conservatism, this chapter will include both democratic globalists and democratic realists within the rubric of the neo-conservative family. In sum, neo-conservatives can be best seen as 'balance of threat' (as opposed to balance of power) realists, with some supplementary assumptions:

> that institutions exert negligible independent effects (shared with neo-realists); that domestic regime type profoundly shapes a state's intentions (shared with democratic-peace liberals); that regime type affects whether a state generates terrorists; and that certain states might not easily be deterrable (the latter two being claims on which the other approaches do not pronounce).
>
> (Alexander 2007: 42)

Neo-conservatism and the Bush Administration

As such, then, what was neo-conservatism's relationship to the Bush administration? Neo-conservatives were junior members of the Bush administration. Approximately twenty secured administration posts in 2001. The highest ranking was Paul Wolfowitz, Deputy Defense Secretary. The neo-conservatives were neither CEO types such as Bush, Cheney and Rumsfeld, Texan loyalists such as Karl Rove, Alberto Gonzalez and Karen Hughes, nor Christian evangelicals such as John Ashcroft. Mostly Jews in a heavily gentile party, and intellectuals in a party mostly unmoved by abstract thinkers, neo-conservatives were generally 'not natural comrades of a president who judged people by the content of their hearts rather than the quality of their minds' (Micklethwait and Wooldridge 2004: 200).

As Micklethwait and Wooldridge note, neo-conservatives have – like all politically active Americans in Washington – interconnections, favoured think tanks and journalistic homes, more or less reliable fundraising sources, and discrete agendas. Crucial to their influence was not a deliberate campaign, but simply the attacks of 9/11:

> the policies that Bush followed after September 11 were no longer just neo-conservative policies. They had become conservative policies – policies that resonated throughout the Right Nation ... America's neo-conservative foreign policy

was not so much a question of conversion, let alone hijacking. Rather, the views of one hitherto eccentric part of the coalition suddenly coincided with the movement as a whole. The neo-cons were not so much conspirators, operating under cover of night, as articulators, saying out in the open what so many conservatives privately found themselves thinking. After September 11, the neo-con solution seemed, to conservatives at least, to be the American solution.

(ibid.: 209–10)

Some of the elements of the crossover of nationalist realist and neo-conservative forces was evident prior to 9/11. In withdrawing from the Anti-Ballistic Missile Treaty, declining to sign up to the Kyoto Protocol or the International Criminal Court, and evincing a tepid enthusiasm for the United Nations the pre-9/11 administration pleased both conservative nationalists and neo-conservatives. Any element of a far-reaching 'forward agenda of freedom' was, however, conspicuously absent. The forces of conservative/nationalist realism were far more ascendant than those of neo-conservatism.

The events of 9/11 altered this, not by transforming the administration but by encouraging it to enlist and adapt certain neo-conservative arguments in support of its policies. Even here, however, the extent to which neo-conservatism – still less neo-conservatives – gained the reins of power, rather than finding a stronger convergence with the assertive nationalists dominating the foreign policy decision-making of the administration, requires careful consideration. Three examples are illustrative: Afghanistan, Iraq and the Israel-Palestinian conflict.

The decision to invade Afghanistan was hardly neo-conservative inspired. Once it became clear that al Qaeda was responsible for the 9/11 attacks and that the Taliban would not hand Bin Laden over, a US military intervention was inevitable. Moreover it was widely supported across the political spectrum, with only one dissenting vote in Congress on the authorisation of military force in 2001. But the subsequent linkage of rogue states, WMD and terrorism as the primary threat to the US – and the explicit addition of prevention, regime change and democratisation as key principles of grand strategy in the National Security Strategy of 2002 – suggested to many an embrace of precisely the vision articulated by many neo-conservatives. The notoriously incurious president now seemed to have latched onto a vision beyond a narrowly defined US national interest.

The clearest example of the new conservative convergence was Iraq. The neo-conservatives' most vociferous opponents – realist conservatives, rather than the left – have depicted Iraq as a neo-conservative war (Rosen 2005). They are not alone. Ikenberry (2004: 7) even suggested that the 'conquest of Iraq was the neo-conservative's (*sic*) defining goal and their crowning achievement'. But while it is true that some neo-conservatives had long wanted to topple Saddam, and actively lobbied for this over 2001–3, casting Iraq as a neo-conservative war is not persuasive. Neo-conservatives certainly supported the war. But the decision to go to war was made by a war cabinet whose principals comprised Bush, Cheney, Powell, Rumsfeld, and Rice – none of whom were neo-conservatives (indeed, it was the supposed Cheney who, as Defense Secretary in 1991, was complicit in the 'Realist' decision to leave Saddam and his army intact at the Gulf War's end). Regime change was justified not in terms of democratising the Middle East but in the US national interest. Rumsfeld was also invested in his pet project of demonstrating the validity of the Revolution in Military Affairs. The Defense

Secretary was 'a shark who swam with the neo-con fish. But he wasn't one of them; like Cheney, he is better characterised as a nationalist hawk' (Weisberg 2008: 201).

Moreover, much of the key impetus for war came not from neo-conservatives but from liberal interventionists such as Blair and erstwhile Democratic Party presidential aspirants Hillary Clinton, Joseph Lieberman, John Edwards, Joe Biden and Christopher Dodd. Outside government, journals and individuals as varied as, respectively, the *National Review, The Economist* and *New Republic*, and Henry Kissinger, Christopher Hitchens, Thomas Friedman, Andrew Sullivan, Fareed Zakaria and Michael Kelly all supported the war. The single most forceful case was authored not by a neo-conservative but by former Clinton NSC operative Kenneth Pollack. The 'democratic peace' argument central to neo-conservative thought was mostly absent from these, as well as administration, rationales for war until long after its conclusion and the onset of the Iraqi insurgency.

In addition, typically, neo-conservatives differed over both the principle and execution of the war. On the former, while Kristol, Kagan and Krauthammer strongly supported the war, James Q. Wilson and others viewed the effort to implant a democratic state in Iraq as doomed to fail. On the latter, Frederick Kagan (2002) had strongly criticised the 'Wolfowitz model' of a light US footprint during the initial phases of the Afghan War and prior to that in Iraq. Indeed, proponents of the neo-conservative 'hijack' thesis might usefully ponder how the most powerful neo-conservative within the administration found himself in a deeply uneasy relationship with his boss, the Defense Secretary, to the point where long prior to the Iraq War they were 'barely on speaking terms' (Weisman 2007: 170):

> [Deputy Secretary of State, Richard] Armitage grew used to receiving calls from Wolfowitz after their bosses had attended a Principals Committee meeting at the White House to ask what had happened, since Rumsfeld refused to tell him. Adding to the awkwardness was a decree enforced by Rumsfeld that the secretary and deputy secretary could not both be away from Washington at the same time. Hence Wolfowitz was frequently forced to cancel long-planned trips because Rumsfeld suddenly decided to take himself off, thus forcing his subordinate to stay behind and mind the store.
>
> (Cockburn 2007: 102)

The third and final example worth consideration is Israel. The common charge that neo-conservatives caused Bush to invade Iraq for Israel not only mischaracterises the administration's decision-making calculus but also misses the most salient point about Israeli strategic interests: most Israelis opposed the democratisation strategy for the region precisely because its success would likely yield outcomes – such as an elected Hamas in Gaza – that could worsen rather than improve Israel's strategic position. If the administration had truly been at war for Tel Aviv's preferences, it would either have dealt first with Iran rather than Iraq or would have left a 'friendly' authoritarian in office in Baghdad rather than the tumult of a nascent and fragile Arab democracy dominated by Shias. To the extent that Bush and Rice explicitly repudiated 'sixty years' of US administrations favouring tyranny over democracy to yield stability while failing to achieve it, the neo-conservative imprint worked against, not with, the grain of Israel's self-conception of its national interest. Moreover, as even the neo-conservative rejectionist Fukuyama (2006: xi) concedes, the prospects for a successful settlement of the Israeli-Palestinian conflict were minimal in Bush's first term, regardless of the nuances of Washington's approach. As such, a pressing question remains: how can the Bush foreign policy be genuinely considered neo-conservative?

How neo-conservative was Bush's foreign policy?

Supporters and critics alike assert that Bush's foreign policy was 'neo-conservative'. A common response to rebuttals of such claims is not only to pursue the geo-political Cluedo equivalent of 'who-dunnit?' in terms of personnel and social links but also to note the administration's official declarations. An important case here suggests that, even if they began as conservative nationalists, the administration's principals were transformed into neo-conservatives, not least the president himself. After all, in his second inaugural speech, in January 2005, Bush declared that, 'It is the policy of the United States to seek and support the growth of democratic movements and institutions in every nation and culture, with the ultimate goal of ending tyranny in our world.' As neo-conservatives were steadily exiting his administration, the president was declaiming that 'History has an ebb and flow of justice, but history also has a visible direction, set by liberty and the Author of Liberty.' To some, Bush was 'adopting a faith-flavoured version of their fantasy foreign policy' (Weisberg 2008: 215). Or, as Heilbrunn (2008: 267) put it, 'The longer his presidency went on, the more of a neo-conservative Bush became – and the less power the neo-conservatives themselves exercised directly.' In short, whatever the identity of the principals occupying the administration's offices, the principles informing its policies were neo-conservative.

In personnel terms, the neo-conservative presence was certainly diminishing with each successive year. In Bush's first term, Perle had been required to give up his chairmanship of the Defense Policy Board that advised the Pentagon (though he remained a board member). Wolfowitz left the Pentagon to head the World Bank. As Bush's second term progressed, such leading neo-conservative figures as there were steadily left, whether through scandal (Wolfowitz, Libby) or a combination of force of circumstances and a desire to return to the private sector (Abrams, Feith).

But whether or not Bush had personally embraced neo-conservatism remains murky. As in his first term, the president occasionally ventured the kind of speeches – albeit markedly less frequently – that suggested he had moved a distance from the Realist statecraft of his father. In the spring of 2008, at the World Economic Forum in Egypt, he even publicly excoriated Middle Eastern regimes that locked up their political opponents.

But for most neo-conservatives, the verdict on Bush became progressively less positive. As Perle summed up the emerging consensus in a speech to the Hudson Institute in May 2007, 'He came ill-equipped for the job and has failed to master it':

> I think he's a decent guy who has been courageous and is trying to do the right thing. But he just can't execute. He can't run the government. He's proven again and again he can't get his arms around the government for which he takes responsibility. And on the issues I care most about, it has gotten substantially worse since Condi went to the State Department.
>
> (Weisman 2007: 237)

A comprehensive neo-conservative audit of the Bush foreign policy would necessarily offer a mixed verdict. Bush did not appoint any neo-conservatives to the decisive policy-making positions in his administration. He did, however, symbolically supplement traditionally conservative nationalist positions – that sustaining American primacy mattered for US security and according a veto on US action to the UN, NATO or anyone else was to be rejected – with an apparent embrace of distinctively neo-conservative ones, in particular, the notions that regimes mattered as much as power balances and that the USA should be in the business of democracy promotion. The wars in Afghanistan and Iraq were supported strongly by neo-conservatives as strategically sound, although their execution ultimately proved anything but, mostly at the behest of conservative nationalists such as Cheney, Rumsfeld and Rice. Nonetheless, under intense pressure after the Democrats' 2006 midterm victories to accept the 'Realist' recommendations of the Baker–Hamilton Iraq Study Group in 2006–7, Bush instead accepted the 'surge' strategy advanced by Frederick Kagan and General Jack Keane. As Stelzer evaluated the balance:

> the neo-cons, although not all powerful, certainly have reason to claim a policy triumph, even if a limited one. The policy of deferring to the United Nations has been replaced with a policy of ignoring that body if American interests so require; the policy of treating terrorist attacks as criminal acts has been replaced with a policy of treating them as acts of war (the first attack on the World Trade Center in 1993 resulted in a criminal trial; the second and more successful attack in 2001 resulted in a war on terrorists in Afghanistan and Iraq); the policy of responding to attacks with ineffectual isolated missile launches has been replaced with a policy of applying massive force, followed if necessary by occupation and nation-building.
>
> (Stelzer 2004: 17)

Against this, as noted earlier, the rationales for war in Afghanistan and Iraq were not justified by appeals to neo-conservative ideas about the importance of values, ideas and nation-building. Nor did their execution follow the kind of nation-building precepts that leading neo-conservatives advocated. Whether in his rhetorical commitment to a 'balance of power that favours freedom' or his follow-through on the ground, Bush's approach was more that of a conservative nationalist than a neo-conservative. His administration's commitment to nation-building in Afghanistan and Iraq was limited, contingent and unenthusiastically embraced. Had he been able opportunistically to withdraw US forces immediately, he surely would have. The nation-building efforts were ones of necessity, not choice. Moreover, Bush's commitment to conditioning aid and diplomatic relations on political reform was almost non-existent in regard to Pakistan, Egypt, Saudi Arabia and elsewhere. There may have been sound reasons for such decisions. But these did not represent neo-conservative prescriptions.

In addition, Bush's willingness to engage in extended negotiations with North Korea, to eschew decisive action against Tehran over its nuclear ambitions, and to reject pressure for regime change from Islamabad and Riyadh to Cairo and Caracas contradicted the soaring rhetoric of his second inaugural. Hence, if 'ideology' provides a necessary part of an explanation of Bush's foreign policy, it is a small part, the key explanatory variables residing outside the realm of ideas: 'if we believe that that foreign policy is neo-conservative then we do not understand it' (Hurst 2005: 77).

In part, the tensions between Bush and neo-conservatives derived from a familiar divide between the realms of ideas and policy. Both unelected policy wonks and candidates for public office are political entrepreneurs locked in a mutually parasitical relationship. The former require the latter to champion their ideas in order to see them realised as policy. The latter require the former to provide them the 'vision' and proposals by which pressing problems might be addressed. In this regard, one of neo-conservatism's most influential voices offered a qualified but robust defence of Bush against his critics. Noting that, like Reagan before him, Bush was a politician rather than an ideologue, Podhoretz pointed out that prudential considerations that did not burden academic critics inevitably intervened when major decisions had to be made:

> None of this meant that those of us who shared Bush's ideas and ideals, but who laboured under neither utopian nor realist delusions, were barred from questioning the soundness of his prudential judgment in this or that instance. But by the same token, we had an intellectual responsibility to recognise and acknowledge that he had already taken those ideas and ideals much further than might have been thought possible, especially given the ferocity of the opposition they had encountered from all sides and the difficulties they had also met with in the field. Indeed, it was a measure of his enormous political skills that – at a time in 2004 when things were not looking all that good for the Bush Doctrine's prospects in Iraq – he had succeeded in mobilising enough support for its wildly controversial principles to run on them for a second term and win.
>
> (Podhoretz 2007: 186–7)

The future of neo-conservatism

The disbandment of the Project for a New American Century in 2006 appeared to some as a symbolic burying of the neo-conservative sensibility. With Fukuyama (2006: ix) also breaking with his prior brethren in an embittered coda, dismissing neo-conservatism as a 'political symbol and a body of thought' as 'something I can no longer support', and even some neo-conservatives conceding that, had they known of the cost of the Iraq War's mismanagement they would not have supported it, few mourned the apparent passing into the night of neo-conservatism.

But neo-conservatism has been pronounced dead on previous occasions. Indeed, it was Irving Kristol himself who offered that verdict in 1996 – one he was later to retract. From John Ikenberry, who pronounced 'the hard-right turn in American foreign policy' both 'intellectually and politically untenable' (2004: 7–8) to Robert Jervis (2005) who similarly claims the Bush Doctrine is 'unsustainable', critics of neo-conservatism have been quick to declare its recent demise. In terms of policy substance, as we saw above, even its advocates have cast doubt on its continued salience in Bush's second term. But, as Kristol argues, the persuasion manifests itself over time in an erratic fashion. As such, there appear three reasons why, even if the 'neo-conservative moment' has passed, it may yet return once again.

First, in the short term, there are factors shaping the foreign policy politics of both political parties that augur well for the neo-conservative persuasion. While the Republican Party struggles to stay competitive under the Bush brand and its deeply compromised legacy, its activists had the wisdom – inadvertent or otherwise – to select as their 2008 presidential standard bearer the one Republican who articulated independent stances throughout his national career. As one conservative commentator asked about McCain in the middle of 2008, in a rather typical caricature of the neo-conservative 'black and white', 'democracy at the point of a gun' approach:

Has he become more neo-con than Bush? In the past McCain has been known as a pragmatist and realist, able to see when American interests have to come before American rhetoric or sentiment. But in the past few years, as the Iraq debate has polarised so many, he has become shriller and more demagogic on the war in the Middle East, more prone to Bush-style declarations about good and evil than subtler assessments of how best to mix force, diplomacy and multilateralism to the West's advantage.

(Sullivan 2008)

As one more sober analyst of the ebb and flow of neo-conservative ideas and influence has suggested, 'No one could do more than McCain to revive the neo-conservative cause' (Heilbrunn 2008: 279–80). This is more than a matter of the Arizona Senator's strong and lonely support, long prior to the 'surge', for more ground forces in Iraq. For while his early congressional career saw him take fairly conventional conservative/ nationalist positions on foreign policy and exhibit a scepticism to US interventions abroad, the 1990s saw McCain evolve as a leading voice in favour of the kind of expansive foreign policy typically favoured by neo-conservatives. McCain was supported by Bill Kristol over Bush in the 2000 primaries precisely because the latter was promising a more 'humble' foreign policy in the mould of his Realist father rather than the 'national greatness' conservatism favoured by McCain. Although McCain's foreign policy advisors in 2008 drew on a range of schools – from Kristol and Kagan to Brent Scowcroft and Kissinger – his inner circle, and some policy positions, exhibited 'a decidedly neo-conservative flavour' (Ambinder 2008: 33). Moreover, his chief foreign policy coordinator, Randy Scheunemann, had been a PNAC director and founded the Committee for the Liberation of Iraq in 2002.

Perhaps the most consequential issue in this regard is not so much whether neo-conservatives will continue to articulate their ideas to the next administration, from the inside or outside, but which ideas they choose to stress. In this respect, a new fissure in neo-conservative ranks may be emerging between those who adhere to the notion that there exists no remedy for the multiple maladies of the Middle East other than democratisation, and those who are now turning instead towards forging a 'league of democracies' against autocracies of whatever political, ideological or religious stripe. There exists something of an irony here inasmuch as it is Kagan (2008) – a democratic globalist supporter of the Iraq War and Middle East transformation – who now stresses the broader threat from autocracies while Krauthammer remains steadfast in his adherence to democratic realism and the priority of regime change across the Arab world.

The prospects for a McCain presidency were, at the time of writing, at best slim. Even an Obama administration, however, might find the siren song of neo-conservative influence difficult entirely to resist. Partly, this stems from the electoral exigencies of national security. As Campbell and O'Hanlon (2006) advised, to win the presidency, 'hard power' Democrats not only need to offer a greater competence than the Bush administration – not difficult – but need also to 'take a leaf from the neo-con playbook' in terms of vision. A Democratic administration that eschews idealism – whether in terms of democracy promotion, human rights, liberty or women's emancipation – is unlikely to secure popular American support. As such, while the pressures of partisan politics and the incentives of election campaigns typically emphasise difference and change, the dynamics of governing can often yield similarity and continuity.

Commenting on a call by Dana Allin, Michael O'Hanlon and Philip Gordon (all pro-minent and vociferous neo-conservative critics) for a future Democrat administration to show 'respect' for leading allies, for example, Anatol Lieven observed that: 'It is difficult to show respect, however, while categorically rejecting someone's advice. In this regard, much of the content and even the language of the *Progressive Internationalist* declaration is indistinguishable from neo-conservative tracts' (Lieven 2004: 77).

An Obama administration would be highly unlikely to wage another preventative war, to use the sometimes undiplomatic rhetoric of Bush's first term, or to appoint as US Ambassador to the UN an individual who has openly derided the organisation. Whether it would also abandon Iraq, Israel and the Arab states of the Middle East; refuse to countenance military action against an imminent nuclear Iran if 'muscular diplomacy' failed; give up on nation-building in Afghanistan; declare the war on terror over, won or lost; or close US military bases around the world all seem much less certain.

The second factor sustaining neo-conservative influence in Washington is genera-tional in nature. In this regard, too myopic a focus on the results of the 2008 pre-sidential election should not obscure the broader issues affecting neo-conservative fortunes. One critic (Heilbrunn 2008: 278) argues that 'it will take an insurgency inside the GOP itself to dislodge the neoconservatives', a prospect that he views as 'dubious'. The old-style Realists of the James Baker, Scowcroft and Kissinger ilk have become a diminishing presence in the party as its electoral coalition has taken on an increasingly southern and western (that is, conservative nationalist), and decreasingly north-eastern, cast. While the neo-conservatives began as rebels against the 1960s rebellion, and while many self-consciously celebrate that anti-establishment identity still, they have increas-ingly taken up a *de facto* residence as a powerful intellectual force within the foreign policy ranks of the twenty-first-century Republican Party and, in particular, its institu-tional and media expressions within the Washington Beltway.

That by no means guarantees the translation of ideas into policy results. Neo-conservatives require the active support or passive acquiescence of conservative/ nationalist realists, which is far from assured. Moreover, both the paleo-conservative and libertarian currents within the conservative coalition, personified by Pat Buchanan and Ron Paul (R-TX), respectively, represent important sources of resistance to both neo-conservatives and conservative nationalists. In addition, as Stelzer (2004: 25) argues, the future survival and influence of neo-conservative ideas will 'depend crucially on the neo-cons' ability to eliminate the contradiction between their foreign policy goals and their domestic policies. Muscular foreign policy, and the accompanying expanded military, cost money.' While the neo-conservative analysis of the threats to US security remains compelling, and the tragic necessity for wars on terror likewise – even to those outside the neo-conservative persuasion (Bobbitt 2008) – squaring the circle of how to enhance American capacities to address those threats will remain a powerful challenge. But the persistence of major challenges and security threats in the international arena – above all from the nexus of mass fatality terrorists and WMD – is likely to guarantee a continued hearing for neo-conservative remedies.

That leads on to the third and final factor suggesting the resilience rather than the passing of the neo-conservative moment: the nature of American political culture. As Lieven noted, by 2004, Iraq had meant that neo-conservative influence on the Bush administration was waning compared to the more assertive nationalism of Cheney/ Rumsfeld and the more multilateral approaches of Powell and Rice. Nonetheless, 'the deeper tendencies in American political culture which the neo-conservatives exploited will remain; indeed ... their democratising messianism is widely shared within the Democratic Party' (Lieven 2004: 153).

As Kristol argues, neo-conservatism is essentially an American persuasion. Nonetheless, politicians and public intellectuals outside America may occasionally embrace its central tenets. Even an unrelenting Europhile and social democratic opponent has recently deigned to concede that while there is 'still something of the neo-con night' about his thought, the 'arch neoconservative' Kagan's call to create a league of democracies 'deserves a hearing and a debate' (Hutton 2008). Indeed, one of the victories that such critics inadvertently accord neo-conservatism is their recent attempts to develop supposedly alternative foreign policy paradigms. Typically, these encompass efforts to combine Realist insights about power and its limits with idealist emphases on values and institutions. Thus, Fukuyama (2006) prescribes in neo-conservatism's stead 'realistic Wilsonianism'. Lieven and Hulsman (2006) offer 'ethical realism'. However sincere and merited the attempts, such efforts are arguably the tribute that cosmopolitan virtue pays the alleged American vice of neo-conservatism. Either such ploys are semantic masks for 'neo-conservative lite' or, alternatively, represent efforts to will the ends of the Bush Doctrine while reverting to means – increased reliance on diplomacy and greater deference to the UN as policy – that are no different to traditional Realist and liberal internationalist schools (Lynch and Singh 2008).

Fukuyama may be correct that neo-conservatism has become 'irreversibly identified with the policies of the administration of George W. Bush in his first term, and any effort to reclaim the label at this point is likely to be futile' (2006: ix). But what was significant about the rhetorical rationales of Bush foreign policy in the first term, and the substance of that policy through Bush's two terms in office, was 'not the prevalence of neo-conservative ideas but their almost complete absence' (Hurst 2005: 90). If, as Hurst rightly contends, the Bush foreign policy was more 'fundamentally influenced by conservative nationalist rather than neo-conservative ideas' (ibid.: 92), the appositeness of identifying neo-conservatism with Bush's first term is highly questionable. As such, the future revival of neo-conservatism may be less futile than Fukuyama suggests. In theory, and perhaps in policy too, neo-conservatives – sweet, sour or otherwise – may well exercise an important influence on US foreign policy long after the Stones have finally ceased rolling.

Conclusion

The liberal historian, Arthur Schlesinger Jr., argued that American history was essentially cyclical. In years to come, something analogous may be written of the history of neo-conservatism and its influence on US foreign policy. Neo-conservatives have offered powerful analyses of the international order, compelling diagnoses of the weaknesses of rival approaches to international affairs, and prescriptions for US policy that have proven controversial. The traumatic events of 9/11 generated sufficient political agreement among both conservative nationalists and some liberal interventionists with these to ensure the interventions in Afghanistan and Iraq. But Iraq was not a 'neo-conservative war' either in design or execution. Whether or not Bush embraced and then abandoned neo-conservative views is a matter that only his memoirs may resolve. But his administration only invoked neo-conservative rationales after the wars took place and, preoccupied by an occupation that paid insufficient, not excessive, attention to neo-conservative thought and with a diminishing neo-conservative presence even in its secondary echelons, Bush effectively gave up on neo-conservatism in substance by early 2005. Had the execution of the post-war stage of the Iraq war been more effective, the fate of neo-conservatism and the shape of US policy could conceivably have been different. Nonetheless, the success of the 'surge' and the continuing threats to US security from radical Islam and assorted autocracies assure the continued salience of neo-conservative strategic thought. Even though the ranks of self-described neo-conservatives remain modest in number, the forces within the Republican coalition and the broader American polity sustaining the neo-conservative persuasion remain powerful and resilient.

Further reading and websites

Stelzer (2004) and Murray (2006) offer the best sympathetic guides to neo-conservative thought. Heilbrunn (2008) provides a critical historical overview. Although they offer a variety of perspectives, the following think tanks offer good sources of neo-conservative worldviews:

www.aei.org
www.hudson.org
www.manhattan-institute.org

References

Alexander, Gerard (2007) 'International Relations Theory Meets World Politics', in Stanley A. Renshon and Peter Suedfeld (eds), *Understanding the Bush Doctrine: Psychology and Strategy in an Age of Terrorism*, New York: Routledge, pp. 39–64.

Ambinder, Marc (2008) 'The McCain Squadron', *National Journal*, 17 May, 28–37.

Bobbitt, Philip (2008) *Terror and Consent: The Wars for the Twenty-first Century*, London: Allen Lane.

Bolton, John (2007) *Surrender Is Not an Option: Defending America at the United Nations and Abroad*, New York: Threshold Editions.

Brooks, David (2004) 'The Neocon Cabal and Other Fantasies', in I. Stelzer (ed.), *Neoconservatism*, London: Atlantic Books, pp. 41–2.

Brzezinski, Zbigniew (2007) *Second Chance: Three Presidents and the Crisis of American Superpower*, New York: Basic Books.

Campbell, Alastair and Stott, Richard (eds) (2008) *The Blair Years: Extracts from the Alastair Campbell Diaries*, London: Arrow Books.

Campbell, Kurt M. and O'Hanlon, Michael E. (2006) *Hard Power: The New Politics of National Security*, New York: Basic Books.

Cockburn, Andrew (2007) *Rumsfeld: An American Disaster*, London: Verso.

Daalder, Ivo H. and Lindsay, James M. (2003) *America Unbound: The Bush Revolution in Foreign Policy*, Washington, DC: Brookings Institution Press.

Ehteshami, Anoushiravan and Zweiri, Mahjoob (2007) *Iran and the Rise of its Neoconservatives: The Politics of Tehran's Silent Revolution*, London: I.B. Tauris.

Fukuyama, Francis (2006) *After the Neocons: America at the Crossroads*, London: Profile Books.

Gottfried, Paul Edward (2007) *Conservatism in America: Making Sense of the American Right*, New York: Palgrave Macmillan.

Halper, Stefan and Clarke, Jonathan (2004) *America Alone: The Neo-Conserevatives and the Global Order*, Cambridge: Cambridge University Press.

Heilbrunn, Jacob (2008) *They Knew They Were Right: The Rise of the Neocons*, New York: Doubleday.

Hurst, Steven (2005) 'Myths of Neoconservatism: George W. Bush's "Neo-Conservative" Foreign Policy Revisited', *International Politics*, 42(1): 75–96.

Hutton, Will (2008) 'West Versus the Rest', *The Observer*, Review, 8 June, p. 22.

Ikenberry, G. John (2004) 'The End of the Neo-Conservative Moment', *Survival*, 46(1): 7–22.

Jervis, Robert (2005) *American Foreign Policy in a New Era*, London: Routledge.

Kagan, Frederick (2002) 'Cheap Hawks Can't Fly', *Weekly Standard*, 4 November.

Kagan, Robert (2008) *The Return of History and the End of Dreams*, London: Atlantic Books.

Kaplan, Lawrence F. and Kristol, William (2003) *The War over Iraq: Saddam's Tyranny and America's Mission*, San Francisco: Encounter Books.

Krauthammer, Charles (2005) 'In Defense of Democratic Realism', in Gary Rosen (ed.), *The Right War? The Conservative Debate on Iraq*, New York: Cambridge University Press, pp. 186–200.

Kristol, Irving (2004) 'The Neoconservative Persuasion: What It Was, and What It Is', in Irwin Stelzer (ed.), *Neoconservatism*, London: Atlantic Books, pp. 33–7.

Leonard, Mark (2008) *What Does China Think?* London: Fourth Estate.

Lieven, Anatol (2004) *America Right or Wrong: An Anatomy of American Nationalism*, London: HarperCollins.

Lieven, Anatol and Hulsman, John (2006) *Ethical Realism: A Vision for America's Role in the World*, New York: Pantheon Books.

Lynch, Timothy J. and Singh, Robert S. (2008) *After Bush: The Case for Continuity in American Foreign Policy*, Cambridge: Cambridge University Press.

Micklethwait, John and Wooldridge, Adrian (2004) *The Right Nation: Why America Is Different*, London: Allen Lane.

Murray, Douglas (2006) *Neoconservatism: Why We Need It*, San Francisco: Encounter Books.

Podhoretz, Norman (2007) *World War IV: The Long Struggle Against Islamofascism*, New York: Doubleday.

Rosen, Gary (ed.) (2005) *The Right War? The Conservative Debate on Iraq*, New York: Cambridge University Press.

Scheuer, Michael (2008) *Marching toward Hell: America and Islam after Iraq*, New York: Free Press.

Stelzer, Irwin (2004) 'Neoconservatives and their Critics: An Introduction', in I. Stelzer (ed.), *Neoconservatism*, London: Atlantic Books, pp. 3–28.

Sullivan, Andrew (2008) 'Would the Clintons Kindly Leave the Building', *The Sunday Times*, News Review, 1 June, p. 4.

Thompson, Michael (ed.) (2007) *Confronting the New Conservatism: The Rise of the Right in America*, New York: New York University Press.

Weisberg, Jacob (2008) *The Bush Tragedy: The Unmaking of a President*, London: Bloomsbury.

Weisman, Alan (2007) *Prince of Darkness: Richard Perle – The Kingdom, the Power, and the End of Empire in America*, New York: Union Square Press.

4 Liberalism and neoliberalism

Timothy J. Lynch

Introduction: what is liberalism?

There are few isms in political theory that have as many prefixes as liberalism: classical, commercial, economic, Great Society, neo-, political, republican, social, sociological … the list is very long. This speaks to the centrality of a liberal tradition in Western thought. Simply put, the West has evolved from a pre-liberal era in which claims to power were grounded in blood (monarchy), metaphysics (religion), racial or national superiority (fascism) or class supremacy (communism) to one in which government was legitimate only if it derived its power from the consent of those it governed. Thus, 500, 100 or even 25 years ago, such governments were relatively few; now they are legion (see Fukuyama 1992: 49–50; and Doyle 1997: 261–4). To be sure, liberal regimes are not identical. They do, however, tend to share a concern with the appropriate limits of governmental power. It is no accident that liberal International Relations (IR) theorists have elevated the explanatory power of individuals in world politics, since these are the 'units', the progress and protection of which is the first duty of the state (see Rosenau 1992: 276–8).

Unlike realists, liberals rarely define themselves against core principles. Realists have, among others, Hans Morgenthau (1904–80) to define their paradigm. He went so far as to enumerate 'six principles of political realism' (Morgenthau 1993: 4–16). Liberals have no such enumeration. That American neoconservatives (see Singh, Chapter 3 in this volume) *and* their detractors can both claim to be liberal is indicative of the rather slippery and fuzzy boundaries within which liberal theorists operate. Nevertheless, while we cannot identify liberal laws or principles, it is appropriate to speak of important liberal traits or assumptions. The individual, or more particularly groups of individual*s*, receive considerable attention in liberal IR theory. Men and women, and their supposed rationality and decency, have tended toward the improvement and progress of societies over time. This assumption might be contrasted with that of realists who understand human nature to be essentially fixed. Thucydides, writing in the fifth century BC, remains central to the realist canon because people and states have not changed in their fundamental natures (see Thucydides 1974). For liberals, states are not autonomous entities; they are amalgamations of people with different tastes and interests that are reflected in their governments. As people change, so do their governing institutions. For liberals, international relations evolve and improve, for realists, they are static and prone to conflict. Liberals explain peace, realists predict war.

Much follows from such divergent premises. Liberals are generally hopeful that the world can be and has been made better; progress is a self-evident liberal truth. For realists, progress is a chimera. Historical elitism is basic to liberal politics and analysis. It is a prejudice to which the United States is especially prone. Inscribed on the Thomas Jefferson Memorial in Washington DC are the following words:

> I am not an advocate for frequent changes in laws and constitutions. But laws and institutions must go hand in hand with the progress of the human mind. As that becomes more developed, more enlightened, as new discoveries are made, new truths discovered and manners and opinions change, with the change of circumstances, institutions must advance also to keep pace with the times. We might as well require a man to wear still the coat which fitted him when a boy as civilized society to remain ever under the regimen of their barbarous ancestors.
>
> (Jefferson 1816)

For realists, the ancient Greeks have as much to teach as the contemporary United Nations – and probably a good deal more. In liberal discourse, the past is usually presented as a place where racism, sexism, imperialism and war were basic to human affairs – an arena from which we have need of escape. The same holds true for liberal IR theorists. It often goes without saying that international politics today, while not perfect, are better than they were before. Francis Fukuyama – whose liberalism is complicated and yet powerful – suggested that the supremacy of liberal democracy at the end of the cold war, in the early 1990s, was so total, its potential rivals so discredited, that it represented 'the end of history' (Fukuyama 1992). He did not call this progress, as such. He did argue that the likelihood of something replacing it was remote. Liberal democracy was the 'end point', he argued, 'of mankind's ideological evolution' and possibly the 'final form of human government' (ibid.: xi). His thesis synchronized so well with the US foreign policy tradition that no president since the end of the cold war has rejected the logic and certainty of the democratic peace. If communism had Marx, liberalism has Fukuyama.

Not all liberal theorists subscribe to this thesis and even Fukuyama denied it was a manifesto for aggressive democratization. For some, the notion of Western supremacy explicit to Fukuyama's interpretation violates their cultural relativism (see Smith 2007: 92–3) and the 'end of history' is increasingly regarded as an unproductive research program within the academy (see Maliniak *et al.* 2007: 30).[1] Most, however, do acknowledge that international relations have improved as a consequence of the proliferation of liberal regimes and the accompanying contraction of their opponents – who prized state control as a means to individual freedom and ended up with neither – in the second half of the twentieth century. State character has evolved because the people within states have changed. Whereas in the past, states defined themselves along ethnic and/or ideological lines, in the brave new world, leaders were prepared to pool sovereignty, to love 'transnationalism', to embrace 'complex interdependence' and to applaud social diversity.[2] These rather nebulous concepts, each accorded significant affection, are common in the liberal discourse on IR. In the Preface to the seminal text of neoliberal institutionalism, one of the most durable and popular versions of IR theory, Robert O. Keohane and Joseph S. Nye bemoaned the rigidities of realism and its stale insistence that IR theory is first and last about explaining why wars happen. '[W]e soon became uneasy about this one-sided view of reality, particularly about its inadequate analysis of economic integration and of the roles played by formal and informal international institutions' (Keohane and Nye, 2001: viii).[3] The knock-on effect of all this was to lessen the explanatory power of *states* in international relations – the central units of analysis for realists – and to increase the explanatory power of all sorts of sub-state actors and non-governmental organizations (NGOs) – the impact of which realists remain decidedly skeptical of but an arena where most neoliberals found themselves working.

Where realists see simplicity, liberals see complexity. The consequence of this is a liberal paradigm which is remarkably diverse, with thousands of scholars studying thousands of international interactions at any and all levels of analysis (see http://www. irtheory.com/know.htm). For this reason, liberalism is often used synonymously with pluralism, a term implying a host of positive connotations for those embracing it; who would not want to be considered a pluralist in contemporary politics and academia? Of course, realism has distinct strands within itself but they are relatively clear-cut. If you work within this more rigid paradigm, you are likely to be labeled in one or two of only four or five ways: as either a classical, neoclassical, structural (or neo-), defensive or offensive realist (Jervis 1978; Waltz 1979; Morgenthau 1993; Mearsheimer 2005). The list of labels for liberal IR theorists is longer simply because the range of factors being observed is so much greater. There are only 190 or so states for realists to theorize; they are over 6.6 billion people open to liberal investigation. Liberal IR theory is consequently vast.

We use the term neoliberals to describe liberal IR theorists since the 1970s – because they followed, chronologically, the liberal thinkers of the preceding 200 or so years.[4] Immanuel Kant (1724–1804) was a *liberal* institutionalist (see Kant 1795), Robert Keohane (b. 1941) is a *neo*liberal institutionalist (see Keohane 1984). They are united in their belief that international institutions can ameliorate the war propensity of governments; get those institutions right and, Kant predicted, we can enjoy a 'perpetual peace'. In the 1990s, the most exciting neoliberal IR subfield was the theory of the 'democratic peace' – also known as republican liberalism – with many scholars working to explain why democracies seemed to avoid wars with each other (see Owen 1994; Brown *et al.* 1996; Doyle 1997; Barkawi and Laffey 2001).[5] Today, despite the endurance of the democratic peace as a research focus, neoliberal theory increasingly concerns itself with questioning the efficacy and inherent limits of American power – especially its harder varieties. Joseph Nye, one of the most influential liberal IR theorists of the past fifty years (in partnership with Keohane, he essentially invented neoliberalism in the 1970s), has managed to frame much of the current debate over American foreign policy with his brilliant, because simply, enumeration of hard and soft power (Nye 2003, 2004, 2005).[6] What such thinkers refer to as the fungibility or complexity of power sets them apart from realists who have a far narrower conception. For scholars, like Nye, calibrating the balance of hard and soft power is essential to foreign policy success.

If anything, the rather optimistic assumptions of the democratic peace have been replaced by a pessimism that a preference for hard power – especially in the American pursuit of the democratization of foreigners – is ruinous of a cooperative international order. Even Fukuyama – sounding remarkably like Karl Marx in his demand that God save him from Marxists – has disavowed the democratization-by-force waged in his name (Fukuyama 2006). The debate is framed not by a neat split between one kind of liberal and another but by scholars working across the social sciences, each adopting and adapting their own liberal suppositions in order to explain contemporary IR. These include sociologists (Mann 2003, 2004; Linklater 2007), institutionalists

(Keohane and Nye 2001; Dai 2007), internationalists (Reus-Smit 2004; Smith 2007), cultural and critical theorists (Lebow 2008; Rengger and Thirkell-White 2007), cosmopolitans (Kaldor 2004; Held 2003), theorists of republican liberalism (Doyle 1997). The intersections of these and many other liberal theories are manifold.

Current and future trends

A basic comparison of the major in-house journals for liberal and realist IR scholars, *International Organization* (*IO*) and *International Security* (*IS*) respectively, is instructive of both recent trends and inbuilt analytical and normative biases across both paradigms, see Figure 5.1.

The contrasts in approach are especially apparent in the use of concepts like 'the citizen', 'climate change', and 'complex interdependence', which liberals are over five times more likely to use than realists; 'Diversity', is favored 2 to 1 by liberals; 'Terrorism', perhaps because of its security implications, is used four times more by realists than liberals.[7] You are twice as likely to read about 'gender', and 'equality' as phenomena in international relations in *IO* than in *IS*. The title of the 2008 American Political Science Association annual conference (in Boston) – 'Categories and Politics of Global Inequalities' – suggests the supremacy of a liberal agenda in the discipline.[8] In the conference program, variations of the word 'liberal' appeared 78 times, variations of 'realism' only nine. According to a recent survey in *Foreign Policy*:

> The picture of the discipline that emerges is a complex one. Some stereotypes are strengthened. Sixty-nine per cent of international relations professors, for example, describe themselves as liberal; a scant 13 per cent see themselves as conservative. They overwhelmingly opposed the U.S. war in Iraq, almost unanimously believe that the United States is less respected in the world because of it, and they

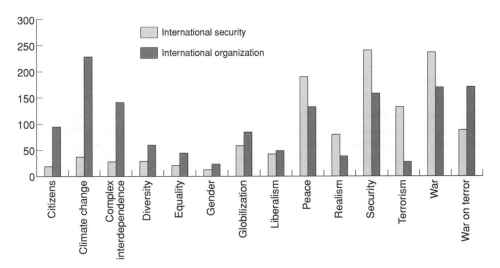

Figure 5.1 A comparison of the frequency of specific terms used in the two most influential journals of IR theory, 2001–2008
Sources: *IO*: http://journals.cambridge.org/action/advanceSearch;
    IS: http://www.mitpressjournals.org/search/advanced

think that this loss of respect poses a significant problem for U.S. foreign policy. Seventy-seven per cent of them support free trade, and only 10 per cent believe the United States should beef up its military budget.

(Maliniak *et al.* 2005)

Liberalism's multilateral bias

The preference for multilateral solutions has become as sentimental to liberal IR theorists as George W. Bush's embrace of unilateralism was instrumental. Liberal thinkers have shown a marked reluctance to abandon the hope that the United States, the foremost creator of international rules and institutions, might one day be bound by them. G. John Ikenberry, the world's eighth 'most interesting' IR scholar (according to Maliniak *et al.* 2007: 18), has noted the incongruity between American internationalist ideals and its actual statecraft. 'The United States has been the greatest champion of multilateral institutions in the twentieth century,' he observes, but has also 'been reluctant to tie itself too closely to these multilateral institutions and rules' (Ikenberry 2003: 49). This paradox has obtained for some time. President Woodrow Wilson, the great liberal hero, invented the League of Nations in 1919 but was unable to get his nation to join it.

So much of neoliberal institutionalism is derived from the observed connection between international institutional cooperation and peace that to circumvent those institutions, according the theory's proponents, invites trouble. The more foreign policies are filtered through the thicket of international processes and rules, the more benign, progressive and 'cosmopolitan' they will become. To remove one's foreign policy from such filtration – as America, it is alleged, has too often done – actually weakens the sum total of global security and of US security in particular. Multilateralism, in several liberal accounts, is a moral value to be upheld in statecraft despite its actual efficacy. The instrumentality and effectiveness of acting alone cannot supplant the moral imperative of acting together. The Iraq War was illegal to many liberal theorists not because of the initially botched reconstruction – this was as possible with the United Nations on-side as without – but because the American intervention did not receive the imprimatur of 'the international community'.

The overthrow of a decidedly non-liberal regime in Baghdad in 2003 earned less liberal applause than the method of America's doing it earned liberal opprobrium. How regime change is effected matters more than what regime is changed. 'Liberal auditing of the war on terror thus becomes a hunt for erroneous procedure on the behalf of the Bush administration' (Lynch and Singh 2008: 100). The Bush betrayal of multilateralism is documented and condemned by Jean-Marc Coicaud (2007), head of the UN University in New York. Among his various charges was George W. Bush's refusal to accept 'the socialization of international life' (ibid.: 199) – a tenuous concept rather more assumed than defined by the author.[9]

Christian Reus-Smit (2004) also relies significantly on notions of 'world community', 'multilateralism', and 'procedural solidarism'. Their dilution under the terms of the Bush doctrine, he argues, calls into question the moral claims made on behalf of that doctrine. It follows for Reus-Smit that any US foreign policy pursued outside of 'the framework of international procedural and substantive rules and norms', even one adopted in self-defense, is by definition immoral. Circumventing the UN Security Council (UNSC) is wrong, he writes, because this institution has 'moral and practical value' (ibid.: 126, 127). The UNSC, which empowers two of the least liberal regimes – Russia and China – with a veto over the behavior of the strongest liberal regime – the United States – is not a contradiction in terms for scholars like Reus-Smit and Coicaud. Rather, this institutional brake on America's 'unilateral opportunism' is to be welcomed as a way of bolstering 'international society' (ibid.: 128, 127). '[U]nbalanced American primacy' (ibid.: 133) will be resisted, he notes, and hopes. Whoever does that balancing, it follows, will be welcomed.

Neoliberal institutionalism, because it prizes so highly the pacification produced by international institutions, necessarily chides foreign policies which pay them less heed. It should be recalled that neoliberalism was a product of the cold war. Its interpretation of that conflict continues to fashion the neoliberal approach to contemporary foreign policy. According to this interpretation, America did better in proportion to its willingness to work with other nations in formal alliances. The cold war's success stories were fundamentally multilateral: NATO, the World Trade Organization (formerly GATT), even the European Union.[10] Less successful were the isolated incidents of American unilateralism. Vietnam, which, save for a brave but small Australian contribution, was fought essentially alone – and to defeat – by the United States.

After the cold war, neoliberalism has come to equate US success with multilateral cooperation, and failure with its absence. The enlargement of NATO was a remarkable success because of the formal partnerships that propelled it. The Iraq War in 2003 was a disaster because it was perceived as insufficiently multilateral and as a repudiation of the UN (even as the action sought to uphold the 16 or so UN resolutions of which Saddam Hussein was, or had been, in violation). It follows in the works of neoliberals that US actions taken in tandem with 'world opinion' – like the Kyoto Protocol on climate change – or that integrate America formally into international institutions – like the International Criminal Court – are to be welcomed (the USA of course signed up to neither, to much liberal chagrin). G. John Ikenberry argues that America has been so vital to the creation and maintenance of international order because it has 'set limits' on its own power (Ikenberry 2001: xi). It has been prepared to bind itself institutionally, making its abundant power less threatening. The more institutionally-bound any state becomes, the less likely it is to fight other states. This provides a working definition of neoliberalism institutionalism. And is indicative of the affection for multilateral action – irrespective of utility – increasingly basic to liberal IR theory.

The exasperation of much liberal analysis since 2001 is owed to a misreading of recent foreign policy history and of the character of the American regime itself. There is an enduring resistance among liberal theorists to the notion that international institutionalism has been tangential to the success of US foreign policy – rising from obscurity to global supremacy in under 200 years – or that the United States is an exceptional rather than a typical liberal democracy. The consequence is a set of liberal theories of IR which privilege multilateralism over less morally pristine, and thus less effective, forms of international strategy, namely, unilateralism or informal 'coalitions of the willing'. Such coalitions were popularised by George W. Bush (2002) and demonised by his detractors, but hardly represent a departure in US foreign policy. Alliances of utility – rather than ideological solidarity, let alone global communitarianism – are basic in American history. The republic itself would have been stillborn but for the alliance with France in the revolutionary war, 1776–83. During its rise to globalism, America had need of some dubious partners, such as the Soviet Union in

World War II, that reflected not a desire to build a world government but to realise American national security.

NATO was effective not because it formalised cooperation and restrained US power but because it was the more effective means of containing the Soviet threat. The organization was embraced not for the multilateralism of its procedures or its international legality but because of the character of the state that was predominant within it: the United States. NATO worked because it gave the lesser nations within it some confidence that the USA would stand against the threatening red blob to their east. International law saved very few people from communism. It is unlikely to save many from the terrorism of the current era. It was the security 'good' that America provided that gave its cold war strategy legitimacy, not international law or institutions. Neoliberal institutionalism thus took the wrong lesson from the cold war and continues to apply it today. It was not complex interdependence, international law and multilateralism that kept the peace but the character and supremacy of American power. We are presented then with a peculiar dilemma for both liberal and realist theorists. Liberals insist international institutions and law matter but US foreign policy belies this claim. Realists dismiss the explanatory power of state character and yet the liberal democratic character of the American regime is the most consequential guide to its behaviour abroad.

This observation speaks to a wider problem in liberal analysis. Because so much liberal theory is predicated on the character of the system, rather than on the individual character of particular states within it, there is an assumption that all liberal regimes are fundamentally similar and are becoming more so as the state withers away and globalisation and transnationalism replace it. Multilateralism is better than its alternative, by this reading, because it increases the number of units and actors involved in any given action. The higher the quantity of involvement, the greater the quality of any subsequent action. The expansion of the European Union is predicated on the superior moral value of size; the bigger the better. The more states formally bind together, the less individual states matter. The less the state matters, the less war-prone international relations become. All wars, especially in Europe, before the dawn of its federal-bureaucratic vision after 1945, were the products of one state attacking another to realise state advantage – defined in national, ethnic and/or ideological terms. To reduce this war propensity, states must be made to matter less and their interdependence to matter more – a twin phenomenon that many neoliberals observe and advocate.

The United States has had a very different experience to that of Europe. An increase in state power in Europe led to disastrous wars. In America, as the state expanded its power and its autonomy relative to others, the nation did rather well. Its power augmented abroad and its liberal rights at home grew; the civil rights movement was an American cold war phenomenon not a European one. As Europe pooled its sovereignty to realise peace, the United States reaffirmed the sovereignty of its 'supreme' Constitution and realised an unprecedented rise to global power.

Much liberal theory observes, assumes and hopes that the state is in decline (see Booth 1991; Linklater 1989). But the preeminent power of Washington suggests otherwise. Thus, we have a disconnection between the analytical concerns of liberal IR theorists – who privilege the explanatory power of sub-state actors – and the reality of American power and, indeed, American-led war – which suggests the decline of the state has been exaggerated. International institutions have had a considerable impact on state behavior in Europe; they have been decidedly marginal in altering American foreign – and especially national security – policy. So, has liberalism lost its foreign policy relevance? The answer is both yes and no.

Q: Has liberalism lost its foreign policy relevance?
A: Yes.

There are at least two reasons to doubt the relevance of liberalism to the actual making of US foreign policy. First, liberal IR theories have increasingly been co-opted by realist ones, and vice versa (see Lynch and Singh 2008: 84–110). The substantive differences across the paradigms are getting smaller. The rise of *neoclassical realism*, as a blending of realist precepts with traditionally liberal levels of analysis, is indicative of this convergence (see Sterling-Folker 1997, 2004; Rose 1998; Ratti 2006; Lobell *et al.* 2008).

Second, too many liberal IR theorists have become mired in a reflexive anti-Bushism which will look increasingly redundant as we move into the post-Bush era, leaving them with many prescriptions but no target. Indeed, the relevance of IR theory for the actual formulation of policy has never been obvious (see Kurth 1998; Lepgold 1998; Lepgold and Nincic 2001; Wohlforth 2000), but for liberals it is perhaps even less so. Liberal internationalism, which has played an important, if over-stated, role in US foreign policy since 1945, has certainly fared less well in an era when the United States lacked a significant opponent and thereby feels less inclined to listen to others. In the cold war, liberal internationalism offered a way of bringing allies into the larger struggle. With that struggle won, this version of liberalism carries less diplomatic weight and has declining domestic appeal. It is, according to Kupchan and Trubowitz (2007), indicative of a 'dead center' in American foreign policy.

If we exempt neoconservatives from the liberal paradigm – as most liberal scholars would prefer – then there is a marked absence of liberal voices, let alone liberal academic voices, in the formulation of modern American foreign policy, despite the enduring attraction of a social science theory – the democratic peace – to US policy-makers. In their national security primer for the Democrats in 2008, Kurt M. Campbell and Michael E. O'Hanlon (2006), cite only one IR theorist – Joseph S. Nye, whose work inspired their title, *Hard Power* – to any significant extent (ibid.: 7). While think tank research is much debated, university research receives very little serious consideration. As a rule, practitioners go on to be scholars rather than the other way around.[11] The earnest liberal analysis offered at meetings of the American Political Science Association and in any number of social science departments on university campuses is almost entirely tangential to the deliberations of the US government. Even the more influential theorists, like Nye, have been those that have enjoyed periods of government service.[12] Indeed, the exclusion of conservative thinkers from the academy in large part accounts for the rise in the vibrancy of Washington think tanks – to where these men and women relocated.[13] Liberals theorists who want to make a difference to policy join Brookings rather than teach and endure the tribulations of securing academic tenure.[14]

Q: Has liberalism lost its foreign policy relevance?
A: No.

This pessimism about liberalism's career prospect ignores two important features of the IR discipline as it is currently constituted. First, that realists, the neoliberal's chief opponent, have hardly covered themselves in analytical glory in recent years. Realism has not been able to fill the vacuum left by the demise of Soviet power and the end of bipolarity. To mix realist metaphors, when this big red billiard ball was pocketed, the remaining balls did not try and balance against the big US ball. Rather, in repudiation of realist predictions, they rushed closer to it. American power has not been balanced by nervous lesser powers in the post-cold war era. India and China have moved toward the USA, not away. In the absence of such balancing behavior, what are realists to do save adopt a commentary increasingly similar to liberals, who form the bulk of their university colleagues? Important realist scholars, such as Mearsheimer and Walt (2007), once disparaged the explanatory power of domestic variables – like ethnic lobbies – in IR, now they embrace them. Indeed, if anything, it is realists who have sounded more like liberals in their denunciations of the new unpopularity of American foreign policy abroad (see Buchanan 2004; Gold 2004; Halper and Clarke 2004, 2007; Tucker and Hendrickson 2004; Mearsheimer 2005; Goldberg 2006; Lieven and Hulsman 2006; Mearsheimer and Walt 2007). Whereas analytically the two paradigms have been oppositional, in terms of their normative bias, they have converged (see Beardsworth 2007).

Second, the relevance of democratic peace theory endures in policy-making circles and in the universities, despite the unwillingness or inability of the latter to penetrate the former. According to IR scholars themselves, the democratic peace remains the single 'most productive' research program in their discipline (Maliniak *et al.* 2007: 29).[15] The relevance of international institutions is inconsistent and unproven. But the democratic peace hypothesis transformed a social science theory into the central pillar of US strategy after the cold war. No liberal idea has dominated the policy debate like the theory which holds that spreading democracies spreads peace. Contention is over the means to this end; it is not over the end itself. The more robust and policy-relevant version of neoliberal IR theory remains the democratic peace hypothesis. Indeed, it is only through this prism that the National Security Strategy of 2002 (Bush 2002) makes any sort of sense.

At the next several presidential inaugurals, as with the last few, we are unlikely to hear neoliberal institutionalism given rhetorical form and expression. Rather, the universality and inevitability of freedom and democracy will remain basic to the conceptualization of international relations offered by the president. He, and eventually she, will do this not simply for reasons of rhetoric but for reasons of utility. The democratic peace is the surest way of effecting a lasting American security. One does not have to share this conclusion. It is, however, more difficult to deny that the democratic peace, as a social science, enjoys a respect among government officials not seen since the scientific socialism of Marxist dogma – but with better prospects of actually being proved right.

Republican liberalism and the bulk of modern IR liberal theory are increasingly at cross-purposes. The loudest works of liberal IR theory in recent years have been those dedicated to denouncing the illusory neoconservative turn in US foreign policy. As we have observed, particular ire is reserved for the notion of democratic universalism. This may account for the designation by scholars of the 'end of history' as the 'least productive' research program in IR (Maliniak *et al.* 2007: 30). Tony Smith's (2007) denunciation of 'liberal fundamentalist jihadism' is now more the rule of liberal IR theory than the exception – despite his claims that liberal theorists themselves are responsible for facilitating overweening American ambition abroad. Republican liberalism or the democratic peace, however, has shown a more steady attachment to the once basic liberal assumption that democracy is a better form of government than its alternatives. It is better not just because democracies are better places in which to live and work but because they do not go to war with each other. Becoming a democracy is hard and prone to conflict (see Mansfield and Snyder 2007) but what, if you are a liberal, as Condoleezza Rice (2005) implored, is the alternative to democratization by coercion or cajolement?

The popularity of a league or concert of democracies, a theme that spanned both presidential platforms in 2008, speaks not to the reemergence of liberal intuitionalism as a foreign policy approach – the league part – but to the ongoing and renewed relevance of *democracy* – and thus to the logic of the democratic peace – in American foreign policy.

Conclusion

In this chapter we sketched the evolution of liberal theories of international relations and observed some of the emerging trends within the discipline. The chapter argued that the analytical bias inherent in many liberal, especially neoliberal, theories actually weakens their explanation of American foreign policy. The insistence that states matter far less than international institutions avoids dealing with the problem of American economic and military preponderance – which actually has very little to do with the decline of 'the state', in fact, quite the reverse.

The chapter concluded by arguing that the democratic peace or republican liberalism is the more robust version of neoliberal IR theory – and is likely to endure, even though several liberals have questioned its orthodoxy and accuracy. The democratic peace explains the content of American foreign policy since the end of the cold war better than alternative approaches within the liberal paradigm. Indeed, the power of the liberal peace hypothesis is so great that, whether one agrees with it or not, it is impossible to conceive of contemporary international relations without recognizing its explanatory power (for scholars of IR) or normative attraction (for the makers of US foreign policy) – an attraction likely to endure into the 2010s and beyond.

Notes

1 Though Fukuyama's pessimism is often overlooked. He was not triumphalist about liberal democracy. Like Tocqueville (2000; writing in 1835) and Nietzsche, he feared democracy would create 'men without chests' (Fukuyama 1992: 300–12). The second half of the book's title – *The Last Man* – is as important as the first though often overlooked.
2 Anne Marie Slaughter (2004) defined 'complex interdependence' as the fundamental constraint on modern US foreign policy.
3 The Prefaces to the first and second editions are included in the third (2001) edition of Keohane and Nye. The seminal text of liberal institutionalism is usually credited to Immanuel Kant's *Perpetual Peace* (1795).
4 Neoliberal institutionalists argue that peace between states is the product of diverse institutions interacting within them and across them. In contradistinction to *neorealists*, neoliberal institutionalists argue that cooperation among non-state actors causes states to be more pacific toward each other. Neorealists argue institutions cannot alter the basic conditions of international anarchy which only national governments can attempt to navigate (see Baldwin 1993).
5 According to the neorealist Kenneth N. Waltz, it is incorrect to call the democratic peace a theory: 'It is a thesis, or a purported fact, but not a theory' ([1959] 2001: x).

6 In 2007, Keohane and Nye were ranked, respectively, by their peers, the first and seventh 'most influential' IR scholars of the last twenty years (see Maliniak *et al.* 2007: 17).

7 This admittedly rather crude measure is based on a simple count of the specific words or phrases as used anywhere in *IO* and *IS* between January 2001 and summer 2008. Of course, not all authors and articles in *IO* are liberal and not all in *IS* realist but the results are indicative of trends in both paradigms. According to Maliniak *et al.* (2007: 20) the two journals were rated as having 'the greatest impact on the way IR scholars think about their subject'. *IO* was no. 1, by a considerable distance, *IS* no. 2.

8 According to the website:

> Categorization and differentiation of ideas, people, institutions, and nations has continued as an unabated intellectual force in the 100-year history of political science as a professional discipline. Changes in world political economy and social organization like globalization, democratization, and international migration, highlight the dynamic character of the distinctions manifest in categories, and invite a close examination of the construction, interpretation, and maintenance of categorical boundaries.
>
> (http://www.apsanet.org/content_2665.cfm)

9 Richard Falk (2003) makes a series of similar claims from a more entrenched leftist position.

10 The General Agreement on Tariffs and Trade, formed in 1948, was the progenitor for the WTO, formally created in 1995. The EU project has been supported by successive US administrations.

11 Henry Kissinger is the most notable exception, moving from Harvard to government in 1969.

12 Nye was an Assistant Secretary of Defense in the Clinton administration.

13 These include think tanks such as the American Enterprise Institute, the Heritage Foundation, and the Hudson Institute.

14 This point was readily conceded by Brookings scholar Pietro Nivola (2008). Ivo Daalder (2007), a foreign policy advisor to Barack Obama in 2008, for similar reasons, declined an academic career path.

15 Some 45 per cent listed it in the top three. Next was 'Non-state Actors/Transnational Social Movements' (36 per cent), 'Rationalism vs. Constructivism' (34 per cent), 'The New Institutionalism' (27 per cent), 'Agent–Structure Debate' (21 per cent), and 'Clash of Civilizations' (21 per cent).

References and further reading

Allison, G. and Zelikow, P. (1999) *Essence of Decision: Explaining the Cuban Missile Crisis*, 2nd edn, New York: Addison-Wesley Longman.

Baldwin, D.A. (ed.) (1993) *Neorealism and Neoliberalism: The Contemporary Debate*, New York: Columbia University Press.

Barkawi, T. and Laffey, M. (eds) (2001) *Democracy, Liberalism, and War: Rethinking the Democratic Peace Debate*, Boulder, CO: Lynne Rienner.

Beardsworth, R. (2007) 'Cosmopolitanism and Realism: Towards a Theoretical Convergence?', paper at British International Studies Association Annual Conference (December).

Booth, K. (1991) 'Security and Emancipation', *Review of International Studies*, 17(October): 313–26.

Brown, M.E., Lynn-Jones, S.M. and Miller, S.E. (eds) (1996) *Debating the Democratic Peace: An International Security Reader*, Cambridge, MA: MIT Press.

Buchanan, P. (2004) *Where the Right Went Wrong: How Neoconservatives Subverted the Reagan Revolution and Hijacked the Bush Presidency*, New York: Thomas Dunne Books.

Bush, G.W. (2002) *National Security Strategy of the United States*, September, Washington, DC: The White House.

Campbell, K.M. and O'Hanlon, M.E. (2006) *Hard Power: The New Politics of National Security*, New York: Basic Books.

Coicaud, J.-M. (2007) *Beyond the National Interest: The Future of UN Peacekeeping and Multilateralism in an Era of U.S. Primacy*, Washington, DC: United States Institute of Peace Press.

Daalder, I. (2007) Roundtable discussion with students, at the Institute for the Study of the Americas, University of London, 22 March.

Dai, X. (2007) *International Institutions and National Policies*, New York: Cambridge University Press.

Doyle, M. (1997) *Ways of War and Peace*, New York: W.W. Norton.

Falk, R. (2003) *The Great Terror War*, New York: Olive Branch Press.

Fukuyama, F. (1992) *The End of History and the Last Man*, New York: Free Press.

—— (2006) *After the Neocons: America at the Crossroads*, London: Profile Books.

Gideon, R. (1998) 'Neoclassical Realism and Theories of Foreign Policy', *World Politics*, 51 (October): 144–72.

Gold, P. (2004) *Take Back the Right: How the Neo-Cons and the Religious Right Have Hijacked the Conservative Movement*, New York: Carroll and Graff.

Goldberg, J. (2006) 'Breaking Ranks: What Turned Brent Scowcroft against the Bush Administration?', *New Yorker*, 31 October.

Gore, A. (2002) 'Iraq and the War on Terrorism,' presentation given at the Commonwealth Club of California, San Francisco, 23 September.

Halper, S.A. and Clarke, J. (2004) *America Alone: The Neo-Conservatives and the Global Order*, New York: Cambridge University Press.

—— (2007) *The Silence of the Rational Center*, New York: Basic Books.

Held, D. (2003) *Cosmopolitanism: A Defence*, Cambridge: Polity Press.

—— (2005) 'The Principles of Cosmopolitan Order', in G. Brock and H. Brighouse (eds) *The Political Philosophy of Cosmopolitanism*, Cambridge: Cambridge University Press, pp. 10–32.

Ikenberry, G.J. (2001) *After Victory: Institutions, Strategic Restraint, and the Rebuilding of Order after Major Wars*, Princeton, NJ: Princeton University Press.

—— (2003) 'State Power and the Institutional Bargain: America's Ambivalent Economic and Security Multilateralism', in R. Foot, S.N. McFarlane and M. Mastanduno (eds) *US Hegemony and International Organization: The United States and Multilateral Institutions*, Oxford: Oxford University Press, pp. 49–72.

Jefferson, T. (1816) Letter to Samuel Kercheval, July 12. In *Jefferson, Thomas, 1743–1826, Letters*, Electronic Text Center, University of Virginia Library, p. 1401.

Jervis, R. (1978) 'Cooperation under the Security Dilemma', *World Politics*, 30(2): 167–214.

Johnson, C. (2007) *Nemesis: The Last Days of the American Republic* (American Empire Project), New York: Metropolitan Books.

Judis, J.B. (2004) *The Folly of Empire: What George W. Bush Could Learn from Theodore Roosevelt and Woodrow Wilson*, New York: Lisa Drew/Scribner.

Kaldor, M. (2004) 'American Power: From "Compellance" to Cosmopolitanism?', in D. Held and M. Koenig-Archibugi (eds) *American Power in the Twenty-First Century*, Cambridge: Polity Press, pp. 181–213.

Kant, I. (1795) 'Perpetual Peace: A Philosophical Sketch'. Online. Available at: http://www. mtholyoke.edu/acad/intrel/kant/kant1.htm.

Keohane, R.O. (1984) *After Hegemony: Cooperation and Discord in the World Political Economy*, Princeton, NJ: Princeton University Press.

Keohane, R.O. and Nye, J.S. (2001) *Power and Interdependence*, 3rd edn, New York: Longman.

Kupchan, C.A. and Trubowitz, P.L. (2007) 'Dead Center: The Demise of Liberal Internationalism in the United States', *International Security*, 32(2): 7–44.

Kurth, J. (1998) 'Inside the Cave: The Banality of IR Studies', *National Interest*, (Fall): 29–40.

Lebow, R.N. (2008) *A Cultural Theory of International Relations*, Cambridge: Cambridge University Press.

Lepgold, J. (1998) 'Is Anyone Listening? International Relations Theory and the Problem of Policy Relevance', *Political Science Quarterly*, 113(1): 43–55.

Lepgold, J. and Nincic, M. (2001) *Beyond the Ivory Tower: International Relations Theory and the Issue of Policy Relevance*, New York: Columbia University Press.

Lieven, A. and Hulsman, J. (2006) *Ethical Realism: A Vision for America's Role in the World*, London: Pantheon Books.

Linklater, A. (1989) *Beyond Realism and Marxism*, New York: St. Martin's Press.

—— (2007) 'Towards a Sociology of Global Morals', *Review of International Studies*, 33: 135–50.

Lobell, S.E., Ripsman, N.M. and Taliaferro, J.W. (2008) *Neoclassical Realism, the State, and Foreign Policy*, Cambridge: Cambridge University Press.

Lynch, T.J. and Singh, R.S. (2008) *After Bush: The Case for Continuity in American Foreign Policy*, New York: Cambridge University Press.

Maliniak, D., Oakes, A., Peterson, S., and Tierney, M.J. (2007) 'The View from the Ivory Tower: TRIP Survey of International Relations Faculty in the United States and Canada', in Program on the Theory and Practice of International Relations, Arts and Sciences and the Wendy and Emery Reves Center for International Studies at the College of William and Mary, Williamsburg, Virginia (February). Online. Available at: http://www.wm.edu/irtheoryandpractice/trip/surveyreport06–07.pdf.

Maliniak, D., Peterson, S. and Tierney, M.J. (2005) 'Inside the Ivory Tower', *Foreign Policy*, 151: 62–8.

Mann, M. (2003) *Incoherent Empire*, London: Verso.

—— (2004) 'The First Failed Empire of the Twenty-First Century', in D. Held and M. Koenig-Archibugi (eds) *American Power in the Twenty-First Century*, Cambridge: Polity Press, pp. 52–82.

Mansfield, E.D. and Snyder, J. (2007) *Electing to Fight: Why Emerging Democracies Go to War*, Cambridge, MA: MIT Press.

Mearsheimer, J.J. (2005) 'Hans Morgenthau and the Iraq War: Realism vs. Neo-conservatism', *Open Democracy*, 21 April. Online. Available at: http://www.opendemocracy.net/content/articles/PDF/2522.pdf.

Mearsheimer, J.J. and Walt, S. (2007) *The Israel Lobby and US Foreign Policy*, New York: Allen Lane.

Morgenthau, H.J. (1993) *Politics among Nations: The Struggle for Power and Peace*, rev. edn, New York: McGraw-Hill.

Nivola, P.S. (2008) Roundtable discussion at the Future of American Conservative Movement Conference, University of Oxford, 10 May.

Nye, Jr., J.S. (2003) *The Paradox of American Power: Why the World's Only Superpower Can't Go It Alone*, Oxford: Oxford University Press.

—— (2004) 'Hard Power, Soft Power, and "the War on Terrorism"', in D. Held and M. Koenig-Archibugi (eds) *American Power in the Twenty-First Century*, Cambridge: Polity Press, pp. 114–33.

—— (2005) *Soft Power: The Means to Success in World Politics*, New York: Public Affairs.

Owen, J.M. (1994) 'Give Democratic Peace a Chance? How Liberalism Produces Democratic Peace', *International Security*, 19(Fall): 87–125.

Ratti, L. (2006) 'Post-Cold War NATO and International Relations Theory', *Journal of Transatlantic Studies*, 4(1): 81–110.

Rengger, N.J. and Thirkell-White, T.B. (2007) *Critical International Theory after 25 Years*, Cambridge: Cambridge University Press.

Reus-Smit, C. (2004) *American Power and World Order*, Cambridge: Polity Press.

Rice, C. (2005) 'The Promise of Democratic Peace: Why Promoting Freedom Is the Only Realistic Path to Security', *Washington Post*, 11 Dec.

Rosenau, J.N. (1992) 'Citizenship in a Changing Global Order', in J.N. Rosenau and E.O. Czempiel (eds) *Governance without Government: Order and Change in World Politics*, Cambridge: Cambridge University Press, pp. 272–94

Slaughter, A.M. (2004) *A New World Order*, Princeton, NJ: Princeton University Press.

Smith, T. (2007) *A Pact with the Devil: Washington's Bid for World Supremacy and the Betrayal of the American Promise*, New York and London: Routledge.

Snyder, R.C., Bruck, H.W., Sapin, B., Hudson, V.M., Chollet, D.H. and Goldgeier, J.M. (2002) *Foreign Policy Decision-Making (Revisited)*, New York: Palgrave.

Sterling-Folker, J. (1997) 'Realist Environment, Liberal Process, and Domestic-Level Variables', *International Studies Quarterly*, 41(March): 1–25.

—— (2004) 'Organizing the Inter-national: Neoclassical Realism and the Third Image Reversed', paper presented at the ECPR, The Hague, Netherlands, September 9–11.

Thucydides (1974) *History of the Peloponnesian War*, trans. R. Warner, London: Penguin.

Tocqueville, A. de (2000) *Democracy in America*, trans. Harvey C. Mansfield and Delba Winthrop, Chicago, IL: University of Chicago Press.

Tucker, R.W. and Hendrickson, D.C. (2004) 'The Sources of American Legitimacy', *Foreign Affairs*, 83(6): 18–32.

Waltz, K.N. ([1959] 2001) *Man, the State, and War: A Theoretical Analysis*, New York: Columbia University Press.

—— (1979) *Theory of International Politics*, New York: McGraw-Hill.

Wohlforth, W.C. (2000) 'A Certain Idea of Science: How International Relations Theory Avoids Reviewing the Cold War,' in O.A. Westad (ed.) *Reviewing the Cold War: Approaches, Interpretations, Theory*, London: Frank Cass, pp. 126–48.

5   Marxism and US foreign policy

Doug Stokes

Introduction

With the terrorist attacks on 9/11 coupled with the increased militarization of US foreign policy and the invasions and occupations of both Afghanistan and Iraq, analysts and students of International Relations (IR) have increasingly sought to employ critical IR theories that can interrogate not just the dominant discourses and social constructions of the discipline, but also the political and economic aspects of the social world itself. Today, neo-liberal globalization is increasingly exacerbating concentrations of global wealth, with the richest 2 per cent of the world's people owning more than half of global household wealth. The bottom half of three billion people own barely 1 per cent. The UN Food and Agriculture Organization has shown that by the time you finish reading this sentence, a child will have died of hunger (a child dies every 5 seconds).[1] They conclude that 24 *billion* dollars are needed to save five million children from starvation every year and yet the US-led war and occupation in Iraq could cost over three *trillion* dollars, which is a 'conservative' estimate according to Joseph Stiglitz, former Chief Economist of the World Bank (Stiglitz and Bilmes 2008). This alone gives a clear indication of social priorities. Moving from a global to a national scale, wealth and power is still deeply concentrated with US households in the top 20 per cent of the income distribution earning more than 80 per cent of the nation's wealth.

According to Marxist theorists, these concentrations of wealth and power are an inevitable result of capitalism, an economic system in which a minority own and control the means of production and the great majority are forced to sell their labour power in order to survive. The purpose of this chapter is not to provide a 'Marxism 101' introduction to Marxist theory *per se*. This has been done in numerous books. Rather, this chapter seeks to show how Marxism is being used to understand the role of the USA within global politics and the international political economy. As the key capitalist power within the global economy, the American state has been crucial in underwriting and supporting the expansion of capitalism as a mode of production across the globe throughout the post-war period. This support has ranged from economic reforms that have sought to maintain an 'open-door' global economy conducive to global business interests to strategic interventions to overthrow governments that are or have been considered hostile to either capitalist social relations or US political hegemony within the post-war order. Today, America's power and the way it is used have become a crucial concern of IR, with a 'long war' declared against nebulous enemies while increased resource competition between great powers intensifies. This concern with the exercise of American power is best illustrated with the return of the concept of an 'American Empire' across a broad range of theoretical and political sentiment.

Crucially, the world that I have described above did not form itself, but was in fact created through human actions and choices, as well as wider structural processes of historical transformation. As students of IR and US foreign policy we must thus ask: how did we arrive at a point in human history whereby the richest people on the planet, who often in turn come from the richest families, earn more in an hour than the poorest people earn in a lifetime? What can Marxism tell us about current trends in world politics and, as the world's dominant state, how can we analyze the role that US foreign policy has played in the construction and defense of global capitalism?

Imperialism

Traditional Marxist approaches to US power are rooted within competing theories of imperialism. Interestingly, Marx himself did not really provide a theory of International Politics and it was left to later Marxist scholars to do this. Imperialism itself can be defined as the policy process of extending a nation's authority through territorial acquisition (for example, the British Empire) or by the establishment of economic and political dominance over other nations and it can and often does take two forms. The first is a more formal type of imperialism that involves overt conquest, territorial control, direct military rule, and so on. The second type is a more informal form of imperialism that often involves more indirect means of control through, for example, economic dominance through the imposition of 'free trade' regimes whereby trade arrangements are imposed on weaker countries by the imperial powers where they are strong (and thus guaranteeing economic preponderance) while ignoring these principles in areas where they are weak. A contemporary example would be use of tariff barriers by the rich nations to support domestic markets such as farming, while insisting on 'free trade' regimes for the poorer nations. In this way, surplus extraction occurs through a global market mechanism with no necessary need to use more formal types of imperialism such as military conquest.[2] In both types of imperialism, then, the ends remain the same: the extraction of surplus value, profits and raw materials from subordinate regions, while the means may differ.

Importantly, within the Marxist tradition, imperialism is intimately bound up with the historical internationalization of capitalism as a mode of production across the globe. That is, as capitalism as a mode of economic organization has historically extended beyond the rich and powerful nations, powerful states imposed their economic interests on other non-capitalist regions and thereby incorporated them within the capitalist global economy that they effectively controlled. One only has to briefly examine the history of European colonialism to see the legacy of this process or indeed the disastrous consequences of US foreign policy in the Middle East in the post-war system that has overthrown democratically elected governments and often supported authoritarian oligarchies so as to ensure access to and control over oil.

However, while there are agreements within Marxism about these common features of imperialism, there are quite strong divergences over the motivations for imperial expansion, what imperialism means for the international system in terms of war and peace and more importantly for this chapter, the role that the state and interstate relations play within contemporary forms of global imperialism. The two key differences are deeply rooted in the early Marxist debates between two contending theories of imperialism. The first is Lenin's inter-imperial rivalry (IIR) thesis that posits the inevitability of rivalry and conflict within international politics as a result of the expansion of rival imperialisms. The second is Kautsky's ultra-imperialism (UI) thesis that posits the possibility of peaceful cooperation between imperial powers. I now outline these different theories and how they feed in to contemporary Marxist debates on US foreign policy.

Lenin: inter-imperial rivalry

Turning to Lenin's IIR thesis, he argued that the processes of political and military domination of the world by the great powers was a logical outcome of the steady internationalization of those same state's economic interests. That is, as capitalism developed, hand in hand with the economic dynamism of industrialization, those states that had the lead in this process, namely the European Great Powers, had also expanded their economic interests abroad to encompass other territories and countries. Given the tight integration between the state and business elites, it was logical that the military power of the state would be used to defend its economic interests as well.

Cecil Rhodes, one of the early British imperialists who helped divide up large parts of British-controlled Africa, captured this logic well when he argued that

> [the British] must find new lands from which we can easily obtain raw materials and at the same time exploit the cheap slave labour that is available from the natives of the colonies. The colonies would also provide a dumping ground for the surplus goods produced in our factories.
>
> (Ellwood 2001: 13)

As the quote amply demonstrates, the process of imperial expansion and military domination was intimately bound up with a process of market expansion and incorporation.

For Lenin's thesis, the most important part of this process was less the fact of overseas capitalist expansion, but what this meant for interstate relations between the capitalist powers. For Lenin, as these states expanded their imperial interests abroad, an inevitable rivalry would increase as they jockeyed for power and raw resources throughout the world. As Lenin argued:

> The epoch of the latest stage of capitalism shows us that certain relations between capitalist associations grow up, *based* on the economic division of the world; while parallel to and in connection with it, certain relations grow up between political alliances, between states, on the basis of the territorial division of the world, of the struggle for colonies, of the 'struggle for spheres of influence' ... The more capitalism is developed, the more strongly the shortage of raw materials is felt, the more intense the competition and the hunt for sources of raw materials throughout the whole world, the more desperate the struggle for the acquisition of colonies.
>
> (Lenin 1916)

As Lenin makes clear, businesses and capital will naturally seek to expand beyond the home state's borders as they grow larger and this process is driven by the fact that capital needs productive outlets in overseas markets and tends towards monopolisation (smaller firms get swallowed up by bigger firms) while national markets are not big enough to soak up the products produced. Overseas markets also provide new outlets for goods. However, as powerful nations carve up the globe in their economic and political interests, there is the ever present threat of interstate war as states' interests collide. As such, according to the IIP theory, there is zero-sum logic to the internationalization of capitalism whereby processes of imperial expansion always threaten war as imperialist powers interests are threatened by other Great Powers jockeying for political and economic hegemony. In many ways, Lenin's IIR thesis is similar to realist analyses of IR, except that realists tend not to unpack how the 'national interest' is derived and, of course in the Marxist case, rivalry is rooted within the expansive logic of capitalism, not the logic of anarchy.

In applying the IIR thesis to present-day US foreign policy, the thesis received a massive fillip with the US invasion and occupation of Iraq, with many commentators using the concept to understand the motivations of the US war drive in the Middle East. After all, here is a region that has long been subject to Western imperialism and possesses an abundance of one of the most important raw resources in the world: oil (Iraq, for example, was itself a creation of the British Empire in 1922, and was stitched together from a series of provinces created under the Ottoman Empire that collapsed following World War I).

Foster captures this argument well when he argues that:

> [I]ntercapitalist rivalry remains the hub of the imperialist wheel ... In the present period of global hegemonic imperialism the United States is geared above all to expanding its imperial power to whatever extent possible and subordinating the rest of the capitalist world to its interests.
>
> (Foster 2003: 13)

By extension, contemporary US imperialism is seen as the result of the unified interest of the predominant sectors of US business, which need to ensure and manipulate export markets for both goods and capital. Accordingly, business interests are thus seen as essentially controlling the American state with military competition between competing powers an extension of international economic competition, which is in itself driven by the expansionist nature of capitalism.

As we have seen above, then, inherent in the IIR thesis, as well as more recent analyses of American foreign policy is often an instrumentalist theory of the state. Simply stated, instrumentalist accounts argue that the state is a mere 'instrument' in the hands of national elites. As Miliband, one of the chief proponents of state instrumentalism, argued, 'the ruling class of a capitalist society is that class which owns and controls the means of production and which is able, by virtue of the economic power thus conferred upon it, to use the state as its instrument for the domination of society' (Miliband 1969: 13). This theorization of the American state (and by extension, US foreign policy), tends to reduce American decision-making to the economic interests of the American capitalist class, with the American state's primary function one of ensuring the necessary conditions for profit maximization for US corporations throughout the globe. Inherent within this theory of the American state is an economic reductionism whereby the political and strategic logics of US statecraft are subordinated to the economic interests of American capital, with the state the central organizational conduit of this process. The projection of American power is thus seen as little more than the extension of an iron fist for corporate interests (we will critique this position later in the chapter).

In sum, then, the IIR thesis posits the close interrelationship between the state and the capitalist class of a given society. As capital expands abroad through investments, as well as the need to secure access to raw materials that are crucial to industrial processes (for example, oil), the state will also seek to expand and carve up the world to defend the interests of their respective capitals. We can read much of the history of European colonialism through this lens whereby French and British imperialism competed with each other to colonize large parts of the planet. Importantly, within this conception is the view that as we have the expansion of capitalism across the globe we will also see increased interstate warfare as states jockey for position and to defend the interests of their capitalists.

Kautsky: Ultra-imperialism and the liberal post-war order

Counter-posed to Lenin's stark portrait of interstate relations stands the ideas of Lenin's contemporary Karl Kautsky, who coined a rival theory of imperialism now termed 'ultra-imperialism'. Unlike Lenin, Kautsky posited the potential for the powerful capitalist nations to develop common interests in exploiting the globe and for their respective capitalists to prefer collaboration and spheres of influence rather than the costly and often deeply destabilizing phenomenon of war. Rather than reading interstate relations and the internationalization of capitalism as a zero-sum game, Kautsky instead argued that businesses and states will instead prefer to fashion forms of cooperation and coordination between themselves. That is, states can cooperate within a common framework and, crudely put, agree to carve up the globe between them. This form of coordination and collaboration can be seen in the operation of US foreign policy in the post-war period when the US emerged as the key hegemonic power within the global economy.

How did the US emerge as the key power within the capitalist global economy? The US role as the leading state within world capitalism became increasingly clear with the decline of Britain, the custodian of global free trade prior to the end of the Second World War. US power in the post-war period was underwritten by its unrivaled military, political and economic power. At the end of the war, for example, the USA had almost half of the world's manufacturing capacity, the majority of its food supply and nearly all of its capital reserves. In this new role, post-war US foreign policy was formulated around a dual strategy: the maintenance and defense of an economically liberal international system conducive to business expansion coupled with a global geo-strategy of containing social forces considered inimical to capitalist social relations.

Importantly, in this endeavor, the American state acted not just in its own interests but also in the interests of other core powers that relied upon the American state to contain the spread of world communism, roll back Third World nationalism and to underwrite the institutions and enforce the rules of the liberal international order. This liberal order was concretized through the American-dominated Bretton Woods institutions that helped fashion the post-war order, the internationalization of American capital and business models (primarily through American foreign direct investment) and US dominance of the strategic frameworks of other core powers, for example, NATO for Europe and the Japan-US Security Pact.

US hegemony was thus positive-sum, and the post-war order was a form of ultra-imperialism, in so far as US power benefited other core capitalist powers and provided a coordination mechanism where common interests where represented by the US state. Importantly, this positive-sum generic reproductive function for global capitalism has formed a key component of American power and has undergirded its hegemony in the post-war international system. In a sense, then, American power has played a system-maintaining role that has benefited a number of core states as well as America itself, and US foreign policy in the post-war system has acted to expand and defend capitalism throughout the globe while attempting to (largely successfully) pacify geo-political rivalries between the Great Powers through providing a common public-good conducive to their interests. As such, we can describe the post-war order that the US was instrumental in creating as a form of ultra-imperialism.

US Cold War policy

US foreign policy during the Cold War era thus sought a number of key objectives. First, it sought to build up and integrate a revitalized Western Europe and Japan-centered East Asia under its hegemony. Although this process benefited these regions, this was not a multilateral order as many liberal theorists claim, but was in fact what could be called a 'conditional multilateralism' insofar as multilateral forms of order were acceptable to US planners as long as it suited Washington's interests. Henry Kissinger captured this Cold War power reality in the early 1970s when he argued that the 'United States [had] global interests and responsibilities' while '[o]ur European allies' merely 'have regional interests'.[3] Importantly, US hegemony relied upon consent as well as force, and its forms of highly successful economic success based on innovative Fordist-type industrialization methods provided attractive models for other capitalist states keen to recover from the devastation of World War II. In this way, the American state emerged as the key power within the capitalist global economy, a hegemony that it continues to enjoy today.

Second, the American state sought to play a system-maintaining role whereby US power was used to defend the liberal international order against threats from anti-systemic movements and it thus benefited other core capitalist states and allowed them to prosper both economically through the build-up of economic interdependence and also strategically as US power was used both to prevent Soviet expansion within Western Europe, and also to police the developing world. This policing function was driven by a desire not only to contain Soviet-inspired insurgencies but also forms of independent nationalism that threatened crucial raw resources (for example, oil) or that posed symbolic threats to US global hegemony by challenging the US-led global system. To this end, the US sought to install and support authoritarian forms of rule as developing world democracies were often seen as potentially dangerous as there was always the threat that these democracies might prove to be too responsive to majoritarian interests that invariably favored wealth redistribution, given the often extreme concentrations of wealth found in the developing world. The anti-democratic nature of US policy in the developing world ran throughout the Cold War period as the various US-backed anti-democracy coups in Iran (1953), Guatemala (1954), Indonesia (1965), Chile (1973) and Nicaragua (1984) amply illustrate. The logic of this orientation within US policy was captured succinctly by one of the central architects of the post-war order in what was at the time a top secret planning document in 1948. George Kennan argued that the US has about 50% of the world's wealth, but only 6.3% of its population ... In this situation, we cannot fail to be the object of envy and resentment. Our real task in the coming period is to devise a pattern of relationships that will permit us to maintain this position of disparity.

(Kennan 1976: 524–5)

Kennan explained that in dealing with dissent during the Cold War, the final answer 'may be an unpleasant one' but the US 'should not hesitate before police repression by the local government'. Kennan considered this repression not only to be strategically necessary but also to be ethically correct, as 'the Communists are essentially traitors'. He continued that '[it] is better to have a strong regime in power than a liberal government if it is indulgent and relaxed and penetrated by Communists'.[4] Aside from Kennan's blanket designation of opposition to US interests as constituting 'communism', the human cost of this support was enormous with all but two hundred thousand of the twenty million people who died in wars between 1945 and 1990 dying in the Third World. In essence, then, US interventions during the Cold War were frequently justified with anti-communist rhetoric but they frequently extended far beyond real or imagined Soviet-aligned communists to encompass a wide range of progressive social forces that sought social change in their often highly class-stratified societies. In a profound sense, then, US foreign policy during the Cold War was often closely aligned with a wide range of reactionary and anti-progressive regimes that by the nature of US global interests formed a containment mechanism for the prevention of social change in the developing world.

Crucially, Marxist scholars seek to broaden the understanding of Cold War US foreign policy from a simple narrative of Soviet containment by also incorporating the economic interests of the USA as a key capitalist power, as well as the strategic and political logics of US statecraft. US foreign policy is thus embedded within wider structures that are not exhausted by a realist logic of strategy or a liberal strategy of what we might call a 'muted idealism' during the Cold War.

Given this historical sketch, it seems rather obvious in the current historical conjuncture that Kautsky's theory of ultra-imperialism seems to have more analytical purchase that Lenin's rather stark theory on the inevitability of interstate war between capitalist powers. Interstate war between the EU and the USA is practically unthinkable, not least because of economic interdependency and strategic cooperation and thus the internationalization of capitalism in the industrial core economies has served to pacify rivalries rather than amplify them. Aside from this point, however, outside of the core capitalist economies, the story has been very different with major wars, covert interventions and mass politicides justified in the name of anti-communism and increasingly counter-terrorism.

I now turn to develop the ways in which contemporary Marxist theorists have taken these theories of imperialism and applied them to US foreign policy after 9/11. In particular, I am interested in examining the work of the 'global capitalist' school.

Globalization and post-Cold War US foreign policy

The concept of globalization has risen to increased prominence, especially after the end of the Cold War when the toppling of the Berlin Wall seemed to capture the feeling that the barriers between countries were finally beginning to dissipate. Aside from the metaphors, however, the end of the Cold War also freed the capitalist world from the constraints placed upon it by the existence of the Soviet Union, and the global economy became truly integrated under Western hegemony, with neo-liberal shock therapy applied throughout the Third World and also the former Soviet Union; a hitherto tightly closed sector of the global economy. Capital literally 'went global' and the barriers to the circulation of international finance were torn down with a wave of privatizations and neo-liberal reforms. Alongside the emergence of an increasingly globally integrated economy, there emerged a broad range of academic sociological and political works that analyzed these trends under globalization.

In particular, there has emerged a key body of work known under the broad rubric of global capitalist approaches. These new approaches argued that accompanying the rise of an increasingly globally integrated economy, new global state and class structures were also forming. This new form of global empire increasingly bypassed or transformed state structures. Perhaps the best known of these approaches was the surprise best-seller *Empire* by Hardt and Negri (2000). However, the most cogent work within Marxism has been developed by William Robinson who examines transnational trends under globalization and the ways in which the transnationalization of capital is impacting upon forms of contemporary US foreign policy. For Robinson, the new global economy has allowed an increasingly transnationally based capital to reorganize production relations that supersede national economies and national states with national systems of production becoming fragmented and integrated into a new global configuration.

Robinson contends that we are witnessing the increased transnationalization of the state as capital becomes increasingly transnationalized. Transnationally orientated states provide the national infrastructure that is necessary for economic activity, adopt policies that assure internal economic stability and maintain social order through both coercive and consensual means. In short, transformed nation-states adopt and implement neo-liberal reform which is the primary policy modality of capitalist globalization which in turn integrates them as circuits within the transnational circulation of capital. The transnational state (TNS) thus encompasses both the transformed and transnationally orientated neo-liberal nation-states *and* supranational economic and political forums such as the IMF, the World Bank and the World Trae Organization (WTO) which, as yet, do not have any centralized institutional form reminiscent of a formal state but which nonetheless provide a coordinating mechanism necessary for global capital accumulation. Concomitant with the rise of this TNS is the emergence of a new global class: the Transnational Capitalist Class (TCC). This new global class is directly related to the changes in the global organization of production and the rise of a nascent TNS. Importantly, this reconfiguration of global class relations changes the dynamics of competition between nation-states with the potential for inter-imperialist rivalry and war shifting from competing nation-states to new global oligarchies competing within a transnational environment (Robinson 2004).

Robinson's portrait of contemporary globalization has very clear implications for the analysis of contemporary imperialism and US foreign policy, insofar as traditional analyses tend to foreground the nationally bounded nature of the imperial project (as we saw above). However, Robinson argues that to analyze the USA as an imperialist power misses a crucial nuance in contemporary capitalist globalization. That is, rather than competing nation-states, or even competing blocs (for example, East Asian versus European capital), the age of transnational capital now means that there is a diffusion of capitalist interests so that one can no longer territorialize interests within a bounded nation-state. Robinson takes the example of the East Asian economic success and its alleged threat to US economic preponderance. He contends that:

> East Asian dynamism is inseparable from the massive entrance of transnational capital, and local elites have sought, not a regional circuit of accumulation in rivalry with circuits elsewhere, but a more complete *integration* into globalised circuits. 'US' investors have hundreds of billions of dollars invested in Asia. Economic dynamism benefits those investors as much as it benefits local elites.
>
> (Robinson 2004: 131)

He thus rejects outright a theory of world order as characterized by the potential for inter-imperial rivalry between competing capitalist states. Importantly, this does not mean that leading capitalist states are no longer central to the maintenance of global capitalism, and Robinson contends that the US state continues to be the global hegemonic capitalist state. However, and this is the crucial point, for Robinson the US state now acts as the central agent of *transnational* capital, rather than a nationally grounded US ruling class, with US military preponderance acting not to secure *American* hegemony *vis-à-vis* potential geopolitical rivals, but acting for the interests of transnational capital as a whole. Instead of a *US* empire, a notion which foregrounds an imperial project bounded by a nation-state and *national* capital, he argues that the USA has 'taken the lead in developing policies and strategies on behalf of the global capitalist agenda' because globalization 'has emerged in the period of worldwide US dominance, and the concentration of resources and coercive powers within the US national state allows it to play a leadership role *on behalf of* a transnational elite'. Accordingly, the US state seeks not to intervene to secure the interests of *American* capital *per se*, but to underwrite and police the world for transnational capital. Robinson is unequivocal about this, and he argues that:

> US military conquest does not result in the creation of exclusive zones for the conquerors' exploitation ... but the colonization and recolonization of the vanquished for the new global capitalism and its agents ... the US military apparatus is the ministry of war in the cabinet of an increasingly globally integrated ruling class.
>
> (ibid.: 140)

In relation to US intervention in oil-rich regions, this *transnational*, positive-sum organizational role played by the American state is most clear. Rather than interpreting US intervention in, for example, Iraq as a case of US imperialism using its military might to exclude oil corporations from competing nations (for example, France or Russia), it is far more accurate to view US intervention as part of the generic role that the US state has long performed in 'stabilizing' market-orientated political economies throughout the Middle East for the generic interests of global capitalism as a whole. That is, by underwriting transnationally-orientated political economies in the Middle East, the USA has deliberately guaranteed the security of the oil supply to *world* markets. As such, US intervention in these regions (of which the Iraq invasion was the most recent example) has benefited other core capitalist states as much as it has the USA. This is the case through guaranteeing a relatively cheap supply of crucial energy to their respective national economies and through the ordering of states and political economies along lines that are conducive to the liberal international order as a whole (which in turn benefits all core regions). As Robinson argues, recent US intervention in Iraq was in fact a 'blueprint for the transnational agenda in the region', and was not a 'US imperialist plan to gain the upper hand over French, German, and Russian competition' through monopolizing Iraq's natural resources including its crucial oil reserves (ibid.: 140).

The destination of oil from the Persian Gulf illustrates this point most clearly: although the USA enjoys strategic primacy in the Middle East, it only draws 10 per cent of its total oil supplies from the region. The remainder is shipped primarily to Japan, Europe and increasingly China. IIR theorists who analyze the intervention in Iraq in stark terms thus presume that other capitalist states do not have an equally important interest in the USA working to guarantee both regional political economies open to capital penetration and state structures able to discipline social forces (be they nationalist, Islamist or explicitly anti-capitalist) that may threaten the security of oil supplies to *world* markets.

In sum, Robinson builds upon Kautsky's argument by arguing that we have thus entered an era of decentered and deterritorialized transnational empire that escapes the territorialized logic of earlier imperialisms and the geopolitical competition inherent within inter-imperial rivalry theories. Needless to say, his conclusions also have major ramifications for the analysis of US foreign policy and American intervention within the global economy. I now turn to consider some problems with the 'global capitalist' approach and its application to US foreign policy.

The dual logic of US foreign policy

Along with other 'global capitalist' theorists, Robinson provides a much-needed corrective to the overly statist and instrumentalist accounts of traditional historical materialist analyses of the US Empire. The more economically reductionist Marxism has always been weak on the development of the liberal order in the post-war system and on the role that geo-politics and strategy have played in US foreign policy (while realist and liberal approaches to US foreign policy have in turn been weak on the political economy of US foreign policy or have ignored the often destructive and destabilizing role that Western economic intervention has played).

However, while his work serves as a useful corrective to these approaches, I wish to argue that he also fails to capture the full logic of contemporary US foreign policy, and in particular underplays the role that the USA performs in securing interests for *the US state* as the lead actor within the globalized capitalist environment.

When arguing that the USA intervenes in order to pursue a *transnational* capitalist agenda on behalf of the TCC, Robinson fails to take full account of the overwhelming preponderance that *territorialized* US capital has within the global market system. This nationalized dominance of the global economy is most clearly seen in the geographical location of key members of the so-called TCC. For example, in 2007, the USA headquartered 162 of the world's 500 largest businesses. The second largest was Japan with 67, while US Foreign Direct Investment (FDI) inflows are projected to increase massively between 2007 and 2011 with over $250 billion annually on average (16.75 per cent of world total), with the UK being the next leading recipient at under half of the USA's share with just below $112 billion (7.54 per cent of world total).[5] The securities industry is the world's top industry in terms of revenue, and all six of the top securities houses are US based. Similarly, of the world's richest members of the so-called TCC, the majority are American, with eight of the world's ten richest people holding US citizenship.

More significantly, the interests of *American* capital are secured throughout the structures and institutions of transnational capitalism, primarily by ensuring that the preponderance of US market power can be exercised in the absence of any significant restraints. As just one example, US foreign policy has been instrumental in implementing neo-liberalism throughout Latin America, both through its multilateral agreements with states in the region, and its domination of the international institutions that are implementing neo-liberal reforms. The Free Trade of the Americas Act (FTAA) built upon the North American Free Trade Agreement (NAFTA) was passed by the US Congress, Canada and Mexico in 1993. NAFTA sought to integrate the economies of North America, Canada and Mexico into a single trading bloc, to dismantle trade barriers, to privatize state-owned industries and to loosen the restrictions on the movement of capital. Like NAFTA, the FTAA seeks to link the economies of all the Latin American nations (with the exception of Cuba) into a single trade bloc. The FTAA is based on a corporate-led model of development that will accelerate post-Cold War neo-liberal reforms of national economies throughout Latin America, and at first glance can be viewed as a classic case of the USA acting according to Robinson's logic (i.e., to affect a transnational outcome beneficial to the TCC).

However, the FTAA contains a number of provisions that have strengthened the power of specifically *American* capital, due to the removal of all barriers restraining the sheer preponderance of US market power within the transnational system (informal imperialism).

At the time of its implementation in 2000, the gross domestic product (GDP) of North, Central and South America was $11,000 billion. However, the US share of this GDP was 75.7 per cent, with Brazil, which was the next largest, at 6.7 per cent, Canada's was 5.3 per cent while Mexico's was 3.9 per cent. The other 31 nations comprised only 8.4 per cent. Per capita GDP in the USA was $30,600 in 2000 while the lowest, Haiti, stood with just $460.[6] The FTAA and other neo-liberal variants will serve to deepen the already overwhelming power of US capital by dismantling national trade barriers to allow easier penetration by US capital and US-subsidized exports, an increase in the privatization (and consequent foreign ownership) of state-owned industries, and the more rigorous enforcement of the intellectual property rights of (mainly) US corporations (Katz 2002: 27–31). What we have, then, is, subject to resistance, the US state acting to secure a transnational outcome which will benefit a number of capitals and the transnationally orientated elites of the respective nations. But due to both the US preponderance of market power and capital internationalization, this will *primarily* benefit US corporations and capitalists.

This dynamic is brought home most clearly within another context: the US Congress's ratification of the World Trade Organization (WTO) Treaty. The WTO is one of the key institutions of global economic governance and is seen by the global capitalist theorists as one of the principal institutional forms for the emergent TNS. However, Section 301 of the US trade act allows the US Congress to unilaterally reject WTO provisions that may threaten key US industries or economic interests. As Gowan has argued, the US has participated in international economic regimes when it suits its economic interests but US acceptance of WTO jurisdiction is 'conditional upon the

WTO's being "fair" to US interests. And all who follow international trade policy know that the word "fair" in this context means serving and defending US economic interests' (Gowan 2004: 477). Washington thus reserves the right to reject the very free trade regimes prevailing within the global economy if these regimes threaten key economic interests. This forms of rules-based rejectionism runs counter to the transnationalized theories examined above. If capital has truly escaped the boundedness of the nation state, how do we explain instances like this?

If we extend this argument to US military capacity, it is inaccurate to view the US military apparatus primarily as 'the ministry of war in the cabinet of an increasingly globally integrated ruling class'. Instead, continued US global military hegemony, whereby it is *the* dominant military power within capitalist globalization (spending more than the rest of the G7 countries combined, with its military budget eight times larger than the Chinese budget, which is the second largest), helps to determine the nature and structures of contemporary globalization, including the interactions between different capitals, *so as to reinforce US primacy* vis-à-vis *potential rivals*. If we take US intervention in the Middle East, for example, given the often fragile social basis of a number of the regimes in the region, US power insulates them from both external and internal forms of opposition that further entrenches the importance of US strategic primacy for the prevailing global oil order. Thus, not only have core powers come to rely on US strategic primacy to police the internal conditions necessary to maintain conditions conducive to capitalist social relations, and through which their energy needs are met, the American state also gets to set the agenda as to what constitutes the 'threat' as well as the responses. This threat definition–brigading–pacification equation thus places the USA at the heart of strategic policing for the global economy, consolidates the reliance of others on its power projection capacity as well as allowing the American state to 'brigade' core powers through mediating the relations between these threats (be they state threats such as a rising China or anti-systemic threats such as Al Qaeda-type terrorists) and states reliant on US primacy.

Importantly, this is not a reversion to the instrumentalist accounts of inter-imperial rivalry theorists that we examined above, whereby the US state acts solely to benefit concrete national capitalist interests. Indeed, such theorizations overlook what Nicos Poulantzas called the 'relative autonomy' of the state. By this, Poulantzas meant that the state enjoys a degree of autonomy from the sectoral interests of its capitalist class, as the state's primary function is to reproduce the necessary conditions for the *long-term* functioning of a given society. Given the global interests of the American state that I have sketched above, the structural requirements of the capitalist system as a whole are not necessarily synonymous with the interests of sections of the American capitalist class. The state's structural role is thus one of long-term *political* management which could well be compromised by catering too strongly to the interests of a particular sector of capital (for example, oil transnationals). As such, Poulantzas' theory of the relative autonomy of the state serves as a useful corrective to overly instrumentalist accounts that denude the state of any political autonomy free from the immediate requirements of the economic interests of capital (Poulantzas 1978). It also serves as a corrective to analysts who frequently paint a straw-man Marxism that is economically reductionist. Panitch and Gindin summarize this state logic when they argue:

> It is not so much that states are autonomous from the capitalist economy or from capitalist classes, as that capitalist states develop certain capacities to act on behalf

of the system as a whole (autonomy), at the same time that their dependence on the success of overall accumulation for their own legitimacy and reproduction leaves those capacity bounded (relative).

(Panitch and Gindin 2005: 102)

We need to internationalize this notion when examining the American state and this 'relative autonomy' is especially clear, given that it has acted as the key hegemonic state within world capitalism throughout the post-war period, and as such has served to underwrite and police the liberal international order within which it enjoyed primacy. In so doing, it has developed specific capacities to act for global capitalism as a whole (and not just for American capitalism), and has served both national *and* transnational interests. This 'dual logic' of US foreign policy has seen Washington playing a systems-maintaining role, which has been widely accepted because the US state has not just been pursuing its own interests at the expense of all its rivals (Lenin's IIR) but has also helped maintain the conditions for the expansion of capital as a system (Kautsky's ultra-imperialism).

Conclusion

In conclusion, this chapter has highlighted contending theories of imperialism which is the primary concept utilized by Marxism to analyze the global economy and interstate relations. I have attempted to draw out the salient points in relation to US foreign policy. Throughout the post-war order and up to the present there have been of course numerous debates among US foreign policy elites as to the precise strategies that should be pursued. However, there seems to be very little divergence over the objectives of US foreign policy: the continuation of American political, military and economic hegemony which has (so far) been fairly beneficial to *all* core capitalist states. We are thus at a strange place in the world, whereby we have a dual logic at work in US foreign policy: on the one hand, it must manage its own national interests while correlating these with the interests of its subordinate, but nonetheless *potential* rivals. This in turn places the USA in a bind in many ways. As new security threats emerge and economic competition intensifies, so does the temptation to use its primacy to pursue a more narrow or unilateral order. This in turn threatens the very order that the US was instrumental in creating and that has served its own interests well. However, if it chooses to work within the rules-based order, there is the ever present threat that others may attempt to constrain American power, or what Kagan has termed a Gulliver complex whereby the sleeping giant is constrained by a thousand multilateral strings (Kagan 2003).

At present, many analysts are analyzing the USA as an Empire in decline and it does seem that the quagmire in Iraq, whereby a ragtag insurgency can effectively blunt the multi-billion dollar US military machine, and the ongoing problems in the Anglo-Saxon hyper-liberal financial markets do point to the decline of American power. If we accept this, the question is, how do we manage this decline and perhaps more pertinently, what comes after?

Notes

1 United Nations (2007).
2 For the classic article on this distinction, see Gallagher and Robinson (1953).

3 Kissinger, quoted in Hersh (1983), p. 636.
4 George Kennan, quoted in Schmitz (1999), p.149.
5 *World Investment Prospects to 2011: Foreign Direct Investment and the Challenge of Political Risk*. Online. Available at: http://www.cpii.columbia.edu/pubs/documents/WorldInvestment-Prospectsto2011.pdf. p.34.
6 *Le Monde Diplomatique,* April 2001.

Further reading

Blum, W. (1986) *Killing Hope. US Military and CIA Interventions Since World War II*, Monroe: Common Courage Press.

Brewer, A. (1991) *Marxist Theories of Imperialism: A Critical Survey*, London: Routledge.

Domhoff, William G. (2001) *Who Rules America?: Power and Politics in the Year 2000*, New York: Mayfield.

Gowan, P. (1999) *The Global Gamble: Washington's Bid for World Dominance*, London: Verso.

Harvey, D. (2003) *The New Imperialism*, Oxford: Oxford University Press.

Herman, E. and Chomsky, N. (1988) *Manufacturing Consent: The Political Economy of the Mass Media*, New York: Verso.

Kolko, G. (2006) *The Age of War: The United States Confronts the World*, Boulder, CO: Lynne Rienner.

Panitch, L. and Gindin, S. (2003) *Global Capitalism and American Empire*, London: Merlin Press.

Rupert, M. and Smith, H. (eds) (2002) *Historical Materialism and Globalization*, London: Routledge.

Stokes, D. and Cox, M. (eds) (2008) *US Foreign Policy*, Oxford: Oxford University Press.

Websites

The National Security Archive provides a great deal of declassified documentation relating to US foreign and security policy, and its role throughout the world: http://www.gwu.edu/~nsarchiv/

Democracy Now! is a national, daily, independent, award-winning news program hosted by journalists Amy Goodman and Juan Gonzalez. Pioneering the largest public media collaboration in the US: http://www.democracynow.org/

Human Rights Watch and Amnesty International are at the forefront of documenting the end results of various states' security policies. Their reports can provide excellent empirical material for research purposes: http://www.hrw.org/, http://www.amnesty.org

The Monthly Review has a good selection of critical analyses from a Marxist perspective: http://monthlyreview.org/

ZNet has a good selection of critical approaches: http://www.zmag.org/ZNET.htm

References

Ellwood, W. (2001) *The No-nonsense Guide to Globalization*, London: Verso.

Foster, J. (2003) 'The New Age of Imperialism', *Monthly Review*, 55: 3.

Gallagher, J. and Robinson, R. (1953) 'The Imperialism of Free Trade', *The Economic History Review*, VI:1. Online. Available at: http://www.mtholyoke.edu/acad/intrel/ipe/gallagher.htm.

Gowan, P. (2004) 'Contemporary Intra-Core Relations and World Systems Theory', *Journal of World System Research*, X: 2. Online. Available at: http://jwsr.ucr.edu/archive/vol10/number2/pdf/jwsr-v10n2gs-gowan.pdf.

Hardt, M. and Negri, A. (2000) *Empire*, Cambridge, MA: Harvard University Press.

Hersh, S. (1983) *The Price of Power. Kissinger in the Nixon White House*, London: Simon & Schuster.

Kagan, R. (2003) *Of Paradise and Power: America and Europe in the New World Order*, New York: Knopf.

Katz, C. (2002) 'Free Trade Area of the Americas. NAFTA Marches South', *NACLA: Report on the Americas*, 4(February): 27–31.

Kennan, G. (1976) *Foreign Relations of the United States, 1948. Report by the Policy Planning Staff*, Washington, DC: General Printing Office.

Lenin, V.I. (1916) 'Imperialism, the Highest Stage of Capitalism'. Online. Available at: http://www.wutsamada.com/msu/IAH206/imperialism.html.

Miliband, R. (1969) *The State in Capitalist Society*, New York: Basic Books.

Panitch, L. and Gindin, S. (2005) 'Superintending Global Capital', *New Left Review*, September–October: 102.

Poulantzas, N. (1978) *Classes in Contemporary Capitalism*, New York: Schocken Books.

Robinson, R. (2004) *A Theory of Global Capitalism: Production, Class and State in a Transnational World*, Baltimore, MD: Johns Hopkins University Press.

Schmitz, D. (1999)*Thank God They're on Our Side. The United States and Right-Wing Dictatorships 1921–1965*, Chapel Hill, NC: The University of North Carolina Press.

Stiglitz, J. and Bilmes, L. (2008) *The Three Trillion Dollar War: The True Cost of the Iraq Conflict*, New York: W.W. Norton.

United Nations (2007) 'Press Conference by United Nations Special Rapporteur on Right to Food', 26 October. Online. Available at: http://www.un.org/News/briefings/docs/2007/071026_Ziegler.doc.htm.

Part II
Non-state actors in US foreign policy

6 Parties, partisanship and US foreign policy

The growing divide

Steven Hurst

A chapter on the relationship between political parties and US foreign policy is itself something of a new direction in books about US foreign policy. A brief survey reveals a distinct lack of attention to this relationship (Dumbrell 1990; Brewer 1992; Deese 1994; Wittkopf and McCormick 1999; Jentleson 2004). Implicit in this absence is the assumption that political parties play no significant role in US foreign policy. This ignoring of parties does not, however, reflect a wider neglect of actors internal to state and society, since the roles of Congress, public opinion, interest groups and the media are not ignored. Rather, a combination of the following beliefs seems to be at work:

1 that foreign policy is generally 'bipartisan' and that parties and their ideologies therefore have no explanatory significance;
2 that Congress is the only arena in which party matters, where it acts as an organizing principle and structures behaviour. The foreign policy-making process, however, is dominated by the executive branch of government and the presidency, which are much less shaped by partisan influences. The irrelevance of Congress thus ensures the irrelevance of parties.

While these arguments may have been valid in the past (and the second one retains a significant degree of relevance even today), however, a continued neglect of the role of parties is a mistake. Over the past 40 years we have seen two, mutually dependent, developments which have markedly increased the importance of parties to US foreign policy-making:

1 a steady and increasing homogenization and polarization of the US political parties;
2 as a direct result of that, an increase in Congressional opposition to presidential foreign policy initiatives when the President is of the opposite party to the Congressional majority.

The result of these developments is that parties now matter, both because of the policy differences between them (who thinks a President Al Gore would have invaded Iraq?) and because the foreign policy-making process has become suffused by partisan conflict.

The rest of this chapter will flesh out this argument, looking first at the factors that led to the breakdown of the 'Cold War consensus' and the increase in partisan political conflict during the second half of the Cold War. It then goes on to explore the impact of the end of the Cold War, and asks whether that event contributed to an increase in partisan conflict over foreign policy. Finally, we look at the presidency of George W. Bush and the impact of the events of September 11th 2001. Some have argued that those events have led to the restoration of a bipartisan consensus and the reassertion of executive branch dominance. This chapter concludes that those claims are exaggerated and that bitter partisan conflict and Congressional attempts to block presidential foreign policy initiatives remain the norm in the post-Vietnam era.

The collapse of the 'Cold War consensus', 1945–89

The discounting of parties as foreign policy actors is a product of the 'Cold War consensus' which existed between the late 1940s and the early 1970s. Agreement on the need to contain the 'Soviet threat' united a broad coalition stretching across both parties (Bax 1977; Wittkopf and McCormick 1990). Consensus on the objectives of foreign policy meant, in turn, that presidents could generally rely on Congressional support for their foreign policy initiatives. (Meernik (1993) found bipartisan support for the position of the President on nearly 62 per cent of foreign policy votes between 1947 and 1972.[1]) Parties, in short, were unimportant because they were in agreement on the objectives of foreign policy and prepared to let presidents pursue those objectives with a free hand.

Since the early 1970s, however, that bipartisan consensus has progressively eroded and conflict over American foreign policy has become both more extensive and more partisan. This change can be attributed to a combination of factors:

1   growing ideological cohesion within both parties and growing polarization between them;
2   institutional reforms in Congress;
3   an increase in the incidence of divided government;
4   the impact of Vietnam and the changing international environment.

Growing ideological cohesion within both parties and growing polarization between them

Before the 1960s, the Democrats were a party of two halves: Northern liberal Democrats representing urban areas and conservative Southern Democrats representing rural areas.[2] This unwieldy alliance was injured by the war in Vietnam – which divided hawkish southern Democrats from increasingly dovish Northern Democrats – then mortally wounded by the issue of race. The support of liberal Democrats for African-American civil rights led increasing numbers of southern white conservatives to transfer their allegiance to the Republican Party (Carmines and Stimson 1989). Those departing whites were partially replaced by socially and economically liberal African-Americans added to the electoral rolls after the 1965 Voting Rights Act. The Republican Party thus gained a new conservative, southern, white electorate (the Republican share of southern House seats rose from 8 per cent in 1960 to 58 per cent in 2007) – while the remaining Democratic electorate in the South became more liberal (Rohde 1994). Over the ensuing decades, the working out of these processes has transformed the Democrats into a homogeneously liberal party and the Republicans into a coherently conservative party.

Previously split between a minority conservative Western wing and a dominant North-Eastern liberal wing, the Republicans have moved steadily rightwards as the growing southernization of the party and a South-West conservative alliance has marginalized the influence of North-Eastern liberals (Trubowitz 1998; Black and Black 2002). Squeezed between the growing conservatism of the Republican base and the drift of socially liberal voters towards the Democratic Party, the liberal wing of the Republican Party went into terminal decline. The drift of those northern liberals towards the Democrats, along with the transformation of the Southern electorate, has meanwhile been pushing the two halves of the Democratic Party together and towards a more homogeneously liberal worldview (Rae 1989; Jacobson 2000; Stonecash *et al.* 2002).

The effects of these processes took time to be fully felt, but the number of 'partisan non-conformists' in both parties began to decline in the 1980s and accelerated in the 1990s. Republican liberals and moderates constituted more than half of all Republicans in some Congresses in the 1960s but had fallen to less than 10 per cent by the 1990s. The percentage of moderate and Conservative Democrats in Congress only began to fall in the early 1980s, but by the 106th Congress (1999–2000) they constituted just 16 per cent of Democrats in the House of Representatives and 2 per cent in the Senate (Fleisher and Bond 2000).

Institutional reforms in Congress

This first development in turn proved the catalyst for a second which compounded it. In the 1970s, Democratic liberals in Congress grew unhappy at the way the seniority rule and the autonomy of Committee chairs created a situation in which a minority of long-serving conservative Southern Democrats chairing key committees were aligning with Republicans against the majority of the Democratic Party. In response, House Democrats instigated changes designed to strengthen the party at the expense of committee chairs. The House Democratic Caucus was given the power to appoint and remove chairs, who were also to be chosen at the start of each Congressional session by a secret ballot within the Caucus. In addition, the party leadership was strengthened, primarily by placing the Rules Committee under the clear control of the Speaker. Increasingly homogeneous and polarized parties thus came to have stronger leadership structures able to enforce their partisan agendas (Rohde 1994: 80–1).

An increase in the incidence of divided government

A further development exacerbating the impact of partisan polarization is the increase in the incidence of divided government.[3] In the 40-year period from 1968 to 2008 there have been just 11 years of united government (1977–80, 1993–4, 2001, 2003–6). Given increased unity within parties and deeper division between them, an increase in divided government leads inevitably to increased executive-legislative conflict, an assumption confirmed by Meernik's finding that divided government was the most significant predictor of Congressional opposition to the use or threat of force by a president (Meernik 1995).

The impact of Vietnam and the changing international environment

The post-Vietnam era not only saw increased partisan polarization, but also a breakdown in the foreign policy consensus. The American defeat in Vietnam led a significant portion of the American political elite to reject the militarized form of containment which they had supported since the early 1950s (Holsti and Rosenau 1984). Nor was Vietnam the only factor provoking dissent. There was a widespread perception that, after two decades of global superiority, the USA was entering a period of decline. The Soviet Union had achieved strategic nuclear parity and China was emerging as a major global power, while European and Japanese companies were out-competing US firms in world markets. US predominance was further brought into question by its abandonment of the Bretton Woods system in 1971 and the oil crisis of 1973–4. This perceived decline in American power led to the breakdown of the Cold War consensus and its replacement by 'competitive and conflictual belief systems' (Rosenau and Holsti 1983: 373), two of which – Cold War internationalism (CWI) and post-Cold War internationalism (PCWI) – became the poles around which mainstream US foreign policy debate came to revolve.

For post-Cold War internationalists, the defeat in Vietnam and the developments of the 1970s marked a watershed. Faced with the reality of decline, America had to adjust its policies accordingly. Multi-polarity, global economic interdependence and 'producer power' were the new realities. New forms of cooperation, the management of interdependence and North–South relations now joined the US-Soviet conflict on a complex foreign policy agenda. The US role in this world would inevitably be more limited given the constraints on its power. The USA would provide selective leadership on key issues and support multilateral institutions in order to promote a stable and peaceful world order. This worldview shaped the initial policies of the Carter administration.

Cold-War internationalists, in contrast, rejected the notion of American decline and insisted that the fundamentals of international politics remained unchanged. Despite the apparent rise of China, West Germany and Japan, the international system remained bipolar and the USSR remained the primary threat to US interests. Economic interdependence and the rise of Third World 'producer power' were illusory and/or of marginal significance compared to the balance of military power. America's global role remained that of sole leader of the non-Communist world and the keys to success were the maintenance of alliance commitments and US defence spending rather than the bolstering of international institutions. This worldview was given practical application by the Reagan administration (Halliday, 1983: 213–42; Rosenau and Holsti 1983: 379).

Initially, at least, the division between these two worldviews did not correlate to the partisan divide but rather to that between liberals (PCWI) and conservatives (CWI) (Holsti and Rosenau 1984: 383). However, as party homogenization and polarization progressed and as ideology and partisan identity came to overlap more and more, so the correlation between Republicanism and CWI and that between Democrats and PCWI grew much stronger.[4] The growing partisan divide was thus reinforced by an emerging conflict of foreign policy worldviews.

In sum, from the late 1960s onwards, a combination of developments led to the collapse of the Cold War consensus and its replacement by partisan conflict over foreign policy. The key factor was the transformation of the parties themselves into two ideologically coherent and polarized organizations – a development compounded by the emergence of conflicting foreign policy worldviews which came to reinforce the partisan divide. The effects of these ideological developments were further exacerbated by the institutional reforms of the 1970s and an increase in the occurrence of divided government.

The effects of these developments were evolutionary rather than revolutionary. In the early 1980s, there were still enough conservative southern Democrats in the House of

Representatives to enable Ronald Reagan to secure massive increases in defence spending in the absence of a Republican majority. If it is at all meaningful to speak of a specific turning point, however, then it arrived with the second Reagan administration (Fleisher and Bond 2000). There had already been evidence of change in Reagan's first term in the shape of the Democratic opposition to the administration's efforts to support the Contra rebels in Nicaragua. The passage of the two Boland Amendments (1983 and 1984) revealed an emergent partisan divide and willingness on the part of Congressional Democrats to overturn presidential preferences. In his second term Reagan found the Congressional Democrats repeatedly opposing him across a wide range of issues including sanctions on South Africa, the size of the defence budget, the Strategic Defense Initiative (SDI), reflagging of Kuwaiti tankers, the banning of nuclear weapons testing, trade rules and compliance with the terms of the non-ratified SALT 2 treaty.

Moreover, such anecdotal evidence is confirmed by more systematic analyses. Studies examining the evolution of the Cold War consensus are as one in finding that it breaks down in the late 1960s and the early 1970s. McCormick and Wittkopf (1990) identified the high point of bipartisanship in the House of Representatives as being the 86th Congress (1959–60) when President Eisenhower received bipartisan support on 80 per cent of foreign policy issues. The low point arrived in the 99th Congress (1985–6) when Reagan got bipartisan support on just 14 per cent of issues. Overall, the average level of bipartisan support for pre-Vietnam Presidents was 52 per cent in the House and 58 per cent in the Senate. For post-Vietnam presidents, it was 32 per cent and 50 per cent respectively. In a similar study, Meernik (1993) found bipartisan support for the President on nearly 62 per cent of foreign policy votes from 1947–72 but on only 39 per cent of votes thereafter. Peake (2002) meanwhile, found a clear increase in foreign policy 'gridlock' post-Vietnam. Whereas 47 per cent of bills seriously considered by Congress prior to the 93rd Congress (1973–4) failed to be passed, that figure rose to 77 per cent after that date. (See also Cooper and Young 1997; Fleisher and Bond 2000; Prins and Marshall 2001; Marshall and Prins 2002; Scott and Carter 2002.)

What all these studies show, in short, is a marked decrease in bipartisan support for presidential foreign policy and its replacement by increased partisan opposition to executive branch foreign policy initiatives.

From the end of the Cold War to 9/11

Subsequent to the trauma of Vietnam, the next profoundly transforming event for US foreign policy was the end of the Cold War, from which event at least two consequences are claimed to have resulted. The first, inevitably, was the reconsideration of existing foreign policy belief systems in the light of the changed international environment. In the view of some observers, the outcome of this process was a significant blurring of the boundaries between the two dominant foreign policy worldviews. According to this argument, while some previously hawkish Republican Cold War internationalists became noticeably more cautious about the use of force in the absence of the Soviet threat, previously dovish post-Cold War internationalists became more supportive of military intervention for purposes such as peace-keeping and humanitarian intervention (Smith 2007). The hawk = Republican/dove = Democrat division, which had been quite clear from the end of the Vietnam War until the end of the Cold War, thus broke down.

While there is a degree of truth in this claim, it is a gross exaggeration to claim that Republicans and Democrats ceased to hold quite distinct worldviews as a result of the end of the Cold War. While a minority of Republicans did become less interventionist (Kirkpatrick 1990; Kristol 1991), the vast majority remained resolutely hawkish. Indeed, the key development within the Republican Party since 1989 has been the increasing dominance of the right of the party and its advocacy of an aggressively unilateralist, militarist and hegemonic foreign policy (Halper and Clarke 2004). Similarly, while the concept of 'liberal interventionism' did gain some traction within the Democratic Party, the Democrats remained fundamentally faithful to the tenets of post-Cold War internationalism, with the Clinton administration prioritizing economics and globalization, emphasizing 'world order' issues and demonstrating continued support for multilateral institutions and international law (Dumbrell 2002).

The second alleged effect of the end of the Cold War is that the decrease in the level of threat resulting from the collapse of the Soviet Union encouraged members of Congress to be even more assertive in relation to foreign policy. According to Lindsay (1999), the key determinant of the balance of power between presidents and Congresses in foreign policy-making is the nature of the international environment. In the absence of overt threats to national security, Americans are more likely to accept the merits of wider public debate because fewer risks are involved. In contrast, when threats are perceived to be great, the public demands strong presidential leadership and sees Congressional activism as dangerous meddling. (Prins and Marshall 2001; Rosner 2005)

The first apparent demonstration of this change occurred during the Persian Gulf Crisis of 1990–1. When President George H.W. Bush altered course away from reliance on sanctions and towards the use of military force in autumn 1990, he encountered stiff opposition from Congressional Democrats. Despite repeatedly insisting that he had the Constitutional authority to act without Congressional authorization, Bush ultimately felt compelled to ask Congress for a declaration of support. In the subsequent vote the House passed a resolution authorizing the use of force 250–183 with 86 Democrats joining 164 Republicans in support. In the Senate the resolution passed by a far narrower margin – 52 to 47 – with 45 of 55 Democrats opposed (Hess 2006).

Bill Clinton faced a Congress controlled by his own party for the first two years of his presidency, but the Democrats lost control after the 1994 mid-term elections. Under the direction of new House Speaker Newt Gingrich, the Republicans returned to Washington determined to assert themselves in the foreign policy sphere. Consequently, in the 104th Congress (1995–6), they challenged Clinton on a range of issues from defence spending and foreign aid to relations with China and Russia and the organization of the State Department. They also sought to undermine Clinton's efforts to revive US multilateralism by persistently attacking the UN, refusing to pay US dues owed to that organization, and opposing US troops serving in peace-keeping missions. In 1995–6, Clinton won only half of the votes on national security issues in Congress, the worst success rate since records began (Mann 1996: 5). Congressional resistance to Clinton was such that by 1996 he looked 'impotent' in foreign policy (Deibel 2000: 25).

After Clinton's 1996 re-election, the Republicans continued to slash his foreign aid requests and over Clinton's two terms they cut spending on international affairs programmes from $20.6 billion to less than $19 billion. They also forced him to accept a more extensive National Missle Defence (NMD) programme than he wanted and to support the objective of regime change in Iraq against his own better judgement. The

Kosovo crisis of 1999 produced a typically rancorous conflict, with all votes on the subject showing deep partisan divisions. The highlight of Republican opposition came in the form of a resolution that would have prohibited the use of Department of Defense funding for the deployment of ground forces which passed by a vote of 249 to 180, with the Republicans voting unanimously in favour (Towell 1999a). On Kosovo, Clinton would ultimately get his way. Not so, however, in the case of the Comprehensive Test Ban Treaty, which the Senate Republicans refused to ratify.

Partisan conflict over foreign policy thus continued throughout the 1990s, but it is unclear that the end of the Cold War produced the increase in conflict suggested by Lindsay and others. Prins and Marshall (2001) found 26 per cent bipartisan support for presidents from 1973–89 but only 20 per cent from 1989–98 (see also Fleisher *et al.* 2000). Scott and Carter (2002: 158), however, found that Congressional opposition to the president on foreign policy rose steadily from the late 1940s until the mid-1980s and then stayed at roughly that level after that point. Wittkopf and McCormick (1999) also discovered an ambiguous picture, with Clinton receiving less bipartisan support in the Senate than Ford, Carter or Reagan, but doing better than them in the House.

It does not appear, therefore, that the end of the Cold War made a significant difference to the degree of partisan conflict over foreign policy, bringing into question the emphasis of Lindsay and others on the international environment. Rather, it would seem, it is partisanship and the ideological divide between the parties which is the primary cause of increased executive-legislative conflict over foreign policy. This is certainly the conclusion of Wittkopf and McCormick who, after testing the significance of a variety of variables, including the end of the Cold War, concluded that loyalty (shared partisanship between Congress and the White House), partisanship and ideology, in that order, were most important in explaining Congressional foreign policy behaviour (ibid.: 454).

September 11th 2001 and after: a return to consensus?

Wittkopf and McCormick's conclusion was reached before the events of September 11th 2001, which altered things dramatically, in more ways than one. Lindsay (2003) argues that this attack fundamentally altered the nature of the foreign policy-making process. In short, there was a massive surge in popular support for President George W. Bush and the public returned to the Cold War mode of demanding strong executive-branch leadership and Congressional deference. The partisan divide was consequently nullified and Democratic opposition to Bush curbed. This argument is complemented by another which suggests that the 'War on Terror' has overcome the splintering of foreign policy worldviews that resulted from Vietnam. The new threat, it is claimed, has forged a new consensus combining the Democrats' support for humanitarian intervention and nation-building with the Republicans' commitment to unilateralism and readiness to use military force (Parmar 2009; Smith 2007).

In the immediate aftermath of September 11th, the Democrats certainly became compliant with President Bush's demands. On 14 September 2001, Congress passed, with a single dissenting vote, a Gulf of Tonkin-like resolution allowing Bush to 'use all necessary and appropriate force against those nations, organizations or persons he determines planned, authorized, committed, or aided the terrorist attacks that occurred on September 11 2001'. Compliance also extended to matters beyond the immediate terrorist threat. Before September 11th, Senate Democrats had opposed Bush's stated intention to withdraw from the Anti-Ballistic Missile (ABM) treaty of 1972 and had cut $1.3 billion from the administration's request for NMD. After September 11th, they restored the money and said nothing when Bush announced US withdrawal from the ABM Treaty in December 2001 (Lindsay 2003).

The Democrats also put up only limited resistance to Bush's determination to attack Iraq. Like his father, Bush requested Congressional support, but with Congressional mid-term elections coming up, the Democrats found themselves in a difficult position given a political environment in which a majority of Americans believed the administration's claim that Saddam Hussein had links to the events of September 11th. With the Republicans playing the security card during the election campaign, the Democrats were backed into a corner and, in early October 2002, both Houses voted overwhelmingly to support the Resolution (Lindsay 2003; Hess 2006).

There is also evidence to support the claim that a new bipartisan foreign policy consensus is emerging. A comparison of the two parties' presidential platforms from the 2004 election finds the Republicans stating that 'there is no greater danger to our people than the nexus of terrorists and weapons of mass destruction', while the Democrats declared that 'there is no greater threat to American security than the possibility of terrorists armed with weapons of mass destruction'. The Republicans insisted that the threat posed by terrorists and WMD 'cannot be contained or deterred by traditional means' but requires, on occasion, pre-emptive action. Not to be outdone, the Democrats declared their 'willingness to direct immediate, effective military action when the capture or destruction of terrorist groups and their leaders is possible'. The Republicans also argued that 'the United States must use the opportunity to extend the benefits of freedom across the globe'. The Democrats concurred: 'promoting democracy, human rights and the rule of law is vital to our long-term security' (Republican National Committee 2004; Democratic National Convention Committee 2004).

The extent of this new consensus, however, is limited. While it encompasses the primary threats to US security and core foreign policy objectives, it does not extend to the means for dealing with those threats or achieving those objectives. Many Democrats voted to give Bush the authority to go to war but, with the odd exception like Senator Joseph Liebermann, this reflected less a genuine conviction than a combination of political calculation and the Bush administration's distortion of the intelligence about Iraqi WMD. Moreover, the vast majority of Democrats, while they did not oppose the removal of Saddam Hussein in principle, clearly did oppose the idea of the USA acting unilaterally and without the authority of UN resolutions. Their preferred course was for Bush to build an international coalition, work through the UN and only to go to war once it was clear that Iraq had not complied with the UN weapons inspectors and was still in possession of WMD (Judis 2002).

The Democrats' 2004 platform revealed a similar distinction between agreement with Republicans on the objectives of policy and disagreement with regard to the means. Bush was lambasted for isolating the USA when it needed cooperation; 'his doctrine of unilateral pre-emption has driven away our allies and cost us the support of other nations' when 'the only possible path to victory will be found in the company of others, not walking alone'. In contrast to the Bush administration's contempt for international law, the Democrats argued for the strengthening of 'international agreements and efforts to enforce non-proliferation'. They agreed that Iran and North Korea must not be allowed to possess nuclear weapons, but argued that 'this is why strengthening the Nuclear Non-proliferation Treaty is so critical' (Democratic National Convention Committee 2004).

The 2008 presidential election campaign only served to reaffirm the divide between the parties. Without exception, the Democratic candidates condemned the Bush administration for its excessive reliance on military power – 'We must learn once again to draw on all aspects of American power, to inspire and attract as much as to coerce' (Clinton 2007: 5) – and argued for a greater embrace of 'soft' or 'smart power', with John Edwards calling for a 'Marshall Corps' of civilian experts in the style of Kennedy's Peace Corps (Edwards 2007). Most obviously, all the Democrats regarded getting out of Iraq as the necessary prerequisite to establishing a new and more effective strategy in the 'War on Terror', rather than seeing the occupation, as did the Republicans, as the centrepiece of that effort. Barack Obama spoke for all the Democratic candidates when he said that 'Iraq was a diversion from the fight against the terrorists' (Obama 2007: 4).

There remains, therefore, a sharp distinction between Democrats, who still believe in multilateralism, international law and an approach to international relations that seeks the mutual benefit of America and others in a stable world order, and Republicans who regard international organizations and multilateralism as constraints on American power and believe the USA can only secure its interests by acting unilaterally and militarily (Judis 2002). Take into account disagreements between Democrats and Republicans on issues such as trade policy and global warming and the notion of a new foreign policy consensus seems premature, to say the least.

Continued divisions would be rendered moot, of course, if the heightened perception of threat from terrorism cows Congressional opposition to presidential foreign policy. However, while the Congressional Democrats were acquiescent to Bush's demands in 2001 and 2002, this did not represent a return to pre-Vietnam norms of behaviour. While the October 2002 vote authorizing the use of force passed 296 to 113 in the House and 77 to 23 in the Senate, virtually all the no votes came from Democrats while Republican support was more or less unanimous. Partisanship, rather than bipartisanship, remained the order of the day.

The Cold War consensus was not based merely on a shared perception of an external threat and fear of the political retribution that would result from a failure to support the president. It was also rooted in weak partisan commitments and genuine policy agreement. While September 11th may have restored some shared perception of threat, it did not lead to renewed agreement on policy, nor has it eliminated the deep partisan enmity in US politics. If anything, the Bush presidency has deepened the degree of partisan polarization (Klinker 2006). A comparison between the Vietnam and Iraq Wars serves to make the point: Gallup polls from the 1960s never found a gap of more than 18 percentage points between Democrats and Republicans in response to the question of whether the war was a mistake. A 2006 poll, in contrast, revealed a 63 per cent gap, with 77 per cent of Democrats saying the Iraq War was a mistake compared to just 14 per cent of Republicans (Dimock 2006).

There is even a case to be made that partisanship, far from being rendered irrelevant by September 11th, was actually critical to the success of Bush after that point. Partisanship has now become so strong in Congress that 'members of the [Republican] majority party … act[ed] as field lieutenants in the president's army rather than as members of an independent branch of government' (Ornstein and Mann 2006: 79). Republican control of Congress and strong loyalty to the president, as much as, or more than, the perception of threat, explains the failure of the Democrats effectively to oppose Bush (Howell and Pevehouse 2007).

The continued importance of partisanship has been confirmed by events since the Democrats regained control of Congress in the 2006 mid-term elections. In March 2007, the House Democratic leadership announced its intention to pass legislation that would require the withdrawal of all US combat troops from Iraq by August 2008. In April, that bill passed the House by a vote of 218 to 208 with 216 of 218 Democrat votes in support and 195 of 197 Republican votes against. Bush vetoed the bill on May 1st 2007 and the next day the House fell short of the two-thirds vote necessary to override the veto.

These events set a pattern for the rest of the year. The Democrats sought repeatedly to impose a timetable for the withdrawal of US combat troops, only to be stymied by their lack of veto-proof majorities and the partisan solidarity of the Republican minority. In July, the House again passed a bill that would have required troop withdrawals, but the Senate failed to do likewise. In November, the House Appropriations Committee wrote a war spending bill that would have redirected Iraq policy. Having passed the House, it fell seven votes short of the 60 necessary to end a Republican filibuster in the Senate. Throughout 2007, in fact, the Senate Republicans repeatedly used the filibuster as a means to defeat Democratic efforts to impose conditions on the President's conduct of the Iraq conflict. The closest the Senate Democrats came to success was a vote on an amendment proposed by Senator Jim Webb that would have required US troops to receive as much time outside a war zone before returning to it as they had just spent in one. This passed 56 to 44 (Republicans 6–43, Democrats 49–0, Independent 1–0), four votes short of the necessary 60.

The events of 2007 do not suggest there has been a return to a bipartisan consensus on US foreign policy. Quite the opposite, in fact. Once they had control of Congress again, the Democrats used it to launch a sustained attack on Bush's conduct of the Iraq War. Both parties behaved in a highly partisan fashion and, had the Democrats had veto-proof majorities in both chambers, they would undoubtedly have imposed a deadline for troop withdrawals.

Conclusion

Despite the events of September 11th 2001, partisan conflict continues to characterize the US foreign policy-making process. This represents a dramatic change from the pre-Vietnam period, when bipartisanship and Congressional support for presidential foreign policy were the norm. So great is the change that some analysts have concluded that Wildawsky's 'two presidencies' thesis, which argued that presidents were much stronger in foreign policy than domestic, has been rendered redundant (Fleisher *et al.* 2000). That is probably an overstatement, since the presidency's institutional resources and constitutional prerogatives continue to advantage it in its struggles with Congress, particularly in the realm of war powers. In the end, George H. W. Bush got his way in 1991, as did Bill Clinton in Bosnia and Kosovo and George W. Bush in Iraq.

Nevertheless, increased conflict over foreign policy and an increase in the number of times presidents fail to get their way are the post-Vietnam norm. Marshall and Prins (2002) found that, pre-1974, presidents won approximately 81 per cent of foreign policy votes, a figure that drops to just under 60 per cent post-1974. A 25 per cent drop in presidential success is a significant change, and the primary reason for that change is the increased salience of parties and partisanship. The increase in partisan polarization post-1968, reinforced by institutional change, divided government and the breakdown of the foreign policy consensus, has made parties and the partisan divide crucial factors in the foreign policy-making process. Under conditions of divided government, Congressional opposition to presidential foreign policy initiatives has become the norm rather than the exception. The end of the Cold War did not alter this fact (though nor did it reinforce it) and neither did the events of September 11th 2001. Despite a temporary lull in Democratic criticism of George W. Bush in the face of a surge in public support for the president and unified Republican control of the Federal Government, the recapture of Congress by the Democrats in 2006 soon saw a return to the post-Vietnam norm.

Notes

1 Bipartisan is defined as receiving support from a majority of both parties.
2 The cause of this strange alliance was the American Civil War. The Democrats were the party of the South and the Republicans the party of Lincoln and the North. For a hundred years after the war, southern whites could not bring themselves to vote for the party of Lincoln. In the meantime, the Democrats themselves were transformed by the advent of the New Deal and the reinvention of the party as the representative of the ethnic and religious minorities and the poor. The Northern and Southern halves of the party were held together by a common interest in economic liberalism and support for an internationalist foreign policy (Ladd and Hadley 1978).
3 Divided government refers to a situation in which a president of one party faces a Congress where one or both chambers are controlled by the opposition party.
4 The transfer of their political allegiance from the Democratic Party to the Republicans by southern white conservatives has a foreign policy parallel in the defection of the first generation of 'neo-conservatives' from the Democrats in response to the latter's drift towards post-Cold War internationalism (Ehrman 1995).

References

Bax, Francis (1977) 'The Executive-legislative Relationship in Foreign Policy', *Orbis*, 20: 881–904.

Black, Earl and Black, Merle (2002) *The Rise of Southern Republicanism*, Cambridge, MA: Harvard University Press.

Brewer, Thomas L. (1992) *American Foreign Policy: A Contemporary Introduction* 3rd edn, Englewood Cliffs, NJ: Prentice Hall.

Carmines, Edward G. and Stimson, James A. (1989) *Issue Evolution: Race and the Transformation of American Politics*, Princeton, NJ: Princeton University Press.

Clinton, Hillary (2007) 'Security and Opportunity for the Twenty-first Century' *Foreign Affairs*, 86(6): 2–18.

Cooper, Joseph and Young, Garry (1997) 'Partisanship, Bipartisanship and Crosspartisanship in Congress since the New Deal', in Lawrence C. Dodd and Bruce I. Oppenheimer (eds), *Congress Reconsidered*, 6th edn, Washington, DC: CQ Press, pp. 246–73.

Deese, David A. (1994) 'The Hazards of Interdependence', in David A. Deese (ed.) *The New Politics of American Foreign Policy*, New York: St Martins Press, pp. 2–34.

Deibel, Terry L. (2000) *Clinton and Congress: The Politics of Foreign Policy*, New York: Foreign Policy Association.

Democratic National Convention Committee (2004) *Strong at Home, Respected in the World: The 2004 Democratic National Platform for America*, Washington, DC: Democratic National Committee.

Dimock, Michael (2006) 'The Iraq Vietnam Difference' Pew Research Center Publications. Online. Available at: http://www.pewresearch.org/pubs/25/the-iraq-vietnam-difference (accessed 22 May 2007).

Dumbrell, John (1990) *The Making of US Foreign Policy*, Manchester: Manchester University Press.

—— (2002) 'Was There a Clinton Doctrine? President Clinton's Foreign Policy Reconsidered', *Diplomacy and Statecraft*, 13(2): 43–56.

Edwards, John (2007) 'Reengaging with the World: A Return to Moral Leadership', *Foreign Affairs*, 86(5): 19–37.

Ehrman, John (1995) *The Rise of Neoconservatism: Intellectuals and Foreign Affairs, 1945–1994*, New Haven, CT: Yale University Press.

Fleisher, Richard and Bond, John R. (2000) 'Congress and the President in a Partisan Era', in Richard Fleisher and John R. Bond (eds), *Polarized Politics: Congress and the President in a Partisan Era*, Washington, DC: CQ Press, pp. 1–8.

Fleisher, Richard, Bond, John R., Krutz, Glen S. and Hanna, Stephen (2000) 'The Demise of the Two Presidencies', *American Politics Quarterly*, 28 (1): 3–25.

Halliday, Fred (1983) *The Making of the Second Cold War*, London: Verso.

Halper, Stefan and Clarke, Jonathan (2004) *America Alone: The Neo-Conservatives and the Global Order*, Cambridge: Cambridge University Press.

Hess, Gary R. (2006) 'Presidents and the Congressional War Resolutions of 1991 and 2002', *Political Science Quarterly*, 121(1): 93–108.

Holsti, Ole R. and Rosenau, James N. (1984) *American Leadership and World Affairs: Vietnam and the Breakdown of Consensus*, Boston: Allen and Unwin.

Howell, William G. and Pevehouse, Jon C. (2007) 'When Congress Stops Wars: Partisan Politics and Presidential Power', *Foreign Affairs*, 86(5): 95–108.

Jacobson, Gary C. (2000) 'Party Polarization in National Politics: The Electoral Connection', in Richard Fleisher and John R. Bond (eds), *Polarized Politics: Congress and the President in a Partisan Era*, Washington, DC: CQ Press, pp. 9–30.

Jentleson, Bruce W. (2004) *American Foreign Policy: The Dynamics of Choice in the Twenty-First Century*, New York: W.W. Norton.

Judis, John B. (2002) 'The Real Foreign Policy Debate: It's Not Just Democrats vs. Republicans. It's Locke vs Hobbes', *The American Prospect*, 13(8), May 6: 102–3.

Kirkpatrick, Jeanne (1990) 'A Normal Country in a Normal Time', *The National Interest*, Fall: 40–3.

Klinker, Phillip A. (2006) 'Mr Bush's War: Foreign Policy in the 2004 Election', *Presidential Studies Quarterly*, 36(2): 281–96.

Kristol, Irving (1991) 'Defining Our National Interest', in Owen Harries (ed.) *America's Purpose: New Visions of America's Foreign Policy*, San Francisco: Institute of Contemporary Studies, pp. 53–69.

Ladd, Everett C. and Hadley, Charles D. (1978) *Transformations of the American Party System: Political Coalitions from the New Deal to the 1970s*, New York: Norton.

Lindsay, James M. (1999) 'End of an Era: Congress and Foreign Policy after the Cold War', in Eugene R. Wittkopf and James M. McCormick (eds) *The Domestic Sources of American Foreign Policy*, 3rd edn, New York: Rowman and Littlefield, pp. 173–83.

—— (2003) 'Deference and Defiance: The Shifting Rhythms of Executive-Legislative Relations in Foreign Policy', *Presidential Studies Quarterly*, 33(3): 530–47.

Mann, Jim (1996) 'Clinton's Foreign Policy Success May Rely on Making Peace with Congress', *Los Angeles Times*, 11 November: 5.

Marshall, Bryan C. and Prins, Brandon C. (2002) 'The Pendulum of Congressional Power: Agenda Change, Partisanship and the Demise of the Post-World War Two Foreign Policy Consensus', *Congress and the Presidency*, 29(2): 195–212.

McCormick, James M. (1985) 'Congressional Voting on the Nuclear Freeze Resolution', *American Politics Quarterly*, 13: 122–36.

McCormick James M. and Wittkopf, Eugene R. (1990) 'Bipartisanship, Partisanship, and Ideology in Congressional-Executive Foreign Policy Relations, 1947–88', *Journal of Politics*, 52(4): 1077–100.

Meernik, James (1993) 'Presidential Support in Congress: Conflict and Consensus on Foreign and Defense Policy', *Journal of Politics*, 55(3): 569–87.

—— (1995) 'Congress, the President and the Commitment of the US Military', *Legislative Studies Quarterly*, 20(3): 377–92.

Obama, Barack (2007) 'Renewing American Leadership', *Foreign Affairs*, 86(4): 2–16.

Ornstein, Norman J. and Mann, Thomas E. (2006) 'When Congress Checks Out', *Foreign Affairs*, 85(6): 67–82.

Parmar, Inderjeet (2009) 'Foreign Policy Fusion: Liberal Interventionists, Conservative Nationalists and Neoconservatives, The New Alliance Dominating the US Foreign Policy Establishment', *International Politics*, 46(2/3): 177–209.

Peake, Jeffrey S. (2002) 'Coalition Building and Overcoming Legislative Gridlock in Foreign Policy, 1947–98', *Presidential Studies Quarterly*, 32(1): 67–83.

Prins, Brandon C. and Marshall, Bryan W. (2001) 'Congressional Support of the President: a Comparison of Foreign, Defense and Domestic Policy Decision Making during and after the Cold War', *Presidential Studies Quarterly*, 31(4): 660–78.

Rae, Nicol C. (1989) *The Decline and Fall of the Liberal Republicans from 1952 to the Present*, Oxford: Oxford University Press.

Republican National Committee (2004) *2004 Republican Party Platform: A Safer World and a More Hopeful America*. Online. Available at: http://www.gop.com/images/2004platform.pdf (accessed 20 February 2008).

Rohde, David W. (1994) 'Partisan Leadership and Congressional Assertiveness on Foreign and Defense Policy', in David A. Deese (ed.) *The New Politics of US Foreign Policy*, New York: St Martin's Press, pp. 76–101.

Rosenau, James N. and Holsti, Ole R. (1983) 'US Leadership in a Shrinking World: The Breakdown of Consensus and the Emergence of Conflicting Belief Systems', *World Politics*, 35: 368–92.

Rosner, Jeremy D. (2005) *The New Tug of War: Congress, the Executive Branch, and National Security*, Washington, DC: Carnegie Endowment for International Peace.

Scott, James M. and Carter, Ralph G. (2002) 'Acting on the Hill: Congressional Assertiveness in US Foreign Policy', *Congress and the Presidency*, 29(2): 151–70.

Smith, Tony A. (2007) *A Pact with the Devil: Washington's Bid for World Supremacy and the Betrayal of the American Promise*, London: Routledge.

Stonecash, Jeffrey M., Brewer, D. and Mariani, Mark D. (2002) *Diverging Parties: Social Change, Realignment and Party Polarization*, Boulder, CO: Westview.

Towell, Pat (1999a) 'Congress Set to Provide Money, but No Guidance, for Kosovo Mission', *CQ*, 1 May: 1036–7.

Trubowitz, Peter (1998) *Defining the National Interest: Conflict and Change in American Foreign Policy*, Chicago: University of Chicago Press.

Wittkopf, Eugene R. and McCormick, James M. (1990) 'The Cold War Consensus: Did It Exist?', *Polity*, 22(4): 227–53.

—— (eds) (1999) *The Domestic Sources of American Foreign Policy*, 3rd edn, New York: Rowman and Littlefield.

Websites

The Democratic Party: http://www.democrats.org

Eben Kaplan, 'US Parties and Foreign Policy': www.cfr.org/publication/9488

The Republican Party: http://www.gop.com

Yahoo's US government directory: http://www.dir.yahoo.com/Government/U_S-Government/Politics/Parties

7 What were they thinking?

Think tanks, the Bush presidency and US foreign policy

Donald E. Abelson

Introduction

Decades from now, when historians and political scientists look back at the turbulent years of the Bush presidency, they will undoubtedly ask – what were they thinking? What was President Bush thinking when he ordered the invasion of Iraq? What advice were his closest advisers – Dick Cheney, Donald Rumsfeld, Paul Wolfowitz, Condoleeza Rice and Colin Powell – giving him as insurgents in and around Baghdad were wreaking havoc on US and allied soldiers? And what, if any, role did policy experts brainstorming at the nation's leading defense and foreign policy think tanks play in advising the Bush administration on how to establish a more stable world order?

Until the memoirs of leading policy-makers involved in Bush's inner circle and the briefing notes summarizing high-level meetings between the president and his principal advisers become available, one can only speculate on what ultimately influenced the Bush administration's decision to resort to force. Moreover, until this and other relevant information surfaces, it will be difficult to confirm why, in the face of considerable public opposition, the president sacrificed thousands of lives and billions of dollars to fight an unpopular and inherently destabilizing war. Although it may take years to piece together an accurate and complete assessment of what led to this foreign policy debacle, it is nonetheless possible to shed light on some of the key domestic influences on US foreign policy during the Bush years.

In the aftermath of 11 September 2001, the American and foreign media, hundreds of interest groups and several other non-state and non-governmental organizations took part in the national conversation over the war on terror. While a study detailing the involvement of these and other actors in the foreign policy-making process would most certainly raise critical questions about the impact of ideas on the Bush administration, in this chapter we will focus solely on how one set of institutions – think tanks – sought to leave an indelible mark on US foreign policy. In doing so, we can further explore how policy experts – who are neither appointed, or elected to public office – can become important actors in the foreign policy-making process.

The aim of this chapter is not to chronicle the evolution of think tanks in the United States, nor is it to engage in a lengthy discussion about the different types of think tanks that populate the policy-making community. These and other issues related to the growth and diversity of American think tanks have been addressed elsewhere (Abelson 1996, 2002, 2006; Rich 2004). Rather, the purpose here is to address what clearly has become a major shortcoming in the burgeoning literature on think tanks. Although scholars who study think tanks in the United States and in other industrialized and developing countries have gone to great lengths to explain how and under what circumstances these organizations become involved in policy-making (Stone 1996; McGann and Weaver 2000; Stone and Denham 2004), the majority of studies have neglected to consider how to assess or evaluate their impact. As a result, although we know far more about the types of think tanks that have emerged in recent years and the various public and private channels on which they rely to market their ideas (Weaver 1989; Abelson 1996, 2002), the extent to which they are able to wield influence at different stages of the policy-making process largely remains cloaked in mystery.

In an effort to address this deficiency, this chapter will explore how a small group of think tanks sought to influence US defense and foreign policy during the Bush administration. Particular emphasis will be placed on how the Project for the New American Century (PNAC) and the American Enterprise Institute (AEI) were able to share their insights on how to wage war in Iraq and in other conflict-ridden countries with key advisers in the Bush White House.

While there is little doubt that think tanks specializing in defense and foreign policy made a concerted effort to influence President Bush's thinking during his tumultuous terms in office, it is important to clarify how and under which circumstances they appeared to have had an impact. For instance, shortly after the United States invaded Iraq, journalists in North America and in Europe claimed that the Project for the New American Century had in effect become the architect of Bush's foreign policy. However, as the war progressed, it appeared that scholars at AEI may have played an even more important role in convincing the Bush administration not only to stay the course in Iraq, but to increase the number of troops being deployed. Support for the 'surge' in Iraq has been closely linked to several projects undertaken at AEI.

Still, as tempting as it may be to make sweeping claims about how influential some think tanks are in official policy-making circles, scholars must be better equipped to analyze the nature and degree of their involvement. As we will discover in the pages that follow, some think tanks have been able to make important contributions to foreign policy by generating timely and policy relevant studies that promote lively discussion and debate among key stakeholders. In doing so, they have made great strides in informing and educating the public and policy-makers about how to meet the many challenges confronting them in the twenty-first century. However, it will become equally apparent that establishing close ties to high-level decision-makers does not guarantee that think tanks will be able to achieve policy influence. Unless and until policy-makers are prepared to listen to their advice, there is little think tanks can do to translate policy recommendations into concrete public policy. For think tanks to succeed in the marketplace of ideas, policy-makers on Capitol Hill, in the White House and throughout the bureaucracy, must be prepared to trust their judgement. Otherwise, scholars residing at think tanks will be left to debate among themselves and members of the attentive public about the virtues and vices of US foreign policy.

In the first section of the chapter, a brief discussion of the many methodological obstacles scholars need to address in studying think tank influence will be provided. This will be followed by a detailed case study of how PNAC and a handful of other conservative think tanks attempted to influence both policy discussions and public debates over the war on terror. Finally, we will discuss why it is important to understand the management style of presidents in any assessment of think tank influence at the highest levels of government.

Assessing the influence of think tanks: challenges and opportunities

As scholarly interest in the role of think tanks in the policy-making process has grown in recent years, far more consideration has been given to the various channels on which they rely to compete in the marketplace of ideas. It is widely known, for instance, that think tanks depend on the media, the internet, workshops, conferences, seminars, as well as on a wide range of publications targeted at different stakeholders, to promote their ideas. It is also generally accepted that although think tanks vary enormously in terms of size, financial and staff resources, research programs and ideological orientation, the 2500 or more think tanks headquartered in the United States share a common desire to shape public opinion and public policy (McGann and Johnson 2006). However, as noted, while several scholars have carefully chronicled the evolution and proliferation of American think tanks since the turn of the twentieth century, little attention has been devoted to evaluating their policy impact.

Scholars who study think tanks acknowledge, among other things, that assessing or measuring the influence of think tanks is inherently problematic. They realize that even the most basic questions about how to study policy influence give rise to a host of methodological concerns. Should policy influence be measured by tracking the number of times think tanks and/or their resident scholars are referred to or interviewed by the media? Would keeping a close watch on the number of publications downloaded on their websites, the number of appearances their scholars make before legislative committees, and the number of publications produced in a given year provide a more accurate measurement of a think tank's influence? Or, alternatively, should we simply record the number of think tank staff appointed to high-level positions in the government to confirm the level of think tank influence? Put simply, do some indicators provide a more accurate measurement of policy influence than others?

Although data on each of these indicators may reveal the amount of exposure think tanks and their staff generate, they cannot confirm how much or little influence policy institutes have in shaping public opinion and/or the policy preferences and choices of policy-makers. Data on media citations, for instance, may tell us which institutes are effective at making the news. However, the frequency of media citations provide little insight into whether the comments made by scholars at think tanks have helped shape, reinforce, clarify or change the minds of policy-makers and the public. Indeed, we cannot even be certain that policy-makers or members of the attentive public are even familiar with what various think tanks have stated in the media. Similarly, when think tanks testify before legislative committees, we can rarely confirm if their statements made a difference to how policy-makers approached particular policy issues. Other indicators such as the number of publications think tanks produce or how many of their staff receive high-level appointments, may tell scholars even less about the influence of think tanks in policy-making.

In addition to considering how to measure policy influence, or if in fact, it can be measured at all, scholars must overcome several other obstacles in evaluating the impact of think tanks. They must, for example, determine how to isolate the views of think tanks from dozens of other individuals and governmental and non-governmental organizations that actively seek to influence public policy. As the policy-making community becomes increasingly congested, tracing the origin of an idea to a particular individual or organization gives rise to its own set of problems. For some students of public policy, examining the various organizations and individuals who coalesce around particular policy issues, offers a useful point of departure (Heclo 1978). By studying the interaction between policy-makers and representatives from non-governmental organizations in specific policy communities, some important insights can be drawn. In addition to identifying the organizations and individuals most actively involved in discussing a particular policy concern with government officials, scholars can, through interviews and surveys, determine which views generated the most attention. However, unless policy-makers acknowledge that their policy decisions were based primarily on recommendations from a particular individual or organization, something they are rarely inclined to do, it is difficult to determine how much influence participants in the policy process have had.

Since it is unlikely that these and other methodological obstacles will easily be overcome, it may be more appropriate to discuss the relevance of think tanks in the policy-making process, than to speculate about how much policy influence they exercise. In other words, rather than trying to state categorically that, on the basis of a handful of indicators, some think tanks appeared to be more influential than others, scholars should determine if, when and under what conditions, think tanks can and have contributed to specific public policy discussions and to shaping the broader policy-making environment. In the following section, we can begin to answer these questions by assessing the extent to which a small group of think tanks became engaged involved in policy discussions and public debates on the war on terror. This case study will help to illustrate that think tanks can and do exercise influence in different ways and at different times in the policy-making process.

The war of words over the war on terror

Despite the increase in terrorist activity during the 1980s and 1990s, little was being done in the intelligence community to protect the United States against future attacks, a concern expressed by Stephen Flynn of the Council on Foreign Relations. In an article published in his think tank's flagship journal, *Foreign Affairs*, before the terrorist attacks of 11 September 2001, Flynn outlined a scenario whereby bin Laden 'might exploit our perilously exposed transportation system to smuggle and detonate a weapon of mass destruction on our soil' (Flynn 2004: xi). To his delight, the article sparked interest in the policy-making community and eventually led to briefings about the vulnerability of America's transportation system. Unfortunately, Flynn's fears about terrorism and the unwillingness of policy-makers to take necessary precautions to protect the American homeland were not widely shared. As he points out, 'The common refrain I heard was, "Americans need a crisis to act. Nothing will change until we have a serious act of terrorism on U.S. soil"' (ibid.: xii).

When terrorists did strike the United States, policy-makers had no alternative – at least no viable alternative – but to react. However, how they reacted, and the effectiveness of their response, have spawned an intense debate in the academic and think tank communities in the United States and abroad. As the initial shock and horror of what occurred on 11 September 2001 began to wear off, scholars in the nation's think tanks and universities took time to reflect on why the attacks took place and what the United States had to do to protect its citizens. For policy experts on the left, the story line was clear: Islamic terrorists had made their way to the United States to punish America's leaders for their foreign policy in the Middle East and in particular, their steadfast support for Israel. Once the United States adopted a more even-handed approach to resolving the Israeli-Palestinian conflict and abandoned its imperialist goals, the threat of terrorism would be significantly reduced (Callinicos 2003; Ross and Ross 2004). If the United States did this, it would no longer have to worry about the bin Ladens of the world. Order, rather than chaos and fear, would come to reflect the state of the international community. As an added bonus, America's strained relations with the United Nations and with much of Western Europe would improve dramatically and the rising tide of anti-Americanism sweeping across the globe would gradually subside.

But for those on the right who believed that this solution could only work in fairy tales, America's response to dealing with terrorism had to convey a very different message. Rather than coddling terrorists and the states that either directly or indirectly support them, what was needed, according to many conservative policy experts, was a clear and forceful demonstration of American resolve. As David Frum and Richard Perle of AEI state in their book, *An End to Evil*:

> The war on terror is not over. In many ways, it has barely begun. Al-Qaeda, Hezbollah, and Hamas still plot murder, and money still flows from donors worldwide to finance them. Mullahs preach jihad from the pulpits of mosques from Bengal to Brooklyn. Iran and North Korea are working frantically to develop nuclear weapons. While our enemies plot, our allies dither and carp, and much of our own government remains ominously unready for the fight. We have much to do and scant time in which to do it.
>
> (Frum and Perle 2003: 4)

For Frum and Perle, the invasion of Afghanistan in October 2001 was a good start. Among other things, it enabled the United States and its coalition partners to topple the Taliban regime and to destroy bin-Laden's terrorist training camps. An even better idea, according to the two AEI residents, was invading Iraq in 2003, a much overdue intervention that allowed the United States to remove another dictator from its roster of enemies. However, they insist that for America to win the war on terror, much more has to be done, including removing terrorist mullahs in Iran, ending the terrorist regime in Syria and adopting tighter security measures at home, recommendations that, if adopted, would no doubt lead to new and more virulent waves of anti-Americanism.

Frum and Perle's recipe for defeating terrorism has found strong support among several conservative members of Congress and think tank scholars, including Brooking's Ken Pollack whose book, *The Threatening Storm* (2002) made a strong case for the invasion of Iraq. But, not surprisingly, their recommendations for future interventions have generated considerable controversy in more liberal policy-making circles. The absence of an exit strategy in Iraq (Preble 2004), combined with an escalating body count, has produced little tolerance for additional conflicts. Regardless of how well or poorly Frum and Perle's grand plan for winning the war on terror has been received, their insights help to shed light on the complexity of waging a war that, according to several critics of the Bush administration, must be fought but may never be won. Their well-publicized views also help to explain why many conservative think tanks should assume some responsibility for creating a political climate that fosters anti-American sentiments.

In their ongoing efforts to dissect the Bush administration's handling of the war on terror, journalists and scholars will continue to offer different explanations for what motivates American foreign policy. They may also comment on the think tanks that are best positioned and equipped to influence the policies of the incoming administration, and may again succumb to the temptation of assuming that proximity to those in power guarantees policy influence. This was the mistake that several journalists, scholars and pundits made in claiming that the blueprint for the Bush administration's foreign policy was drawn up entirely by PNAC.

By the time George W. Bush entered the Oval Office in 2001, it had become Washington's worst kept secret: a small think tank with modest resources, but powerful connections to key members of the Bush team, was rumored to have developed a comprehensive foreign policy for the incoming administration. The think tank that had become a favorite topic of discussion for journalists covering Washington politics and for pundits searching for any clues that would help them predict Bush's behavior in his first 100 days in office, was not the Heritage Foundation or AEI, the darlings of the conservative movement. The heir apparent was PNAC, a neo-conservative think tank whose foray into the policy-making community in 1997 sparked considerable interest among, and support from, several high-level policy-makers, including Dick Cheney, Donald Rumsfeld, Paul Wolfowitz, Scooter Libby and Jeb Bush, the former Governor of Florida and the president's younger brother.

If there were any doubts about which sources of information would help the president manage American foreign policy after 11 September 2001, they were put to rest when the decision was made to invade Iraq. When journalists and scholars skimmed through PNAC's September 2000 study, *Rebuilding America's Defenses*, they thought they had discovered the key to the Holy Grail. In its study, PNAC made several policy recommendations that closely resembled initiatives being pursued by the Bush administration. In fact, the recommendations they made four months before President Bush assumed power (PNAC 2000), such as 'defending the homeland and fight[ing] and win[ning] multiple, simultaneous major theater wars', may as well have been taken directly from his play book.

Could this have been just a coincidence? Not according to several journalists and scholars who made the connection between PNAC, members of Bush's inner circle and the foreign policy the United States had embraced. Writing in *The Guardian* in the Fall of 2003, Michael Meacher, a British Labour Member of Parliament, stated:

> We now know that a blueprint for the creation of a global Pax Americana was drawn up for Dick Cheney, Donald Rumsfeld, Paul Wolfowitz, Jeb Bush, and Lewis Libby. The document, entitled *Rebuilding America's Defenses* (italics added), was written in September 2000 by the neoconservative think tank, Project for the New American Century (PNAC).
>
> The plan shows Bush's cabinet intended to take military control of the Gulf region whether or not Saddam Hussein was in power. It says, 'while the unresolved conflict with Iraq provides the immediate justification, the need for a substantial American force presence in the Gulf transcends the issue of the regime of Saddam Hussein.' The PNAC blueprint supports an earlier document attributed to Wolfowitz and Libby which said the US must 'discourage advanced industrial nations from challenging our leadership or even aspiring to a larger regional or global role.'

Meacher's assessment of PNAC is similar in tone to the one presented by Andrew Austin (quoted in Hamm 2005: 55) who writes:

> Not content with waiting for the next Republican administration, Wolfowitz and several other intellectuals formed PNAC, a think tank 'to make the case and rally support for American global leadership.' Top corporate, military, and political figures aligned themselves with PNAC ... Powerful economic interests [also] threw their support behind PNAC.

Similar comments about PNAC's origins and its strong ties to the policy-making establishment and to the business community continue to make their way into the academic literature on the neo-conservative network in the United States (Halper and Clarke 2004; Micklethwait and Wooldridge 2004). However, as discussed below, evaluating the extent of PNAC's influence is not as straightforward as Meacher and others maintain.

If it looks like a duck and swims like a duck ... : PNAC's influence in perspective

Gary Schmitt, the President of PNAC and a senior adviser to Republican presidential nominee Senator John McCain, spent years in the academic community and in government before running a think tank. He understood the world of Washington politics and how decisions were made in Congress, in the White House and in the bureaucracy. And he understood and appreciated that the right ideas presented at the right time could make a profound difference. Founded in 1997 to promote American global leadership, PNAC spent its early years developing a new conservative approach to foreign policy. This approach or strategy was based on the belief that the United States could and should become a 'benevolent global hegemon'. As William Kristol and Robert Kagan (1996: 20, 23) stated in their essay, 'Toward a Neo-Reaganite Foreign Policy':

> American hegemony is the only reliable defense against a breakdown of peace and international order. The appropriate goal of American foreign policy, therefore, is to preserve that hegemony as far into the future as possible. To achieve this goal, the United States needs a neo-Reaganite foreign policy of military supremacy and moral confidence.

Kristol and Kagan's article struck a responsive chord with several conservative policy-makers and policy experts who encouraged the authors to create an organization that would promote their vision of American foreign policy. As Schmitt points out, 'We got approached by a lot of people saying, why don't you try to institutionalize this?' (Abelson 2006: 214). After Kristol and Kagan convinced Schmitt to become PNAC's president, they secured sufficient funding to launch the new institute.

Building on the success of their 1996 article, Kagan and Kristol, both project directors at PNAC, published an edited collection in 2000 entitled, *Present Dangers*, which further explored the options and opportunities available to the United States as it set out to redefine its role in the international community. Among the many topics addressed by the long and impressive list of contributors were: regime change in Iraq, Israel and the peace process and missile defense, all of which became hot button issues for President Bush. But it was the release of *Rebuilding America's Defenses* in September 2000, a 76-page document endorsed by several people who would come to occupy senior positions in the Bush administration, that propelled PNAC into the national spotlight.

Written by Thomas Donnelly, Donald Kagan and Gary Schmitt, the report was intended to encourage debate among policy-makers and the public about America's military strength and how it could be harnessed to achieve the country's foreign policy goals. Based on a series of seminars in which participants with specialized areas of expertise were encouraged to exchange ideas about a wide range of defense and foreign policy issues, the document left few stones unturned. But did this document or blue-print, as it is often described, amount to an 'extreme makeover' of US foreign policy, or did it simply propose some minor modifications? Moreover, were PNAC's plans for advancing American national security interests in a world in which the United States could market itself as a 'benevolent global hegemon' the product of original thinking, or were their ideas recycled from other sources?

The PNAC document, as Schmitt acknowledged, was intended to provide a more coherent conservative vision of American foreign policy.

> We weren't satisfied with what the isolationists and realists were saying about for-eign policy [and felt] that they were very much drawing the United States back from the world at large ... We thought that even though the cold war had ended, the principles of conservative foreign policy enunciated during the Reagan years, were still applicable to the world today.

In this sense, the PNAC study offered new and innovative ways of promoting American interests in the post cold-war era. Ironically, when the study came out, 'its real impact was on the Clinton folks, not on the Bush people' (Abelson 2006: 215–16).

But when it comes to evaluating the work of his institute, Schmitt, like any responsible policy entrepreneur, can ill afford to be modest.

> I think we do a good job of getting our vision on the table because I think we're very good at what we do ... We get a lot of feedback from editorialists and you can tell they read the stuff. If you make a poignant argument and present a case that's well reasoned and brief, you have a lot of impact, or you can at least have some impact.
>
> (ibid.: 217)

Scholars studying PNAC's ascendancy in the political arena cannot possibly overlook the fact that several of the original signatories to its statement of principles received high-level positions in the Bush administration. As Ted Koppel, formerly of *ABC News* pointed out, you do not have to be a conspiracy theorist to acknowledge the intimate ties between some of Bush's closest advisers and PNAC (ibid.). Still, acknowledging these important connections is a far cry from making the claim that PNAC was the architect of Bush's foreign policy. The president appointed Rumsfeld, Wolfowitz and other foreign policy experts to serve in his administration, not because they were card-carrying members of PNAC or of any other think tank. They were recruited because they were people Bush could trust.

PNAC may have been considered the architect of President Bush's foreign policy, but there were several other think tanks in and around the nation's capital that had become preoccupied with assessing the domestic and global implications of the war on terror.

The Brookings Institution, Rand, the Heritage Foundation, the Center for Strategic and International Studies, the Council on Foreign Relations and a number of other institutes specializing in defense and foreign policy had produced dozens of studies, held workshops, seminars and conferences and testified before Congressional committees and subcommittees about various aspects of US foreign policy. Indeed, in the immediate aftermath of 11 September 2001, it was difficult to pick up a newspaper, listen to the news or watch one of many political talk shows without hearing the views of policy experts from various think tanks. Interestingly enough, while several think tanks struggled for air time, others were being secretly courted by senior officials in the Bush administration.

President Bush and his small circle of advisers known as 'the vulcans' were well aware of PNAC's recommendations for revamping the US military (Mann 2004). Since several of Bush's key advisers had lent their name to PNAC's recently released study, it is likely they would have raised any pertinent ideas contained in the report with the president. However, it appears that PNAC did not have all the answers the president and his advisers were looking for. Shortly after the terrorist attacks, Paul Wolfowitz, Deputy Secretary of Defense, contacted his old friend, Christopher DeMuth, who, until recently, was the longtime president of AEI. His reason for contacting DeMuth, according to veteran journalist Bob Woodward, was to ask him to form a working group of the nation's top Middle East experts to provide the Bush administration with guidance on how to address the political and military problems associated with waging war in this historically-troubled region (Woodward 2006: 83–5).

DeMuth agreed to assemble the working group on short notice and on 29 November 2001, the group met 'at a secure conference center in Virginia for a weekend of discussion' (ibid.: 84). After hours of discussion, DeMuth produced 'a seven-page, single-spaced document entitled "Delta of Terrorism"' which included several policy recommendations. Although DeMuth was not prepared to provide Woodward with a copy of the document, he stated that 'We concluded that a confrontation with Saddam was inevitable. He was a gathering threat – the most menacing, active and unavoidable threat. We agreed that Saddam would have to leave the scene before the problem would be addressed' (ibid.: 84–5).

The conclusions reached by the group did not take long to make their way to the president's top advisers. According to Woodward, Vice-President Cheney noted that the report helped the president to focus 'on the malignancy' of the Middle East and National Security Adviser Condoleeza Rice found the report to be 'very, very persuasive' (ibid.: 85). Although several members of the group DeMuth assembled were not affiliated with AEI, it is difficult to ignore the important role the think tank president played in generating and disseminating ideas to the Bush White House. This would not be the last time AEI had a profound impact on helping the Bush administration manage the war on terror.

In December of 2006, two AEI scholars, retired general Jack Keane, a former vice chief of staff of the Army and a member of the advisory Defense Policy Review Board, and Fred Kagan, a military historian, met with Vice-President Cheney to discuss their plans for a 'surge' in Iraq, based on months of work they conducted at AEI, Keane and Kagan found an ally in Cheney and in Senator John McCain, who played a key role in selling the idea to President Bush (DeMuth 2007; Barnes 2008). Although the involvement of AEI in promoting the surge warrants a detailed case study, for now, it is useful in illustrating an earlier point – that scholars must be careful in making claims about the nature and extent of think tank influence. As noted, while PNAC should be credited with bringing scholars and policy-makers together to reconsider how to pursue US defense and foreign policy interests in the twenty-first century, it would be an exaggeration to suggest that this organization was solely responsible for laying the foundation for US foreign policy during the Bush years. There were several other think tanks, including AEI, that played a key role in disseminating ideas to senior officials in the Bush administration. However, as the final section will discuss, even if think tanks are equipped with the best ideas, they cannot hope to leave an indelible mark on US foreign policy unless the president and his principal advisers are prepared to listen.

Is anybody listening? President Bush and his foreign policy

If anyone needed a crash course in international relations, it was George W. Bush. The eldest son of the 41st president of the United States shared his father's love of baseball, but showed little interest in world affairs. This was reflected in the limited number of trips Bush took abroad. By the time he became president in 2001,

> Bush's foreign travels [had] been limited to three visits to Mexico, two trips to Israel, a three-day Thanksgiving visit in Rome with one of his daughters in 1998 and a six-week excursion to China with his parents in 1975 when his father was the U.S. envoy to Beijing.
>
> (Associated Press 2000)

What Bush did not learn about foreign policy on his travels or from his advisers, he learned on the job. When terrorists struck the United States on 11 September 2001, millions of Americans prayed that he was a quick student. To the surprise of many political pundits, including AEI's David Frum (2003), a former speech writer for President Bush, the president was up to the challenge. According to Frum, like many world leaders, Bush found his voice in a time of crisis – he had come of age. The inexperienced and untested leader, who months earlier, could not answer some basic questions about foreign affairs, had become America's war president, a position that in time he would come to relish. According to Daalder and Lindsay (2003: 2):

> As Air Force One flew over Iraq, Bush could say that he had become an extra-ordinarily effective foreign policy president. He had dominated the American political scene like few others. He had been the unquestioned master of his own administration. He had gained the confidence of the American people and persuaded them to follow his lead.

Shortly after Bush's campaign against terrorism went into full-swing, his leadership style had clearly begun to change. The insecurity and sense of vulnerability that accompanied him to the Oval Office was replaced by a growing confidence and bravado that other commanders-in-chief, including Ronald Reagan, John F. Kennedy, Franklin Roosevelt and Theodore Roosevelt, had exhibited (Deconde 2000). No longer content assuming the role of student listening diligently to his teachers, Bush began to assert his leadership. Although he continued to rely on the advice of Condoleeza Rice, Donald Rumsfeld and the other 'vulcans', it became clear to those outside the inner sanctum that for the most part, the president had little interest in expanding his circle of advisers. To put it bluntly, for policy experts residing in think tanks and at universities, the foreign-policy making process at the highest levels of government was, for all intents and purposes, closed. As Daalder observed:

> This is a very, very, very closed system. I think the president does rely on a small group of people [but] I don't think he's listening to the arguments. I think the arguments in of themselves are being muted more and more. When [Bush] became president, he was always in receiving mode. He'd just sit there and listen. Now he's in broadcasting mode. He spends all his time telling other people what he thinks. Foreign leaders who met with him in his first year thought he was interested in listening to them and now it's all about telling them what he thinks needs to be done. He still listens, but he already knows what he wants. I think he's becoming more confident that he knows what he's doing and he doesn't need anybody's advice. So for these reasons, it is true that the process is not particularly open to outside influence.
>
> (Abelson 2006: 220–1)

The relatively closed policy-making environment that has come to characterize the Bush White House may have impeded the access of policy experts from outside government, but it does not appear to have undermined Bush's ability to make policy decisions. Rather, limiting the number of participants involved in high-level policy matters has allowed the president to wage the war on terror more effectively. According to Daalder and Lindsay, the president has a clear vision of what he wants to accomplish and will not allow even his closest and most trusted advisers to interfere with his agenda. Moreover, contrary to the assertions of countless journalists and scholars that a small band of neo-conservatives have hijacked the Oval Office, they claim that the president has remained the master of his destiny. As the two think tank scholars (Daalder and Lindsay 2003: 16) point out:

> The man from Midland [Texas] was not a figurehead in someone else's revolution. He may have entered the Oval Office not knowing which general ran Pakistan, but during his first thirty months in office he was the puppeteer, not the puppet. He governed as he said he would on the campaign trail. He actively solicited the counsel of seasoned advisers, and he tolerated if not encouraged vigorous disagreement among them. When necessary, he overruled them. George W. Bush led his own revolution.

If President Bush has indeed exercised as much control over foreign policy as the two authors claim, it stands to reason why the majority of think tanks and other NGOs interested in defense and foreign policy issues have had difficulty gaining access to the highest levels of government. Clearly, there have been exceptions as the discussion about PNAC and AEI reveal. But, if Bush's management of foreign policy has been as restrictive as some suggest, what does this tell us about the ability of think tanks to wield policy influence?

Conclusion

Think tanks prepared for the debates over the war on terror much like armies prepare for battle. They took stock of their resources, assessed their capabilities, designed a strategy and determined the most effective ways in which it could be executed. Although their efforts may not always have paid off, think tanks have and continue to stake out and defend their positions in the war of ideas. Through their publications, conferences and seminars, Congressional testimony and ongoing interaction with the media, America's leading defense and foreign policy think tanks have made a significant contribution to shaping the national conversation.

How much of an impact think tanks have had in influencing the substance and direction of the Bush administration's campaign to eradicate terrorism is a question that has yet to produce any definitive answers. In evaluating the extent to which they have made a difference, scholars must, like any competent detective, review what they know and what they do not know about the involvement of think tanks in this controversial policy debate. What scholars who have monitored the debates over various aspects of the war on terror know is that several think tanks, including RAND, CSIS, AEI, Brookings, Heritage, PNAC, the Council on Foreign Relations, the Carnegie Endowment and the Center for Security Policy (CSP) have relied on multiple channels to convey their ideas to the public and to policy-makers on a wide range of issues. Among other things, think tanks have discussed the problems and prospects of homeland security, the advantages and disadvantages of supporting a surge in Iraq, the need to overhaul intelligence agencies both at home and abroad and whether the USA needs to mend fences with its European allies. In short, scholars acknowledge that when it comes to ideas about how to fight a successful war against terrorists, think tanks have spoken loudly and clearly.

Several scholars and journalists have also acknowledged that some think tanks have been better positioned than others to capture the attention of policy-makers. Indeed, the consensus is that no think tank has been more effective at communicating its ideas to the Bush White House than PNAC. In the press and in much of the academic literature that has surfaced since President Bush assumed office, a lot has been made of the strong ties between PNAC and key members of his administration. Even more has been made of how closely the policy recommendations outlined in several of its publications and letters to policy-makers, closely resemble the policies Bush has pursued since 11 September 2001.

However, by probing more deeply into the relationship between PNAC and the Bush administration, we were able to uncover further information. For instance, we learned that the ideological underpinnings of the Bush doctrine, which among other things, helped to justify the war in Iraq, did not originate at PNAC, but were closely linked to recommendations made by several members of his cabinet. As Gary Schmitt acknowledged: 'It's perfectly obvious that Bush's war on terror was not something we articulated before 9–11 … Bush pulled together a strategic vision based on the advice he received from Cheney, Wolfowitz and Rumsfeld' (Abelson 2006: 217). We also learned that AEI played an important role in advising the Bush administration on several key issues related to fighting the war on terror.

Over the course of the past thirty years, think tanks have come to play a more active and visible role in US foreign policy. As a result, it is critically important for students of foreign policy to understand how they seek to become involved in the foreign policy-making process and what, if any, impact they may have had in shaping public opinion and the policy preferences and choices of leaders. Determining how much or little impact think tanks have had will likely continue to give rise to a host of methodological issues – issues that unfortunately, are not easy to resolve. However, the alternative – to simply make unwarranted claims about the nature of think tank influence – is a path we cannot afford to take. Think tanks will continue to grow in number and in stature in the United States and beyond. The challenge will be to determine the most effective ways to evaluate their contribution to public policy.

References

Abelson, D.E. (1996) *American Think Tanks and their Role in US Foreign Policy*, London and New York: Macmillan and St. Martin's Press.
—— (2002) *Do Think Tanks Matter? Assessing the Impact of Public Policy Institutes*, Kingston and Montreal: McGill-Queen's University Press.
—— (2006) *A Capitol Idea: Think Tanks and US Foreign Policy*, Kingston and Montreal: McGill-Queen's University Press.
Associated Press (2000) 'Bush Turns to Foreign Policy Experts,' 16 December.
Barnes, F. (2008) 'How Bush Decided on the Surge,' *The Weekly Standard*, 13(20).
Callinicos, A. (2003) *The New Mandarins of American Power: The Bush Administration's Plans for the World*, Cambridge: Polity.
Daalder, I.H. and Lindsay, J.M. (2003) *America Unbound: The Bush Revolution in Foreign Policy*, Washington, DC: Brookings Institution Press.
Deconde, A. (2000) *Presidential Machismo*, Lebanon, NH: UPNE.
DeMuth, C. (2006) 'Think-Tank Confidential: What I Learned during Two Decades as Head of America's Most Influential Policy Shop', *The Wall Street Journal*, 11 October.
Flynn, S. E. (2004) *America the Vulnerable: How Our Government Is Failing to Protect Us from Terrorism*, New York: HarperCollins.
Frum, D. (2003) *The Right Man: The Surprise Presidency of George W. Bush*, New York: Random House.
Frum, D. and Perle, R. (2003) *An End to Evil: How to Win the War on Terror*, New York: Random House.
Halper, S. and Clarke, J. (2004) *America Alone: The Neo-Conservatives and the Global Order*, New York: Cambridge University Press.
Hamm, B. (ed.) (2005) *Devastating Society: The Neo-Conservative Assault on Democracy and Justice*, London: Pluto Press.
Heclo, H. (1978) 'Issue Networks and the Executive Establishment', in A. King (ed.) *The New American Political System*, Washington, DC: The American Enterprise Institute.
Kagan, R. and Kristol, W. (2000) *Present Dangers: Crisis and Opportunity in American Foreign and Defense Policy*, San Francisco: Encounter Books.
Kristol, W. and Kagan, R. (1996) 'Toward a Neo-Reaganite Foreign Policy', *Foreign Affairs*, 75(4): 18–32.
Mann, J. (2004) *Rise of the Vulcans: The History of Bush's War Cabinet*, New York: Viking.
McGann, J.G. and Johnson, E.C. (2006) *Comparative Think Tanks, Politics and Public Policy*, London: Edward Elgar Publishing.
McGann, J.G. and Weaver, R.K. (2000) *Think Tanks and Civil Societies: Catalysts for Ideas and Action*, New Brunswick, NJ: Transaction Publishers.
Meacher, M. (2003) 'This War on Terrorism is Bogus', *Guardian*, 6 September.
Micklethwait, J. and Wooldridge, A. (2004) *The Right Nation: Conservative Power in America*, New York: Penguin Books.
Pollack, K. (2002) *The Threatening Storm: The Case for Invading Iraq*, New York: Random House.
Preble, C. (2004) *Exiting Iraq: Why the U.S. Must End the Military Occupation and Renew the War against Al Qaeda*, Washington, DC: The Cato Institute.
Project for the New American Century (2000) *Rebuilding America's Defenses: Strategy, Forces and Resources for a New Century*, Washington, DC: The Project for the New American Century.

Rich, A. (2004) *Think Tanks, Public Policy, and the Politics of Expertise*, New York: Cambridge University Press.

Ross, A. and Ross, K. (eds) (2004) *Anti-Americanism*, New York: New York University Press.

Stone, D. (1996) *Capturing the Political Imagination: Think Tanks and the Policy Process*, London: Frank Cass

Stone, D. and Denham, A. (eds) (2004) *Think Tank Traditions: Policy Research and the Politics of Ideas*, Manchester: Manchester University Press.

Weaver, R.K. (1989) 'The Changing World of Think Tanks', *PS: Political Science and Politics*, 22(2): 563–78.

Woodward, B. (2006) *State of Denial*, New York: Simon & Schuster.

Further reading

McGann, J.G. (2007) *Think Tanks and Policy Advice in the United States: Academics, Advisors and Advocates*, London: Routledge.

NIRA (2005) *NIRA's World Directory of Think Tanks 2005*, 5th edn, Tokyo: National Institute for Research Advancement.

Parmar, I. (2004) *Think Tanks and Power in Foreign Policy*, London: Palgrave.

Ricci, D.M. (1993) *The Transformation of American Politics: The New Washington and the Rise of Think Tanks*, New Haven, CT: Yale University Press.

Smith, J.A. (1991) *The Idea Brokers; Think Tanks and the Rise of the New Policy Elite*, New York: The Free Press.

Websites of select American think tanks

The American Enterprise Institute: www.aei.org
The Brookings Institution: www.brook.edu
The Carnegie Endowment for International Peace: www.ceip.org
The Council on Foreign Relations: www.cfr.org
The Heritage Foundation: www.heritage.org

8   Intellectuals and US foreign policy

Aggie Hirst

Introduction

Examining the roles and influence of 'intellectuals' in US foreign policy can provide an insight into the operation of power at the highest levels. In an era in which the circulation of ideas is increasingly rapid and widespread, taking the activities and interventions of intellectuals into account can be instructive in gaining an understanding of how such ideas impact upon society and what productive effects these ideas have on the making of foreign policy. In order to address this topic, this chapter develops a case study of a group of neo-conservative intellectuals active during the presidency of George W. Bush. The ways in which this group of neo-con intellectuals contributed to the development of particular narratives and ideas in the post-9/11 security environment will be explored and their influence will be shown to have been significant in three main ways *vis-à-vis* the decision to invade Iraq in 2003. Before this case study is examined, however, we must first explore what is meant by an 'intellectual', and relatedly, what kinds of influence they can be said to wield in the foreign policy-making realm.

Who or what is an 'intellectual'?

The intellectual is perhaps more difficult to define than might at first seem the case. We tend to associate this label with those who embark on a career in the academic sphere, and also perhaps with certain types of writers, artists, scientists, or professionals who have achieved a certain level of notoriety for their work. An intellectual could be, then, someone who achieved some degree of recognition in society for his or her contribution. However, this definition of who counts as an intellectual could be as limited as to include only those to have completed a PhD or similar qualification, such as university professors, doctors or lawyers, or as broad as extending to anyone who claims to be an authority on a particular subject, for instance, journalists, political commentators or novelists. We are presented at the outset, then, with a difficulty in defining who the intellectual we are discussing is.

Edward Said has suggested that an intellectual is someone who makes some kind of contribution to the study of society; someone who makes a public statement that furthers our analysis of or investigation into how society operates. An intellectual is, for Said, someone who understands that 'freedom must include the right to a whole range of choices affording cultural, political, intellectual, and economic development', which leads him or her to 'a desire for articulation over silence'. He continues, 'This is the functional idiom of the intellectual vocation' (Said 2001: 31). For Said, then, the intellectual is someone who understands that we must address a whole range of issues and problems when trying to understand the world, someone who is consequently inclined to make some kind of statement, who prefers to 'speak' rather than remaining silent. The intellectual understood in this way is someone who plays an active role in the discussion of ideas about society, who makes their voice heard by putting forward their position regarding a particular issue.

This account of the intellectual implies that the voices of these individuals can be and are heard in society; intellectuals thus seem to be people with access to channels of communication, which might include the mass media, the publication of books or articles, appearances on television or radio programmes, and so forth. This indicates that intellectuals are individuals who wield some degree of social power; that their ideas are successfully disseminated and received by the public suggests they must be involved in or have connections with those who produce various kinds of public media. This might also suggest that intellectuals are connected to the workings of political power, since access to the mass media is often closely related to the political; as Said comments, 'all the main [media] outlets are, however, controlled by the most powerful interests' (ibid.: 29). These characteristics, actively intervening in public discourse, involvement in the media, and engagement with the workings of power, are central to understanding who or what an intellectual is.

Why study intellectuals?

Intellectuals have a significant impact upon the culture within which they operate. The ways in which intellectuals affect society has been the subject of long-standing debate. Said has argued that the intellectual tells 'truth to power' (ibid.: 25). Similarly, Chomsky has suggested that, 'it is the responsibility of the intellectual to speak the truth and expose lies' (Chomsky 1967: 2). This implies that the intellectual remains outside the formal workings of politics, examining and commenting upon the activities of those in the establishment and bringing to light things that they might have preferred remained unnoticed. Conversely, others such as Karabel, have argued that the intellectual is often embedded within the workings of politics, whether though holding official government posts, through systems of patronage and funding for their work, or simply in the sense that they support the system which has placed them in a position of relative advantage. They have suggested that these political responsibilities and connections have the consequence of influencing what the intellectual can say or write, or indeed what he or she wants to say or write, leading many to espouse ideas which reinforce the norms of the status quo. The intellectual can then be conservative or radical, and operate within or outside the institutions of power; he or she might have a vested interest in working to maintain or to disrupt the prevailing order.

This argument of whether the intellectual tells truth to power or consolidates and reinforces the political establishment can be further developed if we consider the problem of 'truth'. While telling the truth and exposing lies might seem self-explanatory, when we consider the role of the intellectual in contributing to the formation of what the truth is, this becomes more problematic. The intellectual is in a position, due to expertise, training, resources and social position, to conduct investigations or inquiries into particular topics and consequently to inform society of his or her findings. In this sense, the intellectual does not, perhaps, simply *tell* the truth so much as contribute to *forming* the truth, to what counts as knowledge, defining what the acceptable way to approach a subject is, what sorts of questions can be asked and what kinds of answers attained. The intellectual can thus be said to have a productive role in the formation of ideas and cultural practices and beliefs; their work is not merely descriptive of the existing order but rather actively contributes to forming what is deemed to be 'truth' or 'knowledge' in society. In this sense, intellectuals can be seen to wield a significant kind of power inasmuch as they are 'cultural producers', in the words of one commentator (Bourdieu 1991: 656). They are privileged in forming and transmitting ideas and are recognised in society for playing this role, and as such they can contribute to directing how things are seen; how the public, or indeed those in the political realm, engage with a particular notion or issue is impacted upon through the interventions of intellectuals.

What kinds of influence can intellectuals wield?

The influence of intellectuals could be described and accounted for in many ways. For our purposes here, three types of influence will be explored. While it is worth discussing these as separate instances of the ways in which intellectuals intervene in the development or maintenance of ideas and beliefs in society, it should be remembered that these three types of influence are very closely related, indeed they reinforce and complement one another.

1   *Direct influence*: Direct influence refers to the ways in which intellectuals intervene directly in the policy-making sphere, in other words, those who have a close relationship with the workings of political power. This would include those intellectuals who hold government posts, for instance, in the White House or Departments of Defense or State. It would also include those who present their work in the form of reports or speeches to those who make decisions at the highest levels of the political establishment, whose findings are listened to and incorporated into policy-making processes. Additionally, interest or lobby groups which are closely affiliated with the policy-making realm would be significant here, as well as other formal associations of intellectuals who share a particular position or agenda.

2   *Indirect influence*: Indirect influence refers to the ways in which intellectuals have an impact on policy making through channels other than direct involvement in the political realm. This would include those intellectuals who hold journalistic positions, who write for journals, newspapers and magazines that deal with issues relating to policy making. It would also include those who publish books and monographs intended for a broad public audience rather than exclusively designed for consumption by the political elite. This type of influence is also exerted by those who are called upon as experts to address the public in television or radio broadcasts, and those who are invited to give their opinions in news or current affairs programmes. Indirect influence operates, then, through the support or criticism offered by intellectuals regarding particular decisions made by those in the policy-making establishment; intellectuals wield influence here by addressing both policy makers and the public through their activities in the media, including broadcasts, publications and interviews.

3   *Influence on the broader 'climate of opinion'*: the 'climate of opinion' refers to the system of norms, values and assumptions that forms the basis of any political decision, in that it provides the context and system of rules through which policies or decisions make sense. In other words, the climate of opinion is the network of prevailing narratives that present the issues of the day in a particular light, indeed, which delimit what is deemed politically important and what is not. Intellectuals

have a strong influence in this sphere, particularly to the degree that they can intervene in the ways in which a particular subject is perceived and discussed, or is not, in the political and public realms; their expertise and opinion tend to be respected and are hence influential. This is not the same as claiming that intellectuals somehow have complete control over how important political issues are discussed; it suggests rather than they have to power to either encourage or discourage a particular way of understanding such issues, and can thus intervene in and shape what becomes the common-sense understanding, in other words, the dominant narratives surrounding a given issue. This will become clearer as we examine our case study of neo-conservative intellectuals and their influence on recent US foreign policy making.

Case study: neo-conservative intellectuals, 9/11, and the invasion of Iraq

This study will put into context the propositions regarding the role and influence of intellectuals discussed above by arguing that the decision to invade Iraq in 2003 was influenced in all three of these ways by the activities and ideas put forward by a group of neo-conservative intellectuals who rose to prominence under the presidency of George W. Bush. The invasion of Iraq can be seen to effectively illustrate the ways in which intellectuals can influence policy making; indeed, it can be read as one of the most poignant examples of this in recent US political memory. Before proceeding, however, we must take into account some cautionary points.

To suggest that some sort of conspiracy or coup occurred which saw neo-con intellectuals assume complete control over the making or executing of US foreign policy is not the intention here; a great deal has been published in the media and elsewhere which presents the neo-cons as some kind of sinister cabal which conspired to wrest power from other factions in the administration to pursue their ends. Not only is this a caricature of the situation which risks oversimplification, it also detracts from and depoliticises the study of the neo-con intellectuals and their influences and agendas, which ought to be investigated in detail if we are to have a clearer picture of the effects of these intellectuals in the making of foreign policy.

It is also important to note that the neo-cons are not, nor have they even been, a unitary or homogeneous group. On the contrary, they comprise several different generations, are influenced by many philosophers and thinkers, and have on some occasions disagreed about particular policies or principles. For instance, Irving Kristol, a leading neo-con intellectual, has remained uncharacteristically quiet over the question of Iraq, while Francis Fukuyama has enacted what might be described as an unprecedented U-turn as the consequences of this policy have become apparent. That said, the roles played and influence exerted by particular neo-con intellectuals during the build-up to the invasion of Iraq is clearly discernible and will be the subject of what follows.

Who are these neo-con intellectuals?

The neo-cons are a distinct group on the right of the US political spectrum who attained notably increased levels of influence during the Reagan and George W. Bush administrations, indeed several prominent neo-cons held high-ranking government positions in both. An unusually large proportion of neo-cons can be considered to be 'intellectuals', understood as defined above. Many began careers in the academic sphere, shifting to politics later, often moving back and forth over time, while others have held positions in both government and the academy for many years simultaneously. While an exhaustive list of these individuals is beyond the scope possible here, suffice it to comment upon some of the most high profile and well known of these neo-con intellectuals.

Perhaps most influential neo-con intellectual during the George W. Bush administration was Paul Wolfowitz in his role as Deputy Defense Secretary from 2001 until 2005. Wolfowitz made the transition from academia into politics during the 1970s, leaving Yale University to serve in the Defense and State Departments, but he returned to the academy for a period as Visiting Professor at the Johns Hopkins School for Advanced Research in 1980–1, and again as Dean between 1994 and 2001. He thus straddled the divide between the academic and political realms, bringing his ideas and expertise periodically from the one to the other. Wolfowitz began his academic career at Cornell University, but moved to the University of Chicago where he studied for a PhD in Political Science, which he obtained in 1972.

Abram Shulsky is another notable neo-con intellectual who studied at the University of Chicago, also receiving his PhD in 1972. Shulsky played a significant role in the period of interest here as Director of the Office of Special Plans, an organisation set up by Wolfowitz, the function of which was to re-analyse intelligence relating to Iraq prior to the invasion (see below). Shulsky also served during the Reagan administration under Richard Perle who was Assistant Secretary of Defense. He has published widely, including many collaboration pieces with other prominent neo-con intellectuals, on topics such as new US strategy towards Asia, the rise of China and the world of intelligence gathering.

Richard Perle served during the Reagan administration from 1981 until 1987, then under George W. Bush as a member of the Defense Policy Board until 2003. He was educated at the London School of Economics, moving to the University of Southern California and then to Princeton where he received an MA in Political Science in 1967. Unlike some of the other prominent neo-con intellectuals, Perle's links to universities are not notably strong but his involvement in many think tanks and interest organisations is striking, ranging from a position as a resident fellow in the American Enterprise Institute, to the Jewish Institute for National Security Affairs, to chairing research and study groups such as in the Council on Foreign Relations. He has also published material relating to the War on Terrorism and US security, most influentially, *An End to Evil: How to Win the War on Terror*, co-written with David Frum (Frum and Perle 2004).

William Kristol has also been a highly active neo-con intellectual during this period. He is the son of Irving Kristol, a central figure in the development of the neo-conservative persuasion. William Kristol attended Harvard University, where he received his PhD in Political Science. Although he took up the positions in the Office of the Secretary of Education between 1985 and 1988, and in the Office of the Vice President in 1989 until 1992, Kristol's main influence is felt via *The Weekly Standard*, which he founded and continues to edit. He has published widely, in this and many other journals, newspapers and magazines and has also published books on the subjects of the war in Iraq and America's mission in the War on Terror. In addition to his journalistic contributions, Kristol is notable for co-founding the Project for the New American Century (PNAC) with Robert Kagan, to which all the neo-con intellectuals discussed here belong. In addition, he has affiliations with numerous other think tanks and lobby groups including the American Enterprise Institute, the Foundation for the Defense of Democracies, the Shalem Foundation, the Committee for the Liberation of Iraq, and the Ethics and Public Policy Center.

Robert Kagan, co-founder of PNAC, can also be deemed a neo-con intellectual. He received his education at Yale University, then at the Kennedy School of Government at Harvard, receiving his PhD in History from the American University. He served in the State Department as Deputy for Policy in the Bureau of Inter-American Affairs between 1985 and 1988, and before that in the Office of the Secretary of State as a speechwriter between 1984 and 1985. Since then, like Kristol, Kagan has operated mainly outside the formal workings of government, as co-Director of PNAC, through publications in *The Washington Post* and *The Weekly Standard* and through think tanks and interest groups including the Carnegie Foundation for International Peace, the Center for Security Policy, the Council on Foreign Relations and the Committee for the Liberation of Iraq.

Charles Krauthammer is also a noteworthy neo-con intellectual. Like both Kristol and Kagan, Krauthammer spend a relatively brief period in the political sphere between 1978 and 1980, but his main contribution has been through the writing of journalistic and media publications. He was educated at McGill and Oxford universities before acquiring the title of MD at Harvard in 1975. He has published widely in journals and newspapers including *The Washington Post*, *The Weekly Standard* and *The National Interest* and *The New Republic*, on topics such as the new unipolar world, the War on Terrorism, and has held several editorial positions.

Elliott Abrams, Special Assistant to the President since 2002, is also a noteworthy neo-con intellectual. Before assuming this position in government, Abrams served under Reagan as Assistant Secretary of State for Inter-American Affairs between 1985 and 1989. He was educated at Harvard University, moving to the London School of Economics in 1970, then to Harvard Law School to complete his studies by 1973. He, like Perle, is highly active in interest and lobby groups having served as President of the Ethics and Public Policy Center and holding current or past membership in the Middle East Forum, the American Jewish Committee, the Center for Security Policy, the Committee of US Interests in the Middle East, the Committee for Peace and Security in the Gulf and the Nicaraguan Resistance Foundation.

While there are a great many other important neo-con intellectuals who warrant comment in their own right, these individuals will be the focus here as their activities, publications and other contributions can most directly be seen to have had a significant impact on the decision to invade Iraq in 2003. This influence has to a large extent been linked to PNAC, which might be described as the most forthright and active of the neo-con institutions as far as the promotion of their foreign policy aims is concerned. PNAC was established in 1997, with the intention of promoting what its members termed a 'neo-Reaganite' foreign policy style. It has consistently exerted pressure on both the Clinton and Bush administrations to incorporate the ideas and policy aims of the neo-con intellectuals into US foreign policy, as will be shown in what follows.

Direct influence

The neo-con preoccupation with Iraq

Many of these neo-con intellectuals exerted direct influence on the policy-making establishment during the period leading up to the invasion of Iraq in 2003. Several of them were directly involved in the formation of foreign policy, and their activities and interventions are particularly evident following the 9/11 attacks. However, their pre-occupation with the question of Iraq is in evidence well before the 9/11 attacks. There is available a trail of documents and letters which clearly shows that these neo-con intellectuals and their allies were exerting pressure on the Clinton as well as Bush administration to focus on Iraq as a priority in foreign policy.

In 1992, a classified document entitled the 'Defense Planning Guidance' was drafted several times by a group of neo-con intellectuals including Wolfowitz, Shulsky and I. Lewis Libby and leaked to the *New York Times*. The main emphasis of the document is an evaluation of the threats faced by the USA following the dissolution of the Soviet Union. The document details potential threats and suggests strategies in reference to almost every corner of the globe, including Iraq and the broader Middle East. A section of the document reads as follows:

> In the Middle East and Southwest Asia, our overall objective is to remain the predominant outside power in the region and to preserve US and Western access to the region's oil ... As demonstrated by Iraq's invasion of Kuwait, it remains fundamentally important to prevent a hegemon or alignment of powers from dominating the region.
>
> (Wolfowitz *et al*. 1992: 22)

While removing Saddam is not directly mentioned here, in 1992, we can already see neo-con intellectuals focusing on Iraq, in particular on ensuring US dominance in the region is maintained and its oil and other interests preserved.

The focus on ousting Saddam can be seen to develop through the 1990s. In 1996, Richard Perle led a study group which produced a document entitled 'A Clean Break: A New Strategy for Securing the Realm' (Perle *et al*. 1996). This paper focused on the threats faced by Israel and suggested strategies for enhancing the latter's security. It details ideas and plans for dealing with threats from many Middle Eastern nations, but importantly for our purposes states that:

> Israel can shape its strategic environment, in cooperation with Turkey and Jordan, by weakening, containing and even rolling back Syria. This effort can focus on removing Saddam Hussein from power in Iraq – an important Israeli strategic objective in its own right – as a means of foiling Syria's regional ambitions.
>
> (ibid.: 4)

Here we can clearly see that the removal of Saddam from power has become part of the foreign policy agenda advocated by neo-con intellectuals within the political sphere.

This was followed on 26 January 1998 by the sending of an open letter to President Clinton from PNAC, signed by many prominent neo-con intellectuals including Abrams, Kagan, Kristol, Perle and Wolfowitz. The letter begins:

> We are writing you because we are convinced that current American policy toward Iraq is not succeeding, and that we may soon face a threat in the Middle East more serious than any we have known since the end of the Cold War.

Not only do we see here evidence that neo-con intellectuals were focusing on the problem of Iraq and making the case that a new, more aggressive strategy was necessary, but also that the Middle East is described as threatening to a comparable degree as was the Soviet Union during the Cold War, that conflict with the region seems to be on the horizon. The letter continues that there is a new opportunity in the President's State of the Union Address to confront this increasingly serious threat:

> We urge you to seize that opportunity, and to enunciate a new strategy that would secure the interests of the U.S. and our friends and allies around the world. That strategy should aim, above all, at the removal of Saddam Hussein's regime from power.

Here again, the intention to remove Saddam from ruling Iraq is stated in no uncertain terms. The existing policy of 'containment', the letter states, has been 'steadily eroding over the past several months', with Saddam resisting UN inspections and hence the monitoring of his development of weapons of mass destruction (WMD) becoming increasingly difficult. Significantly, the question of WMD is already circulating here as one reason why Saddam ought to be removed. Saddam will 'almost certainly', the letter claims, be able to develop WMD if the USA continues with the existing policies of sanctions and diplomacy. Indeed, the objective is put very clearly:

> Given the magnitude of the threat, the current policy, which depends for its success upon the steadfastness of our coalition partners and upon the cooperation of Saddam Hussein, is dangerously inadequate. The only acceptable strategy is one that eliminates the possibility that Iraq will be able to use or threaten to use weapons of mass destruction. In the near term, this means a willingness to undertake military action as diplomacy is clearly failing. In the long term, it means removing Saddam Hussein and his regime from power. That now needs to become the aim of American foreign policy.

Here we have the clearest statement yet regarding the policy aims of neo-con intellectuals during this period. Two objectives are unequivocally presented: first, the use of military force to achieve that which diplomacy has failed to accomplish, and, second the removal of Saddam Hussein's regime.

In addition to this, in a 2000 PNAC project report entitled 'Rebuilding America's Defenses: Strategy, Forces and Resources for a New Century', the neo-con intellectuals argue that permanent military bases should be installed in the Gulf region, and operations there maintained:

> In the Persian Gulf region, the presence of American forces, along with British and French units, has become a semipermanent fact of life. Though the immediate mission of those forces is to enforce the no-fly zones over northern and southern Iraq, they represent the long-term commitment of the United States and its major allies to a region of vital importance. Indeed, the United States has for decades sought to play a more permanent role in Gulf regional security. While the unresolved conflict with Iraq provides the immediate justification, the need for a substantial American force presence in the Gulf transcends the issue of the regime of Saddam Hussein.

> (p. 14)

Here, as well and at other points in this document, we can clearly see the issue of Saddam's regime is centrally important. That there is an 'unresolved conflict' with the regime seems to indicate that further action is needed to resolve the issue; the document proceeds to argue that greater 'consideration to the force requirements [is] necessary not only to defeat an attack but to remove these regimes from power and conduct post-combat stability operations' (p. 19). There is little doubt, then, that a continued or permanent presence in the Gulf region was a policy aim for the neo-con intellectuals operating within the formal political sphere, and that the removal of Saddam Hussein from power has loomed large in this broader policy aim since the early 1990s.

9/11 and the invasion of Iraq

The events of 9/11 2001 provided in new space within which the realisation of this long-standing policy aim became increasingly feasible. The publication and circulation of documents and letters such as these, which were directed at and read by those at the very top of the Bush administration, show the ways in which neo-con intellectuals intervened in foreign policy making, attempting to bring renewed attention to the question of Iraq, specifically the removal of Saddam Hussein by military means. The 9/11 attacks provided a context within which this policy aim could be realised; the neo-con intellectuals began immediately after the attacks to bring the issue of Iraq into public and political debate, indeed, they began a process of conflating the 9/11 attacks with the issue of Saddam Hussein's Iraq.

During this period, the neo-con intellectuals began speaking of 9/11 and Iraq in conjunction with each other, forming the sense of an association or link between them. This can be seen as early as 20 September 2001, only days after the 9/11 attacks. In a letter to President Bush from PNAC, the signatories, who included Kristol, Perle, and Kagan as well as many others, stated:

> It may be that the Iraqi government provided assistance in some form to the recent attack on the United States. But even if evidence does not link Iraq directly to the attack, any strategy aiming at the eradication of terrorism and its sponsors must include a determined effort to remove Saddam Hussein from power in Iraq. Failure to undertake such an effort will constitute an early and perhaps decisive surrender in the war on international terrorism.

Here we can see that Iraq and the removal of Saddam are linked directly to the broader War on Terror, indeed it is portrayed as an integral front in this war. The apparent indifference regarding the need for any proof of Iraqi complicity is noteworthy; the statement seems to suggest that whether or not such evidence is available, Saddam should be ousted all the same.

This question of the importance of proof of Iraqi culpability *vis-à-vis* the 9/11 attacks warrants further investigation. The intention to conflate the two threats and hence justify the pre-existing policy aim of invasion can be clearly seen in the activities of the Office of Special Plans (OSP), the intelligence body established at Wolfowitz's behest and run by Shulsky. Neo-con intellectuals integrated themselves into the intelligence community, through which they gathered and interpreted information which, they argued, proved that Saddam was linked to terrorism and 9/11. From her experience in the Office of the Secretary of Defense from 2001, Karen Kwiatkowski states that following 9/11, these neo-cons gained significant influence in the Defense Department, bringing with them their pre-existing policy aim of regime change in Iraq. Of the material produced by the OSP that Kwiatkowski saw, the most significant seems to be the 'talking points' on Iraq, WMD and terrorism.

Much of the intelligence contained in these 'talking points' came from Ahmad Chalabi, leader of the anti-Saddam Iraqi National Congress (INC). Perle and Wolfowitz had known Chalabi personally since 1985 and in their co-authored book, Perle and David Frum blamed the instability of Iraq on the refusal of moderates, including then Secretary of State Colin Powell, to support the reinstatement of Chalabi as ruler (Frum and Perle 2004). The INC was paid $340,000 each month for its central role in the 'Intelligence Collection Program' by the Defense Department despite the fact that Chalabi was labelled a fraud in 1996 by the CIA. Kwiatkowski states that the content of the 'talking points,' based on intelligence from Chalabi and the INC, included claims to the effect that Saddam Hussein was 'becoming an imminently dangerous threat to his neighbors', that he had 'harbored al-Qaida operatives and offered and probably provided them with training facilities', that he was 'pursuing and had WMD of the type that could be used by him, in conjunction with al-Qaida and other terrorists, to attack and damage American interests, Americans and America' (Kwiatkowski 2004). All of these were subsequently disproved. There were also other claims made in original drafts of the 'talking points' that were later dropped when they became public and shown to be groundless. One draft stated that Iraqi intelligence agents met Mohammad Atta in Prague, which was used to link Saddam to the 9/11 attackers. Another was the allegation that Saddam had attempted to purchase yellowcake uranium from Niger. The FBI's records of the whereabouts of Atta showed the former to be untrue, and the documents suggesting the latter were declared forgeries by the office of Sub-Saharan African Affairs.

It would appear, then, that such intelligence was problematic, both in terms of its origins and content. The reliability and credibility of the evidence gathered by Shulsky and his team can be seen to be, then, unreliable at best. That many neo-cons showed their indifference to the need for proof in the letter to President Bush cited above is perhaps not unrelated to this; efforts were made to provide some grounds for the conflation of these two disparate issues, Islamic terrorism and Saddam Hussein, but ultimately, even without such evidence, the policy of the invasion of Iraq should, they maintained, be pursued anyway. All of this shows the ways in which neo-con intellectuals exerted direct influence on the making of foreign policy during this period; they exerted pressure through their official positions within the policy-making and intelligence-gathering establishments, through the activities, letters and statements of PNAC, and via the publication of reports and advisory documents from interest and research groups to encourage the realisation of their preconceived policy aim of regime change in Iraq.

Indirect influence

As well as these direct interventions by individual neo-con intellectuals in government, and the activities and publications of PNAC, other forms of influence that encouraged the policy of regime change in Iraq are discernible. Indirect influence was exercised by the neo-con intellectuals which impacted not only upon those in power but also upon a broader audience, through channels such as the mass media, including journalistic publications, speeches and interviews. Indeed, this type of influence was integral to the process of threat conflation which made possible the invasion of Iraq. Even a brief study of the journalistic and public statements made by neo-con intellectuals following 9/11 clearly shows that the threat posed by Islamic terrorism and that posed by Saddam Hussein were treated as synonymous. This conflation of the two threats in the broader social realm can be seen as a means by which neo-con intellectuals influenced the public to accept the necessity of the invasion of Iraq.

In public addresses, neo-con intellectuals were, almost immediately after 9/11, speaking of al-Qaeda and Saddam in the same breath when describing the new enemy America faced. For instance, Wolfowitz claimed in October 2001 that

> their decision-making is not subject to the same constraints that earlier adversaries faced. Usama bin Laden [and] Saddam Hussein ... answer to no one. They can use the capabilities at their disposal without consultation or constraint – and have demonstrated a willingness to do so.
>
> (Wolfowitz, 2001: 5)

So soon after the 9/11 attacks, statements such as these encouraged the public to begin to associate the two distinct issues as part of the same problem. This intervention into the public sphere conflating terrorism and Iraq began immediately following 9/11 and increased in intensity and frequency thereafter. For instance, in 2002, Krauthammer commented in the *Washington Post* that:

> time is running short. Saddam has weapons of mass destruction. He is working on nuclear weapons. And he has every incentive to pass them on to terrorists who will use them against us. We cannot hold the self-defense of the United States hostage to the solving of a century-old regional conflict.
>
> (Krauthammer 2002a)

Here, Krauthammer unequivocally states that Saddam and terrorism are linked and that the former is likely to arm and aid terrorists in their attempts to attack the USA. Similarly, later the same year, he argued:

> Hawks favor war on the grounds that Saddam Hussein is reckless, tyrannical and instinctively aggressive, and that if he comes into possession of nuclear weapons in addition to the weapons of mass destruction he already has, he is likely to use them or share them with terrorists. The threat of mass death on a scale never before seen residing in the hands of an unstable madman is intolerable – and must be pre-empted.
>
> (Krauthammer 2002b)

This reinforces again the notion that Saddam was connected to and in league with terrorists, the issue of weapons of mass destruction serving to heighten the sense of danger and the severity of the situation. By 2003, Krauthammer was no less insistent on the scale and imminence of the impending threat of the combination of Saddam and terrorism: 'On Sept. 11, 2001, the cozy illusions and stupid pretensions died. We now recognize the central problem of the 21st century: the conjunction of terrorism, rogue states and weapons of mass destruction' (Krauthammer 2003).

Many other neo-con intellectuals seemed to concur with Krauthammer, echoing his sentiments regarding the combined threats of terrorists and Iraq. For example, Kristol argued in the *Weekly Standard* in 2003 that:

> We committed ourselves to reshaping the Middle East, so the region would no longer be a hotbed of terrorism, extremism, anti-Americanism, and weapons of mass destruction. The first two battles of this new era are now over. The battles of Afghanistan and Iraq have been won decisively and honorably.
>
> (Kristol 2003)

Notwithstanding the possible problems associated with describing the Iraq adventure as a victory, this statement shows again how the two distinct issues of terrorism and Saddam Hussein were conflated in the publications of neo-con intellectuals.

Thus, we can see how the conflation of these two distinct issues, fundamentalist Islamic terrorism and Iraq, were linked together by neo-con intellectuals, with the intention of realising their pre-conceived policy aim. Although less 'direct' than the influence exerted on top government officials by those in the political sphere, this more 'indirect' mode of influence is just as significant; the impact of this kind of pressure can be seen to be equally great. The intention of statements such as those cited above is clearly to influence and convince the reader or listener; the style of writing, use of rhetoric, and manner of delivery were intended to persuade the public of the connection between the two disparate issues. That as many as 66 per cent of the US population believed in 2002 that Saddam was directly involved in the 9/11 terrorist attacks, and 88 per cent in early 2003 that he supported or aided the terrorist groups responsible for 9/11, attests to this (Jackson 2005: 163).

Influence on the broader 'climate of opinion'

In addition to these direct and indirect influences exerted by neo-con intellectuals, their impact can be seen to extend to having helped construct the now dominant 'climate of opinion' or 'discourses' surrounding the War on Terrorism. As mentioned above, the issue of the climate of opinion relates to the development and maintenance of specific ideas about a particular issue, in this case the threat faced in the War on Terror. The ways in which this threat has been narrated and understood, and the consequent responses to it which emerge from a particular characterisation, is an instance of the productive dimension of the role intellectuals can play *vis-à-vis* the climate of opinion.

To illustrate this, consider the different threat faced in the Cold War. During this period, the threat faced was presented by intellectuals and commentators as having a particular nature (a superpower, communist), which demanded particular means by which to potentially combat it (conventional and nuclear capacities, as well as others means such as the space race). The possible responses to the apparent threat of the USSR were thus dictated by the way in which they threat was perceived and the enemy understood. The respective merits of the possible responses to the USSR is not what is at stake here, rather the important point to note is that each of these responses could only have been suggested, could only have made sense, given a certain understanding of the nature of the threat posed by the USSR. The ways in which the threat posed by the USSR was narrated, they ways in which it was characterised and understood and the range of options put forward to combat it, developed due to the accounts and arguments put forward by many different kinds of people, but notably for our purposes, intellectuals played a critical role here.

The same is true of the ways in which the threat faced in the War on Terrorism is portrayed. What is important here is attending to the flow of ideas and assumptions through society that lead people to think in specific ways about the nature of threats faced, in other words, a 'climate of opinion' is produced and in turn reflects ideas about the nature of threats faced and possible strategies for dealing with it. This means that the ways in which a threat is portrayed always has political and social consequences, and is not 'innocent' or self-evident; the possible responses are delimited in advance by the ways in which the threat is characterised. In other words, a climate of opinion surrounding what the threat is, who represents it, and importantly how to combat it, is formed and in turn gets solidified in public and political discourse relating to the issue, taking on the appearance of the 'truth' about what the threat is, even though the threat could have been presented differently. The significance of this here becomes clear when we examine the ways in which neo-con intellectuals sought to portray the nature of the threat faced in this War on Terror context.

The neo-con intellectuals propounded a particular conception of the nature of the threat faced, and it is this conception that became prominent in the broader climate of opinion surrounding the War on Terrorism. What is interesting here is the extent to which their account came to dominate the political sphere, other accounts being delegitimated and subjugated, so that non-neo-cons came to take on and reflect ideas which originated in the neo-con intellectuals' writings and speeches. While other groups and individuals did initially suggest different conceptions of the nature of the threat faced, and proposed different strategies for tackling it, for instance, many in the so-called 'realist camp' sought to tackle the issue of 9/11 in isolation from the issue of Iraq, focusing on such issues as the conflict in the Middle East and the grievances of Palestinians *vis-à-vis* Israeli activities and policies, their interpretations failed to achieve discursive dominance. The neo-con campaign to conflate the two issues of terrorism and Iraq worked to discredit, even to make nonsensical, other accounts, for instance, those who sought to inquire into the possible motivations of the 9/11 attackers were labelled 'appeasers' and 'apologists' in the publications of neo-con intellectuals. Thus, neo-con intellectuals can be said to have influenced foreign policy making in this third way; their presentation of the threat faced and appropriate ways of dealing with it came to dominate the climate of opinion, excluding and subordinating other accounts, and was taken up by many outside the neo-con tradition as it came to be seen as the 'correct' way to view the issue.

Conclusion

We can thus see that the neo-con intellectuals influenced the foreign policy establishment in three distinct but related ways. The neo-con intellectuals' influence can been seen to have contributed to what became the prevailing narratives surrounding the 9/11 attacks, Iraq, and the War on Terrorism more broadly through direct intervention in policy making, through indirect influence on the public and politicians via the media, and in terms of achieving discursive dominance in the broader climate of opinion. That the National Security Strategy 2002 reflects the neo-con ideas and agenda perhaps attests to this. While others in the administration and the academy were calling for a different understanding of the threat faced, neo-con intellectuals successfully dominated the discourses surrounding these issues and won the battle for setting the agenda and influencing the climate of opinion. That even now presidential candidates Obama and Clinton are compelled to espouse ideas closely linked to the neo-con ideas camp, such as the 'making the world safe for democracy' and the exceptionalism and special mission of the USA, perhaps demonstrates the pervasiveness of the influence of the neo-con intellectuals *vis-à-vis* discourses surrounding the War of Terror. While it would be an overstatement to claim that it is only because of the neo-con intellectuals' influence that Iraq was invaded, it seems likely that their influence contributed in a very significant way to creating favourable conditions in the US' political establishment and broader society for the invasion to proceed; their direct, indirect and discursive interventions were profound and persistent.

References

Where page references are absent, they did not appear in the original documents.
All PNAC documents and letters available at www.newamericancentury.org
All *Washington Post* material available at www.washingtonpost.com
All *Weekly Standard* material available at www.weeklystandard.com

Bourdieu, P. (1991) 'Forth Lecture. Universal Corporatism: The Role of Intellectuals in the Modern World', *Poetics Today*, 12(4).
Chomsky, N. (1967) 'The Responsibility of Intellectuals', *The New York Review of Books*, 23 February.
Frum, D. and Perle, R. (2004) *An End to Evil; How to Win the War on Terror*, audio recording, read by Richard M. Davidson, New York: Random House Inc.
Jackson, R. (2005) *Writing the War on Terrorism, Language, Politics and Counter-Terrorism*, Manchester: Manchester University Press.
Karabel, J. (1996) 'Towards a Theory of Intellectuals and Politics', *Theory and Society*, 25(2): 205–33.
Krauthammer, C. (2002a) 'We Can't Blow it Again', *The Washington Post*, 19 April.
—— (2002b) 'What Good is Delay?', *The Washington Post*, 7 October.
—— (2003) 'Holiday from History', *The Washington Post*, 14 February.
—— (2004) 'In Defense of Democratic Realism', *The National Interest*, Fall.
Kristol, W., (2003) 'The Era of American Weakness and Doubt in Response to Terrorism is Over', *The Weekly Standard*, Vol. 008, Issue 32, 28 April.
Kwiatkowski, K., (2004) 'The New Pentagon Papers', *Salon*, 10 March. Online. Available at: http://www.umdfacultyagainstwar.com/~bmcclure/archives/46_The_New_Pentagon_Papers.html.
Perle, R., Colbert, J., Fairbanks, C. Jnr, Feith, D., Loewenberg, R., *et al.* (1996) 'A Clean Break: A New Strategy for Securing the Realm', report prepared by The Institute for Advanced Strategic and Political Studies' 'Study Group on a New Israeli Strategy Toward 2000'.
Said, E. (2001) 'The Public Role of Writers and Intellectuals', Deakin Lecture delivered in Melbourne, 19 May.
Wolfowitz, P. (2001) 'Building a Military for the 21st Century', Prepared Testimony to Senate Armed Services Committee, 4 October.
Wolfowitz, P. *et al.* (1992) 'Defense Planning Guidance'.

9 Christian evangelicals and US foreign policy

Stuart Croft

Introduction

American Christianity is an amazingly wide-ranging phenomenon; and one that, in so many ways, is full of political purpose. The nature of American Christianity has been extensively surveyed. Those who research on the subject can be members of the Association of Statisticians of American Religious Bodies, a body which produces its own ten yearly 'Religious Congregations Membership Study' (http://www.asarb.org/index. html). Individuals can engage in online assessments of how 'normal' their own religious belief is. Were I a college-educated American Protestant male aged between 36 and 55, I would be among 42 per cent of my cohort if I attended church every week or more; among 23 per cent if I believed that 'The Bible should be taken literally, word for word'; and among 83 per cent who believe that Jesus is the 'son of God' (Association of Religion Data Archives 2005). *The Pew Forum on Religion and Public Life* has produced from its detailed work a profile of faith across the United States; and from this, it is clear that America is an overwhelmingly Christian nation, with over 79 per cent of the population professing some form of Christianity (Table 9.1).

Of this range of Christian traditions, that which is most often focused on in terms of politics is the grouping that can be termed the Christian Right, or what Woodberry and Smith (1998: 25) term 'Conservative Protestants'. The *Princeton Religion Research Report* has shown how 'evangelicals' have increased steadily, from 34 per cent in 1975, to 45 per cent in 2000 (Wheaton College 2002). The National Association of Evangelicals has 30 million members, in 45,000 churches (http://www.nae.net/) and the Southern Baptist Convention over 16 million members in 42,000 churches (http://www. sbc.net/aboutus/). Around 78 per cent of those who might be termed Conservative Protestants who voted turned out for George W. Bush in the 2004 presidential election on a turnout of some 63 per cent, a 10 per cent gain on the vote in 2000 (Pew 2004).

Yet despite these characteristics, it has been relatively rare to consider how Christianity, and how Christian groups, might impact upon the foreign policy-making of the American state. In *The Review of Faith and International Affairs*, a group of authors suggested that 'only recently has the role of religious faith in shaping foreign policy been taken seriously' (Guth *et al.* 2005: 3). Most of that interest has followed the attacks of 11th September 2001, and most of the focus has been on faith in states outside America. But what if we turn the lens inward? What impact could faith have on American foreign policy-making? As Marsden has argued, 'Since the events of 9/11, the Christian Right have had greater opportunity to influence US foreign policy than ever before' (Marsden 2008: 245).

Table 9.1 Faith in America

Religious tradition			
Christian	(%)	Others	(%)
Evangelical Protestant	26	Jewish	2
Mainline Protestant	18	Muslim	1
Historically Black Protestant	7	Buddhist	1
Catholic	24	Hindu	< 0.5
Mormon	2	Other World Religions	< 0.5
Orthodox	1	Other faiths	1
Jehovah's Witness	1	Unaffiliated	16
Other Christian	< 0.5	Don't know/refused	< 0.5
Total	79		

Source: Religious Landscape Survey, *Pew Forum on Religion and Public Life*. Online. Available at: http://religions.pewforum.org/maps.

Note: ± 0.6% margin of error, 35,556 cases.

This chapter examines these issues in three sections. First, common assumptions about the influence of Christianity on the Bush Administration are explored. The next two sections then examine the ways in which particular organisations, who are associated with Conservative Protestantism have developed foreign policy perspectives, either focusing on making an impact on the way in which individuals should live their lives around the world (the National Association of Evangelicals, and International Christian Concern), or on those that seek to change policy at the level of inter-state relations (the Family Research Council and the Friends of Israeli Communities). What connects these organisations is a belief that Christianity requires believers to engage in politics beyond the borders of the United States, a belief that the foreign policy of the American state should be engaged in helping to deliver those Christian outcomes, and an organisational drive to influence the Administration, Congress and key opinion formers that there should be policy changes in these directions.

American Christianity and the Bush Administration

The issue of the influence of the Christian Right on the Bush Administration has been most powerfully portrayed in Kevin Philips' *American Theocracy* (Philips 2007). Philips argues that Bush has been part of a movement that has created America's first religious party; that the Administration has developed the global war on terror, and strategic issues such as gay marriage, into a new fundamentalist moment; that this has led to a hostility to science (the 'disenlightenment'); and that this has led to increasing 'Biblical' focus on the Middle East. In the UK, the comparative religion author, Karen Armstrong (2006), made a similar argument:

> Is there a connection between a religiously motivated mistrust of science, glaring social injustice and a war in the Middle East? Bush and his Administration espouse many of the ideals of the Christian Right and rely on its support. American fundamentalists are convinced that the second coming of Christ is at hand; they have developed an end-time scenario of genocidal battles based on a literal reading of Revelation that is absolutely central to their theology.

The administration of George W. Bush has been frequently connected with the drivers of a wider Christian Right movement, and indeed with theological elements that have little resonance in much of the world, especially in Europe.[1] A popular British television series emphasised the point. In Channel 4's *Faith and Belief*, Tony Robinson fronted an analysis of the influence of the Christian Right on the Bush Administration. Robinson argued that

> The leaders of the End Time movement are rich, well-connected and very powerful ... End Timers are frequent visitors to the White House. No one knows if George W Bush is an End Timer himself, but his policies are at one with those of the evangelical Right and his language is often apocalyptic, such as when he describes the 'war on terror' as 'the epic struggle of good and evil'.
>
> (Doomsday 2006)

These views ascribe a strong link between the president and the Conservative Protestants. And certainly, there is evidence of such a link. John Ashcroft, well known for his evangelism, served as Attorney General. When accepting an honorary degree at Bob Jones University in 1999, Ashcroft had said:

> Unique among the nations, America recognized the source of our character as being godly and eternal, not being civic and temporal ... And because we have understood that our source is eternal, America has been different. We have no king but Jesus.
>
> (Lewis 2001)

The location was important: Bob Jones University Mission Statement is: 'to grow Christlike character that is scripturally disciplined, others-serving, God-loving, Christ-proclaiming, and focused above' (http://www.bju.edu/about/mission.html). Connections with Conservative Protestant educational establishments abound. Patrick Henry College in Virginia has been able to secure 100 places for their evangelical students in the Bush Administration as interns. Foreign policy is one of the subject areas addressed at the College, taught by Dr Paul Bonicelli until his appointment to the position of USAID's deputy assistant administrator responsible for democracy programmes.

However, it would not be reasonable to assert that there was a simple 'hand in glove' relationship between the Bush Administrations and the Conservative Protestant community. The Christian Right differed with neo-conservatives on a number of points, mostly 'issues of conscience'. Although there are many Christian organisations, on foreign policy issues there is something of a consensus around the need to focus on a commitment to Christian solidarity – that an alliance of convenience for the 'global war on terror' cannot override the need to support the persecuted in countries such as Pakistan, Saudi Arabia and Uzbekistan (Croft 2007). Further, many have been worried about the Bush Administration's 'wavering' support for Israel. One example was in April 2002, when fears that President Bush would undermine Biblical Israel by urging Israelis to withdraw from Jenin led to the mobilisation of a rally in Washington which, with only one week's notice, drew a crowd of 50,000; while the president was subjected to around one hundred thousand email protests from Conservative Protestants (Twomey 2002; Wagner 2003). David Kuo, Bush's first-term deputy director of the White House Office of Faith-Based and Community Initiatives, has accused the

Administration of reaping political benefits from the president's apparent commitment to Christian values and priorities even though senior White House officials held religious leaders and the faith-based agenda in contempt (Kuo 2006).

The influence of religion on the Bush Administration has therefore been more complex and subtle than has often been portrayed. To illustrate this, this chapter will examine the foreign policy orientation of Conservative Protestants in two spheres. First, in relation to responsibilities towards other human beings, the National Association of Evangelicals has been working towards developing commitments on global social justice; while International Christian Concern has been one of the organisations that has worked to develop a concept of global Christian solidarity. Second, in relation to the society of states, the Family Research Council has worked on influencing international institutions concerning 'Christian' values, while Christian Friends of Israeli Communities has sought to ensure that Christians work with and for Israel.

Christian foreign policy and global humanity

For many Christian organisations, much of the focus is on social and health policy issues within the United States. However, some concentrate also on the implications of Scripture, as they read it, for humanity as a whole. Although there are many directions for this thinking, this chapter will focus on two: (1) the drive, surprising to some outside the United States, for global social justice; and (2) the effort to mobilise support for persecuted Christians around the world, in the interests of Christian solidarity.

Global social justice

The National Association of Evangelicals (NAE) began in the 1940s from efforts among the leadership of Protestant churches to both move beyond the fundamentalist/ modernist schism of the 1920s and 1930s, and to provide a framework to engage with a variety of churches in the country isolated by distance and weak transportation links (Utzinger 2006). From humble beginnings, the NAE has grown to its current size, with 45,000 churches across 61 denominations (http://www.nae.net/index.cfm?FUSEACTION= nae.members). Symbolising its development as a site of the Christian Right, the *NiAE* was the host for President Reagan's (in)famous 'Evil Empire' speech about the Soviet Union on 8 March 1983.

A clear Biblical foundation for the NAE is apparent in the Association's Mission Statement, which reads:

> to extend the kingdom of God through a fellowship of member denominations, churches, organizations, and individuals, demonstrating the unity of the body of Christ by standing for biblical truth, speaking with a representative voice, and serving the evangelical community through united action, cooperative ministry, and strategic planning.
>
> (http://www.nae.net/index.cfm?FUSEACTION=nae.mission)

It acts to deliver on that Mission Statement through an organisation that includes the position of Vice President for Governmental Affairs. Held for several years by Rich Cizik, the role is: 'setting its policy direction on issues before Congress, the White House, and Supreme Court, as well as serving as a national spokesman on issues of concern to evangelicals' (http://www.nae.net/index.cfm?FUSEACTION=nae). Cizik has been the key figure in developing the NAE's commitments in the fields of global social justice, and has forcefully played the role of norm entrepreneur. These commitments have been developed through the agreement and publication of 'Statements of Conscience'. The first was in January 1996; another followed in 2002. Largely, these documents were concerned with the second topic for this section: Christian Solidarity. But a new document followed in October 2004, entitled 'For the Health of the Nation: An Evangelical Call to Civic Responsibility'. Here, the NAE – driven by Cizik – moved the agenda from a focus on working for Christians around the world, to a broader focus on the rights of humanity.

Whereas the 1996 and 2002 documents were limited in nature, *For the Health of the Nation* is much more comprehensive, and called for an evangelical engagement in a whole variety of areas of national and international life, public and private. To underpin its authority, the document is littered with Biblical references: for example, examining the 'Principles of Christian Political Engagement' in a number of key claims, not least over family matters, and abortion. But the Preamble is particularly enlightening in this regard:

> Evangelical Christians in America face a historic opportunity. We make up fully one quarter of all voters in the most powerful nation in history. Never before has God given American evangelicals such an awesome opportunity to shape public policy in ways that could contribute to the well-being of the entire world. Disengagement is not an option. We must seek God's face for biblical faithfulness and abundant wisdom to rise to this unique challenge.
>
> (NAE 2004: 1)

There is, therefore, something specific about now – 'special circumstances of this historic moment' (ibid.: 1) – and it is a particularly American moment. Evangelism is so pervasive that evangelicals can now influence the policy of the United States, and therefore impact upon the whole world. There is a duty, to behave Biblically, to bring God's will to the world, and to use the foreign policy of the state towards that end. Although evangelicals take a variety of positions on many different issues, there is, the paper argues, a common bottom line: 'commitments to the protection and well-being of families and children, of the poor, the sick, the disabled, and the unborn, of the persecuted and oppressed, and of the rest of the created order' (ibid.: 1). So what calls are there to impact upon the nature of US foreign policy?

The document moves on page 8 to a section entitled 'We seek justice and compassion for the poor and vulnerable'. After a discussion about the nature of economic justice in the United States – and a statement that the Bible calls for equality of opportunity – the paper declares: 'We further believe that care for the vulnerable should extend beyond our national Borders' (ibid.: 9). This of course is crucially important, because it states that in terms of rights, there are no particular benefits that should (as of right) accrue simply being a citizen of 'God's Country'. Therefore, in terms of global political economy, 'we should try to persuade our leaders to change the patterns of trade that harm the poor and to make the reduction of global poverty a central concern of American foreign policy' (ibid.: 9). It is a call that would not be out of place at a *Live 8* event: they of course had declared that, 'We couldn't have made it clearer that we expect the politicians of this generation to end the scandal of stupid, immoral poverty' (http://www.live8live.com/whathappened/#).

A commitment to global economic justice, though, inevitably requires other commitments. A whole range of crises in the developing world – 'extreme poverty, lack of health care, the spread of HIV/AIDS, inadequate nutrition, unstable and unjust economies, slavery and sexual trafficking, the use of rape as a tool of terror and oppression, civil war and government cronyism' require efforts to 'correct these political problems and promote just, democratic structures' (NAE 2004: 10). The drive for social justice abroad mirrors that at home:

> America has a tragic history of mistreating Native Americans, the cruel practice of slavery, and the subsequent segregation and exploitation of the descendants of slaves. While the United States has achieved legal and social equality in principle, the legacy of racism still makes many African Americans, Hispanics, and other ethnic minorities particularly vulnerable to a variety of social ills.
>
> (ibid.: 11)

Clear directions for policy emerge from this. 'American foreign policy should reward those countries that respect human rights and should not reward (and prudently employ certain sanctions against) those countries that abuse or deny such rights' (ibid.: 10). Further '[I]f governments are going to use military force, they should use it in the service of peace and not merely in their national interest' (ibid.: 11).

These commitments to change in the nature of American foreign policy are demanded by the largest evangelical – for many, by that read 'Christian Right' – umbrella organisation in the United States. And this was written at an important moment: one year after the invasion of Iraq, and in the developing presidential election campaign. It was a clear statement of difference with the Bush Administration, with both its realist and neo-conservative wings. But this was not all. Most controversially of all, the paper moved into the territory of 'creation care'. As the paper put it:

> We affirm that God-given dominion is a sacred responsibility to steward the earth and not a license to abuse the creation of which we are a part. We are not the owners of creation, but its stewards, summoned by God to 'watch over and care for it' (Gen. 2:15).
>
> (ibid.: 11)

It is a commitment to environmental security.

This has certainly created huge debate among evangelicals. Should there be a commitment to 'creation care', and if so, what should that mean, are the questions debated on – for example – the Evangelical Environmental Network at http://www.creationcare.org/ with its strap line: 'Worshiping God. Loving His People. Caring for His Creation'. Or of their separate website, http://www.whatwouldjesusdrive.org/ which states on the 'Welcome' page that 'We believe the Risen Lord Jesus cares about what we drive.'

'For the Health of the Nation' remains an important part of the policy work of the NAE. On the Association's homepage, Leith Anderson's (2008) welcome ends with the appeal: 'Thank you for visiting the NAE website. Take a few minutes to explore. And, especially take a look at our groundbreaking and visionary "For the Health of the Nation."' The themes are developed by NAE *Washington Insight*, a magazine published by the Association for its churches.

Each month the *Washington Insight* is offered in a Church Bulletin Insert format. These Inserts are provided to help keep the local church current on the important policy issues facing the evangelical community ... We believe the involvement of the local church is the key to changing the world.

> (http://www.nae.net/index.cfm?FUSEACTION=editor.
> page&pageID=128&IDcategory=7)

The Spring 2008 issue discusses the new generation of evangelicals, those led by belief rather than party loyalty, and declared that 'For the Health of the Nation' is a key for that new generation, that it has 'caught on as a "vision" for the evangelical movement' (http://www.nae.net/images/Insight%20Spring%2008%20Personal%20edition %20final.pdf). Certainly, the NAE has led the broader Christian movement into new territory in terms of its demands on American foreign policy.

Christian solidarity

While the National Association of Evangelicals can claim an enormous membership, International Christian Concern is one of many smaller NGOs that campaign for the rights of Christians around the world. There are a significant number of such organisations. Open Doors USA says about itself that it has 'grown into the oldest ministry operating discreetly behind closed borders, serving 200 million persecuted Christians in countries hostile to the Gospel of Jesus Christ' (http://www.opendoorsusa.org/index. php?option=com_content&task=view&id=17&Itemid=70). They provide an interactive map to itemise regional and national problems facing these '200 million persecuted Christians' (http://www.opendoorsusa.org/content/category/4/17/24/). Christian Freedom International declares its mission to be: 'Remembering the Persecuted – The work of Christian Freedom International centers around the words of Hebrews 13:3: "Remember those in prison as if you were their fellow prisoners, and those who are mistreated as if you yourselves were suffering"' (http://www.christianfreedom.org/about-cfi.html). As well as providing assistance, Christian Freedom International also

> combines aid with advocacy. CFI is active in Washington, D.C. speaking out on behalf of voiceless Christians around the world. We invite journalists and sponsor congressional delegations to areas of intense persecution. We carefully document evidence of persecution around the world and present our findings so that policy-makers can make informed decisions regarding trade, aid, visas, and related issues with a particular country.
>
> (CFI 2007)

The Jesus Journal provides a news feed on its 'Christian Persecution Watch' site (http:// www.jesusjournal.com/component/option,com_newsfeeds/task,view/feedid,11/. The Voice of Martyrs, based in Oklahoma has 'a vision for aiding Christians around the world who are being persecuted for their faith in Christ, fulfilling the Great Commission, and educating the world about the ongoing persecution of Christians' (http://www.persecution. com/about/index.cfm?action=vom). For information, they publish their free 16-page monthly newsletter, and the website often includes video pieces about cases, or VOM's activities. Bible League who work with local churches in over 60 countries, also focus on the persecuted church, and they make the threat personal and immediate:

Imagine looking over your shoulder because you are studying a Bible, or worshipping in church. Imagine that if you are caught, you could be jailed, beaten, or even killed. To millions of Christians around the world, this is the stark reality.

(http://www.bibleleague.org/persecuted/index.php)

There are, then, many NGOs active in the area of evangelising, and in seeking to support Christians where they may be in danger of persecution. International Christian Concern's strap line is: 'Serving Christ's Persecuted Body: Assistance, Advocacy and Awareness for the persecuted and suffering Christian Church with integrity towards God and our donors' (http://www.persecution.org/suffering/index.php? PHPSESSID=8d546e7d60a42c8f494edd30933cc384). The organisation agrees with the numbers at risk quoted by Open Doors:

> There are 200 million Christians suffering for their faith every day, from Cuba to North Africa, to the Muslim Middle East, India and the rest of South Asia, North Korea, China, Vietnam and Indonesia, to name a few. Yet they remain largely forgotten by the Church in the West.
>
> (http://www.persecution.org/suffering/churchresources.php)

Their key target is the '10/40 window': this is the 'rectangle' of the world from 10 to 40 degrees north of the equator), in which 97 per cent of the world's 'unreached' live. Contributions are sought by International Christian Concern from a variety of individuals: from those 'outside the USA' who want to report persecution; from those who wish to pray for the persecuted church; from those who wish to make a donation; from those who which to work or intern for the organisation; and from those who wish to support an individual pastor who may be 'beaten, tortured or even killed for their work' (http://www.persecution.org/suffering/supportapastor.php). These 'hundreds of thousands of native pastors and evangelists boldly proclaim the Gospel in the world's most persecuted nations'.

The key work for International Christian Concern relates to information gathering and sharing, and thereby awareness raising. The organisation arranges for citizen lobbying. There are instructions for writing to the President, the First Lady, the Secretary of State, and elected representatives. Citizens are invited to write to embassies in Washington, DC, to 'ask for fair treatment for Christians' (http://www.persecution.org/suffering/what_can_i_do.php). There are also petitions, available both to print and use among those in local churches, as well as online petitions. The petition launched in October 2007 was aimed at Ethiopia: actions urged upon the Government of that country included 'Protect Christians who are being forcefully converted to Islam by extremist Islamists' and 'Bring to justice the people who are behind the killing of Evangelist Taddesse on March 26, 2007' (http://www.persecution.org/suffering/pdfs/ 2007-8PetitiontoEthiopia.pdf).

International Christian Concern shares the view that during the twentieth century, 100 million Christians 'were murdered for professing their devotion to Christ. Christians are still dying for their faith today' (http://www.persecution.org/suffering/html/ idop_prayer_bulletin_screenshots.html). It is a viewpoint made popular by Michael Horowitz, a Jewish neo-conservative, from the publication of what in retrospect has been constructed as a defining article: 'New Intolerance Between the Crescent and the Cross', published in the *Wall Street Journal* (quoted in Goldberg 1995). Horowitz was at the forefront of the new concern: preventing a Christian holocaust. As Horowitz (1997) put it, 'You're only allowed to sit out one Holocaust each lifetime.'

Whereas the campaign for global social justice being led by the National Association of Evangelicals is the duty of Christians, but is in the interests of all faiths, the campaigns for human rights of International Christian Concern are focused on Christians to the exclusion of other faiths. As they declare. 'Although we believe in Human Rights and religious freedom for all religions we only deal in Christian persecution' (http://www.persecution.org/suffering/report_persecution.php). Both organisations stress the importance of their advocacy in Congress, with the Administration, and also with the media.

Christian foreign policy and the world of states

If there is much work in the world of American Christian NGOs seeking to change policy towards humanity and Christianity globally, there are also important NGO projects for changing the nature of US foreign policy at the level of international diplomacy. Two areas stand out. First, the development of an engagement with international institutions based on Christian principles, such as is carried out by the Family Research Council. Second, in relation to ensuring that US foreign policy towards the Middle East is based on Biblical principles, for example, by Christian Friends of Israeli Communities.

Delivering Christian principles through international institutions:

The Family Research Council is a heavily funded lobbying organisation, 'founded in 1983 as an organisation dedicated to the promotion of marriage and family and the sanctity of human life in national policy' (http://www.frc.org/about-frc). The organisation claims that the idea for its formation came out of a White House Conference on Families, driven by James Dobson, a towering figure on the religious Right since the 1970s. Michael Crowley wrote, 'Dobson is now America's most influential evangelical leader, with a following reportedly greater than that of either Falwell or Robertson at his peak' (Crowley 2004). He sought to exercise this influence in 2008 when he said 'I cannot, and will not, vote for Sen. John McCain, as a matter of conscience … If these are the nominees in November, I simply will not cast a ballot for president for the first time in my life' (Stoddard 2008). The Family Research Council's first President, Jerry Regier, was a former Reagan Administration official; he was succeeded by Gary Bauer, a former adviser to President Reagan. The current President is Tony Perkins, a former two-term member of the Louisiana legislature, and Republican candidate for the Senate in 2002. The Family Research Council has been steeped in the practice of American politics. It organises lobbying activities; mobilises activists; endorses candidates in elections; comments approvingly – or otherwise – on candidates.

Tony Perkins declares that he 'has a tremendous burden to reclaim the culture for Christ and believes that this revival will begin in the churches across America, reach across denominations and racial and economic lines, and build on shared values of family and freedom' (http://www.frc.org/get.cfm?i=by03h27). In his book, *Personal Faith, Public Policy: 7 Urgent Issues That We, as People of Faith, Need to Come Together and Solve* (Jackson and Perkins 2008) Perkins and his co-author, Bishop Harry R. Jackson Junior, argue that America is at a crossroads; reform is needed to ensure that God will bestow His blessings on the country for another four hundred years. The seven issues concern the family, religious liberty, life, immigration, poverty and justice, racial reconciliation, and the environment. Illustrating that these issues are as much international in nature as national, Perkins and Jackson argue for the need to stand firm against terrorism; to promote pro-marriage policies and continuing the fight to protect the unborn; and to protect the environment by adjusting America's energy policies. The symbolism of the white President of the Family Research Council co-authoring with Bishop Jackson, a senior African-American preacher among the Christian Right, is also important in the context of bringing together diverse groups among evangelicals, and in creating a new politics. Perkins and Jackson argue against bloc support from evangelicals for the Republicans; rather, they argue for the 'seeding' of both main parties by an evangelical movement that acts as a free agent in the American body politic. Consistent with this policy Perkins refused to back any candidates in the primaries, arguing in news letters instead that polices were more important than the candidate.

The political nature of the Family Research Council is clear from its mission statement:

> Family Research Council (FRC) champions marriage and family as the foundation of civilization, the seedbed of virtue, and the wellspring of society. FRC shapes public debate and formulates public policy that values human life and upholds the institutions of marriage and the family. Believing that God is the author of life, liberty, and the family, FRC promotes the Judeo-Christian worldview as the basis for a just, free, and stable society.
>
> (http://www.frc.org/mission-statement)

That of course creates the framework within which the Family Research Council must interact with the world's major international organisations.

The Family Research Council became active in the United Nations in the late 1990s (Maginnis 1999). It sought 'Consultative Status' in 2001, but was unsuccessful; the following year, however, it was admitted ('NGO Committee' 2001). Since then it has engaged with the General Assembly on human cloning in 2002, 2003 and 2005; participated in the 'United Nations Celebration of the International Day of the Family' in 2003/4; participated in the European Regional Dialogue for the Doha International Conference for the Family; and in New York, both in 2004, and 2005/6, on the Commission on the Status of Women. Altogether, between 2002 and 2006, the Family Research Council has participated in 13 different United Nations meetings, issuing reports, lobbying and often holding is own side meetings (UN 2006).

Despite this, the United Nations is a very problematic organisation for the Family Research Council. First, the Council is clear that its main priority is America; second, the UN is a dangerously liberal organisation. On the first point, as Perkins (2006b) has put it, 'FRC's international involvement normally is limited to using our official Non-Governmental Organization status at the United Nations to promote our pro-family agenda and to block bad policies so they will be less likely to be imported into the United States.' On the second point, Tony Minnery, then Executive Vice President of the Council had declared at the UN that 'For a long time now, this venerable institution, the United Nations, has been the playground of fundamental left-wingers' (press conference in 2000).

Buss and Herman (2003) have examined how organisations such as the Family Research Council have internationalised domestic campaigns against women's rights, gay rights and population policy in the late 1990s and early 2000s in *Globalizing Family Values: The Christian Right in International Politics*. Since then, the United

Nations has been notable in Council statements and policies in two regards. First, as inherently problematic in the pursuit of values. In commenting on *American Idol*, Perkins (2008a) showed how the liberalism of the United Nations had been imported so easily into the United States. He praised the willingness of celebrities to participate to raise funds for the poor. However, organisations such as the United Nations Children's Fund (UNICEF) 'certainly don't have the vote of the pro-life community'. He was more forthright on his radio commentary in commenting on UNICEF and similar international groups: 'They've used their funds to support programs that promote abortion, liberal sex education, and population control. These organizations don't help children – they help to abort them!' (Perkins 2008b). Second, however, the United Nations might act as a positive forum for collaboration between like-minded groups – Christian Right groups, traditional Muslim groups – to set liberalism back. As Philip Jenkins argued (2003), 'The areas for potential cooperation between Christians and Muslims worldwide are enormous. We have seen them, for example, in debates over population at the United Nations.' Perkins (2006a) noted, 'Not that I enjoy holding up the United Nations as an example of moral fortitude, but that international body has shown more leadership than the U.S. Congress by passing a measure calling for a worldwide cloning ban.'

The United Nations, then, is fundamentally flawed, but is useful tactically. There are no such saving graces for the European Union. In reviewing the widespread international consensus on the importance of marriage and the family – the United Nation's Doha Declaration – the Family Research Council's William Saunders (2004) noted that 'The only dissent came from the European Union, which sought to use the occasion to advance various measures that are not part of international consensus and that undermine the family.' The casual hostility of Europeans to the right to life, as the Council would see it, was reported by Tony Perkins (2008c):

> The Council of Europe has passed a resolution of 'unconditional' support for abortion. The body, which shapes policies that are often adopted by the European Union (EU), deals a painful blow to global pro-life efforts. In a rushed move, the group's Parliamentary Assembly allowed just three minutes of discussion on the abortion issue, then proceeded to vote with only 185 of the 316 members present.

The Family Research Council is representative of a group of organisations that, while opposed to international institutions on the grounds that they are agents of a non-Christian, liberal agenda, are prepared to work within them tactically.

Inter-state relations

The Christian Friends of Israeli Communities (CFOIC) was founded in 1995 directly from concern about the Oslo Peace Process. The view taken by those who came together to form CFOIC was that the peace process, and the development of international relations, were a profound issue for the evangelical community in the United States because the withdrawals that were required of Israel under the Oslo Agreements 'ran counter to God's plan for the Jewish nation and would only weaken Israel in future confrontations with her enemies' (http://www.cfoic.com/pages.jsp?pageID=5). The Oslo Accords were 'the devastating series of agreements that ceded land to the Arabs in the heart of Biblical Israel' (ibid.). CFOIC was designed to provide a vehicle for Christian support with 'those Jews who are at greatest risk in Israel – those whose very homes are threatened with destruction, those who face terrorism on a daily basis, those whose core values and daily lives are based on Biblical principles' (ibid.).

The basis for CFOIC's support for Israel is eightfold. God will bless those that bless Israel; Christians owe Jews a debt for the Old Testament heritage; although Jews have not responded to the gospel, they are still part of God's plan; as God promised that the Jews could return to their land, helping is bringing about God's will; the times of the Gentiles are almost fulfilled – that is, the Second Coming is close; because of the Biblical call to comfort God's people; to make reparations for anti-Semitism among Christians over time; and because 'The fullness of the Messianic age is coming' (http://www.cfoic.com/pages.jsp?pageID=8). CFOIC acts upon these Biblical demands by raising funds to support Jewish emigration to Israel – for $1000 a month, you can be a 'Guardian of Biblical Israel'; by lobbying in Washington, DC; and by arranging visits to Israel by Christians. As Lee Marsden (2008: 249) has put it, 'Eschatology has been the major driving force behind Christian Right thinking on Israel.'

Such a posture leads to a very clear line on the 'war on terror'. As Sondra Oster Baras, CFOIC's Israel Office Director put it, 'In combating Arab terrorism today, we are not only protecting the children of Sderot and the children of all societies who value freedom and life. We are also defeating a society which is the very embodiment of death and evil' (CFOIC 2008). There is a newsletter written by a Jewish woman in Israel, who shares reflections on various issues with the CFOIC readership. She ends her 'reflections on terrorism' with the line: 'They will send their children to terrorize us but we will not be destroyed' (Schwartz 2008). CFOIC raises funds for specific projects in particular settlements in Israel. One example is Har Bracha, 'founded in 1982 by a small group of families who were eager to settle the biblical mountain of blessing' (http://www.cfoic.com/db_images/Har%20Bracha.pdf). We learn of the dangers posed to the children from the local Palestinians: 'School-age children go to school in nearby Elon Moreh and must travel on bulletproof buses through an area adjacent to the city of Shechem, which is controlled by the Palestinian Authority' (ibid.). Then comes the call to action: 'Due to the rapid rate of growth, a new playground is needed and *CFOIC* has been asked to assist the community in building it' (ibid.). Finally, the call to duty:

> Let's make this happen for them. Your contribution to this project will not only provide healthy recreation and good fun but it will show moral support for the people of Har Bracha. It will express your faith in the future of this vibrant, growing community. It will send a strong message of love to the brave pioneers of Har Bracha as they face the challenges of raising their families against the backdrop of terrorism and violence.
>
> (ibid.)

The 'Israel Lobby' in the United States, as described by John Mearsheimer and Stephen Walt (2007), include a variety of well-known and highly active groups, such as the American Israel Public Affairs Committee and the American Jewish Committee and individuals who, among the Christian Right include Jerry Falwell (now deceased) and the former President of the Family Research Council, Gary Bauer. Whatever one's views about the Mearsheimer and Walt thesis – and plenty hold that it is but a conspiracy theory (Dershowitz 2006) – there is no doubt that there are significant voices and organisations that speak and influence US policy towards Israel. While those selected for focus by Mearsheimer and Walt are high profile, it is perhaps with groups such as CFOIC that the everyday nature of Christian support for Israel comes to the fore. For many American Christians, the creation of the state of Israel is one of the events that precedes the Second Coming; and for that reason, many will support Israel, and many engage in support for Jewish settlements in the West Bank, and for Jewish migration to Israel. A potent symbol is John Hagee's *In Defense of Israel* (Hagee 2007); Hagee also runs the Christians United for Israel. But it is the practical work of organisations like CFOIC that brings Americans directly into contact with Israel, and allows American Christians to engage in action to help bring about the Second Coming.

Conclusion

Each of the groups examined in this chapter have a normative commitment to political transformation, based on Biblical teaching. Although there are many Christian organisations that seek to remain in some senses pure, many others – such as those examined here – seek to work together with other organisations in a common interest. Marsden (2008: 247) argues that '[T]he Christian Right have been most effective as supporters rather than shapers of US foreign policy.' There is something to that. However, Christian interest in foreign policy is relatively new, and we see it changing in important ways – for example, with the interest in some parts of the community with environmental protection. As Senator Sam Brownback put it, 'This is a young movement ... and it's just starting to get its sea legs. I think you'll now see it spread out into a whole lot of areas' (Goodstein 2005). As it does so, in line with the wide range of interests that are represented in Christian America, it is likely that it will do so in a whole variety of areas, and that it will become harder and harder to talk about a coherent group interest in foreign policy. However, given the influence of Christian movements in American politics and society, it might also become more difficult to make Marsden's judgement hold in the future; certainly the aim, with the development of educational facilities such as Patrick Henry College, Liberty University and Bob Jones University, and with a range of political training facilities such as the Center for Christian Statesmanship, is for Christian America to become a stronger shaper of foreign policy. Given the resources being invested, the possibilities for success in particular areas of policy should be taken very seriously.

Acknowledgements

Thanks in particular to Lee Marsden, Trevor McCrisken and Richard Jackson for a whole variety of invaluable insights.

Note

1 There is an important story to be told about such theological developments in Africa and South Korea, however.

References

Note: all web addresses were accessed in April 2008 except where stated.

Anderson, Leith (2008) President's Speech, National Association of Evangelicals. Online. Available at: http://www.nae.net/index.cfm.

Armstrong, Karen (2006) 'Bush's Fondness for Fundamentalism Is Courting Disaster at Home and Abroad', *Guardian*, 31 July. Online. Available at: http://www.guardian.co.uk/commentis-free/story/0,1833810,00.html.

Association of Religion Data Archives (2005) Survey. Online. Available at: http://www.thearda.com/learningcenter/compare/survey2.asp?attend=5&pray=6&bible=3&bible2=4&jesus=5ender=0&age=2&education=4&religion=1&plm=67&ra=1&go=Continue+Survey.

Buss, Doris and Herman, Didi (2003) *Globalizing Family Values: The Christian Right in International Politics*, Minneapolis: University of Minnesota Press.

CFI (2007) 'How is CFI Different from Other Organizations Such as Voice of the Martyrs?', 19 November. Online. Available at: http://www.christianfreedom.org/faq/31-CFI-Facts/110-how-is-cfi-different-from-other-organizations-such-as-voice-of-the-martyrs.html.

CFOIC (2008) Newsletter, 11 March. Online. Available at: http://cfoic.net/addpages.jsp?pageID=115.

Croft, Stuart (2007) 'Thy Will be Done', *International Politics*, 44(6): 692–710.

Crowley, Michael (2004) 'James Dobson The Religious Right's New Kingmaker', *Slate*, 12 November. Online. Available at: http://slate.msn.com/id/2109621/.

Dershowitz, Alan (2006) 'Debunking the Newest – and Oldest – Jewish Conspiracy: A Reply to the Mearsheimer-Walt "Working Paper"', April. Online. Available at: http://www.hks.harvard.edu/research/working_papers/dershowitzreply.pdf.

Doomsday (2006) *The Doomsday Code*, first shown on Channel 4 in September 2006, quote from http://www.channel4.com/culture/microsites/C/can_you_believe_it/debates/doomsday.html.

Goldberg, Jeffrey (1997) 'Washington Discovers Christian Persecution', *New York Times*, 21 December.

Goodstein, Laurie (2005) 'Evangelicals Open Debate on Widening Policy Questions', *New York Times*, 11 March.

Guth, James L., Green, John C., Kellstedt, Lyman A. and Smidt, Corwin E. (2005) 'Faith and Foreign Policy: A View from the Pews', *Faith and International Affairs*, 3(2): 5–6.

Hagee, John (2007) *In Defense of Israel*, New York: Frontline.

Horowitz, Michael (1995) 'New Intolerance Between the Crescent and the Cross', *Wall Street Journal*, 5 July.

Jackson, Harry R., Jr. and Perkins, Tony (2008) *Personal Faith, Public Policy: 7 Urgent Issues That We, as People of Faith, Need to Come Together and Solve*, New York: Frontline.

Jenkins, Philip (2003) 'Sibling Rivalry Among the Children of Abraham: Global Conflict and Cooperation Between Islam and Christianity – July 18, 2003', Witherspoon Lecture. Online. Available at: http://www.frc.org/get.cfm?i=WT04C01.

Kuo, David (2006) *Tempting Faith: An Inside Story of Political Seduction*, New York: Free Press.

Lewis, Neil A. (2001) 'Critics See Little in Ashcroft Speech to Derail Nomination', *New York Times*, 13 January.

Maginnis, Robert (1999) 'Press Conference by NGO Coalition for Women, Children and Family Sponsored by the United States', 30 March 1999. Online. Available at: http://www.un.org/News/briefings/docs/1999/19990330.prolife.brf.html.

Marsden, Lee (2008) *For God's Sake*, London: Zed.

Mearsheimer, John and Walt, Stephen (2007) *The Israel Lobby and US Foreign Policy*, New York: Farrar, Straus and Giroux.

NAE (National Association of Evangelicals) (2004) 'For the Health of the Nation: An Evangelical Call to Civic Responsibility'. Online. Available at: http://www.nae.net/images/civic_responsibility2.pdf.

NGO (2001) 'NGO Committee Approves Two Organisations for Consultative Status with Economic and Social Council – Defers Action on Two Others', press release, NGO/409 9 May. Online. Available at: http://www.un.org/news/Press/docs/2001/ngo409.doc.htm.

Perkins, Tony (2006a) 'Every Front a Battle', *Washington Watch*, 10 May. Online. Available at: http://www.frc.org/get.cfm?i=WW06E02.

—— (2006b) 'Conservative State of the Union Address', 31 January. Online. Available at: http://www.frc.org/get.cfm?i=LH06A17.

—— (2008a) 'Idol Threat', *Washington Update*, 9 April. Online. Available at: http://www.frc.org/get.cfm?i=WA08D31.

—— (2008b) 'Washington Watch Daily Radio Update', 2 April. Online. Available at: http://www.frc.org/get.cfm?i=CM08D03.

—— (2008c) 'Passport to Controversy', *Washington Update*, 18 April. Online. Available at: http://www.frc.org/get.cfm?i=WA08D47#WA08D47.

Pew Research Center (2004) 'Percentage of Votes by Religion', 6 December. Online. Available at: http://people-press.org/commentary/display.php3?AnalysisID=103.

Philips, Kevin (2007) *American Theocracy: The Peril and Politics of Radical Religion, Oil, and Borrowed Money in the 21st Century*, Harmondsworth: Penguin.

Saunders, William (2004) 'The Doha Declaration – An International Consensus in Favor of Marriage and the Traditional Family', Family Research Council, December. Online. Available at: http://www.frc.org/get.cfm?i=LH05B02.

Schwartz, Shira (2008) 'Reflections on Terror'. Online. Available at: http://cfoic.net/addpages.jsp?pageID=117.

Stoddard, Ed (2008) 'Super Tuesday: Dobson Delivers Blow to McCain Candidacy', *Reuters*, 5 February.

Twomey, Steve (2002) 'Thousands Rallied on Mall to Support Israel', *Washington Post*, 15 April.

UN (2000) 'Press Conference', sponsored by US Mission, UN press release, 15 March. Online. Available at: http://www.un.org/News/briefings/docs/2000/20000315.usmission.doc.html.

—— (United Nations' Economic and Social Council Committee on Non-Governmental Organisations) (2006) 'Quadrennial Reports 2002–5 Submitted through the Secretary-General Pursuant to Economic and Social Council Resolution 1996/31', 14 November. Online. Available at: http://esa.un.org/coordination/ngo/session/views/viewer.asp?Document=E/C.2/2007/2/Add.19&number=1&view=2007_C2_Add_19_e.pdf&jumpto=1&session_db=..%5Cdb%5CPrevious_Sessions%5C2007_Session.mdb.

Utzinger, J. Michael (2006) *Yet Saints Their Watch Are Keeping: Fundamentalists, Modernists, and the Development of Evangelical Ecclesiology, 1887–1937*, Macon, GA: Mercer University Press.

Wagner, Donald (2003) 'The Evangelical Jewish Alliance', *The Christian Century*, June 28. Online. No longer available at: http://www.religion-online.org/showarticle.asp?title=2717, pp. 20–4 (accessed May 2006).

Wheaton College (2002) 'Gallup Survey', Institute for the Study of American Evangelicals. Online. Available at: http://www.wheaton.edu/isae/Gallup-Bar-graph.html.

Woodberry, Robert D. and Smith, Christian S. (1998) 'Fundamentalism et al: Conservative Protestants in America', *Annual Review of Sociology*, 24: 25–56.

Further reading

Baird-Windle, Patricia and Bader, Eleanor J. (2001) *Targets of Hatred: Anti Abortion Terrorism*, New York: Palgrave.

BBC Ethics (undated) 'Millennialism, Premillenialism, Dispensationalism', *BBC Ethics and Religion*. Online. Available at: http://www.bbc.co.uk/religion/religions/christianity/beliefs/endtimes_1.shtml.

Celeste, Rev. Robert M. (2008) 'Only a Miracle Can Save the USA Now!', 18 April. Online. Available at: http://www.christianpatriot.com/04_18_2008.htm.

Haggard, Ted (2006) 'Ted Haggard's Letter to New Life Church', reproduced in *The Gazette*, Colorado Springs, 5 November 2006. Online. Available at: http://www2.gazette.com/display.php?id=1326184.

Left Behind (2004) 'Left Behind Series Featured on Upcoming 60 Minutes', 2 February *Left Behind Series News*. Online. Available at: http://www.leftbehind.com/channelnews.asp?pageid=929&channelID=17.

Lezard, Nicholas (2007) 'Onward to the Apocalypse', *Guardian*, 3 February. Online. Available at: at http://books.guardian.co.uk/review/story/0,2003977,00.html.

Sider, Ronald J. (2005) *The Scandal of the Evangelical Conscience: Why Are Christians Living Just Like the Rest of the World?* New York: Baker Books.

Time (1992) 'The Shouting of the Lambs', *Time*, 4 May. Online. Available at: http://www.time.com/time/magazine/article/0,9171,975442,00.html.

Van Biema, David and Chu, Jeff(2006) 'Does God Want You to Be Rich?', *Time*, 10 September. Online. Available at: http://www.time.com/time/magazine/article/0,9171,1533448,00.html.

Whitaker, Brian (2007) 'The Evolution of Daft Ideas', *Guardian*, 29 May. Online. Available at: http://commentisfree.guardian.co.uk/brian_whitaker/2007/05/the_evolution_of_daft_ideas.html.

10 American foreign policy after the Bush administration

Insights from the public

James M. McCormick

The role of the public in shaping American foreign policy elicits considerable debate among scholars and analysts about its importance and its impact. Indeed, two sharply different theoretical perspectives on this relationship have dominated academic and policy discussions over the past half century. One perspective assumes that the public is largely uninterested, ill informed, and subject to presidential leadership. In the strongest variant of this view, the public does not so much shape foreign policy, instead, it is largely shaped by it. The policy implication of this approach is that public opinion has a very limited role in shaping American foreign policy, and that the public largely adopts a "follower" mentality, mainly driven by the president and other key foreign policy officials. A second perspective starts from the premise that the public's views are more structured and stable than suggested in the past. In this view, the public may not be fully conversant with all the details of foreign policy and may not have a sustained interest in foreign affairs, but their underlying attitudes and views are more consistent and predictive of policy positions than often contended. In the strongest variant of this view, the public can and do shape the direction of policy, even if they do not affect every decision. The policy implication of this approach is that public opinion plays a sustaining role in shaping American foreign policy and that policy-makers are constrained by the public's view.[1]

In this chapter, we adopt the second perspective to address the possible linkage between public opinion and US foreign policy, as we move to a post-Bush administration. First, the chapter begins by summarizing briefly these competing theoretical perspectives. Second, the research identifies several *necessary* and *sufficient* conditions required for the public to have an effect on foreign policy. Third, using some recent polling data, we summarize the public's current general orientation to foreign policy and its position on key issues. Fourth, we assess the foreign policy positions of the new Obama administration, its receptivity (and compatibility) with the public's view, and the likelihood that their decision styles will facilitate public input. Finally, the analysis concludes by identifying several structural and process factors that will arguably facilitate greater public impact on foreign policy.

Competing theoretical perspectives on public opinion and foreign policy

A moodish public?

Ole Holsti (1992, 2004) has aptly summarized the first perspective on the relationship between public opinion and the conduct of foreign policy through his careful assessment of the work of Walter Lippmann, Gabriel Almond, and Philip Converse. As

Holsti (1992: 440–2) noted, Lippmann saw the public as not only uninterested and uninformed about foreign affairs, but as dangerous to effective foreign policy-making because they too often compelled policy-makers to acts in ways that were unwise through their seeming veto. Almond, by contrast, saw the public posing a somewhat different danger with "the instability of mass moods" and "the cyclical fluctuations [of those moods] which stand in the way of policy stability" (Almond 1950, quoted in Holsti 1992: 442). Converse's research implied the same kind of concern about the mass public. He reported that there seemed to be no "constraint" in the public's beliefs. That is, the public's views on domestic issues did not predict foreign policy views, and there appeared to be no ideological structure in the public's thinking on foreign affairs (Converse 1964; Holsti 1992: 443–4). Hence, the public appeared to move from one position to another on foreign policy in a way consistent with Almond's moodish characterization.

Indeed, empirical studies over the years have seemingly provided support for these views. Considerable evidence, for instance, points to the low levels of interest and knowledge of foreign policy among the American public during the time of Almond's and Converse's writing, and the quadrennial Chicago Council of Foreign Relations (now the Chicago Council on Global Affairs) surveys of the American public since the mid-1970s largely confirm this point. From this perspective, the public should not – either on normative or empirical grounds, or both – have an impact on American foreign policy.

A structured and stable public?

By the 1970s and 1980s, however, this first theoretical perspective was increasingly challenged through increased conceptual and empirical work on the public opinion–foreign policy linkage. Several major assumptions and assertions from the first perspective – the volatility of the public mood, its lack of structure, and its lack of policy influence – came under increasing scrutiny and were challenged by a new set of empirically-skilled analysts. Instead, they found that, even though the American public may be relatively uninformed about foreign policy issues and susceptible to presidential leadership from time to time, the public's views are more structured, stable, and "rational" than often assumed and the public's mood is more discernible and less changeable than previously suggested.

Jon Hurwitz and Mark Peffley (1987) demonstrated how the mass publics were "cognitive misers" on foreign policy questions. That is, the public used information shortcuts to arrive at political judgments, and in turn the public could rather consistently relate these attitudinal preferences to specific foreign policy issues. Paradoxically, then, the public can and do hold coherent views, though they may lack detailed knowledge about a wide array of foreign policy issues. In detailed analyses of public opinion surveys over a considerable length of time (from the 1930s to the 1980s), Robert Shapiro and Benjamin Page conclude that public opinion generally has changed slowly: "When it [public opinion] has changed, it has done so by responding in rational ways to international and domestic events" (Shapiro and Page 1988: 211). In this sense, public opinion does not tend to be "volatile or fluctuate wildly," as Almond suggested. Instead, and as their later book title put it, there exists "the rational public," both on domestic and international questions (Page and Shapiro 1992). Using another approach, Eugene Wittkopf (1990) demonstrated that the American public was divided into four underlying belief systems on foreign policy – what he labeled as those who were accommodationists, internationalists, hardliners, and isolationists – and that these belief systems were highly predictive of their positions on foreign policy issues and highly stable over time. In short, a similar message emerged from Wittkopf's analyses: the public's views are structured and consistent. In all, then, such consistency and structure are important *prerequisites* for policy influence.

Other studies have sought to identify the source of the stability and structure in public attitudes on foreign policy. Importantly, Ole Holsti (2004: 231–2), has systematically reviewed an array of these studies on the predictors of foreign policy beliefs (age, gender, race, education, partisanship, and ideology). His principal conclusion is particularly instructive for us: "[T]he closely linked attributes of ideology and party identification consistently have been the most powerful correlates of attitudes on a wide range of foreign policy issues." Put differently, these two factors have consistently predicted the stability and coherence of public opinion on foreign policy issues over the past several decades in a variety of different studies. Indeed, Page and Bouton (2006), through a systematic analysis of a large number of foreign policy surveys, confirmed that this stability and structure have remained.

Identifying necessary and sufficient conditions for public impact

While the evidence of foreign policy attitudinal structure among the public – and the centrality of ideology and partisanship as important contributors to this structure and stability – are *necessary* conditions for public opinion impacting policy outcomes, they are not *sufficient* ones. That is, the opinion of the public must have a way to enter the decision-making process and affect policy. Fortunately, there has also been some research to assess this linkage, but the conclusions over public's policy effectiveness remain divided.

In their five-decade analysis of the directional change in public opinion and public policy, Page and Shapiro (1983) found that policy *followed* opinion, both in domestic and foreign policy matters. On foreign policy issues specifically, they report that policy and opinion were consistent in 62 per cent of the cases examined. In a more recent study of the relationship between the views of the American public and the views of their leaders from 1974 to 2002, Page (and Jacob) with Bouton (Page and Bouton 2006) found what they describe as "the foreign policy disconnect" between the public's view and those of their leaders. That is, the views of foreign policy leaders in three policy domains – defense policy, economic policy, and diplomatic policy – were very different from the public's views. From a fifth to a third of the time in these policy areas, a majority of the leaders surveyed took a position that was at odds with the majority of the public (ibid.: 213). With this disparity, they contend, it is difficult to argue that the public is getting the policy direction that it wants – or that policy is necessarily following opinion.

While these two studies are not directly comparable – since one links opinion and policy and the other examines the congruence of policy positions – both studies fail to demonstrate *how much effect* public opinion has on policy. In this sense, we need to go beyond the aggregate analyses or a description of the current state of opinion between leaders and the public. Ole Holsti (2004: 65) notes that the central task to is develop "carefully crafted case studies" in which the role of public opinion is evaluated in the decision process – whether the decision-makers perceive it, are affected by it (or not), and how it affects the decision chosen.

Some work has been done along these lines, but the results paint a mixed picture about the public's impact on policy choices. In his case analyses of American policy toward Vietnam in the 1960s and 1970s, toward Nicaragua in the 1980s, and toward the Gulf War and Bosnia in the 1990s, Richard Sobel (2001: 240) offers an upbeat conclusion about public opinion and policy: "Public opinion has constrained the US foreign policy decision-making process over the last generation." He acknowledges that the public's effect is more in the realm of policy restraint (the elimination of some available policy options) than in setting the policy *per se* (the prescription of precise policy options). By contrast, Douglas Foyle (1999) offers a more cautionary conclusion about public opinion. In a series of cases spanning the Truman through Clinton years, he found that the public's views are less effective in shaping policy. To the extent that the public's views matter, however, their impact is importantly a function of the policy-makers' belief system and the particular policy context. When the policy-maker is *receptive* to public input and when the decision setting *allows* the public to affect policy, opinion matters. In this way, Foyle nicely identifies the *sufficient* conditions for the public's impact.

Current foreign policy issues and the structure of public opinion

With this background on the role of public opinion and foreign policy, we now turn to assess the current state of public opinion – the public mood, if you will – on key foreign policy issues during the 2008 presidential campaign. In particular, we are interested in discussing the public's general orientation to foreign policy at the present time and cataloguing the public's views on key foreign policy issues. We are also interested in assessing the degree of stability and structure in those views and whether the *necessary* conditions for public impact exist. In turn, we want to assess the degree of receptivity by a new administration to the public's impact on foreign policy, and the decision style of the White House occupant that will affect this receptivity – and thus whether the *sufficient* conditions are also present.

The public and its general orientation to foreign policy

The public's general orientation to foreign policy has remained markedly stable along several dimensions: the role of the United States in the world, the key goals that the United States should pursue, and the instruments of policy to achieve those goals. First, the American public remains committed to an international role for the United States with 69 per cent of the public supporting this view. This level of commitment has not wavered over the past 60 years – either during the height of the Cold War, in the immediate post-Cold War period, or in the post-9/11 and post-Iraq War periods (see Global Views 2006: 14). However, the public does not support a unilateral role with these international involvements, and does not believe that the United States should serve as the world's policeman. Instead, the public believes that the United States should adopt a multilateral approach toward solving international problems. Second, the American public continues to embrace the view that the leading foreign policy goals for the United States should be ones that combine national security and economic security for the American people. Since 9/11, of course, the public recognizes the threat of international terrorism and the spread of nuclear weapons, but it remains equally concerned about protecting the jobs of American workers, maintaining adequate energy supplies, and promoting economic growth (see, e.g., Global Views 2006;

Bouton and Page 2002). Third, the instruments of American foreign policy favored by the American public reflect the past patterns. The vast majority of the public continue to back a multilateral approach over unilateral approach, support the United Nations, and favor utilizing international treaties and agreements to address an array of problems. Regarding a military presence around the world and the use of American military power to achieve its goals, the Iraq War has not measurably altered the public's general view on these issues. While there is an increased interest in the use of American force for humanitarian and peacekeeping roles, the use of American military power in other ways is largely not endorsed (Global Views 2006).

What is important about this portrait of the public's orientation to foreign policy is its relative stability. Neither the role that the United States should play, the key goals that it should pursue, nor the policy instruments have altered very much. In this sense, the public mood exhibits a consistency and structure over recent years, despite some turbulent times at home and abroad.

The public and key foreign policy issues

To address the public's view on some specific foreign policy (and domestic policy) issues, we need some procedure to limit the array of issues for further analysis. In order to make this assessment manageable, we selected some key foreign policy issues identified by the public. Over the past several years, the Gallup Organization has surveyed the American public on the importance of particular issues that the president and Congress should address and on the importance of particular issues in influencing the public's vote for Congress or the presidency in particular years.[2] Figure 10.1a shows our compilation of the percentage of the American public identifying various foreign and domestic issues as "extremely important" from 2001 to early 2008 from various surveys. It is hardly surprising that Iraq and terrorism have largely dominated the agenda during these time periods, but it is interesting to note that immigration and the environment also receive attention as important concerns for the public. As Figure 10.1b illustrates, though, the economy and healthcare usually exceed the role of immigration and the environment as important issues for the American people. (It should be noted that by the time of the 2008 election, the economic problems at home and abroad swamped other concerns, although foreign policy issues remained salient for parts of the electorate [Pew Research Center for the People and the Press 2008]).

Iraq

Unsurprisingly, the war in Iraq has consistently been the major concern of the American public over the past several years (although the economy has eclipsed it as we moved further into 2008). Iraq has been identified by the public when the "most important question" is asked, and it has also been identified by the public "as the single most important issue that Congress and the administration should address" (see Gallup's 2008d, "Pulse of Democracy: The War in Iraq," from which much of the data discussed here are drawn). Much as there has been stability in the public's identification of the issue, there has likewise been stability in the public's views on policy direction, as least in recent years. A majority of the public has been consistently opposed to present American policy in Iraq. Since May 2004, a majority of the American public judged that it was not "worth going to war in Iraq," and a majority of the American public

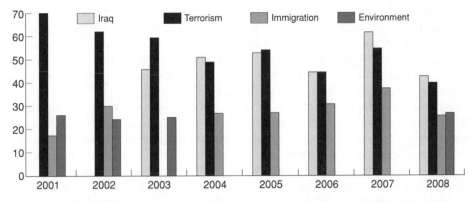

Figure 10.1a Percentage of the American public identifying these foreign policy issues as "extremely important", 2001–2008

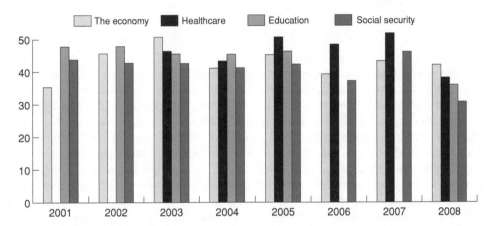

Figure 10.1b Percentage of the American public identifying these domestic policy issues as "extremely important", 2001–2008

Sources: Jones (2001); Moore (2003); Carroll (2005, 2006); Carroll and Newport (2007); and Saad (2008).

Note: The foreign policy and domestic policy data above were obtained from the "extremely important" portion of the following question: "How important is it to you that the president and Congress deal with each of the following issues in the next year – is it – extremely important, very important, moderately important, or not that important?" The data for 2006 and 2008, respectively, were obtained from the question, "how important the candidate's position on that issue will be in influencing your vote for Congress/President this year?"

also judged that things were going "very badly" or "moderately badly" in Iraq even earlier. On the question of whether "the United States made a mistake in sending troops to Iraq," the majority of the American public did not consistently agree with that statement until August 2005. But since then, that majority has increased slightly, although it has largely remained in the upper 50 per cent range, surpassing 60 per cent on only three polling occasions, July 2007, October 2007, and January 2008 (Jones 2008a).

While the public has stable and consistent views on the problem that Iraq poses, it also has some consistent views on policy options. The majority of the public has consistently been opposed to the Congress cutting off funding for the war (Newport and Carroll 2007), even as it has supported a withdrawal of American forces. The public, however, has been more ambivalent about how much time for producing a withdrawal of American forces. A plurality of Americans has fluctuated between supporting a policy that seeks to withdraw within 12 months and supporting a policy that takes as many years as needed (Gallup 2008d).

Party and ideology importantly structure public opinion on Iraq. In general, Republicans support the war, Democrats oppose it, and independents lean in opposition. Moreover, when the public is asked the "mistake" question by party (Democrat or Republican) and ideology (liberal, moderate, or conservative), the impact of party seems more important than ideology. Democrats, whether liberal, moderate, or conservative, see the war as a mistake in overwhelming majorities (from 74 per cent to 91 per cent), while Republicans (whether liberal/moderate, or conservative) do not view the war as a mistake by sizeable majorities (59 and 80 per cent). Significantly, though, independents, by a majority of 53 per cent to 40 per cent see the war as a mistake (Jones 2008b).

Terrorism

On the issue of terrorism, the public has modulated its views since the events of September 11, but it still remains an issue of concern. Immediately after those events, terrorism, of course, moved to the top of the American public's issue agenda – the first time in a number of years that a foreign policy issue was located there. Moreover, terrorism continued to be a significant political issue in the Congressional and presidential elections of 2002 and 2004, respectively. More recently, insecurity among the public has waned a bit (see Gallup 2008c). Immediately after 9/11 and until about mid-December 2004, a sizeable plurality (and occasionally a majority) of the public generally judged that "further acts of terrorism in the United States over the next few weeks" were "somewhat likely." Since mid-December, 2004, the modal response of the public has changed to the view that further such acts are "not too likely." Furthermore, the public has not been very concerned about whether terrorism would directly affect their families for a considerable time. The plurality response to this question since 9/11 (and before) was that the public was "not too worried" that they or their families "will become a victim of terrorism" (see Gallup 2008c). More generally, too, the issue of terrorism has now fallen behind the economy, Iraq, education policy, corruption in government, healthcare, and energy among the issues most important to the public in influencing their vote for president (Saad 2008).

The issue of terrorism, however, differentially affects the views of partisans and independents. For Democrats, only 36 per cent of such respondents in early 2008 viewed terrorism as an "extremely important" or "very important" issue in affecting their presidential choice, ranking 11th out of 14 issues identified in a recent survey. For Republicans, by contrast, terrorism ranks 1st out of the same 14 issues, with 50 per cent of these partisans identifying it as the top issue in their voting for president. For independents, the issue of terrorism falls between its ranking with Democrats and Republicans, albeit closer to the latter than the former (ibid.). This group of voters views the economy, Iraq, and government corruption as the top issues, with terrorism closely behind in fourth place.

In sum, then, the issue of terrorism has diminished a bit as a salient one for a segment of the electorate, principally Democrats, but it has not done so for Republicans and only to a lesser extent among independents. The issue's salience could change, depending upon global events. If an international incident were to occur, the issue could increase in salience, especially for that electorally important segment of the American public, independents, and perhaps for some conservative Democrats..

Immigration

While immigration has gained some salience in particular primaries and caucuses during the 2008 presidential election cycle, its overall salience for the American public generally has been relatively low compared to other issues, ranking behind a large number of other issues. In an early February 2008 survey of 14 issues of importance to Americans in voting for president, "illegal immigration" ranked lowest among these issues. Still, with 60 per cent of the public viewing it as extremely important or very important in judging candidates, the issue does have some public resonance (Saad 2008).

The public's views on immigration over the past 30 years has largely been for seeking a decrease in the level of immigration when presented with the options of decreasing, increasing, or maintaining the present level (Gallup 2008b). Either a large majority or a sizeable plurality favored this option. On only three different occasions has a plurality of Americans supported maintaining the present level of immigration and only 7 to 17 per cent during the various surveys favored increasing the level of immigration. Despite this negative view of increased immigration, the majority of the American public continues to view immigration as good for the country, and the majority favor allowing illegal immigrants the opportunity to become American citizens.

Attitudes on immigration tend to divide along partisan and ideological lines. Republicans are more likely to favor decreased levels of immigration than Democrats, and conservatives are more likely to favor decreased levels of immigration than liberals. Similarly, the issue of illegal immigration is much more important for Republicans than for Democrats. Republicans rank illegal immigration 6th out of 14 issues in importance for their presidential voting decisions, with 34 per cent of these respondents listing it as "extremely important." Democrats rank illegal immigration as least important for their presidential voting decisions, with only 22 per cent of these respondents listing it as "extremely important." The views of independent voters on the immigration issue are closer to Democrats than to Republicans. For independents, the importance of illegal immigration ranks 13th out of 14 issues, with only 24 per cent of them ranking immigration as "extremely important" (Saad 2008).

With the apparent low salience of the immigration issue among the public and with the relative stability of the American views on this issue, it appears unlikely to play a particularly large role in voting decisions nationally. (In particular states, though, the story may be somewhat different.) Yet the immigration issue, much like the terrorism issue, may be a latent one that could be activated by presidential contenders or by the next administration. Indeed, there is some evidence that this has already occurred. At the time of the discussion of the immigration law in the Congress during the summer of 2007, the issue rose on the public's agenda. In fact, the issue was perceived the second highest priority (after the Iraq War) that the president and Congress should address (Carroll 2007).

The environment

The environment is one of those increasing number of intermestic issues with implications for both the domestic arena (e.g., air pollution in the cities) and international arena (e.g., global warming). On this issue, the public's views have been pretty stable and consistent over the past several years. The public has long recognized that global warming has begun, that it is predominantly caused by human behavior, and that environmental quality has been only "fair" in the recent past and getting worse (Gallup 2008a). Further, the public believes that we have made only limited progress in addressing this issue, and the public supports a wider array of activities (stronger federal environmental standards, higher auto emission standards, more mandatory control on carbon dioxide emissions, and more solar and wind power) to improve the environment. Finally, too, a majority of the public have been supporters of the Kyoto Protocol, a position largely at odds with the actions of the Bush administration (see Bouton and Page 2002; Global Views 2006).

The issue of the environment is divided along partisan lines, too. Republicans are more satisfied with the environmental conditions than are Democrats. Democrats are more supportive of environmental efforts than Republicans. Democrats are about twice as likely to view global warming as a "critical threat" than Republicans. Republicans are less likely to view efforts to improve the global environment as key foreign policy goals. At the same time, a majority of Democrats and Republicans support US participation in the Kyoto Protocol, favor aiding other countries to limit greenhouse gases, and believe that environmental standards should be incorporated in international trade agreements (Global Views 2006: 31).

Iran

One final issue that has gained salience among the public in recent years is the future direction of relations with Iran. In October, 2007, a Gallup poll reported that Iran was selected as the "single country" that was considered "the greatest threat to stability in the world" (Carroll 2007). This threat perception of Iran proved to be greatest across the board – with the highest per cent among Republicans at 50 per cent, independents next at 30 per cent, and Democrats the least at 26 per cent – when compared with a series of other countries. Across partisan ties, too, the public generally supported sanctions that were imposed on Iran by the United States in 2007, although high percentages of the public, across party identification did not have much knowledge of such actions.

The salience of Iran to the public is not wholly clear at this point. When the public is prompted to assess the relative importance of Iran compared to a set of other countries that require attention by presidential candidates, it comes out just behind Iraq as most important, and ahead of Afghanistan, China, and list of other countries (ibid.). At the same time, the issue has not shown up in some of the other surveys of crucial issues, apparently for the lack of prompting in the surveys themselves. Hence, Iran appears like some of these other key foreign policy issues: it could be one that emerges as salient for the public in light of international actions.

The public's views and its impact on a post-Bush administration

What is particularly striking about this brief review of the public's general orientation to foreign policy and its views on specific issues is the degree of stability and structure in recent years, even in the face of the events of September 11 and in the face of the ongoing Iraq War. To be sure, the public views are divided by partisan and ideological differences, but these, too, seem remarkably stable. In this sense, American public opinion on foreign policy does appear to exhibit the *necessary* conditions for the public to have a policy effect. But are the *sufficient* conditions present for the public to have an effect?

While there are no assured ways of assessing the likelihood that a mechanism for *public access* to policy-makers and a *degree of receptivity* of the public's views by decision-makers (the sufficient conditions) will be met by a new administration, we can provide some initial assessments about an Obama administration, and then also suggest the likelihood of the public's impact on foreign policy, regardless of the particular person occupying the White House.

An Obama administration

On the face of it, the public's general orientation to foreign policy and its specific views on the key issues seem to meet with considerable receptivity with the views and policy advanced by President Barack Obama. While it is difficult to summarize President Obama's general foreign policy orientation fully given his limited experience in this area, his policy statements seem to suggest largely a liberal internationalist approach. He espouses continued American leadership in the world ("We can neither retreat from the world nor try to bully it into submission. We must lead the world, by deed and by example") (Obama 2007: 4), appears committed to the use of diplomacy as the first option, although he does not wholly eschew the use of force, and endorses the use of partnerships for addressing both security and non-security issues globally. He also embraces a commitment to American values as the basis for foreign policy actions ("Our global engagement cannot be defined by what we are against; it must be guided by a clear sense of what we stand for") (ibid.: 14). Likewise, he supports the promotion of democratic societies ("We need to invest in building capable, democratic states that can establish healthy and educated communities, develop markets, and generate wealth") (ibid.: 14).

In terms of issues, President Obama appears to adopt positions that coincide with the public's views on key foreign policy issues. For instance, he has given a high priority to addressing the issue of nuclear proliferation. This issue appears to be an important one for the American public, and his manner of addressing it – via global cooperation, including the ratification of the Comprehensive Test Ban Treaty and negotiating a global ban on the production of new nuclear weapons materials – are largely in sync with the American public as well. Similarly, he has expressed his intent to deal with global terrorism through a coordinated and cooperative effort worldwide. On trade policy, President Obama has waffled a bit – especially with his critical statement about NAFTA during the primaries. The American public, however, remains divided over the benefits and costs of international trade (Global Views 2006: 23–4); hence, President Obama's position may not be as problematic as some might suggest. Finally, President Obama's position on Iraq coincides more fully with both Democrats and independents, although his Iraq withdrawal proposal is more accelerated than the majority of the public probably supports. In all, then, President Obama's foreign policy orientation and policy positions appear to be in line with the public's views at present.

In an Obama administration, several factors suggest that there may be considerable public access and impact on the direction of foreign policy. First, if Iraq and Iran remain more salient than the issue of terrorism throughout the political campaign, those issues will be the ones that will receive immediate attention with a new administration. As Miroslav Nincic (2008) has recently demonstrated, foreign policy issues and the position of candidates have increasingly proved to be important in voter's choices in recent elections. Although these foreign policy issues proved less salient than economic ones in the 2008 election (Pew Research Center for the People and the Press 2008), an Obama administration will likely feel compelled to address these foreign policy sooner rather than later. Second, his principal foreign policy advisers during the campaign, albeit a mixture of political realists and liberal internationalists, are more likely to be receptive to following the public's view in the overall direction of foreign policy. While Zbigniew Brzezinski and Anthony Lake surely have strongly held view on foreign affairs, they would also be cognizant of the public's views. Third, Obama's relative foreign policy inexperience and presumably his open decision style should make it more likely that the public would have an effect.

Any new administration

While the personal characteristics of the person selected as president surely impact the role of public opinion in shaping foreign policy, other structural and process conditions will also affect the public's role, regardless of who holds the presidency. First, the salience of foreign policy issues has been on the increase in recent presidential elections, and presidents do take policy initiatives based upon their electoral successes. At the same time, although the American and global economic meltdown will likely occupy most of the new administration's immediate attention, the new administration will surely need to address the foreign policy issues in an increasingly dangerous world. Second, the magnitude of the public opinion on foreign policy issues matter, too. Previous political research on foreign policy suggests that the public's view must reach about 60 per cent before necessarily impacting policy. Political scientist Thomas Graham (1994: 196) noted that "public opinion on a foreign policy issue must reach at least consensus levels (60 per cent or higher) before it begins to have a discernible effect on decision making." Needless to say, some foreign policy issues have reached that level or nearly so, and thus they have the possibility to have an impact. Third, the 111th Congress is controlled by Democrats in the House and the Senate, and the margins of that control are wider than in the 110th Congress (Herszenhorn 2008). Hence, the pressures upon a new administration to be more responsive to the public's views as reflected in that body will increase. Finally, even if a new administration is not wholly responsive to the policy options sought by the public, it will have its decision latitude considerably reduced in the foreign policy realm by the pull of public opinion and by the requirements of electoral politics in a democratic setting, especially if the salience of foreign policy continues to increase in an interdependent world.

Conclusion

In this chapter, we began by identifying the two principal theoretical perspectives for understanding the role of public opinion in affecting American foreign policy direction – one that sees the public's views as uninformed and moodish, the other that sees the public's views as structured and stable. Utilizing the second perspective, we identified the necessary and sufficient conditions for public opinion to have a foreign policy impact. In turn, we assessed whether the necessary and sufficient conditions are present in current foreign policy opinion and the Obama administration that will follow the Bush years.

For the necessary conditions, we argued that the public's general orientation toward foreign policy and its stances on key foreign policy issues are largely stable and are generally structured by the effects of party and ideology – and have been for some time. For the sufficient conditions, the receptivity to public opinion by leaders and the degree of access to the policy process for the public, the analysis is more speculative, based upon the policy views and likely decision styles of an Obama administration. In general, the new administration will likely demonstrate greater receptivity to public impact, albeit to varying degrees, than at present. In addition, though, several structural and process conditions in the American political system suggest a larger role for public opinion in the years ahead. What still remains unclear is how much effect the public will have in exercising policy restraint (eliminating some options) for a new administration or in promoting policy choice (prescribing key options). In general, with foreign policy decision-making concentrated in the executive branch, the public's ultimate policy effect likely will be more the former than the latter for any post-Bush administration.

Notes

1 On these theoretical perspectives, see McCormick (2005: 513–43) from which I draw here and below.
2 Our compilation is not exhaustive or complete of the possible issues that could be created from the Gallup surveys, but it does give some sense of the range of issues identified by the public and provides a list of issues to review.

References

Almond, Gabriel A. (1950) *The American People and Foreign Policy*, New York: Frederick A. Praeger.
Bouton, Marshall M. and Page, Benjamin I. (2002) *Worldviews 2002: American Public Opinion & Foreign Policy*, Chicago: Chicago Council on Foreign Relations.
Carroll, Joseph (2005) "Terrorism, Iraq Still Top Priorities for Americans," Gallup, 10 February. Online. Available at: http://www.gallup.com/poll/14884/Terrorism-Iraq-Still-Top-Priorities-Americans.aspx (accessed 25 February 2005).
—— (2006) "Top Midterm Election Issues: Iraq, Terrorism, Healthcare, Corruption," Gallup, 19 January. Online. Available at: http://www.gallup.com/poll/20977/Top-Midterm-Election-Issues-Iraq-Terrorism-Healthcare-Corruption.aspx#1 (accessed 25 February 2008).
—— (2007) "Public: Iran Poses Greatest Threat to World Stability," Online. Available at http://www.gallup.com/poll/102463/Public-Iran-Poses-Greatest-Thre … , (accessed 6 March 2008).
Carroll, Joseph and Newport, Frank (2007) "Iraq, Terrorism, Corruption Top List of the People's Priorities," Gallup, 11 January. Online. Available at: http://www.gallup.com/poll/26104/Iraq-Terrorism-Corruption-Top-List-Peoples-Priorities.aspx#1 (accessed 25 February 2008).
Converse, Philip E. (1964) "The Nature of Belief Systems in Mass Public," in David E. Apter (ed.) *Ideology and Discontent*, New York: The Free Press, pp. 206–61.
Foyle, Douglas C. (1999) *Counting the Public In. Presidents, Public Opinion, and Foreign Policy*, New York: Oxford University Press.
Gallup (2008a) "Gallup's Pulse of Democracy: Environment." Online. Available at: http://www.gallup.com/1615/Environment.aspx?version=print (accessed 24 February 2008).
—— (2008b) "Gallup's Pulse of Democracy: Immigration." Online. Available at: http://www.gallup.com/1660/Immigration.aspx?version=print (accessed 24 February 2008).

—— (2008c) "Gallup's Pulse of Democracy: Terrorism." Online. Available at: http://www.gallup.com/4909/Terrorism-United-States.aspx?version=print (accessed 24 February 2008).

—— (2008d) "Gallup's Pulse of Democracy: The War in Iraq." Online. Available at: http://www.gallup.com/1633/Iraq.aspx?version=print (accessed 24 February 2008).

Global Views (2006) *Global Views 2006: The United States and the Rise of China and India*, Chicago: The Chicago Council on Global Affairs.

Graham, Thomas (1994) "Public Opinion and U.S. Foreign Policy Decision Making," in David A. Deese (ed.) *The New Politics of American Foreign Policy*, New York: St. Martin's Press.

Herszenhorn, David M. (2008) "Senate Democrats Hope for a Majority Not Seen in 30 Years: 60 Seats," *The New York Times*, 7 March. Online. Available at http://www.nytimes.com/2008/03/07/us/politics/07senate.html?_r=1&th&emc=th&oref=slogin (accessed 7 March 2008).

Holsti, Ole R. (1992) "Public Opinion and Foreign Policy: Challenges to the Almond-Lippmann Consensus," *International Studies Quarterly*, 36(December): 439–66.

—— (2004) *Public Opinion and American Foreign Policy*, rev. edn, Ann Arbor, MI: The University of Michigan Press.

Hurwitz, Jon and Peffley, Mark (1987) "How Are Foreign Policy Attitudes Structured? A Hierarchical Model," *American Political Science Review*, 81(December): 1099–120.

Jones, Jeffrey M. (2001) "Americans' Priorities for President and Congress Shift After Attacks," Gallup, 10 October. Online. Available at: http://www.gallup.com/poll/4978/Americans-Priorities-President-Congress-Shift-After-Attacks.aspx (accessed 25 February 2008).

—— (2008a) "Majority Still Favors Timetable for Troop Withdrawal," Gallup, 18 February. Online. Available at: http://www.gallup.com/poll/104398/Majority-Still-Favors-Timetable- ... (accessed 18 February 2008).

—— (2008b) "Majority Continues to Consider Iraq War a Mistake," Gallup, 6 February. Online. Available at http://www.gallup.com/poll/104185/Majority-Continues-Consider Iraq ... (accessed 24 February 2008).

McCormick, James M. (2005) *American Foreign Policy and Process*, 4th edn, Belmont, CA: Thomson Wadsworth.

Moore, David (2003) "Public: Terrorism, Economy Top List of Congressional Priorities," Gallup, 7 January. Online. Available at: http://www.gallup.com/poll/7531/Public-Terrorism-Economy-Top-List-Congressional-Priorities.aspx#2 (accessed 25 February 2008).

Newport, Frank and Carroll, Joseph (2007) "Americans Say Iraq War a Mistake, But Do Not Want Funding Cut." Online. Available at: http://www.gallup.com/poll/26791/Americans-Say-Iraq-War-Mistake ... (accessed 18 February 2008).

Nincic, Miroslav (2008) "External Affairs and the Electoral Connection," in Eugene R. Wittkopf and James M. McCormick (eds) *The Domestic Sources of American Foreign Policy*, Lanham, MD: Rowman & Littlefield Publishers, Inc., pp. 125–40.

Obama, Barack (2007) "Renewing American Leadership," *Foreign Affairs*, 86(July/August): 2–16.

Page, Benjamin I. and Bouton, Marshall M. (2006) *The Foreign Policy Disconnect: What Americans Want from Our Leaders but Don't Get*, Chicago: University of Chicago Press.

Page, Benjamin I. and Shapiro, Robert Y. (1983) "Effects of Public Opinion on Policy," *American Political Science Review*, 77(March): 175–90.

—— (1992) *The Rational Public: Fifty Years of Trends on Americans' Policy Preferences*, Chicago: The University of Chicago Press.

Pew Research Center for the People and the Press (2008) "Inside Obama's Sweeping Victory." Online. Available at: http://pewresearch.org/pubs/1023/exit-polling-analysis-2008 (accessed 10 November 2008).

Saad, Lydia (2008) "Iraq and the Economy are Top Issues for Voters." Online. Available at: http://www.gall\up.com/poll/104320/Iraq-Economy-Top-Issues-Voters ... (accessed 25 February 2008).

Shapiro, Robert Y. and Page, Benjamin I. (1988) "Foreign Policy and the Rational Public," *Journal of Conflict Resolution*, 32(June): 211–47.

Sobel, Richard (2001) *The Impact of Public Opinion on U.S. Foreign Policy: Constraining the Colossus*, New York: Oxford University Press.

Wittkopf, Eugene R. (1990) *Faces of Internationalism: Public Opinion and American Foreign Policy*, Durham, NC: Duke University Press.

Further reading

Clinton, Hillary (2006) "Foreign Policy: Council on Foreign Relations." Online. Available at: http://www.hillaryclinton.com/news/speech/view/?id=1233 (accessed 7 March 2008).

—— (2007) "Security and Opportunity for the Twenty-first Century," *Foreign Affairs*, 86 (November/December): 2–18.

Feaver, Peter D. and Gelpi, Christopher (2008) "American Veterans in Government and the Use of Force," in Eugene R. Wittkopf and James M. McCormick (eds) *The Domestic Sources of American Foreign Policy*, Lanham, MD: Rowman & Littlefield Publishers, Inc., pp. 97–113.

Lippmann, Walter (1955) *Essays in Political Philosophy*, Boston: Little, Brown.

McCain, John (2007) "An Enduring Peace Built on Freedom," *Foreign Affairs*, 86(November/December): 19–34.

—— (2008) "On the Issues: National Security." Online. Available at: http://www.johnmccain.com/Informing/Issues/054184f4-6b51-40dd-8964-54fcf66a1e68.htm (accessed 9 March 2008).

11 Race, African-Americans and US foreign policy

Mark Ledwidge

> So what they're going to try to do is make you scared of me. You know, he's not patriotic enough. He's got a funny name. You know, he doesn't look like all those other presidents on those dollar bills, you know. He's risky.
>
> (Barack Obama Presidential Campaign, 2008)

> I want to see a Foreign Service that looks as if black Americans are part of this great country.
>
> (Secretary of State Condoleezza Rice 2008)

James Meernik and Elizabeth Oldmixon contend that 'an effective foreign policy provides benefits to all those residing in the United States' (Meernik and Oldmixon 2008: 189). This chapter argues first that for much of American history a White Anglo-Saxon Protestant (WASP) power elite has presided over western-centred and racialised foreign policies that are indifferent and divergent to the policy preferences of African-Americans; Second, that scholars have overlooked, and ignored the foreign affairs activities and preferences of (American) non-whites; and, third, scholars have assumed that African-Americans have had no sustained interest in foreign affairs (Plummer 1996: 1). However, changing demographics and increased cultural diversity suggest that the traditional parameters of US foreign policy face emerging challenges from below. This chapter foregrounds race and US foreign policy, an increasingly important but under-researched topic which is interwoven into the political tapestry of American politics.

This chapter is part of a nascent brand of scholarship that provides an introductory analysis of six new directions in US foreign policy scholarship. First, the framers of US foreign policy extended the notion of white supremacy beyond the shores of America. Second, the academy's tradition of separating domestic and foreign affairs has fostered an intellectual rigidity which inadequately acknowledges the permeability of race as a theory of political power. Third, African-Americans have a historic and under-acknowledged tradition of engaging with foreign affairs; in addition to framing their domestic struggle within the broader context of a global struggle against white hegemony. Fourth, at critical historical junctures, such as the cold war, domestic and foreign affairs forced America to modify its foreign policy. Fifth, state repression undermined African-American internationalism pertaining to Africa and the African Diaspora. Sixth, African-American internationalism was largely grounded in racial concerns and identity politics.

The 2008 presidential campaign raised questions with regard to whether race, age, or gender are significant factors which would impact on the worldview or foreign policy agendas of Senators John McCain, Hillary Clinton or Barack Obama. This chapter argues that the intersection of race and US foreign policy has been and is an integral feature of US politics and that few scholars 'have sought to place the construction of whiteness in the context of US foreign policy' (Horne 1999: 437). This chapter challenges the idea that American elites have been impervious to America's racial conventions due to enlightened perceptions of global politics. Moreover, the chapter maintains that issues of race and ethnicity need to be more fully explored with regard to US engagement with global politics. The chapter is divided into seven sections detailing discussions on race, the candidacy of Barack Obama, the foreign policy establishment, African-Americans and US foreign policy, race and ethnicity in contemporary foreign policies, and the future implications of race and US foreign policy.

The politics of race

This chapter conceives racism as a significant factor in the historical and contemporary context of the engagement of African-Americans with foreign affairs. It maintains that 'the situation of African-Americans has been qualitatively different from that of any other racial or ethnic ... [group] ... in the United States' (Lipset 1996: 113). The system of enslavement that Euro-Americans imposed on Africans created a unique system of racial oppression which blocked African-American entry into politics[1] until the 1960s (Winant 2006: 990). Thus, for the majority of US history, African-American political activities have occurred outside of the political establishment. Limited access to political representation has undoubtedly impaired African-American efforts to articulate, promote and defend their group interests within the political arena. The exclusion of African-Americans from domestic politics is significant because it has impeded their ability to address foreign affairs from within the political establishment (Meriwether 2002: 34).

Although economic power does not necessarily translate into political power subsequent discussions will identify the link between group identity, economic status and the ability to influence US foreign policy. Theodore Cross maintains that Euro-American power was used to constrain African-American economic power (Cross 1987: ix); Cross maintains that the 'prior advantage and incumbency' of Euro-Americans (ibid.: ix) hampered the economic development of African-Americans. This is important as this chapter highlights the link between wealth and the ability to create and maintain (organic) group-oriented lobbies. In brief, race is credited as facilitating the exclusion of African-Americans from political appointments and fostering economic inequality *vis-à-vis* Euro- and African-Americans. Since the possessions of political and economic power are useful commodities when it comes to influencing politics and foreign policy, Euro-American hegemony can be viewed as a form of racial power.

Race and American power

US racism represents a power-oriented system of behaviour founded on notions of Euro-American supremacy which has determined the domestic power configuration. Although race can assume a fluid ideological structure composed of alterable beliefs and prejudices, the alleged irrationality of racial doctrines is problematic. American history defines Euro-American racism as a functional system which generated specific behaviour patterns which in turn created, maintained, justified and, when necessary, renegotiated the parameters of Euro-American hegemony. Wellman insists that:

> The subordination of people of colour is functional to the operation of American society as we know it and the colour of one's skin is a primary determinant of people's position in the social structure. Racism is a structural relationship based on the subordination of one racial group by another. Given this perspective the determining feature of race relations is not prejudice towards blacks but rather the superior position of whites and the institutions – ideological as well as structural – which maintain it.
>
> (Wellman 1977: 35)

Irrespective of outward appearances and the pursuit of alternative configurations, the defining feature of US race relations is Euro-American hegemony. Hacker claims that America is a 'white country' (Hacker 1992: 4). The gender and European origins of the 43 US presidents underscore the prevailing logic of US society. Despite the election of Barack Obama, a sober evaluation of US race relations identifies the correlation between racial identity and power. Wellman's hypothesis identifies the logic of racism as Euro-American hegemony over key institutions and the formation of government policy. This raises questions regarding the relative capacity of an individual's racial characteristics to re-orientate the bureaucratic mechanisms charged with framing domestic and foreign policies. Since race represents a significant factor in domestic politics, it is unwise to assume that US foreign policy has been conducted in a race-neutral manner.

International context of American expansionism

While domestic race relations have aroused intense and immense interest in the academy, foreign policy and international relations scholars have generally overlooked how race has been utilised to construct a racialised new world order undergirded by the concept of western or white hegemony (Chowdhry and Nair 2004: 17; Krenn 2006: xiv; Krishna 2006: 89). That is, the emergence and maturation of America occurred during the high point of European expansionism which drew upon notions of race and western exceptionalism to justify European dominance. A dispassionate analysis of the foundations of US politics indicates that the Founding Fathers sanctioned a racial brand of foreign policy including the importation and enslavement of Africans and a frontier foreign policy geared to territorial expansion, 'pacification' and extermination of the Native American population (Hunt 1987, 47).

US history indicates that race determined who could run for political office and determined the identity of the framers of US foreign policy. To be specific, Michael Hunt has argued that US foreign policy has been filtered and fuelled through a racialised lens (ibid.: 48). Michael Krenn argues that, centuries after the American Revolution of 1776, conquests in Latin America and the Pacific were articulated in racial terms that mirrored the language and tenor of European colonialism (Krenn 2006: 50). The identification of race's historic impact on foreign policy presents a holistic analysis of foreign affairs and introduces a neglected and controversial issue into international relations (IR) scholarship (Jones 2008: 2). It also begs the questions: does race matter today and why have foreign policy and IR scholars neglected to emphasise race as a factor in international relations?

President Barack Obama and US foreign policy

Many Americans perceive the candidacy of Barack Obama as their primary reference point to the issue of race and US foreign policy. The Euro-American population contemplated whether racial identity impacts on US foreign policy. Evidently Obama's racial identity and connections to the non-white world pose major questions for the political establishment and sections of the American public. At heart, the inversion of America's racial conventions has generated both excitement and awakened fears related to US race relations (Doyle 2008: 5).

The nub of uncertainty associated with Obama is undoubtedly connected to his African heritage and its meaning in the American context (Mazama 2007; 3). The response to Barack Obama is indicative of some Euro-Americans' concerns regarding his racial identity. The early provision of secret service personnel to protect Obama (Asante 2007: 105) is indicative of the history of racialised violence directed at African-American leaders. In addition, elite and professional pundits' insensitive comments or references regarding the assassination of Obama (http://www.nypost.com/seven/05232008/news/nationalnews/why_hill_wont_drop_out–bobby_kennedy_wa_112232.htm) or Bill O'Reilly's use of the word lynching in regard to Michelle Obama (*Huffington Post* 2008) reflected a callous disregard for the Obamas that seems antithetical and uncharacteristic of a presidential campaign. Given the historical context of US race relations, the racial dynamics of the 2008 presidential elections are quite predictable. While one expects public scrutiny of a presidential nominee's foreign policy, at times, the analysis of Obama has strayed into questions of his suitability that appears to be linked to his race.

The candidacies of Barack Obama and Hillary Clinton indicate that some Americans harbour serious reservations regarding the legitimacy of a female or African-American head of state (*New York Times* 2006). Concerns regarding Hillary's toughness or her reception in the Middle East were predicated on notions that her gender would be a liability in regard to executing US foreign policy. Similarly, Obama's empathetic orientation to the emerging world and his personal connections with Islam fuelled allegations that he would be soft on the war on terror.

The storm surrounding Obama's relationship to Reverend Jeremiah Wright and the allegations regarding Obama's patriotism reflect notions of dual loyalties, and raise questions concerning his commitment to African-American causes (*The Week* 2008: 6). In fact, references to Obama's appeal to white voters were predicated on initial speculation that his candidacy was grounded on racial politics. Issues related to questions concerning his allegiance to the American flag and the absence of a tie pin, and Obama's conspicuous use of the US flag in key speeches were undoubtedly linked to the question of his loyalty; the implication being that Obama's racial identity could distort his policy orientations to the developing world. Given that the US president is expected to have an unflinching loyalty to America, the intense scrutiny of Obama indicates that some Americans questioned his and his wife's patriotic fervour.

The controversy surrounding the Obama campaign suggests that racial identity factors into the electorate's perception of a candidate's suitably in regard to domestic and foreign policy. According to Zbigniew Brzezinski (national security advisor to President Jimmy Carter), 'What makes Obama attractive to me, is that he understands that we live in a very different world where we have to relate to a variety of cultures and peoples' (MSNBC 2007). Brzezinski's comments imply that America's foreign policy could benefit from having Obama at the helm. In the first instance, it would suggest a break with the overtly racialised past. Second, it suggests in a crude way that non-white nations might respond more favourably to foreign policies associated with a non-WASP. Alternatively, it might suggest that historically the Euro-American majority have relied on the president to endorse policies geared to the maintenance of white hegemony in the global context. Irrespective of premature conclusions that the candidacy of Obama represents a racial watershed in US foreign policy, competent scholars cannot assume that the election of Barack Obama would automatically translate into substantial changes in US foreign policy (Asante 2007: 115; Parmar 2008: 47). Given Obama's electoral and funding profile, he is obviously not the quintessential black candidate. Nor does his racial identity ensure a break with the established parameters of US foreign policy.

It would be problematic to assume that Obama's African roots would ensure his pursuit of a more equitable foreign policy towards Africa. If he did, how would America and the foreign policy establishment respond? Whether Obama's African ancestry will or should encourage a favourable foreign policy towards Africa raises important questions regarding whether US policy framers have favoured European states due to racial and western imperatives of global dominance. Nonetheless Obama's campaign website does little to indicate any major commitment to Africa. While Obama's foreign policy section has listed speeches detailing his position on Latin America and the Caribbean, Europe and China, he has no speech specifically directed at Africa. Although the website addresses halting the genocide in Darfur and ending the conflict in the Congo and a commitment to the conviction of the former Liberian President Charles Taylor (Barack Obama Official Website 2008), the foreign policy section provides similar coverage on Iran and Israel.

Despite his Kenyan heritage, Obama's website does not highlight any special emphasis to creating a special relationship with Kenya or other African states. Indeed, given the centrality of the race-neutral discourse, Obama would be at pains to illustrate an even hand in regard to his approach to African states or African-American policy preferences. Ironically, critics will doubtlessly demand a race-neutral brand of foreign policy that ignores the historical biases of America's foreign policy establishment. This raises questions regarding whether the Obama administration could realistically address any Africa-related policy preferences of the African-American constituency, given the pressures of status anxiety and mainstream fears of Obama 'going native'.

According to Richard Cohen of the *Washington Post*, 'nothing in Obama's record suggests he harbors anti-Semitic views' (*Washington Post* 2008). Obama's orientation towards Israel and his reception from Jewish Americans reflects the complexity of domestic and foreign affairs (http://middleeast.about.com/od/usmideastpolicy/a/me080605a. htm). Irrespective of adverse criticism, the Obama website is unequivocal in its support for Israel, emphasising plans

> [To] Ensure a Strong U.S.-Israel Partnership: Barack Obama strongly supports the U.S.-Israel relationship, believes that our first and incontrovertible commitment in the Middle East must be to the security of Israel, America's strongest ally in the Middle East ... Obama supports ... Israel's Right to Self Defense ... [and] Support[s] Foreign Assistance to Israel. He has called for continuing U.S. cooperation with Israel in the development of missile defense systems.

Despite Obama's efforts to disassociate himself from alleged tensions between sections of Jewish and African-American leadership cadre, he has being heavily scrutinised with regard to his plans for the Middle East. It has been argued that 'President Bush used a speech to the Israeli Parliament ... to denounce those who would negotiate with "terrorists and radicals" – a remark that was widely interpreted as a rebuke to Senator ... Obama' (*New York Times* 2008).

While his speech at the American Israel Public Affairs Committee (AIPAC) silenced critics, Obama's speech elicited a different response in the Arab world. The racial and ethnic identity of Senator Obama has elicited immense public scrutiny from mainstream America. False reports of his schooling in a madrassa (*Times* Online 2007), his birth names, especially Hussein, and his alleged ties to Islam, prompted some Americans and sections of the political establishment to question his religious credentials and his relationship with the Muslim world. Jeremiah Wright's championing of Louis Farrakhan lent itself to a litany of rumours regarding the true allegiances of Senator Obama (*Washington Post* 2008). The post-9/11 context and the race, religion and terror paradigm have weaved an amorphous cloud around his candidacy that implied that his race, inexperience and personal relationships were incompatible with his assuming the presidency and directing US foreign policy. Interestingly the American-centred analysis of US politics has not addressed the Muslim world's assessment of Obama.

Sana Abdullah, a correspondent of the *Middle East Times*, maintains that in the Muslim world 'many Arabs and Muslims had hoped his African background and Muslim father would make him more sympathetic to their causes' (http://www.metimes. com/International/2008/06/05/obamas_aipac_speech_shocks_arabs/9021/). Abdullah suggests that the belief of some Muslims that Obama's racial and ethnic identity would encourage Muslim-friendly policies have been dashed by his stance on Israel (ibid.). On balance, Obama's racial identity and his contrary positions on Israel and the Muslim world reflect the combustive politics of America's domestic context and the existing fissures in international politics.

While it is tempting to see the Obama phenomenon as the central concern of this chapter, it is part of a broader canvas pertaining to African-Americans and foreign affairs. The next section will highlight the institutional factors that have impaired African-Americans foreign policy activities.

The foreign policy establishment

Although scholars have acknowledged the existence of a hegemonic white Anglo-Saxon Protestant elite (WASP) with regard to domestic and foreign affairs (Winant 2006: 990), they have under-emphasised the racial and gender homogeneity of this class and failed to examine whether identity configurations impact on the substance of US foreign policy. The controversy pertaining to the identity–foreign policy nexus foregrounds how Euro-Americans (specifically WASP elites) have maintained hegemonic control over US foreign policy and super-ordinate control over the political apparatus.

Although C. Wright Mills identified the existence of a socio-political and economic power elite (Mills 2000: 4) he neglected to highlight the racial orientation of the WASP elite or the racial and ethnic basis of WASP power. The WASP elite is essentially a socio-economic and racial power class with a predisposition and personal interest in Euro-American and western hegemony. The WASP hypothesis implies that WASPs have controlled the political apparatus and determined the character of US foreign policy. It would be erroneous to credit the WASP establishment as possessing unassailable power. A realistic characterisation of WASP power conceives it as an ongoing struggle; periodically reinforced by threat-orientated *nativist*[2] purges (Lauren 1996: 61; Higham 2002: 4; Persaud 2004: 69) designed to reinforce, protect and maintain WASP dominance along racial and ethnic lines. The prevailing logic of the WASP thesis suggests that 'the United States belongs ... to the Anglo-Saxon race' (Higham 2002: 9).

The ethnic parameters of WASP power

While distinctions between race and ethnicity have become increasingly blurred,until recently ethnicity was not a significant factor in foreign affairs literature. A simplified model of the ethnicity paradigm views it as a by-product of cultural, linguistic and religious expressions of a specific group (Kirk 2008: 277). Throughout US history, the ethnicity paradigm was predicated on a group's degree of similarity or divergence from the Anglo-Saxon cultural paradigm. As a result, America developed an informal assimulationist model designed to infuse WASP attributes into white immigrant communities (Winant 2006: 990) which ultimately caused the socio-political integration of white ethnics into the establishment and foreign affairs networks. Despite the emergence of new ethno-racial formations throughout US history, influential foreign affairs networks have been and still are the racial, cultural and religious preserves of the WASP elite. Therefore, other ethno-racial groups have subordinated their conceptions of foreign affairs to accommodate the WASP imperatives which have generally been legitimised as representing the 'national interest'.

The racial, cultural and linguistic attributes of the English-speaking WASP elite has served as a benchmark regarding entry into the political power class. Thus it is conceivable that the ethno-racial conventions of US politics have insulated the foreign policy establishment from the inclusion of African-Americans and non-whites; and if, or when, non-whites have assumed a role in the US foreign policy establishment, their political views have been tailored to WASP requirements. Conversely the integral role of Euro-Americans in formulating US foreign policy might be viewed as a consequence of demographic factors and the possession of the required credentials to direct foreign policy.

Making foreign policy

The demographic status of Euro-Americans provides an inadequate explanation as to why WASPs are still the premier group responsible for framing US foreign policy. Aside from random occurrence, the relative power differentiation between the white and non-white population resulted from racialised immigration policies geared to the maintenance of Euro-American hegemony (Persaud 2004: 73). Limiting the entry of non-whites helped ensure that Euro-Americans retained the lion's share of political power. Majority rule and the possession of super-ordinate socio-economic and political power arguably facilitated Euro-Americans' or WASPS' prevalence in the foreign policy establishment. Despite the historical prevalence of American racism, the racial worldview of Euro-American politicians is frequently under-acknowledged. Indeed, the WASP establishment has assumed a mythical identity, shrouded in notions of rationality and objectivity which suggests that the commitment to white hegemony was abandoned at the water's edge.

However, a broad view of American politics indicates that (prior to the 1960s and to varying degrees) the federal government has sanctioned and reinforced the racial oppression and exclusion of African-Americans from its own institutional frameworks (Omi and Winant 1994: 81; King 1997: vii). While Hunt foregrounds the racial worldview of the progenitors of US foreign policy; other scholars have highlighted the racial prejudice of the architects of the cold war, including President Truman (Dudziak 2002: 24), and key members of his administration such as George Kennan (Borstelmann 2003: 49), John Foster Dulles, James Byrnes, George Marshall, and Dean Acheson (ibid.: 51). Borstelmann maintains that the post-war foreign policy establishment inherited by Truman had 'little interest in any fundamental alterations in the international racial status quo … [And was grounded] … in assumptions of white racial supremacy' and the maintenance of global white hegemony (Borstelmann 1993: 39). If the elite pantheon of the Truman administration (credited with advancing domestic race relations) was predisposed to the retention of global white hegemony, foreign policy specialists should establish the degree to which race has factored into the construction of US foreign policy.

An elite or populist brand of foreign policy

Despite the plausibility of the racial thesis, there are legitimate counter-arguments. Alternative explanations of African-American under-representation in the foreign policy establishment must emphasise that in the first instance access to the formal and informal mechanisms of the foreign policy establishment has been limited for all Americans (Singh 2003: 268), that is, the construction of US foreign policy has generally been shielded from the mechanisms of popular democracy (Dumbrell 1990: 53; Singh 2003: 274). In brief, the institutional mechanisms of the federal government have ensured that US foreign policy was kept under the tutelage of the educated elite. As a consequence, most Americans have had, and continue to have, limited access to the higher echelons of the legislative and executive branch where policy formation occurs. In accordance with notions of popular democracy, pluralists would point to the existence of foreign affairs interest groups as providing additional access points for American citizens, and as a counter-weight to an elite state-centred foreign policy (Jentleson 2007: 45).

Rationality, a foundation of good foreign policy

It has been suggested and perhaps assumed that the engineers of US foreign policy possess a rational and sober disposition which precludes them from being driven by ideological concerns (Hunt 1987: 3). For example, George Kennan propagated an elite-led foreign policy free from ideological constraints in order to promote rational deliberation among elite thinkers and to avoid policy distortion (ibid.: 7). The debacles of the Vietnam War and the (G.W. Bush) war in Iraq undermine the idea that policy elites are able to transcend the ideological imperatives that drove the cold war or drive the current war on terror; both of which have raised questions regarding the deliberative capacities of political elites. G.W. Bush's comparisons between the cold war and the war on terror speak to the ideological congruence linking both conflicts (McCrisken 2007: 161) which were similarly framed as righteous conflicts with immoral, intractable foes.

Vietnam and the war in Iraq indicate that politicians can ignore public sentiment while presiding over flawed policy choices (ibid.: 167); in both cases the rigid adherence to foreign policy prerogatives undermined the Johnson and Bush administrations' domestic standing. The lessons of the Iraq War suggest that foreign policy elites endorsed intra-group policies derived from powerful discourses generated by the executive branch, sections of the media and well-connected neo-conservative think tanks (see Chapter 7 in this volume byAbelson). On balance, elite thinkers are by-products of the ideological and cultural assumptions of American elite society and are thus susceptible to expressing the ingrained aspects of America's political culture. Consequently, we would expect US politicians to be susceptible to notions of racial hierarchy.

Still, the caveat that foreign policy should be insulated from public opinion high-lights the importance of foreign affairs within a state-centric conception of global pol-itics and speaks to the importance of international relations, which is characterised by complex permutations. Advocates of elite stewardship of foreign affairs argue that the public lacks the expertise, educational credentials and required judgement to under-stand global politics. With the proper grounding and required participation in political education, the public can acquire an informed knowledge of international relations. With regard to foreign policy the larger question is 'who governs and who should determine US foreign policy?' Scholars have characterised the formal and informal foreign policy establishment as an Ivy League East coast establishment, comprised of a civil aristocracy (Parmar 2008: 5). Given the limited access of African-Americans to America's Ivy League institutions and the favoured professions of the foreign affairs networks, it is conceivable that the exclusion of African-Americans from the foreign affairs establishment may have been a consequence of failure to meet the professional and educational requirements.

A pluralist[3]or meritocratic view of participation in foreign affairs suggests that within the bounds of competitive interests, when individuals or groups amass sufficient organisational capacity and obtain the required expertise or successfully lobby politi-cians and government agencies, they can insert their foreign affairs goals into the fabric of US foreign policy (Dumbrell 1990: 53).

A pluralist analysis would explain the limited participation of African-Americans in foreign affairs as a consequence of their organisational weakness. Indeed, African-Americans such as Ralph Bunche, Walter White, W.E.B. Du Bois, Andrew Young and other notables have garnered the state's attention, leading to consultation and formal appointments.

During the modern era, the Congressional Black Caucus has played a role in relay-ing African-American concerns to the legislative and executive branch of government (Normington 1996: 16). In addition, the Bush Administration's appointments of Colin Powell (65th Secretary of State 2001–5) and Condeleeza Rice (66th Secretary of State) are indicative of the increasing involvement of African-Americans in elite circles of the foreign policy establishment. And the success of Obama indicates that educational achievement, electoral success and immersion in political networks can ensure African-American inclusion in elite circles, irrespective of their racial identity.

The race-neutral meritocratic analysis, however, masks how Euro-Americans' insti-tutional hegemony allowed them to exclude African-Americans from the federal gov-ernment (and by extension the foreign policy establishment). Limited access to the political networks in Washington has hampered their ability to engage in or influence US foreign policy. Also the assimilationist creed would generally encourage individuals to adopt the WASP worldview as a requirement to gaining entry into elite circles. Note that status anxiety and adherence to group think prevented Ralph Bunches' overt assistance to African-American efforts to assert a racial clause in the UN Charter (Ledwidge 2006: 190).

African-Americans and US foreign policy

Scholars have erroneously argued that the African-American fight for domestic equality undercut their efforts to engage in foreign affairs. Recent research verifies that African-Americans have sought to promote organic models of international politics in addition to lobbying the state apparatus (Plummer 1996: 5; Meriwether 2002: 3; Borstelmann 2003: 28; Ledwidge 2006: 9). For example, Ledwidge (forthcoming) charts the evolutionary development of an African-American foreign affairs community (AAFAC) from 1900–70. While previous generations of scholars have confined the African-American struggle to the domestic context, a small cadre of contemporary scholars are refashioning perceptions of American history and foreign affairs literature by highlighting the significance of African-American efforts to realign America's racial configuration, in addition to reshaping the political context of international relations.[4]

A broader historical perspective paints an unpalatable picture of the US government's orientation to African-American engagement in international affairs; when African-Africans have organised and expressed their desire to undermine Western racial hegemony in the domestic and global sphere; the state has utilised the intelligence apparatus to neutralise or undermine African-American efforts in defence of the global black constituency (Kornweibel 1998; Gaines 2006; Ledwidge 2006).

A number of points need to be stressed. First, organic expressions of African-American policy goals have generally elicited a hostile or indifferent response from Euro-Americans. Second, African-American internationalism has generally been fuelled by Black Nationalist and Pan-Africanist ideologies wedded to their African origins and the liberation of the African Diaspora (Pinkney 1976; Clarke 1992; Cone 1993; Joseph 2006). In short, the Pan-Africanist thrust of African-Americans during the nineteenth and twentieth centuries which sought a unified global constituency and a liberated Africa was considered antithetical to US interests (Clarke 1992). Consequently when deemed appropriate, Euro-Americans have emphasised integration and the singularity of the American Negro in order to minimise their engagement in foreign affairs (Plummer 1996: 23). The evidence indicates that as a consequence of Euro-American hostility to African-American identity politics that African-Americans attempts to influence US foreign policy in relation to several international policies such as the actions of the League of Nations (1919) (Clarke 1974: 12; Lewis 2000: 60; Ledwidge 2006: 92), the Italo-Ethiopian war (1934–6) (Scott 1973: 129; Plummer 1996: 43; Meriwether 2002: 34), the formation of the United Nations (1944–5) (Harris 1991: 142; Anderson 2006: 51; Ledwidge 2006: 194), decolonization (Von Eschen 1997: 3; Borstelmann 2003: 84; Gaines 2006: 12) were consistently framed as antithetical to US interests or immature and flawed attempts of racial tribalism.

In retrospect, the federal government's (progressive) engagement with the African-American foreign affairs network resulted from circumstances arising from its foreign policy requirements dating back to WWI through to WWII and the cold war period (Von Eschen 1997; Layton 2000; Dudziak 2002; Parmar 2004), whereby domestic and global concerns forced the federal government to pay more credence to African-American views on US foreign policy. In brief, race, WASP interests and the structural imperatives of the US political system facilitated the creation of a brand of racialised elitism predicated on notions of ethno-cultural and white supremacy, and determined who could legitimately shape US foreign policy. Yet why haven't African Americans asserted their influence in the non-state arena of interest group politics?

Ethnicity, a resource in interest group development

According to Trevor Rubenzer (2008), successful interest group politics requires the convergence between the government's foreign affairs policies and the goals of the interest group. This is important as African-American attempts to change the domestic and international colour-line were often contrary to US foreign policy. Rubenzer's assertion corresponds to the fact that the influence of African-Americans on US foreign policy increased during the twentieth century as a result of the requirements of the national security apparatus during America's global ascendancy, and in relation to African-American efforts to increase their status within the American polity. The exceptional circumstance of African-Americans also played a pivotal role in their marginality. The success of the WASP elite was partially derived from a strong sense of group consciousness founded on racial and ethno-cultural ties, and the relative preservation of historical origins which, via appropriate adaptations to the American context, generated ethnic ties that augmented their domestic status and influenced their perceptions of international relations.

However, most scholars have ignored how the unique and traumatic entry of African-Americans in the bowels of slave ships and the context of enslavement have fractured their cultural, ethnic and historical connections to Africa, while mainstream projections of African inferiority undermined efforts to construct a self-affirming African-American identity (Meriwether 2002: 17). Given the centrality of culture, ethnicity and historical memory to formulating the ethnic interest group, the travails of US race relations clearly inhibited African-American efforts to construct an ethnic network. Also contemporary data illustrate that within the American context the relative status of an ethnic/racial group's country of origin can enhance their domestic standing and facilitate their international agenda.

Another facet of domestic race relations has also hindered the profile of African-Americans in foreign affairs; prior to the mid-1960s, African-Americans had limited access to the electoral process, which reduced their ability to utilise the vote to support or elect congressional and presidential candidates with favourable orientations to their foreign policy preferences.

Economic under-development

Yet, why is it that there is not a proliferation of African-American foreign affairs interest groups? One of the key factors in curtailing the activities of the African-American foreign affairs network is money. Oliver and Shapiro indicate that the relative wealth discrepancies between Euro-Americans and African-Americans resulted from violent, discriminatory and institutionalised racism (Oliver and Shapiro 1995: 50). The historic economic under-development of African-Americans has limited their capacity to create a self-funded, professionalised lobbying network. For example, African-Americans' most lauded professional foreign affairs lobby, Trans Africa (1977) had only a modicum of success during its mobilisation against apartheid during the

1980s. Despite amassing a membership of 10,000 (Dickson 1996: 144) and receiving funding from the Rockefeller, Ford, and Carnegie Foundations (ibid.: 145), Trans Africa experienced major funding issues. Hence Dickson credited the economic fragility of the African-American middle class as hampering the growth of Trans Africa during the 1980s (ibid.).

While funding is an attractive option, reliance on external funding is problematic and runs the risk of the cooption of group goals due to funding requirements. The successes and failures of Trans Africa are an under-researched topic that requires greater scrutiny in order to explain the marginal impact of African-Americans pertaining to foreign affairs and to test the alleged plurality of the foreign policy establishment. That economic power and a strong group consciousness are both significant factors in the construction of a successful lobby group is important, as white America has consistently impeded the economic development of African-Americans and undermined their efforts to re affirm their African heritage (Gaines 2006: 6).

Contemporary foreign policy

Ethnic diversity and interest group politics

As early as 1975, Nathan Glazer and Patrick Moynihan maintained that ethnic concerns were becoming the 'single most important determinant of American foreign policy' (Glazer and Moynihan 1975: 23). In addition to the contention by Glazer and Moynihan, the cultural wars of the 1990s witnessed the rearticulation of group identity in a manner that would challenge Anglo-centric perceptions of US foreign policy. Notwithstanding a conservative backlash, which coincided with Huntington's clash of civilisations thesis, the insurgent forces' bid for a more inclusive form of foreign policy was undermined by the horrors of 9/11 which stifled calls for a multicultural assessment of US foreign policy. However, with the impending retirement of the foreign affairs elites of the cold war era (Shain 1994: 812), the established character of US foreign policy might be susceptible to a more inclusive brand of foreign policy. Hence the projection of American 'values' in the 2008 presidential elections, where the Christian ethos coupled with a narrow and conservative definition of patriotism may represent a reaction to Islam and the influence of new non-white diasporic communities. These communities are refashioning the cultural and linguistic patterns of the US socio-politic in addition to attempting to realign the parameters of US foreign policy. This is reflected in Huntington's belief that US foreign policy is currently under the thrall of ethnicised special interests that have shifted the emphasis of America's established foreign policy (Huntington 2004: 285–6). These new cadres, organised around ethnic and racial identities, are likely to concern Americans committed to the Western-centric form of US foreign policy.

Huntington's clash of civilisations thesis is reminiscent of cold war internationalism which highlighted communism's threat to America's internal and international security. The emergence of increasingly professionalised diasporic lobbies and their attempts at steering US foreign policy towards their countries of historical origin suggest that Huntington's diatribe against the imposition of special interests regarding the direction of US foreign policy has ethnic and racial undertones, especially since Yossi Shain's claim that 'alongside the more established groups of Greek, Armenian, Irish, or Jewish descent, the more recently empowered diasporas of African, Arab, Cuban, Filipino,

Haitian, Korean, and Mexican [are engaged in shaping US foreign policy towards their countries of origin' (Shain 1994: 812).

Given the relative degree of racial, religious and cultural divergence of these new foreign affairs interest groups, one would expect a degree of tension between the establishment and these emerging groups. Finally, the conservative discourse regarding who shapes foreign policy fails to acknowledge that that the traditional foreign policy establishment could be characterised as an ethno-racial special interest group. Whether American democracy is flexible enough to seriously engage with new policy orientations emanating from non-white interest groups willing to assert a cultural and identity-based approach to foreign affairs will be a significant factor in twenty-first-century foreign policy.

Preconditions for successful lobbies

It is striking that given the relative size of the Jewish and Cuban populations these communities have created strong professionalised and well-financed lobbies while African-Americans have made minimal progress in that regard. It behoves us to examine some key attributes pertaining to interest group development.

Indian Americans

In a recent article, Jason Kirk affirms the importance of a stable group consciousness and economic power as the basis of an ethnic lobby. Kirk identifies the rapid growth of a highly funded and professionalised Indian American lobby network (Kirk 2008: 276). Kirk acknowledges that two of the primary factors regarding the emergence of the network relate to the modern ascendancy of India as a global player; The importance being the alleged correlation between the relative status of India and the Indian American foreign affairs networks. Spectulatory insights suggest that successful ethnic lobbies construct or maintain socio-political and cultural links to their mother country. The second significant factor in the rise of the India lobby was the immigration act of 1965 (ibid.: 276) which facilitated the entry of Indians to America. This reinforces the idea that the racialisation of US immigration has contributed to the ethno-centric character of US foreign policy.

Conversely, the Indian American lobby bears the hallmarks of an ethnic and racially homogeneous diasporic network despite foreign policy analysts concerns, regarding the increase in 'political organisations established along cultural, ethnic, religious, or racial lines' (ibid.: 277). Kirk credits the Indian American lobby with a pivotal role in brokering the 'US India Nuclear agreement' (ibid.: 277). However, in light of the controversy surrounding the Mearsheimer and Walt thesis concerning the Israel lobby, ethnic and racial lobbies are still subject to mainstream scrutiny which hinges on issues of national loyalties (ibid.: 278) and undue influence.

Although it has taken African-Americans centuries to address US foreign policy, it would appear that the India Caucus which was modelled on the Black Caucus (ibid.: 290) has managed this in a few decades. It is hard to imagine that the marginalisation of African-Americans is not related to their unique status in US politics. For example, when the India Caucus was set up in 1994 (ibid.: 289), it established a formidable presence in the House of Representatives and even the Senate. Kirk cites Raghavan who indicates 'its democratic founding co-chair was Hillary ...

Clinton, ... and its initial membership of 20 also included then Majority Leader Bill Frist ... and Minority Leader Tom Daschle' (ibid.: 290). Given mainstream public apathy, well-funded ethnic lobbies will have increasing opportunities to shape US foreign policy.

One wonders what this means to African-Americans whose struggles paved the way for the increased access of other non-white groups and whose original efforts to steer US foreign policy including efforts to unite with newly independent African states were neutralised by the political establishment (Sales 1994: 143).

The importance of domestic issues regarding a group's ability to shape foreign affairs is probably tied to the fact that:

> Economic profile of an ethnic identity group might affect the support it can garner from legislators; Indian-Americans like some other communities frequently linked to powerful ethnic lobbies, such as Jewish and Cuban-Americans have an average, household income that is significantly higher than the average US household.
>
> (Kirk 2008: 280)

This is important as Oliver and Shapiro argue that 'materially, whites and blacks constitute two nations' (Oliver and Shapiro 1995: 7) whereby the earnings of African-Americans and their overall wealth index are significantly lower than that of whites. A recent report claims that 'As we look at the reality of Black-white inequality we see that to this day African-Americans do not even make 60% of the income of white Americans and in terms of wealth are in an even worse position' (Muhammed 2008: 9). In the twenty-first century, America's projection of a liberal, colour-blind society fails to appreciate the legacies of an intensely polarised society in which continued discussion of enslavement, reparations and institutional racism by African-Americans is considered problematic.

The storm surrounding Reverend Jeremiah Wright's views on US foreign policy reflect the African-American tradition of articulating critical and controversial perspectives of domestic and foreign policy, in which leaders including Du Bois, Garvey, Paul Robeson, Walter White, Martin Luther King and Malcolm X authored an alternative take on US foreign policy grounded in Third World politics and notions of Africanist loyalties. Likewise, support for Barack Obama among African-Americans speaks to a latent desire to address previous and contemporary barriers to African-American interests and the authorship of a dignity affirming hyphenated identity (Walters 2007: 22). Their support for Barack Obama represents a historic agenda favouring progressive policies rooted in racial equality and group-oriented tactics and Obama's thematic synergy with African-American aspirations.

Scholarly discourse regarding whether African-Americans can pursue a progressive foreign affairs agenda in relation to Africa reflect the consistent engagement of African-Americans with African issues. However, the numerous structural and institutional manifestations of white supremacy have neutered the emergence of an intellectually organic African-American foreign affairs network. While critics will question the validity or accuracy of fusing racial theories with foreign affairs scholarship, it is imperative that this discussion of foreign affairs is properly contextualised. The persistence of racial discrimination which necessitated President Bush's commentary on the racial implications of noose hangings perpetrated by Euro-American racists, and tensions arising from the perceptions of the Jena six incident[5] undercut notions of

African-American paranoia, causing some African-Americans to question the race neutrality espoused by American elites and mainstream Americans. The biting commentary of Jeremiah Wright highlights his distrust of American politicians founded on the bitter realities of African-American experiences in America.

The future: ethnic tensions in contemporary foreign policy

The ethnic and racial composition of US society is set to become a critical factor in the twenty-first century. Demographic projections indicate that by 2050 Euro-Americans will cease to be the majority population. Two questions: would the demographic ascendancy of the non-white population lead to a greater diversification of the US state apparatus? Will the election of Obama and an increase of non-whites change the policy outlook of the foreign policy establishment? While it is controversial to suggest that contemporary US foreign policy is predicated on the preservation of white hegemony, calls for a US-led Concert of Democracies might suggest

> A sort of alliance of the English-speaking countries – an Anglo sphere, the evolution of a hangover from late nineteenth-century and early twentieth-century Anglo-Saxonism: a racist belief in the innate biologically-determined superiority in economy, industry, government and culture of Anglo-Saxon peoples.
>
> (Parmar 2008: 42)

The clash of civilisations rhetoric and the War on Terror, including Bush's reference to the Crusades, have prompted suspicions of rearticulated residues of the West's religious and racial supremacy. Globalisation and the commitment to promote Western ideals and democracy have been described as a twenty-first-century re-articulation of western dominance founded on a North–South divide originally structured on white hegemony.

Conclusion

The election of Barack Obama will go down in history as a critical juncture in American politics. In short, some analysts believe American foreign policy is in a crisis stemming from the increasing influence of ethnic lobbies bent on securing their narrow interests at the expense of the larger polity. These conservative forces seem to imply that the alleged national interest has never been subject to the narrowly defined interests of a specific group. This is problematic as the existence and persistence of a WASP elite suggest that American foreign policy may have been filtered through the policy directives of a racialised and pro-western WASP elite. In a sense, the current dilemma may reflect a general concern regarding the emergence of non-white ethnic lobbies whose international agendas diverge from the status quo. The advocates of globalisation and American exceptionalism have heralded the exportation of democracy and the West's brand of liberal economics as an irreversible triumph of American civilisation.

Globalisation has increased immigration from the southern to the northern hemisphere which has augmented the presence and participation of ethnic interest groups within America's domestic sphere. In short, the rhetoric of inclusion and the delegitimisation of white supremacy and fluctuating demographics pose serious questions regarding the future character of US foreign policy. If US foreign policy is required to benefit all US citizens, then American elites need to construct an inclusive model of the national interest which extends the boundaries of concern beyond the protection of western democracies. The adherence to western-centred policy preferences belie the increasing need for progressive engagement with the Southern hemisphere and reflect the problems associated with a war on terror overwhelmingly directed at non-Europeans. Brezinsky's championing of Obama spoke to the necessity of America's projection of a more inclusive foreign policy profile. While realists consider that might equals right, global demographics and the relative decline of western power require a new type of foreign policy.

It is disingenuous to assume that the American socio-politic is and has ever been colour-blind. Race is a significant factor in domestic politics. Since domestic politics are arguably determined by a power elite wedded to the core values embedded in American culture, it is reasonable to suggest that foreign policy elites continue to perceive international relations through a racial lens. Although the high profile appointments of Colin Powell and Condoleeza Rice and the Obama phenomenon suggest a withering of WASP privilege, the incorporation of non-WASPS is not wholly progressive as specific individuals are probably selected due to their adherence to the policy preferences of the incumbent elite; and the belief that policy abnormalities will be ironed out during their incorporation. The maintenance of incumbent institutional and ideological frameworks are reflected in the prediction that the successor to George W. Bush will have to maintain the precepts of the Bush administration's foreign policy for a number of years (Parmar 2008: 47). Hence Obama's call for change may have a limited impact on US foreign policy.

If race is a factor in foreign policy and international relations. why have scholars ignored it? First, African-American thinkers have identified the racial aspect of US foreign policy for over a century. However, the marginal position of African-Americans in the academy and the media has limited their ability to propagate their views to mainstream audiences. Second, given academics' tendency to focus on their personal interests, the interests of funding bodies and the academy, the relative absence of non-whites in the academy could affect the subject preferences. Put bluntly, race is an emotive subject which academics, politicians and Americans are inclined to avoid as it undercuts the claims of American democracy. In addition, the neo-conservative rearticulation of the colour-blind society (Winant 2006: 995) has defined African-Americans continued discourse on race as reverse racism. Consequently successful African-Americans (in particular) have been goaded into the avoidance of playing the race card.

During the twentieth century US elites went to great pains to silence African-American activists who violated the taboo of criticising America on foreign soil, while pragmatic foreign policy elites championed the dissolution of Jim Crow in order to silence cold war critics and to win allies in the emerging world. In the aftermath of the identity-based cultural wars championed by African-Americans and the war on terror climate, America is witnessing a twenty-first-century version of ethno-religious and racialised patriotism that threatens to inflame group tensions. These tensions are derived from previous incarnations of race, culture, religion and ethnicity. In brief, the excesses of twentieth-century racism have led to the reframing of racial supremacy in a more acceptable package. For example, Darren Brunk identifies how US elites have an African schema whereby Africa has 'certain meanings for societies and policy makers socialised ... in ... many western societies ... [which includes] ... stories of savage cannibalism, state failure, child soldiers and violent anarchy' (Brunk 2008: 305).

In the final analysis, Brunk points to perceptions about Africa as influencing the decision-making process of US officials regarding Somalia and Rwanda (ibid.: 311) without considering whether race is a factor in US foreign policy towards Africa. Here, despite the distinct echo of racism, America's foreign policy towards Africa seems sufficiently disconnected from its treatment of African-Americans and the deeply engrained racism of the past. Thus, one could be excused for wondering if the West's response to the horrors of Rwanda and Darfur have no connection to previous conceptions of race that placed less value on the lives of people of African descent, whether in Harlem or in Darfur. Indeed, at times. it appears as if centuries of racial practices were successfully eradicated during the racial reforms of the 1960s. Despite the victory of Obama foreign affairs, literature needs to carefully assess to what degree race has influenced or will continue to influence the racial composition of the formal and informal foreign policy establishment and to determine its impact on the character of US foreign policy.

Notes

1 Aside from the post-civil rights era, the short period after the American Civil War has been identified as a highpoint in African-American politics.
2 In the US context, Nativism is associated with reactionary behaviour aimed at preserving Anglo-Saxon hegemony in relation to the control of immigration and the cultural assimilation of immigrant groups.
3 Martin Smith maintains that 'the key feature of pluralism is difference or diversity. The complexity of the modern liberal state means that no single group, class or organisation can dominate society' (Smith 1995: 209).
4 Such as Plummer, *Rising Wind: Black Americans and U.S. Foreign Policy, 1935–1960* (1996); Von Eschen, *Race Against Empire, Black Americans and Anticolonialism, 1937–1957* (1997); Borstelmann, *The Cold War and the Color Line: American Race Relations in the Global Arena* (2003); Layton, *International Politics and Civil Rights Policies in the United States, 1941–1960* (2000); Krenn, *The Color of Empire: Race and American Foreign Relations* (2006); Anderson, *Eyes Off the Prize: The United Nations and the African American Struggle for Human Rights, 1944–1955* (2006).
5 The Jena six refers to a series of incidents in Jena, Louisiana, in 2006 related to racial tensions stemming from white students' hanging of nooses and violent altercations between them and black youths.

References

Anderson, C. (2006) *Eyes Off the Prize: The United Nations and the African American Struggle for Human Rights, 1944–55*, Cambridge: Cambridge University Press.
Asante, K.A. (2007) 'Barack Obama and the Dilemma of Power: An Africological Observation', *Journal of Black Studies*, 38: 105–15.
Asante, M.K. (1995) *African American History: A Journey of Liberation*, Saddle Brook, NJ: The Peoples Publishing Group Inc.
Atwater, D.F. (2007) 'Senator Barack Obama: The Rhetoric of Hope and the American Dream', *Journal of Black Studies*, 38: 121–9.
Barack Obama Official Website (2008) 'Foreign Policy'. Online. Available at: http://www.barackobama.com/issues/foreignpolicy/.
Borstelmann, T. (1993) *Apartheid's Reluctant Uncle: The United States and Southern Africa in the Early Cold War*, Oxford: Oxford University Press.
—— (2003) *The Cold War and the Color Line': American Race Relation in the Global Arena*, Cambridge, MA: Harvard University Press.

Brunk, D.C. (2008) 'Curing the Somalia Syndrome: Analogy, Foreign Policy Decision Making, and the Rwandan Genocide', *Foreign Policy Analysis*, 4: 301–20.

Buchanan, P.J. (2002) *The Death of the West: How Dying Populations and Immigrant Invasions Imperil Our Country and Civilization*, New York: St Martin's Press.

Cameron, F. (2002) *US Foreign Policy after the Cold War: Global Hegemon or Reluctant Sheriff?*, London: Routledge.

Chowdhry, G. and Nair, S. (eds) (2004) *Power, Postcolonialism and International Relations*, London: Routledge.

Clarke, J.H. (ed.) (1974) *Marcus Garvey and the Vision of Africa*. New Jersey: African World Press Inc.

—— (1992) *Notes for an African World Revolution: Africans at the Crossroads*, New Jersey: African World Press Inc.

Cone, J.H. (1993) *Martin and Malcolm and America: A Dream or a Nightmare?*, London: HarperCollins.

Cross, T. (1987) *The Black Power Imperative: Racial Inequality and the Politics of Nonviolence*, New York: Faulkner Books.

Dickson, D.A. (1996) 'American Society and the African American Foreign Policy Lobby: Constraints and Opportunities', *Journal of Black Studies*, 27: 139–51.

Doyle, L. (2008) 'We Are A Better Country Than the Past Eight Years', *The Independent*, 29 August, pp. 4–5.

Dudziak, M.L. (2002) *Cold War Civil Rights: Race and the Image of American Democracy*, Princeton, NJ: Princeton University Press.

Dumbrell, J. (1990) *The Making of US Foreign Policy*, Manchester: Manchester University Press.

Gaines, K.K. (2006) *American Africans in Ghana: Black Expatriates and the Civil Rights Era*, Chapel Hill, NC: University of North Carolina Press.

Glazer, N. and Moynihan, D.P. (1975) *Ethnicity: Theory and Experience*, Cambridge, MA: Harvard University Press.

Hacker, A. (1992) *Two Nations: Black and White, Separate, Hostile, Unequal*, New York: Macmillan.

Harris Jr., R. (1991) 'Racial Equality and the United Nations Charter', in A.L. Robinson and P. Sullivan (eds) *New Directions in Civil Rights Studies*, London: University Press of Virginia, pp. 126–45.

Higham, J. (2002) *Strangers in the Land*, London: Rutgers University Press.

Horne, G. (1999) 'Race from Power: U.S. Foreign Policy and the General Crisis of "White Supremacy"', *Diplomatic History*, 23: 437–60.

The Huffington Post (2008) 'Bill O'Reilly Apologizes for Michelle Obama "Lynching" Remark'. Online. Available at: http://www.huffingtonpost.com/2008/02/22/bill-oreilly-apologizes-n_87949.html?page=4.

Hunt, M.H. (1987) *Ideology and U. S. Foreign Policy*, New Haven, CT: Yale University Press.

Huntington, S.P. (2004) *Who are We?: The Challenges to America's National Identity*, New York: Simon & Schuster.

Jentleson, B.W. (2007) *American Foreign Policy*, New York: W. W. Norton & Company Inc.

Jones, G.B. (ed.) (2006) *Decolonizing International Relations*, Plymouth, NH: Rowman and Littlefield Publishers Inc.

—— (2008) 'Race in the Ontology of International Order', *Political Studies*, 56(4): 907–27.

Joseph, P.E. (2006) *Waiting 'til the Midnight Hour: A Narrative History of Black Power in America*, New York: Henry Holt and Company.

Katz, R.S. (2007) *Political Institutions in the United States*, Oxford: Oxford University Press.

King, D. (1997) *Separate and Unequal*, Oxford: Clarendon Press.

Kirk, J.A. (2008) 'Indian-Americans and the U.S. – India Nuclear Agreement: Consolidation of an Ethnic Lobby?', *Foreign Policy Analysis*, 4: 275–300.

Kornweibel Jr., T.J.R. (1998) *'Seeing Red' Federal Campaigns Against Black Militancy, 1919–1925*, Indianapolis: Indiana University Press.

Kotkin, J. (1992) *Tribes: How Race, Religion and Identity Determine Success in the New York Global Economy*, New York: Random House.

Krenn, M.L. (2006) *The Color of Empire: Race and American Foreign Relations*, Washington, DC: Potomac Books.

Krishna, S. (2006) 'Race, Amnesia, and the Education of International Relations', in G.J. Jones (ed.) *Decolonizing International Relations*, Plymouth, NH: Rowman & Littlefield Publishers, pp. 89–108.

Lauren, P.G. (1996) *Power and Prejudice: The Politics and Diplomacy of Racial Discrimination*, Boulder, CO: Westview Press.

Layton, A.S. (2000) *International Politics and Civil Rights Policies in the United* States *1941–60*, Cambridge: Cambridge University Press.

Ledwidge, M. (2006) 'Race, African-Americans and U.S. Foreign Policy', PhD, Department of Politics, University of Manchester.

—— (forthcoming) *Race and US Foreign Policy*, London: Routledge.

Lewis, D.L. (2000) *W.E.B. Du Bois: The Fight for Equality and the American Century, 1919–63*, New York: Henry Holt and Company.

Lipset, S.M. (1996) *American Exceptionalism: A Double-Edged Sword*, London: W. W. Norton & Company.

Logan, R.W. (1997) *The Betrayal of the Negro: From Rutherford B. Hayes to Woodrow Wilson*, New York: Da Capo Press.

Mazama, A. (2007) 'The Barack Obama Phenomenon', *Journal of Black Studies*, 38: 3–6.

McCrisken, T.B. (2007) 'No More Vietnams: Iraq and the Analogy Conundrum', in D. Ryan and J. Dumbrell (eds) *Vietnam in Iraq: Tactics, Lessons, Legacies and Ghosts*, London: Routledge, pp .159–78.

Mearsheimer, J.J. and Walt, S.M. (2007) *The Israel Lobby and US Foreign Policy*, London: Penguin Books.

Meernik, J. and Oldmixon, E. (2008) 'The President, the Senate, and the Costs of Internationalism', *Foreign Policy Analysis*, 4(2): 187–206.

Meriwether, J.H. (2002) *Proudly We Can Be Africans*, London: University of North Carolina Press.

Mills, C.W. (2000) *The Power Elite*, New York: Oxford University Press.

MSNBC (2007) 'Brzezinski on Obama'. Online. Available at: http://firstread.msnbc.msn.com/archive/2007/09/12/358475.aspx.

Muhammad, D. (2008) '40 Years Later: The Unrealized American Dream', *Institute for Policy Studies*, 4–18.

New York Times (2006) 'The Pattern May Change, if … '. Online. Available at: http://www.nytimes.com/2006/12/10/weekinreview/10nagourney.html.

—— (2008) 'Bush Speech Criticized as Attack on Obama'. Online. Available at: http://www.nytimes.com/2008/05/16/world/middleeast/16prexy.html?hp.

Normington, P.M. (1996) 'The Struggle to Establish an African American Lobby on Foreign Policy for Africa and the Caribbean: From Ethiopia to Haiti', MA thesis, Department of American Studies, University of Manchester.

Obama, B. (2004) *Dreams from My Father: A Story of Race and Inheritance*, New York: Three Rivers Press.

Oliver, M.L. and Shapiro, T.M. (1995) *Black Wealth/White Wealth*, New York: Routledge.

Omi, M. and Winant, H. (1994) *Racial Formation in the United States from the 1960s to 1990s*, London: Routledge.

Parmar, I. (2004) 'Another Important Group That Needs More Cultivation': The Council on Foreign Relations and the Mobilization of Black Americans for Interventionism, 1939–41', *Ethnic and Racial Studies*, 27: 710–31.

—— (2008) 'Not Neo-Conservatism But Conservative Nationalism and Liberal Interventionism: The New Alliance Dominating the US Foreign Policy Establishment: 1–41. Centre for International Politics Working Paper Series No. 36, October 2007.

Persaud, R.B. (2004) 'Situating Race in International Relations: The Dialectics of Civilizational Security in American Immigration', in G. Chowdhry and S. Nair (eds) *Power Postcolonialism and International Relations: Reading Race, Gender and Class*, London: Routledge, pp. 56–81.

Pinkney, A. (1976) *Red, Black, and Green*, Cambridge: Cambridge University Press.

Plummer, B.G. (1996) *Rising Wind: Black Americans and U.S. Foreign Affairs, 1935–1960*, London: The University of North Carolina Press.

Rubenzer, T. (2008) 'Ethnic Minority Interest Group Attributes and U.S. Foreign Policy Influence: A Qualitative Comparative Analysis', *Foreign Policy Analysis*, 4: 169–85.

Sales Jr., W.W. (1994) *From Civil Rights to Black Liberation: Malcolm X and the Organization of Afro-American Unity*, Boston, MA: South End Press.

Scott, W.R. (1993) *The Sons of Sheba's Race: African-Americans and the Italo-Ethiopian War, 1935-1941*, Bloomington, IN: Indiana University Press.

Shain, Y. (1994–95) 'Ethnic Diasporas and U.S. Foreign Policy', *Political Science Quarterly*, 109(5) (Winter, 1994–1995): 811–41.

Singh, R. (1998) *Congressional Black Caucus: Racial Politics in the U.S. Congress*, London: Sage Publications.

—— (2003) *Governing America: The Politics of a Divided Democracy*, Oxford: Oxford University Press.

Smith, M. (1995) Pluralism', in D. Marsh and G. Stoker (eds) *Theory and Methods in Political Science*, New York: Palgrave, pp. 209–27.

Stoddard, L. and Grant, M. (1922) *The Rising Tide of Color against White World-Supremacy*, New York: Charles Scribner's Sons.

The Week (2008) 'A Racial Challenge: Can Obama Get Past His Fiery Preacher?', 354, p. 6.

Times Online (2007) 'Obama "Was Educated in Madrassa"'. Online. Available at: http://www.timesonline.co.uk/tol/news/world/us_and_americas/article1294780.ece.

Von Eschen, P.M. (1997) *Race against Empire: Black Americans and Anticolonialism, 1937–57*, London: Cornell University Press.

Walters, R. (2007) 'Barack Obama and the Politics of Blackness', *Journal of Black Studies*, 38: 7.

Washington Post (2008) 'Obama's Farrakhan Test'. Online. Available at: www.washingtonpost.com/wp-dyn/content/article/2008/01/14/AR2008011402083.html.

Wellman, D.T. (1977) *Portraits of White Racism*, New York: Cambridge University Press.

Winant, H. (2006) 'Race and Racism: Towards a Global Future', *Ethnic and Racial Studies*, 29: 986–1003.

Part III
New policy directions

12 Transatlantic relations and US foreign policy

David Hastings Dunn

Structure and agency in transatlantic relations

George W. Bush's tenure will long be remembered as one of the most tumultuous in transatlantic relations. Never before in the post-war period had the Atlantic community been so comprehensively split and so actively opposed diplomatically as they were over the US-led invasion of Iraq in 2003. What impact the Bush administration's policies have had and what legacy they leave behind for his successor pose a series of questions for the analyst of US foreign policy. Not least of these is the extent to which his successor will be constrained by the problems and commitments which Bush left behind. While the retirement of Bush and his senior advisors in January 2009 marked a distinct end point to his administration, the opportunity for a fresh start for his successor will be severely limited by American commitments in Afghanistan and Iraq, and ongoing challenges in dealing with Iran, North Korea and the Middle East Peace Process. While both contenders to replace him championed 'change' as their themes, how much change it will be possible to deliver in the years to come in many policy areas remains to be seen. That potential for change in part depends on how much scope there is for 'agency' in the 'structure–agency' debate. This is a question with particular relevance for the new administration in dealing with the foreign policy issues which America faces in the new term. It is also one, however, which has particular relevance for the question of transatlantic relations and as such it provides a good case study of this analytical approach. This is the case because there has been much speculation since the low point of 2003 as to how much relations across the Atlantic between the USA and its erstwhile European opponents have improved. While 2003 marked the low point, relations were strained across the Atlantic before this, due to disagreement over climate change, the ABM Treaty, the International Criminal Court, the CTBT and a whole host of other issues. These issues provided the backdrop to the diplomatic confrontations which occurred in the run-up to the invasion of Iraq. Since then, however, and particularly in the past two years, there has been a marked improvement in the tone of the transatlantic dialogue. How much of this is superficial and how much of it is substantive remains the subject of debate. A related question is how much of it is due to changes in the political actors on both sides of the Atlantic and how much their actions have managed to transcend structural changes in relations. In other words, how much has agency changed and rejuvenated transatlantic relations and how much have these changes in political actor mitigated the structural factors that others see as sources of divergence between Europe and America?

To Iraq and back? The nature of the dispute

The current debate over how much was permanently changed in transatlantic relations and how much has been restored subsequent to the Iraq episode must be set in historical context. Historically transatlantic relations have been marked by a series of crises with each successive episode being presented as uniquely different from the previous crisis in this troubled relationship. Michael Howard, referring to this long and troubled history remarked that the relationship was like a 'successful but unhappy marriage' (Howard 1999). The point being that it was somehow inevitable that this odd couple should and would be together but that did not mean that they were always entirely happy about the relationship. This of course does not foreclose the possibility that any new crisis could be the straw that broke the camel's back. And for many observers the depth and nature of the transatlantic dispute over Iraq signified just that, something quite different from previous disputes and therefore a radical departure from this traditional way of thinking about this relationship. For some, it represented the 'tipping point' in a relationship that was already badly fractured in the wake of diverging trends since the end of the Cold War (Daalder 2003; Cox 2005: 210). For this school of thought, Iraq demonstrated that within the transatlantic relationship at least two conceptions of what the alliance meant were in operation. For the Bush administration and its allies the existence of the alliance ought to have ensured European support for America's intervention in Iraq. The failure of many NATO allies to actively support the war and the efforts of some to politically oppose it was seen as disloyalty to the point of betrayal of both the United States as leader of that alliance and of the transatlantic spirit more broadly. For the opponents of this view, Atlanticism had an entirely different meaning. For this school, the transatlantic relationship was premised less on a notion of follow my leader than on a set of shared rules and values, among them being a recognition of the importance of the institutions of the international system including the United Nations, international law and collective decision-making among the major transatlantic powers over matters that materially affected all their interests and security and indeed the stability of the international system as a whole. In a sense, the crisis of Iraq was only a failed attempt by France and Germany to do what America did to France and Britain in 1956 over the Suez Crisis in similar circumstances, and it is only different if you have an unequal view of what the alliance and transatlanticism is more broadly. Thus those critical of the USA over Iraq are also inclined to be critical over the way that America has reacted over criticisms over Iraq.

What the conflict in Iraq did, according to many observers, was to illustrate starkly these two conceptions of what transatlanticism was supposed to represent. From both perspectives the split over the invasion of Iraq was seen as an infidelity from the spirit of transatlanticism which could not easily be forgiven or forgotten by either side because of what that infidelity was seen to represent. Like most extra-marital dalliances while the act itself (the invasion/political opposition to the invasion) was seen as repulsive, more damaging still was what this was seen to represent of how one viewed the other. The relationship between Europe and America has historically operated like the traditional 1940s marriage that it was, not only in terms of its division of labour but also to the fidelity of the ideas which the relationship enshrined. Historically it was like a courtly marriage, a political deal conducted with affection rather than love for mutual benefit. For its critics, however, Iraq has brought into question the basis of that political deal.

For others, however, there is a danger in extrapolating too much from this single event. For these observers, while Iraq demonstrates considerable differences, the overall trend is one of convergence of interests in the context of an external threat rather than divergence of the modalities of dealing with it. Such observers are keen to remind us that on 12 September 2001 the French newspapers declared 'we are all Americans now' and NATO followed this with its historic declaration that the terrorist attacks represented an Article 5 violation, and therefore 'an attack on one is as an attack on all'. The mood then was one of unprecedented unity and solidarity. Modernity was under attack and 'the West' responded with appropriate unity and support. As Gordon and Shapiro note:

> In a twist that few could have predicted before September 11, within a month America was conducting a major war halfway around the world, and the biggest problem for the European allies was that they wanted to send more troops than Washington was prepared to accept.
>
> (Gordon and Shapiro 2004: 1–2)

Nor was disagreement over Iraq on the scale that developed an inevitability, it is argued. Many alternative outcomes were possibly not as damaging to transatlantic relations as the events that followed. 'Iraq was in many ways the perfect storm; there is no reason to believe that the crisis it provoked will be anything like the norm in transatlantic relations' (ibid.: 6). In this respect, a degree of caution is necessary least the mistake is repeated from 1991 when the first war against Iraq was widely interpreted as setting a new pattern for international relations. For the clash of the magnitude that occurred 'resulted not just from structural trends, but also from a strong degree of contingency, personality, misguided diplomacy, poor leadership, Iraqi unpredictability, and bad luck' (ibid.: 8). And it is not difficult to imagine circumstances when either all the Europeans would have supported and contributed to military action or that full Iraqi compliance demonstrating lack of WMD would have prevented American action. James Rubin makes a related point, that if the Bush administration had waited just a few months, 'it would have been Iraqi non-compliance and not spurious claims about an Iraqi threat that would have triggered the war', and as a result 'many more countries would have been willing to contribute substantial troops and substantial reconstruction assistance if such international legitimacy had been obtained' (Rubin, cited by Cox 2005: 27). For Rubin, though this of course was part of the message that Bush was sending by the way he prosecuted the war. Colin Powell, his Secretary of State, did not tour the world drumming up support in the way that James Baker had done a decade earlier. Bush himself stayed off the long distance phone line. America was making the point that it was willing and able to act in its own defence in the way it defined it without having to ask anyone's permission. Although the Bush administration has stepped back from this approach somewhat in its second term, the legacy of this episode lingers and therefore what the final consequence of this approach will have on the future of transatlantic relations remains hotly contested.

Atlantica restored?

Despite the depth of the crisis between the USA and Europe culminating in the invasion of Iraq in 2003, there has been much debate since then as to how much relations across the Atlantic have improved or even recovered. In his farewell tour of Europe in 2008, Bush was even able to utter, without any hint of apparent irony, that 'When the time comes to welcome the new American President next January, I will be pleased to report that the relationship between the United States and Europe is the most vibrant it has ever been' (Baldwin and Bremmer 2008). To the extent that this is true, it has largely been attributed to changes in political actors at the elite level on both sides of the Atlantic: to changes in agency as the instigators of new policy and in mitigation of diverging structural trends. In the second Bush term, these changes have been attributed in part to the elevation of Condoleezza Rice to Secretary of State and the accompanying reduction in role for the combative Vice-President Dick Cheney. Along with these changes came a series of replacement appointments in the top echelon of foreign policy advisors. In came Robert Zoellick, Robert Kimmitt and Robert Gates and out went Donald Rumsfeld, John Bolton, Paul Wolfowitz and Douglas Feith, personalities most associated with the failed ideological approach of the first term (Kupchan 2008: 139). The neo-conservative hubris which saw American primacy without limit and which culminated in the invasion of Iraq, had, by the second term, it was argued, run aground on the rocks of its own over-ambition. The Bush Doctrine, which had been presented as a policy for widespread application, was thwarted by the multiple failures of the policy in Iraq.[1]

Transatlantic relations and therefore US foreign policy towards its principal European allies have also undergone a remarkable turnaround largely as a result of changes in leadership on the Continent. Initially this trend exacerbated the tensions across the Atlantic with those leaders who had supported Bush's Iraq policy losing the confidence of their populations. Thus, José Maria Aznar of Spain and Silvio Berlusconi of Italy lost office to their opposition rivals in elections while Tony Blair lost the confidence of his party and the British population and was eventually replaced as Prime Minister. By contrast, however, elections in France and Germany brought in two new leaders who were much more Atlanticist in their outlook. The departure from the political scene of President Chirac of France and Chancellor Schroder of Germany, the principal opponents of the Iraq War and everything it represented, removed a considerable obstacle to better transatlantic relations. That they were replaced by leaders in the form of President Sarkozy and Chancellor Merkel, elected despite their intentions to improve relations with America, was a further boost to better relations. Berlusconi's re-election in April 2008 reinforced this trend.

Sarkozy's election in particular has been a major boost to the tone of relations across the Atlantic. With his easy *bon ami* and accommodating rhetoric, Sarkozy has quickly become the 'new Blair' in American affections (Ghannoushi 2007). As a result, in his farewell tour of Europe, Bush used the French capital to deliver the centrepiece speech of the tour – calling France 'America's first friend' (bbc.co.uk 15 June 2008). For Washington, according to a US diplomat, Sarkozy is now 'the axis on which our relations with Europe will turn' (ibid.). Rather different from the 'axis of weasel' of 2003. For France too, 'the frost is over', according to an Elysée Palace spokesman, 'We want to show the warmth that now exists between the two countries after the friction of the recent past' (ibid.). In a similar way, the new German Chancellor has demonstrated her credentials in transatlantic relations as far as Washington is concerned by showing her ability to 'identify problems, take initiatives, craft agreements other countries can support, and then turn to the US for the contribution needed to close or enforce the deal' (Schake 2007: 2). Berlusconi's re-election reinforces this trend. The only exception to this rule is the rather curious position of the UK government under Gordon Brown which has taken steps to distance itself from Washington in a number of ways in a rather belated reaction to the excesses of the Bush administration in its first term, on the apparent assumption that it can simultaneously signal its disapproval of the Bush administration while remaining pro-American (Dunn 2008). Although personal relations have cooled at the highest level between the UK and USA, however, on substantive policy issues the UK remains firmly Atlanticist and is the most robust supporter in material terms to American operations in Iraq and NATO and US operations in Afghanistan. Indeed, in terms of the structure–agency debate, although counter to the prevailing trend, the actions of the Brown government reinforce the argument that transatlantic relations are susceptible to the influence of changes in agency as far as the dynamics between the leaders are concerned while the underling structural components of their bilateral relationships remain largely unaffected.

Recent improvements in transatlantic relations have not only been evident at the level of leadership atmospherics, however. There have been real improvements on substantial issues as well as in the mood music. On the American side, the combination of the failure of US policy in Iraq and the subsequent embroilment of the US Army in a major counter-insurgency war there meant that the anticipated extension of the Bush Doctrine to other 'rogue' states has not materialised. Instead a more nuanced form of diplomacy has been adopted in the second term with the USA supporting the EU-led diplomacy towards Iran and the six party talks towards North Korea. A similar consensual approach has been achieved in European and American efforts towards the restoration of the Middle East peace process between Israel and Palestine and the emerging statehood of Kosovo (Kupchan 2008: 139). Despite initial inclinations to the contrary, Europe and America have also maintained a common approach towards the prohibition of arms sales to China and the non-recognition of Hamas in the Gaza Strip. The Bush administration has also abandoned its position of denial with regard to global climate change and has signed up, along with its European and Asian allies, to global targets for carbon reduction (Revkin 2008). In Afghanistan too, all 24 NATO allies are involved in the alliance's operations against the Taliban in what is for the alliance its first military engagement of any scale and its first military venture outside of Europe (mod.uk 11th July 2008). The Bucharest NATO Summit also made substantial progress, according to NATO's Michael Ruehle, on 'the need to move from a geographical understanding of security to a more functional approach … There is broad agreement on the direction of NATO's military transformation, namely toward expeditionary capabilities for operations beyond Europe' (Ruehle 2008). France has also signalled its intention to move towards a more Atlanticist position. Sarkozy has announced the deployment of a further 750 French troops to Afghanistan and published the first major strategic review of its armed forces in 14 years. Among its recommendations are an increase in defence spending, further professionalization of the Armed Forces and the announcement of the intention to rejoin the integrated military command structure of NATO (Bremmer 2008). America's acceptance of the quid pro quo requested by France, that the US accept a distinct EU security dimension within NATO, also represents new ground in transatlantic relations.

The past two years have also seen a substantial shift in European attitudes on two issues which have long plagued transatlantic relations: the related issues of ballistic missile proliferation – and how much of a threat this constitutes, and the appropriateness of missile defence as a strategy to deal with this. Up until this point the European

NATO allies were reluctant to identify ballistic missile proliferation as an imminent threat to European security; to name the source of that likely threat in a NATO context, or to embrace ballistic missile defence as a strategic response. All these positions have recently shifted, however, and the declaration following the Bucharest NATO Summit in April 2008 signalled a significant shift in position towards the American approach on all three issues, stating that:

> Ballistic missile proliferation poses an increased threat to Allies forces, territory and populations. Missile defence forms part of a broader response to counter this threat. We therefore recognise the substantial contribution to the protection of Allies from long-range ballistic missiles to be provided by the planned deployment of European-based United States missile defence assets. We are exploring ways to link this capacity with current missile defence efforts as a way to ensure that it would be an integral part of any future NATO-wide missile defence architecture.
>
> (nato.org, 3 April 2008)[2]

While the Bucharest Summit failed to reach agreement on the time scale by which Ukraine and Georgia should be invited to apply for NATO membership, even on this issue more progress was made than was expected. Indeed, given the growing number of negotiating partners and issues involved, the 2008 summit represented a significant set of achievements. While differences remain, including those on which agreement has been reached, the level of unanimity on important security issues found among the transatlantic partners was unprecedented, given recent events. Whether this consensus represents a significant repair in transatlantic relations or even a recovery in the underlying trust between the USA and its allies remains hotly contested. Where there is room for agreement is that changes in agency have already been responsible for what improvement in relations have taken place. Whether these improvements can be maintained, embedded and built upon is also subject to debate concerning the impact of the next major change of agency, the swearing in of the 44th president of the United States in 2009.

New US president, new relationship?

Given the widespread unpopularity of President George W. Bush, there is understandably great expectations internationally that the election of a new president will herald the dawn of a new age in transatlantic relations and global politics more broadly. This expectation is fuelled further by the candidacy and prospect of victory of Barack Obama, a politician who has adopted 'change' as the theme of his bid for the White House. And yet the expectations on both sides of the Atlantic are so high that they are almost certain to be disappointed to some degree when it comes to matters of substantive policy. Despite the expectations to the contrary, presidential honeymoons are often nightmares for the European allies, and from both sides the expectations are likely to meet entrenched positions. While the Europeans can expect an end to unconstitutional imprisonment at Guantánamo and special rendition; the abandonment of the phrase 'War on Terror' and a return to serious multilateral negotiations on climate change, on other issues there will be limits to how far the new administration will deviate from the pattern of US foreign policy since 9/11. Furthermore, the 44th president will expect a great deal more international assistance to bring stability to Iraq and Afghanistan than the European allies have hitherto offered. Obama has talked of the need for a 'diplomatic surge' and his expectation is that the major economies will play a central role in financing the reconstruction necessary to allow an American drawdown in both countries, starting off in Iraq (Hass 2008). It is questionable whether the USA would wish to grant a correspondingly larger diplomatic role to the Europeans in return for an increase in investment. The legacy of war in Iraq and Afghanistan and the wider war on terror greatly reduces the room for manoeuvre for the new president and what it is possible to achieve, and yet the expectations of him and his expectations of the allies are likely to be high. In practice, the first Obama administration may look more like the second Bush administration than the first Bush term did to the second. Having said that, during the Bush years, due to the absence of genuine US leadership on issues such as climate change and diplomatic efforts with Iran, Korea and Israel/Palestine, the European allies have over time also established a new role in international negotiations. Re-establishing America's international diplomatic position in this context will not be easy and will require adjustments on all sides. Thus, while there are great expectations of the 44th president for improved relations across the Atlantic due to the change in US leadership – a change in agent – the gap between the expectations and the ability to deliver in policy terms may mean that the relationship remains one characterised by tough negotiations and differences of approach. The new president, however, can expect a great deal of good will to be shown to him simply because of the fact that he is not George W. Bush and thus presents an opportunity through the process of democratic renewal for a fresh start in transatlantic relations. Just how sustained that good will will be, and thus how prolonged the renaissance in transatlantic relations will last, in part depends on the interplay of these aspects of political agency and the wider structural cleavages affecting relations across the Atlantic.

Structural changes in the transatlantic relationship

While most commentators recognise and welcome the improvement in transatlantic relations that has been evident in recent years, others argue that structural changes in the international political system have resulted in patterns of divergence in relations between the USA and Europe of a fundamentally transformative nature. Of these trends, two changes in particular are often identified: (1) those which have taken place in Germany and thus relations with the EU and Europe more broadly; and (2) changes in the foreign policy of the USA itself.

The Berlin Republic

Although provoked by the particular circumstances of the Iraqi crisis itself, the transatlantic dispute of 2003 signalled the operation of something much more profound than the future of Iraq itself. Coming as it did 14 years after the collapse of the Berlin Wall and two years after 9/11, the Iraqi crisis represented the culmination of several long-running processes. Although the French-led opposition to the invasion of Iraq was the most obvious demonstration of the rift within the Atlantic alliance, in some regards this was the least radical policy change of the debacle. President Chirac's opposition to the Bush administration while passing a new milestone in actively trying to thwart the strategic intentions of American foreign policy was at least within the traditions of Paris's historical opposition to what is sees as American hegemony. The same could not be said of the stance adopted by the Federal Republic of Germany. Historically, Germany's role within the transatlantic alliance was central to the linkage between Europe and America. Germany's deference towards Washington in matters of security policy was a balancing counterpart to its partnership with France in the construction of the European project. Germany's reliance on America for security was a restraining influence on European opposition to US foreign policy. As a quid pro quo for this restraint, Washington was always careful to accommodate Germany's concerns in recognition of the importance of the Federal Republic's role within Europe and Europe's role within the Cold War stand-off. With the end of the Cold War, the foundations of this grand bargain were nullified but its effects went unnoticed as a result of the benign international environment of the Clinton years combined with the process of German unification that had absorbed much of Bonn's attentions and resources during the 1990s. Throughout this period, however, at a time when Germany's sense of its new identity was rising, the strategic importance of Germany to the USA, and thus the need to accommodate its concerns, was in decline. Where there was a coincidence of interests such as German participation in the Kosovo campaign in 1999, the structural changes in the nature of this relationship remained dormant. Quite what a turning point for German foreign policy the Kosovo War was, however, was masked by the shared objective of the allied participants. What at the time was seen as a demonstration of transatlantic solidarity, however, was in reality an indication of other forces at work. In fact, the decision to take part in this military action was a marker more of a desire to pursue an independent foreign policy than it was a demonstration of alliance solidarity. Thus when the USA indicated its plans to conduct operations in Afghanistan through coalitions of the willing rather than through NATO; and then promulgated its doctrine of pre-emptive warfare, and applied that to Iraq despite no clear UN mandate to do so, the stage was set for Germany to break ranks with Washington and in so doing to break with its post-war tradition of limited sovereignty expressed as a constrained foreign policy. Thus, as Buras and Longhurst explain, Germany's opposition to the Iraq War was an expression of 'normalisation' which

> [For the] Berlin Republic relates to a changed perception of sovereignty and the licence this gives Germany to pursue a foreign policy line steered by conceptions of German interests ... it was Germany's freedom of action that counted [now] and not the coherence of the Western alliance.
>
> (Buras and Longhurst 2005: 57–8)

The significance of this change for transatlantic relations cannot be overestimated. As Andrews argues, 'from a structural perspective, the key change in post-war European politics is Germany's newfound capacity for policy manoeuvre ... a new era of "permissiveness for Germany" has been ushered in which "represents a fundamental change" in transatlantic relations' (Andrews 2005: 71). This is primarily the case not because of the disagreement over Iraq but because of structural changes in the international system. The Iraqi crisis merely demonstrated that such disagreements were possible and set the 'Schroder precedent' for future repetitions. Absent the previously existing imperative of alliance cohesion, the scope for future disagreements is now considerable since not only have the structural conditions changed but so have the German electorate's awareness of those changes. Thus the German government is much more willing to criticise US policy, as it did in 2007 over Washington's planned deployment of ballistic missile system components in Poland without fully consulting Russia (Dombey 2007). As a result, and rather ironically given the Berlin Republic's newfound willingness to contemplate the use of force beyond the confines of narrowly defined self-defence, the ability of the USA to rely on Germany as an Atlanticist partner in matters of security policy has been diminished as a result of the changes in foreign policy outlook which the Iraq crisis brought to the fore. It is for this reason that the USA has failed to convince Germany to lift the restrictions on the deployment and operations of its forces in Afghanistan despite a sustained effort to do so. In this sense, despite the new mood created by the election of Chancellor Merkel, relations with Europe's largest economy and America's formerly staunchest ally remain in a different place to the Cold War period.

Having fewer cooperative allies also feeds other aspects of the structural changes in transatlantic relations. With the end of the Cold War, the security of Europe assured, America is less interested in Europe as the cockpit of international politics, and the support of European states in its international relations is also correspondingly less vital than it was. It is perhaps these structural changes in US foreign policy in the post-9/11 period which may be most influential to transatlantic relations in the long term.

US foreign policy: the implications of the Bush Doctrine

Despite the end of the Cold War, American foreign policy remained focused on Europe throughout the 1990s due in large part to the politics of NATO and EU enlargement and the Balkan wars. Even during the Clinton administration, however, America's new and distinctive position within the international system began to be expressed through an increased tendency to pursue its interests unilaterally, rather than in concern with its traditional transatlantic allies. Absent the Soviet threat, America increasingly found no continuing need to trim its foreign policy inclinations in light of the sensitivities of its European allies. Alliance harmony was no longer a strategic imperative of the post-Cold War period and thus ceased to be a guiding principle of US foreign policy. Not until the arrival of the Bush administration in 2001, however, did this become abundantly clear to America's transatlantic partners. From the outset, the tone and substance of the new Republican administration marked a distinct contrast with the Clinton administration which it had replaced. Bush's inclination to pursue an 'America first' agenda was accelerated in response to the terrorist attacks of September 2001 and the strategic reassessment that followed, even though solidifying previous trends, was nothing less than revolutionary. Given this long secular trend in US foreign policy towards unipolarity, many analysts remain convinced that what has come to characterise Washington's diplomacy in the post-Cold War world is now a structural feature of the international system (Lynch and Singh 2008).

Advocates of this argument point to the adoption of a new strategic doctrine by the Bush administration and to the fact that in doing so it abandoned the tenets of America's post-war approach to grand strategy. Although it made headlines by its advocacy of pre-emptive military strikes, the new strategic doctrine's implications are much broader and more significant than this. For over 50 years the USA relied on a combination of containment and deterrence as the guiding principle of its geopolitical approach. It was this strategy that successfully won the Cold War and it was this approach that was applied to Iraq after the Gulf conflict in 1991 by successive administrations, including, initially, that of George W. Bush. Containment, however, was a reactive and multilateral strategy that was framed in a period when US power was balanced by a rival superpower. At the start of the twenty-first century the geopolitical position of the USA is very different and it is in these circumstances and in the context of the global war on terrorism, that this new doctrine was forged. America's role in the new system appeared to the Bush administration as unconstrained by the structural constraints that had limited its freedom of action in previous periods. As a result, it adopted policies that could be distinguished from previous US strategies in three important ways: (1) its focus on pre-emption; (2) its hegemonic aspirations; and (3) its unilateralism. While all three elements had an enhanced prominence in the new doctrine, they all had their antecedents in previous policy debates, and for this reason, it is argued, have become entrenched in US policy.

Pre-emption

Although the adoption of a policy that actively espoused pre-emptive military action to remove capabilities or regimes that threaten the USA was a significant change in policy, it was also one which had followed a clear evolutionary path. Throughout the Cold War various attempts were made to break away from the constraints and risks that the containment doctrine involved.[3] In the post-Cold War era, the Clinton administration took a small step towards a pre-emption policy in 1993 with the announcement of the Counter-Proliferation Initiative. As part of this policy development, the Pentagon called for the capability to 'delay, disrupt or deny the deployment of weapons of mass destruction, and to disrupt or destroy the supporting infrastructure for weapons of mass destruction and missile capabilities' (Bowen and Dunn 1996). Importantly, however, this initiative aimed to provide a military capability. It did not propose the elevation of pre-emption to the forefront of US foreign policy as a declaratory strategy (Bush 2002: 6).[4]

The rationale of the new policy was the perceived inability to deter the new type of adversary. 'In the Cold War', the National Security Strategy (NSS) (2002) states, 'weapons of mass destruction were considered weapons of last resort whose use risked the destruction of those who used them. Today, our enemies see weapons of mass destruction as weapons of choice', with the result that

> [The] United States can no longer solely rely on a reactive posture as we have in the past. The inability to deter a potential attacker, the immediacy of today's threats, and the magnitude of potential harm that could be caused by our adversaries' choice of weapons, do not permit that option. We cannot let our enemies strike first.
>
> (ibid.)

The way in which the USA viewed its own nuclear weapons was also revised in light of this new doctrine; the Nuclear Posture Review added 'rogue' states to the list of potential targets and removed the pledge not to attack non-nuclear states.

Support for pre-emption was bolstered by the successful use of military force in both Afghanistan and Kosovo. For Washington, these missions developed 'a profound optimism that we can do it – we can invade a country halfway round the world and bring about a reasonable settlement' (Baker 2003: 1–3). It was also a strategy that was developed with a target state in mind: Iraq. It was partly in that context that the strategy was initially judged favourably by members of Congress and the public alike. For many observers, however, there remained serious concerns about its implications both in general terms and with regard to Iraq in particular. For many of the European allies, this policy also raised concerns with regard to the wider implications of the strategy and the distance that it created between them. If pre-emption was legitimate for the USA, then why not for India against Pakistan, or vice versa, or Israel against Iran or any other number of possible scenarios? Concern was also expressed as to the limits of this policy. If Iraq followed on from Afghanistan, then which state would be next after Iraq, and where would the policy end, given Washington's long list of 'rogue' states? The development of this strategy posed a serious problem for the continuity of transatlantic relations as they had previously been understood. While Operation Allied Force – the Kosovo War of 1999 – had provided a multilateral model of intervention in the post-Cold War period, the new operations marked a distinct and deliberate rejection of this model. As a result, and despite the recent improvement in relations, many European allies remain opposed to pre-emption and the unilateral use of force as a strategic doctrine and see little prospect of the USA renouncing its shift to this new strategic outlook in the new strategic environment.

Pre-eminence

Though less widely reported, an equally important aspect of the new Bush doctrine was its statement that the USA would not permit any state to close the military lead that it established after the collapse of the USSR. 'Our forces will be strong enough to dissuade potential adversaries from pursuing a military build-up in the hope of surpassing or equalling, the power of the USA.' Given that US military spending accounts for 40 per cent of global military expenditure, more than the next 20 largest spenders combined, as a statement of fact, this was unremarkable. As a political aspiration, however, it illustrates how the USA viewed the world and its place in it. As a policy statement, it had much in common with the 1992 Defence Planning Guidance Document, known as the 'No Rivals' draft which declared, 'Our first objective is to prevent the re-emergence of a new rival ... Our strategy must now refocus on precluding the emergence of any potential future competitor' (Hass 1997: 53). This document was dismissed at the time as unworkable, unaffordable and unsupportable. To the Bush administration, however, these objectives seemed manageable. It is for this reason that NSS 2002 sets out a world role that is proactive in its advocacy of what it called

> a distinctly American internationalism that reflects the union of our values and our interests. The aim of this strategy is to help make the world not just safer but better. Our goals on the path to progress are clear: political and economic freedom, peaceful relations with other states, and respect for human rights.

It is a strategy that commits the USA to champion free markets, free trade, democracy and human rights. The mechanisms it identified for this purpose are supportive allies, increased but conditional foreign aid and unrestrained military might. More specifically, it pledges to 'defend the peace by fighting terrorists and tyrants ... preserve the peace by building good relations with friends and allies ... [and] extend the peace by encouraging free and open societies on every continent'. The universalism of this last point marks a deliberate departure from previous US policy, especially in relation to the Middle East. This point was reinforced by a further pledge to support 'modern and moderate governments, especially in the Muslim world'. In doing this, the administration was signalling its plans for the democratic transformation of the Middle East, demonstrating the potentially far-reaching implications of this new strategy. For many European states, this aspect of the strategy is both wildly optimistic in its outlook and provocative to many states and regimes in the region. It is also seen as unnecessarily provocative to China as the rising world power in the international system.

Unilateralism

The third and related aspect of the new strategy was its insistence that 'While the United States will constantly strive to enlist the support of the international community, we will not hesitate to act alone, if necessary, to exercise our right of self defense.' In many respects, this has been the most troubling aspect of US foreign policy, particularly in the post-9/11 environment. Nor have recent episodes of more multilateral international engagements entirely convinced many observers that this aspect of US foreign policy has been reversed. America's opposition to the International Criminal Court, to the 'Ottawa Declarations', the recent ban on Cluster Weapons and the Biological Weapons (and Toxins) Convention show no sign of being reversed by the next president. Even the US's recent acceptance of the need to address climate change has not resulted in any actions or policy.

Indeed, in the post-9/11 environment, America's perception of external threat has so strengthened its willingness to use its unique position of power within the international system to solve its problems unilaterally that it is difficult for many observers to imagine any new leader reversing this shift in approach. To be fair to the Bush administration, it has always insisted that it has acted multilaterally, but where it did act in concert with its allies, it was clear that this 'multilateralism' coincided with the US agenda. While President Obama has talked of the need for inclusive diplomacy with America's major allies, he has also talked about the need for a return of American leadership on the world's stage. Whether the rest of the world is willing to follow a new period of American leadership after eight years of President Bush, remains open to question.

Transatlantic consequences

The effects of the structural changes in the international system brought about the end of the Cold War which mostly lay latent and suppressed throughout 1990s have now become the subject of political as well as academic discourse. Major events such as the end of the Cold War, German unification, 9/11, the reaction to the terrorist attacks and the formalisation of that reaction in the National Security Strategy of the United States and the invasion of Iraq, have now brought into question both the basis and the continued operation of the transatlantic community, as it had previously been conceived. For many European observers, the policies and positions adopted by the Bush administration were the culmination of a series of trends in American foreign and security policy which had been present but repressed throughout the Cold War period and latent but contained throughout the 1990s. The triumphalism of the National Security Strategy Document and the strategic aspirations which it advanced and the worldview that this betrayed seemed to represent for many European observers a significant point of departure from what was previously considered to be the basis on which the transatlantic relationship was based. To many Europeans, their conception of transatlanticism was the pulling together of sovereign powers towards common goals in support and furtherance of their common values. It was this set of ideas that they had taken forward with the construction of the EU. As far as the USA appeared to many Europeans, however, Washington was more concerned about geopolitical hegemony expressed as American leadership of political and cultural modernity. So rather than being allies and co-authors of a common future, many European observers now saw themselves through the eyes of the Bush administration as being either supporting acts to this new American strategic project or else largely irrelevant in the new power structure.

The primary response to these developments at a strategic level was for the EU to draft a security strategy document of its own. In this document, 'A Secure Europe in a Better World', drafted by Javier Solana, the European Union's High Representative for Foreign Affairs, the EU offers a reposte to the US strategy statement in a number of ways (Solana 2003). Most immediately it widened the horizons of European security concerns by recognising that Europe's security interest and the threats which are posed to them are global rather than purely regional in their nature. It also set out three pillars of the common strategy. The first pillar called for the extension of the security zone around Europe and recognised the strategic priority of bringing stability to areas on the continent's periphery. The second pillar concerned the mechanics of global governance and called for the reaffirmation of the United Nations as the principal institution of international security. And, third, the EU called for new policies to respond to the twin threats of terrorism and WMD proliferation (see Spear 2003). The main differences between the American and European strategy papers were the complete absence in the latter of any discussion of military pre-emption and the repeated calls to strengthen both international law and the institutions and norms of international order (Asmus 2006: 24). While agreeing more or less on the nature of the security threats presented in the post-9/11 environment, there were significant differences remaining over the appropriate means. The differences in response in the two documents reflects the divide in American and European approaches to questions of global governance: for the Europeans: 'multilateralism was preferred to unilateralism, pragmatism to ideology, root causes prioritised over symptoms, diplomacy over military force, the long term over the short term, the known over the unknown, caution preferred to risk' (Howorth 2006: 30). Perhaps the most important aspect of the European Security Strategy document, however, was that it was written at all. That this was the case is indicative of the fact that the Europeanisation process has been spurred on by the Iraq crisis itself. The lessons learned from the division in Europe over the Iraq crisis which left the Continent's response to Washington divided and ineffective, was that such a division within Europe is best avoided in the future and that the best way for this to be achieved is through the development of common European approaches to foreign and security policy issues. In its diplomacy both towards Iran and North Korea (through the six party talks), the EU has also demonstrated in the years since a consistent ability to act in a coherent and effective manner on the international stage. That this also achieved a better relationship with America in Bush's second term does not detract from the fact that its prime motivation is not to be on the wrong side of American foreign policy decisions unilaterally decided upon. That the Lisbon Treaty is currently stalled due to the Irish referendum in 2008 does not detract from the fact that there remains significant momentum towards the EU developing more competence as an institution in the realm of foreign and security policy.

Conclusion

Transatlantic relations have improved significantly in the second half of this decade in large part as a result of a concerted effort to do so on both sides of the Atlantic. The Iraq crisis of 2003 presented a glimpse of a world in which the West was split and the transatlantic community was divided against itself in a state of political stalemate. It was an unappealing vision and one which new leadership on both sides of the Atlantic have strenuously sought to avoid in their subsequent international relations. In their diplomacy since then over Iran, North Korea, the Middle East and also Afghanistan and Iraq, the transatlantic allies have shown the positive benefits of working together rather than the pitfalls and paralysis of oppositional politics. How much of this can be attributed to changes of agency, new leaders with new policies, and how much it reflects the cyclical pattern of transatlantic relations where structural tensions rise to crisis point before being mitigated, remain open to question. Although changes in both Germany and in the EU itself as an international actor had significant and novel structural effects on the international system affecting the operation of the traditional pattern of relations across the Atlantic, it is changes in the USA itself and the subsequent effect on its relations with its European allies that perhaps present the biggest challenge to the continued conception of transatlantic relations in the twenty-first century. Shifts in the structure of world politics with the end of the Cold War have undoubtedly changed the context of transatlantic relations but how fundamentally these affect the ability of Europe and America to work in concert to deal with the new challenges which this new environment presents is in large part dependent on the nature of changes within the USA itself. If the policies practised by the Bush administration as spelled out in its National Security Strategy document such as pre-emptive warfare, unilateralism and the quest for hegemony represent structural shifts in the conduct of US foreign policy, as a result of the lack of constraint on US actions after the Cold War, and these tendencies are manifested in the administrations which follow that of George W. Bush, it is very difficult to see how transatlantic relations can operate on anything like the basis on which they existed for the 60 years of the post-war period.

On the other hand, if the 'neo-imperial moment' of the Bush administration has passed its zenith and more multilateral and nuanced policies can be expected to emanate from Washington, then the scope for recovery in transatlantic relations remains a possibility. For many Europeans, however, the experience of the Bush administration will not be easily or quickly forgotten. For most of the post-war period the USA has been viewed as standing for liberty, democracy and the rule of law and universal goals over narrow self-interest. During the Bush years, however, America as seen from Europe has exported more fear than hope, prioritised security over liberty, cynically sidestepped its own Constitution and rights, and placed its own conception of its national interests over international law, norms of behaviour and the future of the planet's environmental wellbeing. Rebuilding its image and trust will take time. Whether its new leaders are able to repair transatlantic relations will be an interesting test of the 'structure–agency debate'. There are clearly now many pressures on the USA and on the European allies to act in different ways than the priorities dictated by the Cold

War. Whether and to what extent political agency can mitigate the effects of those pressures will ultimately determine the future of transatlantic relations in the decades to come.

Notes

1 The most immediate impediment to the further application of this strategy was the failure to discover the WMD on which the case for the immediate invasion of Iraq was justified. The lack of any evidence of nuclear, chemical or biological weapons or even of any ongoing programmes to produce them was widely seen as undermining the American case for war. What was true for the worst-case assumptions was also true for the best-case analysis. While the Iraqis might have been glad to be rid of Saddam Hussein, they were not impressed with the inability of the American occupiers to provide security, civil amenities and a semblance of order. The faulty assumptions on which Operation Iraq Freedom was built and justified were a setback for the Bush administration in both practice and in principle.
2 It continues:

> We remain deeply concerned about the proliferation risks of the Iranian nuclear and ballistic missile programmes. We call on Iran to fully comply with UNSCRs 1696, 1737, 1747 and 1803. We are also deeply concerned by the proliferation activities of the Democratic People's Republic of Korea and call on it to fully comply with UNSCR 1718. Allies reaffirm their support for existing multi-lateral non-proliferation agreements, such as the Nuclear Non-Proliferation Treaty, and call for universal compliance with the Nuclear Non-Proliferation Treaty and universal adherence to the Additional Protocol to the International Atomic Energy Agency (IAEA) Safeguard Agreement.

See the text of the Bucharest Summit Declaration at: http://www.nato.int/docu/pr/2008/p08-049e.html.
3 In 1954, President Eisenhower announced his 'Rollback Doctrine' (which sought to 'roll back' the 'Iron Curtain', that is, overthrow communist regimes in Eastern Europe), only to abandon Hungary to its fate in 1956 when that country put this policy to the test. Faced with the risk of confrontation with the USSR, which had invaded Hungary, the Eisenhower Administration reverted to the safety and security of containment. In the 1980s, the Reagan administration sought in its nuclear policies options pre-emptive contingencies for fighting a limited nuclear war with the Soviet Union. Similarly Reagan's enthusiasm for both his Strategic Defense Initiative and, later, for radical arms control proposals, reflected his desire to escape US reliance on nuclear deterrence. Despite his support for these policies, however, deterrence remained US strategy.
4 Interestingly, the adoption of the pre-emption strategy was not the immediate response of the Bush administration to the September 2001 terrorist attacks. In his Congressional address on 20 September 2001, President Bush declared that the new grand purpose for US policy was 'ending terrorism'. The switch to preventing the accumulation of weapons of mass destruction 'in the hands of irresponsible states' was a policy developed gradually during 2002 (Lemann 2002). See also David Hastings Dunn, (2005).

References

Andrews, David M. (2005) 'The United States and its Atlantic Partners', in David M. Andrews (ed.) *The Transatlantic Alliance Under Stress: US-European Relations after Iraq*, Cambridge: Cambridge University Press.

Anon (2008a) 'Bush Compliments Sakozy's Wife', 15 June. Online. Available at: http://news.bbc.co.uk/1/hi/world/europe/7455156.stm.

—— (2008b) 'Defence Secretary makes Washington speech', 11 July. Online. Available at: http://www.mod.uk/DefenceInternet/DefenceNews/DefencePolicyAndBusiness/DefenceSecretaryMakesWashingtonSpeech.htm.

Asmus, Ronald (2006) 'The European Security Strategy: An American View', in Roland Dannreuther and John Peterson (eds) *Security Strategy and Transatlantic Relations*, Abingdon: Routledge.

Baker, Gerard (2003) 'Missing in Action', *Financial Times*, 31 January.

Baldwin, Tom and Bremmer, Charles (2008) 'After Years of the Special Relationship, is France America's New Best Friend?', *The Times*, 14 June.

Bowen, Wyn and Dunn, David Hastings (1996) *American Security Policy in the 1990s: Beyond Containment*, Aldershot: Ashgate.

Bremmer, Charles (2008) 'Sarkozy Marches back into NATO with Army Shake up', *The Times*, 18 June.

Buras, Piotr and Longhurst, Kerry (2005) 'The Berlin Republic, Iraq, and the Use of Force', in Kerry Longhurst and Marcin Zaborowski (eds) *Old Europe, New Europe and the Transatlantic Security Agenda*, Abingdon: Routledge.

Bush, George (2002) *The National Security Strategy of the United States 2002*, cited in full in *The New York Times*, 20 September.

Cox, Michael (2005) 'Beyond the West: Terrors in Transatlantica', *European Journal of International Relations*, 11(2).

Daalder, Ivo (2003) 'The End of Atlanticism', *Survival*, 45(2).

Dombey, Daniel (2007) 'US Lashes out at Kremlin over Missile Dispute', *Financial Times*, 22 January.

Dunn, David Hastings (2005) 'Bush, 9/11 and the Conflicting Strategies of the "War on Terrorism"', *Irish Studies in International Affairs*, 16.

—— (2008) 'The Double Interregnum: UK–US Relations After Blair and Bush', *International Affairs*, 84(6): 1131–43.

Ghannoushi, Soumaya (2007) 'Sarkozy, the New Blair', *Guardian online*, 28 September. Online. Available at: www.guardian.co.uk/commentisfree/2007/sep/28/sarkozythenewblairpleasek.

Gordon, Philip and Shapiro, Jeremy (2004) *Allies at War: America, Europe, and the Crisis over Iraq'*, Washington, DC: Brookings/McGraw-Hill.

Haass Richard (1997) *The Reluctant Sheriff*, New York: Council on Foreign Relations.

Hass, Christopher (2008) 'Obama Calls for a "Diplomatic Surge"', 8 April. Online. Available at: http://my.barackobama.com/page/community/post/stateupdates/gGBcCF.

Howard, Michael (1999) 'NATO at Fifty: An Unhappy Successful Marriage: Security Means Knowing What to Expect', *Foreign Affairs*, 78(3).

Howorth, Jolyon (2006) 'The US National Security Strategy: European Reactions', in Roland Dannreuther and John Peterson (eds) *Security Strategy and Transatlantic Relations*, Abingdon: Routledge.

Kupchan, Charles A. (2008) 'The Transatlantic Turnaround', *Current History*, March.

Lemann, Nicholas (2002) 'The Next World Order', *The New Yorker*, 1 April.

Lynch, Tim and Singh, Robert (2008) *After Bush: The Case for Continuity in American Foreign Policy*, Cambridge: Cambridge University Press.

North Atlantic Treaty Organisation (NATO) (2008) *'Bucharest Summit Declaration'*, 3 April. Online. Available at: http://www.nato.int/docu/pr/2008/p08–049e.html.

Revkin, Andrew (2008) 'After Applause Dies Down, Global Warming Talks Leave Few Concrete Goals', *New York Times*, 10 July.

Rubin, James (2004) 'Political Dynamite', *FT Magazine*, 3 April, p. 27.

Ruehle, Michael (2008) 'NATO's 2008 Summit: Bucharest's Balance Sheet', 12 July. Online. Available at: www.worldsecuritynetwork.com/showArticle3.cfm?article_id=15989 (accessed 14 July 2008).

Schake, Kori (2007) 'The US Elections and Europe: The Coming Crisis of High Expectations', Centre for European Reform, November.

Solana, Javier (2003) 'A Secure Europe in a Better World', European Council, Thessaloniki, 20 June. Online. Available at: http://www.europa-eu-un.org/articles/en/article_2449_en.htm.

Spear, Joanna (2003) 'The Emergence of a European Strategic Personality' *Arms Control Today*, November.

Further reading

Andrews, David M. (ed.) (2005) *The Transatlantic Alliance Under Stress: US-European Relations after Iraq*, Cambridge: Cambridge University Press.

Asmus, Ronald (2006) 'The European Security Strategy: An American View', in Roland Dannreuther and John Peterson (eds) *Security Strategy and Transatlantic Relations*, Abingdon: Routledge.

Bush, George (2002) *The National Security Strategy of the United States 2002*, cited in full in *The New York Times*, 20 September.

Cox, Michael (2005) 'Beyond the West: Terrors in Transaltantia', *European Journal of International Relations*, 11(2).

—— (2008) 'Europe's Enduring Anti-Americanism', *Current History*, 107(707) (May).

Daalder, Ivo (2003) 'The End of Atlanticism', *Survival*, 45(2).

Dunn, David Hastings (2005) 'Bush, 9/11 and the Conflicting Strategies of the "War on Terrorism"', *Irish Studies in International Affairs*, 16.

Gordon, Philip and Shapiro, Jeremy (2004) *Allies at War: America, Europe, and the Crisis over Iraq'*, Washington, DC: Brookings/McGraw-Hill.

Howorth, Jolyon (2006) 'The US National Security Strategy: European Reactions', in Roland Dannreuther and John Peterson (eds) *Security Strategy and Transatlantic Relations*, Abingdon: Routledge.

Kupchan, Charles A. (2008)'The Transatlantic Turnaround', *Current History*, March.

Lindburg, Tod (ed.) (2005) *Beyond Paradise and Power: Europe, America and the Future of a Troubled* Partnership, New York: Routledge.

Lynch, Tim and Singh, Robert(2008) *After Bush: The Case for Continuity in American Foreign Policy*, Cambridge: Cambridge University Press.

Revkin, Andrew (2008) 'After Applause Dies Down, Global Warming Talks Leave Few Concrete Goals', *New York Times*, 10 July.

Schake, Kori (2007)'The US Elections and Europe: The Coming Crisis of High Expectations', Centre for European Reform, November.

Solana, Javier (2003) 'A Secure Europe in a Better World,' European Council, Thessaloniki, 20 June. Online. Available at: http://www.europa-eu-un.org/articles/en/article_2449_en.htm.

Spear, Joanna (2003) 'The Emergence of a European Strategic Personality', *Arms Control Today*, November.

13 US national security

Still an ambiguous symbol? Still an illusion?

Linda B. Miller

Introduction

Writing with his usual prescience in 1962 at the height of the cold war, Arnold Wolfers cautioned that there were serious problems with any concept of "national security" whose authors failed to acknowledge its nature as "an ambiguous symbol". (Wolfers 1962: Chapter 10). Writing decades later after the end of the cold war, but before the 9/11 attacks, Richard Betts warned of similar problems in the leading American journal, *International Security.* Asking whether "strategy" was still an "illusion", he argued that "strategy fails when the chosen means prove insufficient to the ends." He wrote that the "limiting the range of ends" could be as important as limiting the range of means"(Betts 2000). Now, as US policymakers and theorists struggle to incorporate "the war on terror" into existing strategic rationales or try to devise newer concepts of security that make sense either domestically or internationally, how useful are these caveats?

Are concepts of US national security in the twenty-first century fated to be ambiguous? Is strategy still an "illusion"? If so, what are the consequences? Could a return to geostrategic thinking from the cold war, as George Kennan articulated, make a comeback? Do either the much discussed "selective engagement" or "off-shore balancing" avoid these traps?

Placing the Iraq and Afghanistan wars in this longer view offers sobering insights into the limits of both theory and practice. Surveying the period from 2001 to 2009 is a useful way of answering the two questions posed in this chapter's subtitle. Just as most US IR theorists and policymakers missed the end of cold war in the years leading up to 1989, so, too, they missed the significance of terrorism as a challenge to American national security interests in the run-up to 9/11. Many theorists and policymakers also were slow to grasp the deleterious implications of linking the war in Iraq to the ambiguous challenge of a generalized war on terror. Now as the Bush administration has ended, the legacy of these errors is becoming clearer. To give but one example, the unresolved conflict between Iran and the USA demonstrates the mismatch of goals and means that Wolfers, Kennan and Betts observed.

Other illustrations abound. In world politics, every day is not a new tomorrow. Legacies from one administration to another persist. Unanswered questions and unresolved conflicts afflict Washington, regardless of political party. Any search for "new directions" must acknowledge this basic fact.

So it is important to analyze the main lines of argument the Bush administration used to legitimate its policies on both the war on terror and the second Iraq war. For they were to be the building blocks of new directions in 2001. Now, eight years later, were they part of a coherent strategic vision? Or just officials making it up as they went along? In either case, what explains the failure of mainstream theorists to challenge more forcefully the Bush administration's claims of linkage between a second Iraq war, unfinished business in Iran and the self-proclaimed war on terror? Given these realities, what might be the outlines of a non-doctrinal post-Bush/Cheney, post-Iraq strategy for the USA?

Practice

Clearly, no single factor dominated in the unfolding justifications US policymakers repeated to legitimate the global war on terror and the 2003 Iraq war, yet recurring themes are evident. The administration's contempt for the "reality-based community", meaning everyone outside a very limited group in the Executive Branch, is obviously one factor. First articulated in a *New York Times Magazine* article in October, 2004, then later in Ron Suskind's (2004) popular book, *The Price of Loyalty: George W. Bush, the White House and the Education of Paul O'Neill*, a Bush spokesman explained that the administration would elaborate its own priorities and leave the explanations to journalists and other observers whose experience necessarily confined them to less comprehensive world views. A second factor was the unwavering belief in the superiority of the US Executive Branch, especially in the realm of foreign policy. By design, this increasingly contested constitutional control would marginalize both the legislative branch and the judicial branch. Elaborated over the course of the past eight years, this conception of American politics was unprecedented in its scope and was at the heart of the claim that the Bush administration tried to be truly "revolutionary". A third factor was the penchant for reinforcing American hegemony against all other state comers, as advanced in the National Security documents of 2002 (and later in 2006).

Taken together, these three elements go a long way toward understanding the main thrusts of official clarifications (or deliberate obfuscations) of US national security policy in the early twenty-first century. Each proved to be problematic, almost before the ink dried. As discussed later in this chapter, numerous rejoinders from both "liberals" and "conservatives" have appeared which hint at the ways in which fuller challenges will mounted in the next decade. More important, though, is the assertion and assumption of American exceptionalism that undergird the other three factors. Here there is no need to wait for history to render verdicts. Here it is possible to analyze the essential weaknesses of the recent official US world view that has recently distorted national security.

The origins of the belief in American exceptionalism, whether based on geographical location, institutional innovation, or historical experience, found new meaning after the cold war when US superiority in military and economic resources made it seem that diplomacy and treaties could be down graded, that alliances could be neglected, and international crises could be ignored unless they rose to the level of threatening the safety of the "homeland." 9/11 fell into the latter category and therefore offered a test case of whether the rest of the litany was valid. Responses to the terrorist attacks provided a rare instance of whether, in Stanley Hoffmann's memorable phrase, "the sheriff and the missionary" were once again indivisible in US foreign policy (Hoffmann 2006: Chapter 12). If they were, doctrines of preemption would be not only legitimate but also mandatory and might be sold domestically and internationally as self-evident. If they were not, especially if US practice did not fulfill the expectations such hubris created, then both domestic and international acceptance would shatter.

As always, in international relations, results matter, not just rhetoric. As the Iraq war exposed the limited preparation of US civilian and military leaders for the aftermath of combat, it became clear that power projection was the rationale for American deployment of its forces in the Middle East and elsewhere. A huge literature now catalogues the lack of planning for counter-insurgency, the failure to grasp the multiple cleavages in Iraqi society, and the profound ignorance of local customs that doomed this American exercise of global leadership. Yet the election campaigns of 2008 rarely confronted the most critical issues such as whether "global war makes sense as an antidote to terror, whether preventive war works, whether the costs of 'global leadership' are sustainable, and whether events in Asia rather than the Middle East might just determine the course of the 21st century" (Bacevich 2008).

Similarly, the growing literature on Iran, divided between narrow scholarly, academic interpretations and more sweeping journalistic evidence of current events, rarely uncovers strategic rationales for American behavior. Yet as Iran has clearly benefited from the Iraq war, there is more urgency in articulating the US choices, both in terms of "regime change" and non-proliferation of nuclear weapons. Significantly, this discussion is taking place while the USA has no exit strategy from Iraq and Afghanistan. One visitor, Michael Massing, wrote that Michael Ware, CNN's Baghdad correspondent, believes "It is all about Iran [because] their agents of influence go to the top of the Iraqi government." Winning for Iran in Iraq means protecting its political gains there by forging ahead with a nuclear deterrent to resist American pressures to desist from exerting Shiite influence in Iraq. Iranian threats to close the Strait of Hormuz to oil shipments are therefore counter-threats to Washington's persistent warnings about Teheran's uranium enrichment. Ironically, this mutually confrontational posture is mistaken, in part, because Iran and the USA have overlapping, if not common, interests in Iraq: a fragile order rather than chaos and planned reductions in US forces over time rather than a rapid pull-out (Massing 2008).

What explains American reluctance to talk to Iranian political leaders about these obvious agenda items? Perhaps the clearest answer is US reluctance to consider, let alone, abet, Iranian regional hegemony in the Middle East. For this reason, the Bush administration clung to the notion of 60 or so bases in Iraq as part of the stalled Status of Forces Agreement with the al-Malaki government. For this reason, the Bush administration told Congress it wished to spend upwards of $400 million on covert military operations in Iran to destabilize the government and gather intelligence on its nuclear programs. As critics have pointed out, it might be preferable to finish the job in Afghanistan, quell the Taliban resurgence there, and possibly locate Osama bin Laden (see, for example, Robinson 2008).

What confounds many observers is the failure of US officials to explain convincingly why Iran with nuclear weapons constitutes a threat that would warrant American bombing, invasion and occupation, or Israeli air strikes as a substitute. Thomas Powers argues that to assume that because Iran's leadership consists of "religious fanatics crazy enough to use a bomb if they had one" evokes memories of American and Russian worries about Chinese acquisition of nuclear weapons decades ago. Why not assume that Iran, like all other countries that went nuclear since 1945, would face major constraints on any attempts to use such weapons? After all, "the world's experience to date has shown that nuclear powers do not use them, and they seriously threaten to use them only to deter attack." "What changes is that nuclear powers have to be treated differently; in particular, they cannot be casually threatened" (Powers 2008). Seen in this light, the US-Iranian standoff, leaving the American military option on the table down grades diplomacy and sanctions as more viable means to securing a more attainable goal, especially since these two instruments are supported by both the EU and Russia, China and Japan.

In fact, the reasons for the continued exchange of bluster, warnings and threats between the two countries may lie in both their domestic politics as much as in international relations practice. Here intra-Pentagon squabbles over the utility of force are one factor. Equally important, though, is Bush's history. Thus, Thomas Powers writes that in 2008, as in 2003, the 43rd president's predilection for force has deep roots that will leave his successor with uncomfortable options.

> But a war to overthrow Saddam Hussein won't by itself provide a decision outcome in the present case because there are two rogue states with programs to build nuclear weapons in the Middle East. The theory says that both have to go, and if President Bush can be taken at his word, he thinks the same thing. To me [Powers] the implication seems clear: Iraq first, Iran next. We are not free of this danger yet.
>
> (ibid.)

Of all the distortions the wars in Afghanistan and Iraq created for American strategic interests, none looms larger in the on-going confrontation with Iran than the persistent tensions between the uniformed US military and the White House. Dramatized during the firing of Admiral William Fallon, who loudly resisted pressures for the USA to go to war with Iran, it became clear to other uniformed officers that:

> the coherence of military strategy is being eroded because of undue civilian influence and direction of non-conventional military operations. If you have small groups planning and conducting military operations outside the knowledge and control of the combatant commander, by default you can't have a coherent military strategy. You end up with a disaster, like the reconstruction efforts in Iraq.
>
> (Hersh 2008)

Moreover, Iran poses different problems than either Iraq or Afghanistan in terms of its ethnic minorities, geographic constraints, and nationalist impulses. Still, for hawkish American political figures disappointed in the comprised outcomes of the those two wars, the temptation to set things right by a relatively cheap air campaign against Iran sometime during the protracted electoral season was hard to give up.

The idea that intra-Muslim tensions might have more to do with the course of events in Iraq, Afghanistan, and Iran, along with Pakistan and Turkey, dies hard in American domestic politics, for it suggests that the USA faces essentially weak players rather than enemies of global reach and appetites. It undercuts the notion that America is "at war" which premise serves to strengthen executive power in struggles with Congress (Zakaria 2008b). It also calls into question the Bush legacy of extending democracy, American style, to the greater Middle East. Even more threatening, the notion that the USA has not found the right mix of instruments to realize this ambitious end, poses challenges to established ways of conducting US foreign policy.

Since 2001, the ideological bases of US practice hardened as fixed doctrines have yielded rigidity not flexibility and as domestic and international support for a national security policy rooted in exceptionalism and preemption has plummeted. Practice, summed up in the protracted wars in Afghanistan and Iraq, and uncertainties over Iran, has aroused suspicions that the US emperor has no clothes, no Plan B when events do not confirm the policymakers' predictions, no grasp of the importance of social movements or non-state actors in shaping outcomes, especially tarnished ones. The failures of practice have provided fertile ground for theorists. How well have observers done in uncovering mistakes and misapprehensions of policymakers, even if belatedly?

Theory

For observers, the Bush administration's foreign policy practice has provided ample ground for criticism, especially since 2003, when doctrines of preemption led inexorably to the invasion of Iraq. In the six years since, critiques have taken a predictable course, with both "liberals" and gradually "conservatives" arguing that the war was unnecessary, incompetently managed, and fixated on the wrong enemy. By diverting attention from Al Qaeda, by reawakening Sunni-Shiite strife, by empowering Iran, by down grading threats from North Korea and Pakistan, by sidelining the Darfur and Israeli-Palestinian conflicts, Washington policymakers had damaged not only US national security but also world order. Lacking both credibility and influence, the Bush administration would thus limp toward an ignominious conclusion that could take years to undo. Successors would have a difficult task in rejuvenating the institutional foundations that had first attained and then sustained great power entente after World War II.

For those critics who preferred to ground their attacks by offering reasoned, sustained alternatives, it was crucial to point out that the domestic, bipartisan approach that saw the cold war to a successful conclusion had collapsed. It was equally vital to show that the Bush approach was essentially ahistorical in terms of its goals and means. Yet here some critics were probably wrong. More telling was the finding that much of Bush's ambition, if not implementation, had deep roots in one or another US foreign policy tradition. By linking "unilateralism" to "Wilsonian liberalism", at least one observer was able to show that Bush, like Wilson before him, had mistakenly overestimated American power and was obstinate about admitting that goals had to be redefined and narrowed if anything was to be salvaged from his attempt to establish "hegemony on the cheap" (Dueck 2003: 4). Hegemony resting on fragile unipolarity has occupied many scholars in recent years, especially those eager to avoid the labels of liberal and conservative. Christopher Layne, for example, also writing in *International Security*, faults those who think the absence of new great powers or active counterbalancing against the USA is a sign of acceptance of American primacy. Arguing for restraint as expressed in "off-shore balancing" as the next grand strategy, Layne believes that the USA could thereby regain stature and prestige. He also foresees a decline in others' attempts to challenge the USA if such efforts are made soon and effectively. Of course, off-shore balancing is not a new idea, but it would look restrained after recent excesses of US over-involvement in oil-rich Arab or Muslim countries like Iraq (Layne 2006). Essentially, it calls for pre-positioning of US forces away from land bases.

As part of its appeal, off-shore balancing would also acknowledge that with new issues such as global public health and climate change rising on many national foreign policy agendas, America's logistical advantages and military strengths could often be put in the service of relief efforts along with war-fighting, as responses to the Asian tsunami of 2004–05 showed. Fittingly, such a re-positioning would factor in the rise of China, India, and Brazil as well as the residual strengths of the EU, Russia and Japan in co-operative diplomatic efforts toward Iran and other difficult actors. Off-shore balancing could appeal to both liberals and conservatives and those in between who are seeking a way out of the "security trap" caused by US power projections and inevitable backlashes (Dodge 2008). Implied in off-shore balancing, then, is an implicit commitment to energizing sluggish international institutions that must keep pace with global realities of new agenda and new players. Equally significant, judgments about when and where to intervene would result from the interplay of US executive and legislative actors over sustained periods of time.

Still more comprehensive critiques are offered in book-length form by two prominent American theorists, Francis Fukuyama and Tony Smith. Their recent works serve as convenient bookends, representing as they do a "conservative" and a "liberal" take on the Bush years in the context of shifting domestic and international settings. Each is disillusioned with the pretense and passion of true believers or enablers in the American academy or punditry who supported both the war on terror and the Iraq war uncritically and who might endorse war with Iran. Each, without naming names, is disgusted by the refusal of such individuals to speak truth to power.

Each is a maverick in challenging the foundations of prevailing doctrines. Fukuyama, writing as a reformed supporter of the neoconservative agenda, correctly identifies the lacunae in that analysis of globalization and the security implications that flow from it in *America at the Crossroads* (Fukuyama 2006). By the conservatives' failure to account for political and economic development as aspects of national security, he explains why even a US military victory in Iraq would leave the country and region unstable. Yet Fukuyama's welcome call for "rule-bound, accountable" international institutions (ibid.) is at best a partial solution to the security requirements of a post-Iraq world system where the USA may well retreat into a more isolationist foreign policy position. His refusal to give up on quasi-utopian approaches stems from his refusal to abandon what might be any remaining value in conservative, non-evangelical core beliefs about human society.

By contrast, Tony Smith shows how liberal optimism alone is equally ill-suited to the threat of terrorism. Smith, like Fukuyama, who is often quoted in his book, thinks that the excess of liberal enthusiasm for the democratic peace has provided an on-going endorsement of "utopian violence" that might survive the Iraq debacle. But his more important contribution lies in his careful demonstration of how advocates of liberal internationalism developed a focus on human rights and interventions to promote them in the 1990s. It was this endorsement, when married to more conservative theories of aggressive US nationalism, that constructed an impressive rationale linking American power and purpose. This "pact with the devil", in the book's title, prepared the way for the Iraq war by seeming to underwrite a growing consensus for US military action to promote democracy abroad, especially in the Middle East (Smith 2007). At a time when previous fissures between conservative and liberal approaches might have produced more impressive criticisms before the 2003 invasion, was this a fatal flaw? Smith thinks so. By castigating liberals for their intellectual dishonesty, he offers a pessimistic forecast of a post-Iraq strategic reorientation for US policymakers.

Of course, neither Fukuyama nor Smith exhausts the range of critical opinion trying to keep pace with the headlong rush of new directions emanating from the Bush administration. While other theorists busied themselves with exploring the dimensions of eroding state sovereignty and resulting shifts in global balances, Fukuyama and Smith both harked back to the wisdom and insights of George Kennan's hallowed state-based definition of a viable US grand strategy: policies aimed at assuring American interests in Europe, Asia and the Middle East primarily, using various foreign policy instruments as circumstances might require.

Building on these foundations, other observers have striven to put Bush's floundering new directions in the broader context of US foreign policy over two centuries. Often such attempts find authors reaching opposite conclusions. Thus, Robert Kagan asserts that authoritarianism, represented by Russia and China, permits power projections along with democracy as a belief system. Yet his conclusion, that a League of Democracies could be a counterweight, does not necessarily follow (Kagan 2008). Fareed Zakaria is more impressed with the capacities of American business to pave the way for more productive new directions than what governments alone may offer (Zakaria 2008a) From this ferment, productive discussions may follow, aimed as much at the academy and punditry as potential US officialdom. A fluid, shifting context is shaping the contemporary debate against the background of Bush's expansionist thrusts in the Middle East and elsewhere.

Post-Bush, post-Iraq?

To look ahead to future American strategies while the Iraq war and the war on terror continue is perhaps premature, for any plausible doctrines or policy preferences will depend in large part on outcomes there and in the region as a whole, especially unfavorable ones for the USA. It is also important to remember that post-Bush and post-Iraq are not the same thing in terms of American strategy. Insofar as the Bush administration has had any discernible strategy as the Iraq war has dragged on, it has consisted mainly of tactical course corrections that ensure a passing along of the protracted conflict to its Washington successors, together with arms deals for Saudi Arabia and others. All candidates for president in the 2008 election were committed in one way or another to consider redeployment while leaving some US forces in Iraq for the foreseeable future to stave off both Al Qaeda and an even more disastrous civil war. In these circumstances, any potential future strategies will rest not only on the more recent changes Fukuyama, Smith and others analyze, but also on the historical grab-bag that presents itself to any new administration taking office during a war. Institutional memory in Washington is almost always absent when a new administration assumes power.

For this reason, it is useful to review the likely contenders beyond off-shore balancing. These include a renewed commitment to "benevolent hegemony" with world-wide US power projection designed to prevent the rise of other great powers abroad while retaining Bush-like claims on expanded executive authority at home. This already discredited grand strategy might regain traction only if both the war on terror and the Iraq war were widely regarded as successes. Given the resurgence of Al Qaeda and the Taliban, and the lack of political reconciliation in Iraq, these verdicts are unlikely. A second contender would be a reorganization of American resources, both military and economic, an updated Kennan blueprint, to permit selective engagement in regional or global crises depending on particular circumstances. As the name indicates, judgments on individual cases and crises would take precedence. In fact, this latter approach seems the most likely because it would be based on more traditional executive-legislative relations at home and a more nuanced reading of globalization in the wider world. Moreover, such a case-by-case reading of challenges would be the only declared strategy both liberals and conservatives could jointly endorse, especially after Iraq, for it would permit judicious partnerships with the UN, NATO, the EU and other regional organizations and satisfy critics who worry about isolationism at home and chaos abroad.

These concerns were uppermost in the findings of a recent bipartisan commission that called for a revision in the 1973 War Powers Act presumably governing executive-legislative relations in the declaration and conduct of hostilities. Led by James Baker and Warren Christopher, two aging, venerable former Secretaries of State, the commission concluded that Articles I and II of the Constitution failed to specify the tensions between the President's role as Commander-in-Chief and the Congress's role in declaring war. Their proposed remedy, the War Powers Consultation Act, would require the two branches to adopt a complicated procedure of discussion and intelligence sharing so that a joint committee of Congress would review and vote up or down deployments lasting more than a week and permit the cutting off of funds for deployments if approved by two-thirds of the House and Senate. Although unlikely to be presented in its present form, such legislation would signal a return to bipartisanship in foreign policy as a new administration takes power. It nicely complements the desire for selective engagement as a new/old strategic direction, even if necessarily flawed in terms of predicting the behavior of unknown legislative and executive actors.

What were the signs that such a new direction was gaining adherents even before the Bush administration left office? First, US policymakers have recently redefined the goals of both the war on terror and the Iraq war. Far from "wanted dead or alive", the search for Osama bin Laden became a vague unease with Pervez Musharraf's toleration of Taliban and Al Qaeda sanctuaries in Pakistan. Second, Iraq is no longer heralded as a potential democratic light unto the nations in the Middle East, but as a conflict that eventually must end if and when local politicians get their acts together, even at the risk of soft partition. That such reformulations, edging closer to realities on the ground, now pass for acceptable outcomes speaks volumes about the ill-fated conceptions of American grand strategy advanced after 9/11. Of course, there are still hold-outs, for example, William Kristol, writing in *The Washington Post* that, despite Bush's low popularity in the polls, Iraq may still be salvaged by the "surge". Renewed friendships with Japan and India, or Chinese "stability" that compensates for Russian "slippage" will save US foreign policy from disaster, he argues (Kristol 2007).

Yet even this misleading cheerleading cannot overcome the "fatal contradictions" in Iraq policy, writes William Pfaff. As he emphasizes, "Washington itself avowed long-term strategic interests in Iraq that now are clearly incompatible with the demands for troop withdrawal now intense in political Washington and loud elsewhere in the United States" (Pfaff 2007). In these circumstances, broadly defined selective engagement looks like the only viable post-Bush, post-Iraq strategy on offer for the USA in the next decade. But such a seemingly sustainable approach is replete with hazards of its own, especially if it remains grounded in the all-too-familiar pre-Bush trap of insisting on

American maintenance of geopolitical superiority over all comers, reinforced by "muscular" idealism. Efforts to break strategy into regional segments could suffer the same fate, for example, if the Bush administration tries to isolate Iran via a "Green curtain", hoping to build up Sunni Arab players along the lines of cold war Iron Curtain precedents.

Is the international system too complicated or fragmented to imagine successful US grand strategies for the next decade or more? Yes and no. Yes, in the sense that all foreign policy agendas must include a host of functional challenges in health and economics that are difficult to integrate into overarching doctrines that will attract domestic as well as global support. No, in the sense that even diminished or intermittent American leadership may wrest some order from evident chaos if plausible choices result from the Iraq debacle.

Such choices cannot be ideal, but could be at least sensible, for example, if US policymakers resist the urge to heighten tensions with Russia in the vain hope that cold war assumptions are still useful in that complex bilateral relationship. Clearly, the burden of selection that will confront the next administration is heavy, particularly as the social costs associated with maintaining an aging population will stress even US resources. In a recent study, Mark L. Hass warns that isolationism might look even more attractive in these unprecedented times, despite US demographic advantages and despite even greater burdens of this kind for India, China, and the major European countries (Hass 2007). More traditional interstate conflicts might be attenuated, although interstate resource-driven tensions could mount.

Not surprisingly, caution would indicate that the USA could begin the long road back to strategic health by updating and sustaining older practices. Imaginative thinkers will augment this historically proven set of state-based priorities to include the transnational agendas of globalization in trade and health resting on non-state actors as well. Is such a sensible approach beyond consideration? Beyond achievement? Possibly not. Paradoxically, the chances are better if US policymakers eschew public diplomacy or hyped advertising in favor of actions like the closing of Guantànamo or the redirection of aid to education and localized democracy promotion in places like Pakistan and Somalia. For such a strategy to gain domestic support, future administrations would have to tone down or abandon exaggerated claims of executive privilege. They may also have to tone down, if not abandon, claims of American exceptionalism or easy democracy promotion.

Under what circumstances might these two requirements for a new/old grand strategy become compelling? One would surely be the protracted withdrawal from combat stances in Iraq, a difficult process that could take as long as two years. A second would be closer ties with Britain, France and Germany, an equally problematic process that could take even longer, but might result from new leadership in the three countries, along with the USA, in 2009. A third would be a 2008 election that brought to power an administration pledged to refocus on domestic priorities ranging from more equitable health care to repaired infrastructure. Such possibilities are modest, to be sure, but perhaps attainable. The result would be a breathing space that would permit revisiting Wolfers' recommendations about balancing ends and means.

Although national security would still be an ambiguous symbol, and strategy "illusory" in Betts' terms, it would also be less delusional when compared to the Bush II years. It would also mark the return of the suitably chastened "reality-based" community and none too soon.

References

Bacevich, A. (2008) "What Bush Hath Wrought", *Boston Globe*, July 1.

Betts, R.K. (2000) "Is Strategy an Illusion?", *International Security*, 25(2): 5–49.

Dodge, T. (2008) "US Foreign Policy in the Middle East", in M.E. Cox and D. Stokes (eds) *US Foreign Policy*, Oxford: Oxford University Press.

Dueck, C. (2003) "Hegemony on the Cheap", *World Policy Journal*, 20(4): 1–11.

Fukuyama, F. (2006) *America at the Crossroads*, New Haven, CT: Yale University Press.

Hass, M. (2007) "A Geriatric Peace?", *International Security*, 32(1): 112–47.

Hersh, S. (2008) "Preparing the Battlefield", *The New Yorker*, July 7 and 14.

Hoffmann, S. (2006) *Chaos and Violence*, Lanham, MD: Rowman and Littlefield.

Kagan, R. (2008) *The Return of History and the End of Dreams*, New York: Knopf.

Kristol, W. (2007) "Why Bush Will Be a Winner", *The Washington Post*, July 15.

Layne, C. (2006) "The Unipolar Moment Revisited", *International Security*, 31(2): 7–41.

Massing, M. (2008) "Embedded in Iraq", *The New York Review of Books*, July 17.

Pfaff, W. (2007) "The Fatal Contradiction in Iraq Policy". Online. Available at: www.williampfaff. com, July 10.

Powers, T. (2008) "Iran: The Threat", *The New York Review of Books*, July 17.

Robinson, E. (2008) "Bush's Parting Shots", *Washington Post*, July 1.

Smith, T. (2007) *A Pact with the Devil*, New York: Routledge.

Suskind, R. (2004) *The Price of Loyalty: George W. Bush, the White House and the Education of Paul O'Neill*, New York: Pocket Books.

Wolfers, A. (1962) *Discord and Collaboration*, Baltimore, MD: Johns Hopkins University Press.

Zakaria, F. (2008a) *The Post-American World*, New York: W.W. Norton.

—— (2008b) "True or False: We Need a Wartime President", *Washington Post*, July 7.

Further reading

Bacevich, A. (ed.) (2007) *The Long War*, New York: Columbia University Press.

Brzezinski, Z. (2007) *Second Chance*, New York: Perseus Group.

Chollet, D. and Goldgeier, J. (eds) (2008) *America Between the Wars*, New York: Public Affairs.

Gordon, M. and Trainor, B. (eds) (2006) *Cobra II*, New York: Pantheon.

Hunt, M. (2008) *The American Ascendancy*, Chapel Hill, NC: University of North Carolina Press.

Ikenberry, G.J. (2004) "The End of the Neoconservative Moment", *Survival*, 46(1): 7–22.

Kupchan, C. and Trubowitz, P. (2007) "Grand Strategy for Divided America", *Foreign Affairs*, 86(4): 71–84.

Lynch, T. and Singh. R. (2008) *After Bush*, Cambridge: Cambridge University Press.

Rice, C. (2008) "Rethinking the National Interest", *Foreign Affairs*, 87(4): 2–27.

Ricks, T. (2006) *Fiasco*, New York: Penguin Group.

Scoblic, J.P. (2008) *US vs. Them*, New York: Viking.

Woodward, B. (2006) *State of Denial*, New York: Simon & Schuster.

Websites

http://www.whitehouse.gov/nsc/2002/index.html
http://www.whitehouse.gov/nsc/2006/index.html
http://www.gseis.ucla.edu/courses/ed253a/american-exceptionalism.htm
www.cfr.org
www.foreignpolicy.com
www.nyrb.com
www.nytimes.com
www.newyorker.com
www.washingtonpost.com
www.williampfaff.com

14 The US and the Middle East in theory and practice since 9/11

Linda B. Miller

Introduction

Few subjects of US foreign policy reveal a larger chasm between theory and practice than the Middle East since 9/11. Few regions of the world have exposed more gaps between rhetoric and reality than the Middle East since the terrorist attacks. Few topics in American foreign policy invoke more domestic reactions than the Middle East. No survey of "new directions" is complete without analysis of recent and current American policies toward Iraq, Iran, and Israel. Yet paradoxes in US Middle East policy did not begin with the George W. Bush administration, nor will they end there. Still, few, if any, presidential administrations have done more to limit US options while expanding the US role in the region.

Rarely has the American reach so exceeded its grasp as it has in the years 2001–8 in the Middle East, especially as Washington has extended the geographical boundaries of the region to include Afghanistan and sometimes Pakistan, as well as North Africa. This extension, a Bush–Cheney new direction, whether actual or often just rhetorical, has further exposed the chronic gap between goals and means in US foreign policy. Restoring balance, realism and restraint must be a priority for any new administration. As a first step, US policymakers must find the right combination of diplomatic, economic, military and cultural instruments of foreign policy, especially toward Iraq, Iran and Israel, and also toward Egypt, Syria, Jordan and Lebanon.

What are the possibilities for post-Bush new directions, even if grounded in old assumptions? As this chapter explains, old assumptions could well constrain new directions in 2009 and beyond, even if a more sensible view of the region eventually prevails, one that shrinks the geographical boundaries more realistically in the future and, in so doing, narrows the gap between American objectives and instruments. Connecting the dots, to use the popular phrase, is especially urgent since misguided policies could damage US foreign policy elsewhere.

The links between US policies in the Middle East and more general debates and dilemmas in American foreign policy deserve more attention than they generally receive. Worldviews and the changes in them that events shape are especially complex in this volatile region which has figured prominently in US foreign policy since the founding of the Republic. Whether as the site of missionary efforts, proxy battles with the Soviet Union, contested trade routes, or oil deposits, the Middle East has captured attention and sparked frustrations when local players have so often put their own agendas ahead of that of the Americans or have cleverly tailored their own compulsions to US fears of the moment, as the years since 9/11 have demonstrated.

Visions or fantasies?

Understandably, the tension between the demands of Middle East governments and their own peoples (with whom they are often at war or at cross-purposes) and the far-away US is a continuing theme in broad historical narratives of the long history of American foreign policy (Oren 2007). With Arab documents closed, existing accounts are necessarily limited, but there is enough in the public domain to "enable Americans to read about the Barbary Wars and Operation Torch or to follow presidential efforts to mediate between Palestinians and Israelis and see the shadow Teddy Roosevelt and Woodrow Wilson" (ibid.: 506). Caught between the rival demands of communism and nationalism, cold war American presidents from Harry Truman to Ronald Reagan tried to balance US domestic priorities and international imperatives as the British and French withdrew after World War II. Juggling and muddling through, with the occasional covert intervention as in Iran in 1953, or the more general Middle East crises in 1956, 1967 and 1973, in no way indicated any overall architecture in American responses. As the post-colonial regimes in Egypt, Syria, and Iraq challenged America's writ, better relations were established with the Jordanian and Saudi Arabian monarchies, often via arms deals as well as oil purchases.

In the run-up to the 2001 terrorist attacks, that particular danger went largely unrecognized, despite warnings (see Clarke 2004). Only after the Twin Towers fell and the Pentagon was hit, did the US government and the citizenry embark on a rapid, sometimes flawed re-education on the possible sources of such unanticipated violence on American soil. Here the "imperial" nature of US foreign policy over two centuries offered little preparation for how to deal with novel adversaries like the Taliban or Osama bin Laden. To be sure, world politics might reveal that the USA was "imperial" in its expectations of its "right to lay down the rules of trade, commerce, security, and political legitimacy" (Dorrein 2004), but such general thrusts did not provide guidelines on how to deter non-state, non-territorial actors like Al Qaeda from additional murderous attacks. Nor did such dominant status confer a script for how to prepare the American people for a long twilight struggle against shadowy perpetrators living in caves half a world away. That would be the task for US policymakers in the wake of the Afghanistan and Iraq wars.

How remarkable and unfortunate then that the US president at the time should be one without a coherent world view. George W. Bush entered the White House after a protracted legal battle with the much better prepared Al Gore. With scant knowledge of the Middle East, Bush's jumble of ideas rested on established precepts of American military and economic power and a determination not to repeat the over-involvement of Bill Clinton in debilitating negotiations with players like Yasser Arafat's PLO. Bush and Dick Cheney, the Vice President, expected to preside over the status quo rather than embark on new directions. Most significantly, Bush shared with many of his generation a form of triumphalism after the cold war whose successful conclusion consolidated the view that states, hierarchies, friends and foes were the permanent building blocks of international relations. Networks, non-state actors and social movements were the province of IR theorists chiefly, with realists, liberal institutionalists and constructivists working on their familiar terrain.

As self-styled pragmatists, Bush and Cheney, both oil men with little comprehension of the larger currents roiling the Middle East, knew how to construct arms deals and fossil fuel purchases, knew what blandishments were needed with the Saudi princes and with Israeli political leaders. Once, such a limited agenda might have sufficed. But in circumstances of chronic regional underdevelopment and rising fanaticism, of *jihadi* appeals to unemployed young people, the Bush administration was basically clueless. Therefore, the Washington entourage, especially its complement of neo-conservatives, were spectacularly unprepared to deal conceptually with the divergent meanings of 9/11. Gilles Kepel explained this deficiency with respect to the subsequent US choice to embark on the Iraq War. The Washington script called for the fall of Saddam Hussein, the emergence of civil society, and the inevitable emergence of Western-style democracy according to the East European script of 1990–1, none of which happened (Kepel 2004).

Yet the reasons why this script was chosen had little to do with Eastern Europe and everything to do with ensuring that the two pre-9/11 bedrocks of US Middle East policy – Israeli security and access to cheap oil supplies – would survive both terrorism on American soil and turbulence in the region itself. As well, political leaders insisted, reshaped Middle East policies offered the prospect of enhancing executive power in American politics. With Iraq as Enemy #1, and Iran and Syria arrayed closely behind as "evils" to be contained and deterred, official Washington finally appeared to have a post-9/11 vision. But was this depiction another fantasy that could not survive testing on the ground?

As additional cascading threats emerged or were manufactured, presidential rhetoric grew more elaborate. Saddam Hussein had to be linked to the war on terror so that a new vision of the Middle East as a source of democracy rather than autocracy or theocracy could take hold. Leaders like Ariel Sharon and Vladimir Putin who understood how to manipulate US fears would be supported against their own self-defined terrorist challengers regionally and globally. Proponents of such an approach argued that democracies do not go to war against each other but allies make resources like oil available to each other. Of course, the 2006 war between Israel and Lebanon was an important exception to one of these dicta and the Saudi refusal to lower oil prices was the functional equivalent of another. Nevertheless, Secretary of State Condoleezza Rice repeatedly insisted that the Middle East was in the "birth pangs" of a new order. Favored allies, like Saudi Arabia were on the road to democracy, even as others like Lebanon were falling away from such a path. Iraq had had elections, but even administration cheerleaders did not proclaim that stable democracy had resulted by 2005 (Diamond 2005). (See also Kessler 2008.) Flaws in policy planning were self-evident.

The conceptual void left by the passing of the Soviet Union was filled, awkwardly to be sure, by Osama bin Laden and his nefarious colleagues, despite their lack of nuclear weapons or fixed territorial bases. When difficulties arose, as when the 9/11 Commission confirmed that Iraq had nothing to do with either 9/11 or WMD, other rationales, such as human rights or even the democratic peace were invoked. The important task was to maintain a vision, whether fanciful or not, one that could convince enough US voters to ensure continuity. So birth pangs would have to do, at least as a stop gap until the presumably more pragmatic second term was assured.

At the heart of the Bush tinkering and fabricating, as in the dogged efforts to insist that Iran was developing nuclear weapons that could spark World War III, was the flat rejection of the Clinton world view as flawed. Thus, any suggestion that the road to Baghdad should begin with the road to Jerusalem was mocked. Diplomacy in the Israeli-Palestinian on-going drama would take a back seat. As of 2001, the USA would "park the problem", and make pronouncements or send envoys as needed. Observers could sputter and point out anomalies, but the Bush administration appeared to have answers for any doubters. Yet this vision could only be maintained if the Iraq and Afghanistan wars were decisively won, thereby vindicating the expense of American treasure. In fact, Iraq would determine how Iran and the Israel-Palestinian conflict would play out in US policy. To the extent that Iraq remained unresolved, policies toward Iran and Israel would evolve unpredictably and often inconsistently, including during the 2007 "surge" phase of the Iraq conflict.

From this perspective, it is vital to remember that while the USA might use all instruments of foreign policy, absent nuclear weapons, *vis-à-vis* Iraq and Iran, including force and sanctions, it could and would use mainly diplomacy *vis-à-vis* Israel and the Palestinians. This imbalance of means has shaped the goals and explains the partial successes, if any, of its Middle East policies. It also explains why, in its final year, Bush administration policymakers finally agreed to explore and even conduct low-level talks with Iran, along with its previous saber-rattling behavior. Annoyed with the slow pace of Israel-Palestinian talks, shut out of Turkish-mediated Israeli-Syrian indirect negotiations and French attempts to set up a Mediterranean Union, Washington was slow to clarify what remained of its scaled-down visions for the Middle East, its architecture and its infrastructure for change there. The advantage of adding a public diplomatic face to relations with Iran could at least change the conversation during the later phases of the US presidential election campaign, if not eliminate the option of air strikes against Iranian nuclear targets either by the US or Israel.

Roadmaps or realities?

For Israel, Iraq and Iran, the Bush administration developed "roadmaps", to use its expression, that depended more on American predominance in the Middle East and US domestic politics and less on local realities. For this reason, each roadmap encountered difficulties as local actors refused to play Washington's game according to Washington's timetables. For Israel, the US benign neglect of negotiations for six years allowed the Israeli government to proceed with its own agenda vis-à-vis the Palestinians and Iranian threats to go nuclear. For Iraq, the American tendency to regard Iraqi sovereignty as less important than US control of the battlefield allowed sectarian violence to escalate to the point of civil war. For Iran, the US insistence on preconditions for talking to Teheran allowed any differences on nuclear matters between the clerics and the Iranian president to recede. Each roadmap developed pot-holes which no amount of belated US attention could mask.

In addition, unforeseen events, such as the 2005 assassination of Rafik Hariri and the subsequent withdrawal of Syrian forces from Lebanon rendered Washington's plans incomplete, if not unworkable altogether, for they showed that individual roadmaps had to accommodate shifts elsewhere in the region. Two years later, with the "surge" in Iraq trying to remedy the fraught situation there, these other events continued to take their toll. If nothing else, the surge also put paid to any Middle East foundation of America's imperial posture like no other series of events since 1991. The frustration with the course of the war explains not only the Republican defeat in the Congressional elections in 2006, but also the more sobering return to reality by the Executive branch after the excesses of 2001–4. It was a prime factor in the ultimate Bush concessions on a timetable for US troop withdrawals from Iraq when attempts at a more comprehensive agreement with the al-Malaki government stalled in July 2008 (see Meyers 2008).

This "reality" of scaled-down goals would itself often be unclear to observers, if not to policymakers themselves. Again, the ongoing violence in Iraq determined domestic and international reactions to Iran and Israel. When killing escalated in Iraq, bellicose US rhetoric against Iran mounted, but the possibility of a US strike against Iranian nuclear sites diminished. When violence in Iraq abated, American diplomatic overtures toward Iran and Israel-Palestine took center-stage. When national reconciliation in Iraq eluded US policymakers, pressures to restart and sustain direct Israeli-Palestinian talks mounted. Juggling these policies was especially difficult in circumstances of an enlarged regional concept for the USA in the Middle East and Bush's consistent low ratings in American and international public opinion polls. Nevertheless, the Bush administration spokesmen continued to argue that withdrawal from Iraq would unleash regional chaos, evidence to the contrary notwithstanding (Fettweis 2008: 96). Rather than accept the likelihood that US withdrawal would spark either political accommodation or civil strife in the country with an eventual winner, the administration clung to its own unrealistic script.

To sum up, the three central subjects of American Middle East policies were inextricably linked, though in unproductive ways because Iraq remained the independent variable and the other two subjects the dependent variables. The Bush administration contrived to bequeath to its successors a tangled web of interests and anxieties, of unfulfilled promises and murky threats. Prone to events it could not control, the US government placed excessive confidence in leaders like Pervez Musharraf, Ehud Olmert, or Mahmoud Abbas who could not deliver American goals. Well-intentioned roadmaps were overtaken by events, "realities" were transitory. Unwilling to concede that his succession of foreign policy doctrines such as pre-emption were either inconsistent or event-driven, Bush embarked on the final year of his presidency determined to have something to show for his Middle East follies. Staging elaborate conferences and trips to the region, the president struggled for a positive legacy, albeit one dependent on others for even minimal success. Talk of "anything but Clinton" receded, as Bush himself took part in the negotiations and conference rituals. Ceremony rather than substance prevailed.

The Bush administration's new directions, including the much heralded US commitment to a two-state solution for the Israel-Palestinian conflict, proved to be an outcome increasingly overtaken by events like the electoral victory of Hamas in January 2006 and its subsequent takeover of the Gaza Strip. Similarly, as already discussed, US plans for Iraq and Iran stalled when the local players developed interests of their own that often differed from American preferences. Increasingly, Washington's demands for "stability" fell on deaf ears in the region where far-reaching changes, such as the possible soft partition of Iraq or the acquisition of the complete fuel cycle by Iran were in direct opposition to US roadmaps. How would Washington, in the midst of a lengthy electoral cycle in 2008, handle such awkward realities? Even more unsettling to regional stability would be an Israeli decision to bomb Iranian nuclear sites on grounds of an existential threat to the Jewish state's survival (Morris 2008).

Whatever the ideological tenacity of US policymakers, American administrations typically are institutionally capable of dealing with just one main issue at a time. So the preoccupation with Iraq necessarily has meant involving either the EU or the UN in dealing with Iran or the Palestinians. US officials routinely stressed the terrorism agenda and anti-corruption efforts as preconditions of aid to the Palestinians. Israel has been allowed to complete its security fence. Neither the EU nor the UN has adopted these positions. From Washington's point of view, perhaps most important in this dismal recital is the recent tendency for local players to begin contacts with each other, for example, visits between Iraqi and Iranian leaders, or between Israeli and Syrian diplomats, without waiting for US direction. To be sure, agreements between Israel and Syria, officially still at war, would fit in well with American priorities, especially if US officials were candid about the prospects for accords on either water usage, the Golan Heights, security, borders and normalized bilateral relations (Ignatius 2008).

On balance, then, a turn toward pragmatism characterized the Bush approach to the Middle East in the second term, thereby bequeathing a more sustainable checklist to the next administration. Intact, though tattered, are the two bedrocks of previous policy: Israel's security and access to Arab oil supplies. The cost has been abandonment of imperial thrusts in Iraq in favor of a toned-down hope for stability and withdrawal. Entropy entered the scene as the Bush two-term presidency wound down amid hopes for a return to US leadership and worries about an Asian century. For analysts still interested in the gap between goals and means, US policy in the Middle East remains a fascinating case study. Visions or fantasies, roadmaps or realities? What stands out after eight years of trying to preserve the two bedrocks in a rapidly changing world is the US tendency to subordinate local claims and demands to a global threat. Thus, in trying to formulate policies toward Hamas, Washington behaved as if the political movement were "part of a unified, global organization, and (conflated) its aims and motivations with those of other, very different groups, (thereby risking) a self-fulfilling prophecy" (Gordon 2008: 34).

This story would have less staying power if it reflected only one dimension of US foreign policy. In fact, the pulling and hauling in the Middle East reveals some of the major difficulties with US foreign policy overall. The gap between aspirations and attainments stands out, as well as a predilection for short-term fixes rather than long-term planning. The over-dependence on particular leaders when things have gone wrong are familiar trends (Ross 2007). The lack of any Plan B *vis-à-vis* lesser powers or the tendency to downplay the possibilities of soft power to turn the tide in a more favorable direction for American national interests, however loosely defined, is prominent (Nye 2004). The failure to understand, let alone manipulate successfully, other cultures or local imperatives is also obvious. As well, the tendency of American negotiators to ignore issues of accountability and compliance has often doomed even successful agreements (Ross 2007).

Not surprisingly, then, the net result of recent efforts to promote an Israeli-Palestinian agreement, based on a two-state solution by the end of 2008 was likely to produce a "paper disengagement" that could be

> a stroke of political genius that gives all the parties most of what they want. The fiction of an Israeli withdrawal can support the fiction of a Palestinian state run by (Mahmoud) Abbas and Fatah, whose physical security will be insured by the presence of actual Israeli troops on the ground. The Americans can get a diplomatic success that can give added credibility to a diplomatic alliance against Iran, or peacemaking efforts with Iran, depending on how the wind blows in the next six months.
>
> (Samuels 2008)

Such an outcome would be a far cry from the previously declared goal of an American-directed transformation of the Middle East, but an accurate reflection of the legacy of the ill-conceived Iraq war and the diminishing influence of the USA in the still turbulent region.

This abiding verdict in no way reduces the need for the USA to adopt more realistic approaches to the vagaries of the Middle East. Quite the opposite. What, then, would constitute such realism?

What would perpetuate the US tendency to either ignore the region in favor of Europe or Asia and then to refocus on it obsessively? What explains the US tendency to exaggerate the importance of the Middle East in US foreign policy as opposed to relationships with Latin American or African countries? Is there perhaps an end point to US activity in the region as it lurches between "reformation and Armageddon?" (Lynch and Singh 2008: 200).

First and foremost, many observers agree, the US must come to grips with the likelihood of turbulence and backsliding even if a reordered list of US priorities reduces the toxic levels of anti-Americanism evident since 2003. Washington must work toward, though not dictate, a region where politics and economics operate more harmoniously with each other. This means promoting development along with security in US dealings with the array of democracies. theocracies and autocracies in the region. This also means rewarding those individual leaders who stand against terrorist groups determined to damage civilians in random attacks, not with arms deals, but with economic assistance based on good governance as Washington has tried to do in Africa and Latin America. It requires acknowledging that prosecuting a war in Iraq has elevated the stature of Iran regionally (Carter and Innocent 2008: 67).

It may also mean harnessing the inherent advantages of American-style higher education in the Middle East, which stresses science and technology, along with politics and civil rights. Several US universities are already staffing new campuses, for example, in the United Arab Emirates. These positive aims are well accepted below the governmental level in the region and need to be highlighted there, too. Where critics part company is over the question of whether US withdrawal from Iraq will hasten or hinder such a new direction. To this imponderable, there is no easy answer because the circumstances and timing of such a redirection cannot be predicted. Much will depend on the caliber of local leaders as well as those in Washington. Yet there are other obstacles to consider beyond these obvious factors.

The future lies ahead

New directions for US foreign policy in the Middle East will depend upon a complex balancing of reformulated goals, suitable means and a long list of obstacles that always confront any outside powers in the region. Considering this balance from the standpoint of the three countries who were the targets of recent roadmaps demonstrates the complicated nature of the balancing task. Outcomes in Iraq, whether construed as "victory" that justifies the initial war and occupation or more likely as a careless waste of US resources, will expose an inbred American value: "When you have a strong sense of your national destiny, it's practically a religious mission, a divinely-ordained sequence of narrative that won't tolerate revision. You certainly don't want to let anyone else interfere with that" (Banks 2008: 76). This deeply held conviction explains why the flawed Bush doctrines that led to a second Gulf war still resonate with segments of the US public, despite the fact that others loudly acknowledge that the US has been fighting the wrong people in the wrong place. It explains why there is so often a reluctance to use international institutions more fully and earlier in crises like Iraq (see William Pfaff, www.williampfaff, July 15, 2008). It also underscores that the roots of what became that war of choice had roots in the Clinton years when Kosovo was also a war of choice (Chollet and Goldgeier 2008). Then the repeated argument was that the USA was the "indispensable nation".

That sense of indispensability was at the heart of the neoconservatives' insistence on exercising US military power against Iraq and also perhaps against Iran in service of securing Israel's future as well as American security. As this often mentioned vision yielded to realities on the ground, and demands for withdrawal escalated at home, neocons found it difficult to argue that only US military power could protect Middle East oil supplies since that commodity is sold on world markets. As well, the insistence that an Iraq without the American military would provide training grounds for terrorists down played the fact that such training grounds exist elsewhere on the globe and on the internet. And the idea that Afghanistan and Pakistan should receive any US forces withdrawn from Iraq ignored the fact US had little to gain and much more to lose by fighting the Taliban, Al Qaeda and Pakistani tribal elements at the same time, a recipe for disaster.

What US roadmaps in the Middle East show is the underlying beliefs that American democracy is exportable to a region characterized by diverse political systems (Wright 2008) and that the "democratic peace" can take root there. This would be an admirable, if distant, goal if local players espoused it. But they do not and no amount of US rhetoric will make it so. In Israel, the tension between a Jewish state and democracy persists and will only be resolved internally if and when a political centre takes root (Avishai 2008). In Iran, adding diplomacy to the US arsenal will pay off in the future only when the USA realizes it must give up the goal of regime change openly and privately, as well as demands for the cessation of nuclear enrichment before negotiations. Here the North Korean and Libyan examples deserve study. Iranians, too, must compromise and tone down hostile defamation of Israel as their own elections approach. In fact, domestic opinion in Iran indicates a new willingness

> [to] oppose the reckless and self-perpetuating policy of international confrontation apparently for its own sake; clearly damaging economic policies; and perhaps most importantly, the attitude of a president who brooks no criticism and whose ego has crossed the threshold of acceptability.
>
> (Ansari 2008: 93)

Subtle shifts are taking place in the Middle East, with a cooling of the over-heated atmosphere evident to outside observers. This marks what should be a welcome defeat for US policies of isolation and condemnation and a welcome endorsement of practical moves toward dealing with "rogue" actors like Hamas, Hezbollah and the Egyptian Muslim Brotherhood (Slackman 2008). Yet, against this more cheerful background, other problems loom. As one long-time observer notes before the global recession:

> Right now, the region is experiencing an economic boom, creating the opportunity to address the deep-seated political, economic and social problems that have spawned terrorist groups like Al Qaeda. That's certainly what the people of the

region hope. The danger is that the way the rising revenues are spent will more likely worsen the region's instability over time.

(Pollack 2008a)

Local leaders rather than the USA will determine whether useful solutions will follow, for example, whether there will be region-wide attempts to work on water problems or cross-border terrorism (*The Economist*, 19 July 2008).

What can be said with confidence now is that recent American policies have exacerbated tensions in the region and delayed internal accommodations to the newer realities of globalization in the Middle East. This zeal to impose solutions from the outside has resulted in "tarnished outcomes" (Montgomery 1986). Such outcomes are hardly unique. Indeed, what US policy in the Middle East expresses clearly is what John Montgomery foresaw as early as 1986, well before the end of the cold war and the 9/11 attacks. The US requires "skills of patient diplomacy and a national self confidence independent of military assertiveness" in order to be a "great power" rather than a superpower. There should be little disagreement with this sobering assessment now, as the USA itself turns toward internal renewal as do its Middle Eastern allies and adversaries.

The Middle East as a region offers the chance of testing these home truths as the Bush administration fades into history. As well, these possibilities offer a test of whether part of the older US foreign policy wisdom associated with the late George Kennan has staying power in the twenty-first century. He argued that single doctrines for US foreign policy were unsuitable and that the Middle East, along with Europe and Asia, were the enduring subjects of US diplomatic interest and deserved the highest level of attention over time and space. Yet internal developments there would remain essentially beyond US control. Such an approach would correctly place realities before roadmaps, visions before fantasies. Such a challenge awaits the post-Bush administration and its successors, specifically the painful recognition that the new rules of the game in the region are increasingly being written in the region itself rather than in outside capitals like Washington (Khouri 2008), as the 2009 Gaza war demonstrated.

References

Ansari, A.M. (2008) *Iran under Ahmadinejad*, London: Adelphi Papers, #393.
Avishai, B. (2008) *The Hebrew Republic*, New York: Harcourt.
Banks, R. (2008) *Dreaming Up America*, New York: Seven Stories Press.
Carter, T. and Innocent, M. (2008) "The Iraq War and Iranian Power", *Survival*, 49(4).
Chollet, D. and Goldgeier, J. (eds) (2008) *America Between the Wars*, New York: Basic Books.
Clarke, R. (2008) *Your Government Failed You*, New York: HarperCollins.
Diamond, L. (2005) *Squandered Victory*, New York: Henry Holt.
Dorrein, G. (2004) *Imperial Designs*, New York: Routledge.
Fettweis, C. (2008) "On the Consequences of Failure in Iraq", *Survival*, 49(4).
Gordon, P. (2008) "Winning the Right War", *Survival*, 49(4).
Ignatius, D. (2008) 'Talking Into the Sunset", *The Washington Post*, July 24.
Kepel, G. (2004) *The War for Muslim Minds*, Cambridge, MA: Harvard University Press.
Kessler, G. (2008) *Confidante*, New York: St Martin's Press.
Khouri, R.G. (2008) "New Rules for the Middle East", *International Herald Tribune*, May 26.
Lynch, T. and Singh, R. (2008) *After Bush*, Cambridge: Cambridge University Press.
Meyers, S. (2008) "Bush, in a Shift, Accepts Concept of Iraq Timeline", *New York Times*, July 19.

Montgomery, J. (1986) *Aftermath*, Dover, MA: Auburn House.
Morris, B. (2008) "Using Bombs to Stave off War", *International Herald Tribune*, July 18.
Nye, J. (2006) *Soft Power*, New York: Basic Books.
Oren, M. (2007) *Power, Faith and Fantasy*, New York: W.W. Norton.
Pollack, K. (2008a) "Drowning in Riches", *New York Times*, July 13.
Ross, D. (2007) *Statecraft*, New York: Farrar, Straus and Giroux.
Samuels, D. (2008) "The Father of Palestine", *The New Republic*, February 13.
Slackman, M. (2008) "Talks Signal Mideast Shift", *New York Times*, July 18.
Wright, R. (2008) *Dreams and Shadows*, New York: Penguin Press.

Further reading

Freedman, L. (2008) *A Choice of Enemies*, New York: Public Affairs.
Gerges, F. (2005) *The Far Enemy*, Cambridge: Cambridge University Press.
Goldsmith, J. (2007) *The Terror Presidency*, New York: W.W. Norton.
Kagan, R. (2006) *Dangerous Nation*, New York: Alfred Knopf.
Kleiman, A. (2000) *Compromising Palestine*, New York: Columbia University Press.
Lesch, D. (ed.) (2003) *The Middle East and the United States*, Boulder, CO: Westview Press.
Norton, R. (2007) *Hezbollah*, Princeton, NJ: Princeton University Press.
Pollack, K. (2008b) *A Path Out of the Desert*, New York: Random House.
Ross. D. (2004) *The Missing Peace*, New York: Farrar, Straus and Giroux.
Telhami, S. (2004) *The Stakes*, Boulder, CO: Westview Press.
Wittes, T. (ed.) (2005) *How Israelis and Palestinians Negotiate*, Washington, DC: United States Institute of Peace.

Websites

www.abuaardvark.typepad.com
www.carnegieendowment.com
www.cfr.org
www.iht.com
www.juancole.com
www.newamericancentury.com
www.nytimes.com
www.pbs.org
www.theatlantic.com
www.thewashingtonnote.com
www.washingtonpost.com

15 The US and the UN

The return of the prodigal son?

Craig N. Murphy

Throughout the recent, long US presidential campaign, various voices supportive of the United Nations could be heard expectantly predicting that, whichever candidate was elected, the long estrangement of the United States from the UN was about to end. This chapter looks back at not only the last eight years, but also the longer history of the US–UN relationship. That history suggests something different: While it may be unwise to ignore the extreme estrangement caused by recent US policy (as one distinguished French scholar, Jacques Fomerand, did when he noted a "remarkable pattern of continuity with previous administrations" that "runs counter to the comforting notion that we are in a mere fleeting moment of irresponsible insanity"[1]), there is little reason to expect rapid change in the overall pattern that existed throughout the George W. Bush years. The celebrations that will mark the new US embrace of multilateralism in 2009 may well be followed by disappointment within both the UN and the United States. This will not be the fault of individuals – of untested or distracted leaders in Washington or New York. Rather, it will be a consequence of the structural position of the United States within a global political economy that remains governed by the state system (a legacy of the Agricultural Age) even while the outlines of the (necessarily) *global* political system of the Industrial Age are becoming more apparent.

Who, exactly, is the son?

Some of the voices that were the most hopeful about US–UN relations in 2008 were those of the UN's "Mohicans," members of the tontine created by those who worked for the United Nations in its first year when it was part of the Bronx campus of the City University of New York's Hunter College. (Many staffers lived along the Hudson River, where James Fenimore Cooper set *The Last of the Mohicans* and "Uncas," the novel's hero, had a name that sounded like it could be one of the proliferating UN agencies where the irreverent young men and women worked.) Most of the remaining Mohicans have trouble seeing the United States as the estranged child of the UN; if anything, the relationship is the other way around. After all, most of the UN's original staffers were from the United States.

Bruce Stedman's story is typical. The long-time finance chief of the UN's development coordinating body remembers sitting on a US destroyer in the Pacific reading E. B. White's *New Yorker* magazine dispatches from the San Francisco Conference where the original "United Nations" (the wartime alliance) founded today's "United Nations Organization." White's passion made Stedman ache to be part of the struggle to create this American-inspired organization for world peace. In the week he was demobbed, Stedman went to join a new battle, in the Bronx, where he found scores of other idealistic young Americans.[2] Stedman eventually got an unusually important job – over the years, something more than 80 per cent of the UN system's personnel and resources have been devoted to its field offices in the developing world.[3] Yet, even the American Mohicans who ended up in more typical jobs – as statisticians, or stenographers or the like – shared Stedman's sense of mission, and his sense that creating the UN was the logical sequel to the US victory in 1945.

After all, the UN system had largely been an invention of the US government, of Franklin Roosevelt and those who were close too him.[4] John W. Holmes, a Canadian diplomat involved in wartime negotiations, remembers Roosevelt closing the earlier Hot Springs conference with the playing of "The Star-Spangled Banner," a sign, Holmes believed, of what the American sponsor imagined the UN would become.[5] The US acted "on the assumption 'that it was the destiny of mankind to become units in the expanding Republic of God' (established in 1776)."[6] Roosevelt's child, the United Nations, was meant to rally the nations of the world to fulfill that destiny. Instead, to the chagrin of some its earliest American supporters – including Stedman and many of the other aging Mohicans – the UN has become the prodigal son, aiding and giving voice to other visions of humankind's future, those petty dictators who use the UN to aggrandize themselves and more powerful dictators who use it to weaken the democratic ideals once embraced by the United States.

The Mohicans may exaggerate the degree to which Roosevelt's ideals were shared by all Americans and Holmes certainly exaggerates the naïveté and paternalism of the UN's American founders, but it is true that the founders' views were very different from those of most Americans today. The main difference is not so much that, in the 1940s, most Americans preferred multilateralism while, today, many dislike it. In fact, the difference has more to do with *beliefs* than with *attitudes*: The UN was created at a time when most Americans believed that some form of global government – something a good deal more complex than the UN – was inevitable, and in the not too distant future.

The evidence of that belief is overwhelming. Throughout the war, high-level academic-government partnerships assessed the pre-war international institutions and proposed ways in which they might be reformed[7] and leaders of both US political parties competed to develop the most attractive vision of world government. In fact, one of the most popular books in the US from 1943 through 1945 was a compilation of the four most prominent of these visions. It is true that the least radical of the four was developed by a Republican, former President Herbert Hoover,[8] but the most comprehensive was written by Roosevelt's most successful Republican challenger, Wendell Willkie.[9]

The politicians' books and E. B. White's *New Yorker* columns (that Bruce Stedman read at sea) were part of a popular genre that had generated best sellers throughout the Second World War. The books included an outline for an international organization of democracies written by the *The New York Times*'s inter-war correspondent in Geneva, Clarence K. Streit, parts of which read like John McCain's proposal for an alternative to the UN.[10]

Even more remarkable were the world government plans developed by the polymath, Ely Culbertson, already famous throughout the United States as the inventor of contract bridge (a game addictively embraced by many Mohicans and other bright young men and women of the day). Culbertson's second book on world government includes what now seem almost comically laudatory cover endorsements from leading scholars and public intellectuals of the day. Frederick L. Shuman, whose undergraduate text on international relations was the one most widely in the United States from the 1930s until around 1960 wrote, "the structure Mr. Culbertson has reared is so ingenious, so integrated, so beautifully articulated that it is almost irrelevant, not to say irreverent, to suggest knocking off a portico in one place or adding another somewhere else." Duke University political economist, champion of positivist social science and past president of the American Sociological Association, called Culbertson's plan, "the most perfect machinery yet devised by the mind of man to prevent international war." Journalists Dorothy Thompson (considered by *Time* to be one of the two most influential women in the country, almost the equal of Eleanor Roosevelt) and Max Eastman (in the midst of his theatrical, and well-timed disavowal of his old role as a lion of the left) were no less admiring.[11]

Today, the reception of Culbertson's particular plan for world government may seem bizarre, but it is worth recounting just to make clear how much the times have changed. It would be difficult to imagine that (say) Joshua Goldstein (author of the most popular international relations text in the USA today), Robert Keohane, Hillary Rodham Clinton and Francis Fukuyama or Irving Kristol would all embrace a plan for world government developed by the inventor of (say) Guitar Hero®. But the reason it is so difficult to imagine is that none of today's major US scholars, policy-makers or public intellectuals would embrace *any* plan for world government, no matter who invented it.

Things were very different in the 1940s. Then, the only question that divided the different US advocates of world government was what form the evolving system of world government should take: Should it be federal – modeled on the government of the United States and formed via a process of constitutional bargaining similar to the one that gave the USA its Constitution of 1787, or should world government evolve from the specific-purpose-oriented – "functionalist" – public international unions, such as the International Telecommunications Union, that began to emerge in the 1860s and that many observers in the 1940s considered the one successful part of the League system?[12]

Roosevelt's vision was a compromise. It combined functionalism with a kind of great power concert. He worked to reestablish the public international unions on a new, stronger footing. (The Hot Springs conference was about creating the Food and Agriculture Organization, which replicated the pre-League agriculture union – even occupying the same building and retaining the staff.) At the same time, the center of the UN system was to be the great power Security Council, with its Military Staff Committee and unified military force – perhaps a potential center of power for a US-inspired federal government.

Of course, the US worldview of the 1940s had huge blind spots that obscured truths that, today, we can see quite clearly. For example, the wartime literature in the USA rarely discussed a third, equally plausible path to world government, despite the fact that it was largely through this third means that some of the very limited world government we actually have was established.

Not only can world government (1) emerge from the devolution of functions to expert-based organizations, or (2) be established through an act of federation, it also can (3) be created by a predominant power. In theory, there were functionalist, federal, and *imperial* paths to that world that so many Americans in the 1940s expected and desired.

In the 1940s, some might even have argue that this last form of "world government" was the one that had been theorized the best; it was little different than global empire or world supremacy, the putative goal of every state since time immemorial, according to many realists. However, imperialism and colonial empires were out of favor in the USA at the time, especially among the internationalists who supported Roosevelt. Nonetheless, it is ironic that this third possibility was rarely mentioned in the United States at a time when many foreign observers, such as John Holmes, saw this as exactly what the USA was attempting to create.

In recent years, Yale comparative legal scholar Amy Chua has made a great deal of the debatable argument that there have been a small number of actual historical examples of "global" empires or "hyper-powers."[13] She includes George W. Bush's United States among such powers, but agrees with today's common wisdom that, in 1945, the USA was *not* such a power. Nonetheless, the USA created an embryonic world government, the UN System, through means that Chua considers typical of the few successful global powers: Roosevelt's UN was largely the result of an imperialism of soft power, a kind of ethical hegemony that took into account many of the interests and aspirations of the other victorious powers, as well as those of the vanquished.[14]

It is only in relation to that kind of hegemony that the USA now seems to be the way-ward child: It has become something like a true hyper-power, but it is no longer willing to accommodate some of the interests and aspirations of other states, especially many of the national interests and aspirations that are amplified by the UN system. These two developments may be related; that is, a structural change may have led to a change in US policy. Even so, it is worthwhile first to consider the perceptions and attitudes – the worldviews and the policy goals – that are the proximate causes of this change in policy.

How US ideas about the UN have changed and why

The US government's recent lack of support for the interests and aspirations con-cretized within the United Nations is, in part, a consequence of the US's abandonment of the belief in the impending necessity of world government. If world government is not on the horizon, then respect for the institutions that serve as the incubators of such government (according to the functionalists) or as a sort of ethical-hegemonic reflec-tion of one's own aspirations for a governed world order (according to critical realists), is no longer necessary.

The academic view

Such a change in understanding has certainly gone on within the US academic com-munity, which, compared to similar academic communities in other powerful countries, has an unusually strong relationship to government.[15] Yet, many younger international relations scholars may be surprised to realize how late this wartime idea persisted.

In the mid-1960s, it was still the height of political realism to argue, as Hans J. Morgenthau did in his Introduction to David Mitrany's *A Working Peace System*, that the nation-state was obsolete and the traditional politics among nation states would never get us to necessary world state – hence Morgenthau's endorsement of Mitrany's functionalist vision.[16]

Something has happened in the 43 years since then. While some US scholars focus on global governance (perhaps best defined as "what world government we really have") and a very few others imagine the eventual evolution of a world state,[17] most US scholars and policy-makers – most of whom received their higher education since the mid-1960s – understand world affairs as the politics of the state systems that have been with us since the beginning of settled agriculture over 5000 years ago. We live, US scholars tend to argue, in a system defined by state powers and interests and almost everything that really matters in terms of "global governance" takes place as a consequence of strategic interactions that are defined by state power and interests. There is no world government provided by international organizations – no weak, functionalist foreshadowing of what will become, there is no way to achieve world government (except, perhaps, via the temporary military supremacy of a single state), and, as a result, there is no practical way to speak sensibly about a imminent "need" for world government. The UN system is only an instrument of the foreign policies of its various state members, and, given its limited resources, it is a very weak instrument, at that.

The sources of this new, post-1960s consensus are many. Alexander Wendt, perhaps the most prominent US scholar who still sees world government as inevitable, points to the rising scientism of the scholarly discipline that took off in the 1970s and brought with it an unwarranted distrust of teleological arguments.[18]

Yet, much of the "inevitability of global governance" discourse that dominated the first two-thirds of the twentieth century was equally scientistic: It presented evolutionary models of political economy that claimed that only political systems regulating economic life across the entire geographic area of fundamental production can survive. Therefore, because industrial capitalism (or, according to some scholars, the industrial system, *per se*) pushes toward a single global economy, a unified polity will follow.[19] Susan Strange often pointed to the irony that, in the USA, the rise, in the 1970s, of the field called "International Political Economy" led to the dominance of state-system-centered studies of the "Politics of International Economic Relations" that almost eclipsed older traditions of political economy.[20] Perhaps this is part of the reason that the academic interest in world government waned.

Yet, the most significant reason may just be that, by the 1970s, the UN system, the only "world government" we had, became awfully boring to most scholars in the United States.[21] The global security structure that affected the United States was its nuclear balance of terror with the Soviet Union. Moreover, by the early 1970s, the US government institutions that were concerned with the fields of the UN's primary operation – especially development – had become as interesting and as powerful as the UN itself. Arguably, both the academic and the governmental turn away from the UN system was reinforced by the rising competence, and the rising bureaucratic demands, of USAID, the country's bilateral aid agency.[22]

This combination of factors has led to a situation in which today, unlike in 1945 or in 1966, US academics rarely see the UN system as important simply because it is the main precursor we have to world government. In the US hyper-power, post-Soviet world, some scholars, such as Michael Mandelbaum, simply see the US *as* global governance, as "what world government we have."[23] More typical are the views of Stephen Krasner, the nuanced and reflective Stanford University professor who served as Director of Policy Planning in the George W. Bush State Department. In a wide-ranging television interview, Krasner spoke of how the European Union, with its supra-nationalism, pooled sovereignty, and functionalist governance of various industrial problems represented something fundamentally new and different than the classical states of the state system,[24] but he ignored the similarities at a global level, where the UN system, the WTO, and a range of related private standard setters maintain pockets of activities where supra-nationalism, pooled sovereignty, and (certainly) functionalist governance might be seen as well.

Elite and popular attitudes

Outside the academic world, US views about the desirability of some kind of world government have changed less markedly since the 1960s. Surveys taken in the last five years continue to find large majorities of US citizens who want a much stronger United Nations and who consider such a development to be necessary because the world is becoming more "interconnected" and problems are "more of an international nature." More than 60 per cent of the US public would give the UN a standing peacekeeping force and international marshals capable of arresting national leaders accused of war crimes as well as the right to investigate violations of human rights wherever they occur and the power to regulate the international arms trade. On the other hand, only 45 per cent of the US public would approve of international taxes to pay for the UN's work.[25] (However, as my students often point out, perhaps only 45 per cent of US citizens would approve of taxes to support the operation of governments at any level.)

While the US public consistently supports a much stronger role for the UN than has been deemed imaginable or desirable by scholars for more than a generation, elite and popular attitudes toward the *existing* UN have been declining since the 1960s. US views reached their nadir in 2003 and 2004, around the time that Secretary General Kofi Annan made it clear that he considered the US war in Iraq to be in violation of international law. In August 2003, 60 per cent of US citizens polled by Gallup felt that the UN was doing a "poor job" with 37 per cent saying it was "doing a good job." These results were almost the reverse of when Gallup first asked the same questions, 50 years earlier when 55 per cent felt the UN "was doing a good job."[26]

Some students of US foreign policy see this declining affection for the UN as a consequence of the incoherently connected philosophies that have governed elite foreign policy attitudes since the beginning of the Republic. As leaders of a secular "City on the Hill" and model for the world to emulate, these men and women have an almost Manichaean attitude toward the rest of the world: When foreigners follow the US lead, they are good; when they do not, they are bad.[27] Hence, when the UN was simply a reflection of the vision of its US founders, it was good. As the UN became something different, it became something bad. Kofi Annan understood this dynamic quite well, which is one reason that he organized his ambitious program for UN reform (what he hoped would be his great legacy) around the themes of Franklin Roosevelt's original "Four Freedoms" speech in which he named the wartime alliance (the "United Nations") and first spelled out his vision for the postwar world.[28]

Annan's reforms failed due to the opposition of the Bush administration's powerful temporary ambassador to the UN, John Bolton, whose disdain for the organization was extreme. Nevertheless, the broader US opposition to the UN, which has been developing for decades, would doom any attempt to present the current organization as the dutiful child of its founders. In all of the major conflicts that have come to define the UN, US elite opinion (and, in many cases, mass opinion) has come to diverge from that of the UN majority and of the UN's permanent staff (what scholars call the "second" United Nations[29]).

As early as 1965, Hayward Alker and Bruce Russett had discerned the four main conflicts that would divide the UN: (1) the East–West conflict; (2) the North–South conflict between the rich, largely capitalist, countries and the Third World; (3) the conflict over Palestine; and (4) a conflict over the future of multilateralism. Only one of these conflicts, the first, has disappeared. In the remaining three cases, US views have increasingly become those of the minority within the UN system.

The US, of course, welcomed Israel's independence, but US administrations did not become unwavering supporters of Israeli positions until sometime after the 1967 war. (In 1956, Eisenhower opposed the British, French, and Israeli attack on Egypt over Suez.) Moreover, there was no solid UN majority in opposition to Israel until the early 1970s when most Sub-Saharan African governments (the UN's largest regional bloc, by far) switched from supporting Israel, to supporting the views of the Arab states, initially in the wake of what Africans perceived as Israel's unreasonable rejection of the peace proposals made by a commission of ten of Africa's most distinguished heads of state.[30]

The timing of the US's isolation on North–South issues is similar. The US was a designer and the main benefactor of the UN's development system until around 1970. The organization that eventually became the UN Development Programme (UNDP) was the direct descendant of the Marshall Plan and was intended to be something like the Marshall Plan writ large for the whole world. The Marshall Plan's only chief executive officer, Republican businessman Paul Hoffman, was the first head of UNDP and remained in the job until 1971.[31] UNDP and its predecessors, in turn, were instrumental in convincing almost all of the UN specialized agencies (including the World Bank), to begin the development work that has become the central mission of most of the agencies.[32] The centrality of the USA as a supporter of the developing world within the UN ended with the US war in Vietnam and the Nixon administration. That was when the USA cut its financial support for multilateral development organizations (shifting some to USAID) and took a uniquely oppositional position to Third World proposals to reform international economic institutions in the wake of the collapse of the original Bretton Woods mechanisms.[33]

The US government's opposition to further extensions of multilateralism is something of a later vintage, and it, of course, not something supported by majority of the US public even if the opposition may have the tacit support of many in the US academic community. It was the Reagan administration, in 1981, that first signaled a major retreat from multilateralism, initially by calling for a wholesale review of the US's participation in the World Bank and the International Monetary Fund, the specialized agencies that many observers considered to be already the most subservient to the USA. The new US policy was the brainchild of the relatively new, conservative think tank, the Heritage Foundation, which argued for "American withdrawal from a UN system it could no longer dominate."[34]

The special case of the second Bush administration

It is not surprising that Heritage promoted such a position. The Foundation was one of many organizations that contributed to the rise of the political right in the US over the last generation. Many of the organizations were created and bankrolled by conservative, Christian businessmen from the South and West, men such as Fred, David, and Charles Koch, the last of whom is described by one liberal blogger as the richest and most politically connected mogul you've never heard of.

Koch (pronounced coke) heads Koch Industries, the world's largest private company with oil refineries, gas pipelines, cattle ranches, paper mills and financial services that produce an estimated $90 billion in revenue a year. Although Koch is richer than George Soros or Carl Icahn – and spends millions each year to lobby Congress and to bankroll libertarian causes – he is largely unknown outside of his hometown of Wichita, Kansas.[35]

For the UN, the geographic origins of the supporters of the new right were important. From Reagan onward, the Republican Party has gained power by solidifying white majority in southern and western states, regions previously either dominated by the Democratic Party or else competitive between the two parties. The new regional power centers of the Republican Party are areas where, for a variety of historical reasons, isolationism, militarism, and the starkest versions of international Manichaeism are typically found.[36]

Since Reagan's rise, the history of the Republican Party has been the story of the return to the worldview that typified the party before Wendell Willkie. Historians recall that it was the power of Republican isolationists in the US Senate that doomed Woodrow Wilson's vision of the League of Nations. The global economic depression, Hitler's rise, the success of the global alliance that defeated him, and the pressures of the early Cold War left the Republican Party under the control of internationalists through the Nixon administration. Similar internationalists remained at the center of the administration of George H. W. Bush, but his son's views were much closer to those of Reagan.

This view of the UN was well summarized by the hour-long videotape that was widely distributed as part of 2000 electoral campaign: "Global Governance: The Quiet War Against American Independence." The video, narrated by the man who would soon become US Attorney General, John Ashcroft, explains that the Clinton administration has made an unholy alliance with "global bureaucrats" to give the UN "control over American land, natural resources, private property, our economy, and even our children."[37]

The career of John Bolton, Assistant Secretary of State for International Organization Affairs under the first George Bush and temporary UN Ambassador for George W. Bush epitomized these views. The title of Bolton's revealing memoir of his tenure as UN ambassador, *Surrender is Not an Option: Defending America at the United Nations and Abroad*[38] neatly encapsulates the larger vision of which his attitude toward the UN is a part: Because most foreign governments are venal and envy the power and wealth of the United States, in the UN, the USA is always surrounded by a potential global coalition of enemies. Whatever its original, naïve purpose, today, the United Nations merely amplifies the power of this anti-US coalition. Thus, a heroic defender of US interests needs to stand firm against the UN and UN majority, except on those occasions when it is possible to use some of the powers of the UN to serve the immediate goals of the nation.

Bolton was at the center of the Republican attack on the United Nations since that attack's beginning. During Ronald Reagan's first term, a well-intentioned internationalist Republican Senator from Kansas, Nancy Kassebaum, introduced legislation to limit US payment of its UN dues in order to encourage administrative reform of the organization, following on proposals made by the Heritage Foundation. This began a consistent policy of under-funding the UN and many of the Specialized agencies that has been a consistent part of US–UN policy ever since.[39] Assistant Secretary of State Bolton not only played a role in promoting the Heritage idea, he also "led the campaign to withdraw US membership from UNESCO" and threatened to withdraw US funding to the UNDP if it did not funnel millions of dollars to various US nongovernmental organizations on the right, including the Heritage Foundation itself.[40]

Under George W. Bush, Bolton credited himself with thwarting Kofi Annan's attempts to unify and strengthen the administrative capacity of the UN system, with ending the UN career of Annan's powerful deputy, British Liberal Democrat Mark Malloch Brown, and with finding a pliable replacement for Annan in Ban Ki-Moon. However, Bolton came to question the permanence of his "victories." By 2007, he was speaking out against what he considered a failure of nerve on the part of his old boss, an unwillingness to use military force against Iran and North Korea, and a dangerous tendency to rely on the UN.[41]

Most observers point to the same actions as evidence of a new "pragmatism" that took hold in Bush's last two years, a pragmatism that reinforced more traditional internationalists, such as Stephen Krasner, who still worked in a government that had seemed to be dominated by men like Bolton. *Newsweek* editor and Harvard-trained international relations scholar Fareed Zakaria pronounced this shift "What Bush Got Right" and argued that the next administration should not simply "reverse course," but learn from Bush's brief final period of political realism.[42]

Throughout that period, even the Bush administration's understanding of global governance and its attitude toward the UN system – or, at least, multilateralism – seemed to change. After the Russian invasion of Georgia in summer 2008, administration spokesmen warned Russia that the nature of the world had changed. To maintain a powerful, productive, and modern economy, industrial states had to be linked closely to one another; they had to be members in the multilateral clubs in which the rules of the world economy were set, and Russia risked not being unwelcome in those vital forums.

By extension, of course, what was good for Russia was also good for the United States. The old Heritage Foundation argument for withdrawing from any multilateral organizations that the US could not dominate had been rejected. The second Bush administration was not longer a special case.

Will the relationship change?

Still, the Bush administration's late development of foreign policy pragmatism certainly did not mean a fundamental change in official US policy toward multilateralism, global governance, or the UN system. As just one indication: the US debt to the UN, which had sharply declined (from about US\$ 2 billion to 1 billion) after the 2001 terrorist attacks, crept back up to its early 2001 level during Bush's last two years in office.[43]

There are structural reasons for the persistence of US disenchantment with multilateralism. There is a fundamental difference between a global power, even a hyperpower, that can imagine creating a form of world government in its own image, (as the United States did for that brief moment in the 1940s) and a global power that recognizes that most forms of institutionalized international cooperation will be reached through compromise. Unfortunately, for that power's leaders, many of those compromises will not serve the power's interests as well as unilateral action can. Or, to put it another way, a global power is always going to be tempted to use its vast power in its own narrow and short-term interests, rather than in service of its long-term, global vision.

This was clear more than a century ago when Great Britain, another of Amy Chua's handful of hyper-powers, had the vision of creating a liberal world economy controlled by a coalition of limited democracies that is now so popular among US elites today. However, when it came to creating global institutions that could make such a system work – especially institutions under which British commercial and military interests would be held accountable to international norms – the British were unusually cautious. Consider the Hague Conferences of 1899 and 1907, which had vast agendas that were truncated by a few powers. As originally conceived, the conferences would have banned many of the weapons and tactics that became commonplace in the twentieth century (including aerial bombardment) and they would have created binding international commercial law and global trade courts that would have been even stronger than what was created when the weak General Agreement on Tariffs and Trade became the much more powerful World Trade Organization (WTO), in 1995.

In the months before the 1899 conference, British public intellectual W. T. Stead worried (presciently) that British caution might lead his government to limit the issues that would be discussed at The Hague.[44] In 1907, when The Hague agenda was expanded to include all the original proposals, a growing trade conflict between Britain and the most recently industrialized (and, at that moment, more industrially successful) Germany led that young empire to oppose discussion of tariffs, private international law, taxation, rights of foreigners to hold property, standards, and international labor issues – many of them issues in which Germany had been the sponsor and benefactor of international cooperation in the 1890s. In 1907, Great Britain joined Germany in opposing greater institutionalization of the international governance of global transportation and communication and, in other venues, blocked international cooperation on health and sanitation because health regulations might impact British shipping. The British argument that the germ theory of disease was not scientifically proven was very similar to the Bush administration's absurd claims about a lack of scientific consensus on global warming.[45]

The British example illustrates that any similarly strong power will be tempted to use its power for short-term gain rather than to work collectively to institutionalize a longer-term vision, but doing so is a matter of choice: Might not a new US administration resist the temptation? The records of the Carter and Clinton administration should give us pause.

It was, after all, Jimmy Carter – perhaps the most internationalist president after Kennedy – who first pulled the USA out of a UN agency. From 1977 to 1980, Carter temporarily withdrew the USA from the International Labor Organization when US, but not Israeli, concern about the Organization's embrace of the Palestine Liberation Organization was added to persistent opposition of US labor leader, George Meany.[46]

Clinton and his closest advisors also embraced multilateralism. Clinton gave strong hortatory support to the creation of the International Criminal Court and the Kyoto Protocol. Yet, if even if Clinton at some point had the political capital to get Congressional approval of those initiatives (which he may never have had), he certainly did not choose to use it. The man that the Clinton administration supported as UN

Secretary General, Boutros Boutros-Ghali even claims that, for short-term domestic political reasons, Clinton undermined comprehensive UN reform and did nothing to support Boutros-Ghali's bold attempt to make the promotion of democracy a central purpose of the organization.[47]

Boutros-Ghali is not an unbiased source, but his account of these issues is broadly supported by the then number two official in the UN, UNDP Administrator Gus Speth, an American nominated (meaning "appointed") by Clinton. Speth speaks of his surprise at Clinton's last-minute reversal of support for the reform plan that Speth developed. Clearly, Clinton had heard from UNICEF chief, and former Manhattan Borough President, Carol Bellamy, whose independent source of power would be curtailed by the reform. While Speth does not dwell on Clinton's motivation, others point to the aspirations of Hillary Rodman Clinton, who needed the backing of New York's Democratic Party leaders for her planned run for the US Senate.[48]

The difference between the Clinton administration and other recent great power advocates of multilateralism has been marked. Gordon Brown envisioned using the pledges of major aid donors as a kind of collateral that would allow the UN to raise so much capital for economic development that otherwise pie-in-the-sky MDG poverty-reduction goals suddenly seemed plausible.[49] Successive conservative presidents of France have proposed and even begun to institute taxes on "global" transactions (such as airline tickets) to provide the UN with an automatic, independent source of finance.[50] Perhaps the only difference between the Europeans and the Americans is that neither the British nor the French government can gain petty, short-term advantage by working to undermine some aspect of the UN system in the way that every US president can. The US president faces the temptation to make political patronage appointments to those UN jobs that, by tradition rooted in power, are his to make (such as the chief executives of UNICEF and the World Bank). Because the USA still provides by far the largest financial contribution to most UN agencies, the US administration has the power to appease many domestic constituencies by threatening to withdraw funding or support for specific actions, something no other state is in the position to do. Moreover, because the UN system as a whole will, almost inevitably, have some agencies or programs whose actions deviate from norms that are widely shared in the USA, every US administration will, at some point, be under pressure to use that power.

It is perhaps a law of international politics that hyper-powers are fickle (if not feckless) friends of global governance. There may be some validity to Jacques Fomerand's concern that the "irresponsible insanity" of the Bush administration's policy toward the UN will become more the norm than the exception.

Notes

1 See Fomerand (2007).
2 Bruce Stedman, interview with the author, 3 February 2005, for Craig N. Murphy, *UNDP: A Better Way?* (2006).
3 The UN system as a whole includes all the UN Specialized agencies, which include some of the "Public International Unions" established in the nineteenth century and continued under the League of Nations; the UN system includes the World Bank and the International Monetary Fund. Scholars distinguish the "first" United Nations, the club of nations, from the "second" United Nations, the international civil servants and global public administration that is provided by them. (See Claude, 1996.) It is the personnel of the second UN, and the resources that they employ and they distribute, that have been so focused on the developing

world. Sir Robert Jackson's (1969) "Capacity Study," the first, and only, major internal eva-
luative study of the entire estimated an even higher percentage. Given the increase in membership from the developing world since 1969, there is every reason to believe that the UN's
work has become even more focused there. See Jackson (ibid.: 4).

4 The celebrated recent history of the San Francisco Conference emphasizes the role played
by Truman and those close to him in the months after Roosevelt's death (Schlesinger
2003). Schlesinger's perspective is especially relevant to the Charter and the central organs
of the UN, but the history of the UN system as a whole, whose specialized agencies
began to be established as early as 1943, is much more a story of Roosevelt and those
close to him. Eric Helleiner has begun some critically important studies of those connections,
the first of which was published in 2006 as "Reinterpreting Bretton Woods: International
Development and the Neglected Origins of Bretton Woods," *Development and Change*, 37
(5): 943–67.

5 John W. Holmes, "Looking Forward and Backwards," keynote speech to the First Annual
Meeting of the Academic Council on the UN System, 23 June 1988, published as an
occasional paper by the ACUNS Secretariat, Hanover, NH, 1988.

6 Quoted in Fomerand (2007: 274). Fomerand says that Holmes, in turn, described himself as
quoting "an unnamed Canadian social scientist" (ibid.: 278).

7 See. Murphy (1994: 163–6).

8 The work was by Herbert Hoover and Hugh Gibson, "The Problems of Lasting Peace," in
Henry Seidel Canby (ed.) *Prefaces to Peace* (New York: Simon & Schuster, Doubleday,
Reynal & Hitchcock, and Columbia University Press, 1943).

9 See Wendell L. Willkie, *One World* (New York: Simon & Schuster, 1943), abridged in Canby,
Prefaces to Peace.

10 See Streit (1940).

11 All the quotations are from the cover of Ely Culbertson, *Total Peace: What Makes Wars and
How to Organize Peace* (1943).

12 One example of the debate was James Avery Joyce (ed.) (1945) *World Organization: Federal
or Functional? A Roundtable Discussion*, which the title page describes as, "A discussion by
Patrick Ransome, George Catlin, Edvard Hambro, C. B. Purdom and J. A. Joyce, chairman,
held in London, February 5, 1944, which had as its main theme Professor Mitrany's
pamphlet, 'A working peace system.' An introduction by Professor Mitrany and an article by
H. G. Wells have been added." A somewhat similar defense of the functionalist view
appeared in the Nobel Lecture of the 1946 Peace Laureate, Emily Greene Balch, the American founder of the Women's International League for Peace and Freedom and one of first
professors of International Relations, "Toward Human Unity or Beyond Nationalism,"
nobelprize.org/nobel_prizes/peace/laureates/1946/balch-lecture.html.

13 See Chua (2007).

14 This is a standard description of ethical hegemony used by many followers of Antonio
Gramsci. I owe my understanding of it to the late Italian diplomat, Enrico Augelli; see
Augelli and Murphy (1988: 124–34).

15 A point made by many scholars and discussed cogently as the problem of "In and Outers," in
Thomas J. McCormick, *America's Half Century: United States Foreign Policy in the Cold
War* (1989).

16 Hans J. Morgenthau, "Introduction," in David Mitrany, *A Working Peace System* (1966:
7–12). See also Campbell Craig, "Hans Morgenthau and the World State Revisited" (2007:
196–215).

17 Perhaps the most prominent of these is Alexander Wendt, "Why a World State is Inevitable:
Teleology and the Logic of Anarchy," Civitatis Paper of the Month, No. 4, May 2004, www.
civitatis.org/pdf/wstate.pdf.

18 Ibid.

19 Thomas G. Weiss and Sam Daws remind students of the UN of the late Harold Jacobson's
ironic appreciation of such arguments, "World Politics: Continuity and Change since
1945," in *The Oxford Handbook on the United Nations* (2007: 84). Much of this strand of
political economy originated with mid-nineteenth-century authors who were concerned
about the unification of small states (e.g., Germany, the United States, and Italy) to create
larger units that would support industries that could compete with those in Great Britain,

the first industrial nation. See Murphy, *International Organization and Industrial Change* (1994: 144).
20 For example, Susan Strange, "An International Political Economy Perspective" (1997).
21 This is the implication of the argument of Gene M. Lyons, the Dartmouth College professor who helped reinvigorate the study of the UN in the USA in the 1990s; see his *Putting ACUNS Together* (1999).
22 This is an argument that was made forcefully to me by many of the Mohicans I interviewed when I studied UNDP. Some of the evidence is summarized in a section entitled "Running the Gauntlet for US Funds," in Murphy (2006: 154–8).
23 See Mandelbaum (2005).
24 "Conversations with History: Stephen D. Kranser," 6 November 2007, ideo.google.com/videoplay?docid=7645542962499624840&ei=59GySNDiDpDuqwLwsMTqDA&q=Krasner&vt=lf&hl=en.
25 University of Maryland Program on International Policy Attitudes, Americans and the World, United Nations, www.americans-world.org/digest/global_issues/un/un1.cfm.
26 Ibid., and Nichols (2003).
27 See Augelli and Murphy (1988: 35–74).
28 Lee Feinstein of the US Council on Foreign Relations tried to make this connection abundantly clear to an elite audience that had become quite skeptical of the UN. See Feinstein, "Annan's UN Report Seeks to Take Into Account UN Interests," 22 March 2005.
29 See Claude (1996), "Peace and Security."
30 Divisions within that group certainly contributed to its failure, as well. See Touval (1982: 202–24).
31 Murphy (2006: 41–50, 56).
32 Ibid.: 57–60, 82–93.
33 A collapse that was engineered by the Nixon administration. Significantly, the US break from "the South" was not yet definitive even in the Nixon years; the Republican Congressman whom Nixon nominated to replace Hoffman was one of the strongest advocates in the UN Secretariat for the Third World's "New International Economic Order" proposals, something that Nixon understood would be the case when he made the nomination; Murphy (2006: 158–62).
34 See Beigbeder (1987: 12).
35 See Eisenberg (2008), and see the more nuanced discussions of the Koch foundations, on the Media Transparency website: www.mediatransparency.org/funderprofile.php?funderID=9.
36 Michael Lind has written one of the more popular discussions of how these regional origins have changed US foreign policy. See his *Made in Texas: George W. Bush and the Southern Takeover of American Politics* (2003).
37 "Global Governance: The Quiet War Against American Independence," An Eagle Forum Television Special Report, distributed by Cross Media Communications, 1997.
38 Bolton (2007).
39 The US-based Global Policy Forum, often in collaboration with the Friedrich Ebert Foundation, has maintained the most exhaustive and consistent analyses of the chronic UN financial crisis. The starting point for their analysis is, "Background and History of the UN Financial Crisis," www.globalpolicy.org/finance/chronol/hist.htm.
40 Williams (1992), reprinted at www.globalpolicy.org/reform/williams.htm.
41 Meyers (2007).
42 Zakaria (2008), www.newsweek.com/id/151731.
43 Global Policy Forum, "US vs. Total Debt to the UN: 1996–2008," www.globalpolicy.org/finance/tables/core/usvtotalgraph.htm.
44 Stead (1899: 443–8).
45 Murphy (1994: 102–4); Scott (1907: 407–10); Cooper (1989: 178–254).
46 Galenson (1981).
47 Boutros-Ghali (1999).
48 Murphy (2006: 292–4).
49 Announced in Gordon Brown, Remarks to the Royal Institute of International Affairs/Chatham House Conference on Corporate Social Responsibility, 22 January 2003.
50 UN News Centre (2005) "Annan Welcomes France's Airline Ticket Levy to Help Developing Countries."

References

Augelli, Enrico and Murphy, Craig N. (1988) *America's Quest for Supremacy and the Third World*, London: Pinter Publishers.

Beigbeder, Yves (1987) *Management Problems in International Organizations: Reform or Decline?* London: Frances Pinter.

Bolton, John (2007) *Surrender Is Not an Option: Defending America at the United Nations and Abroad*, New York: Simon & Schuster.

Boutros-Ghali, Boutros (1999) *Unvanquished: A US-UN Story*, New York: Random House.

Chua, Amy (2007) *Day of Empire: How Hyperpowers Rise to Global Dominance and Why They Fall*, New York: Doubleday.

Claude, Jr., Inis L. (1996) "Peace and Security: Prospective Roles for the Two United Nations," *Global Governance*, 2(3): 289–98.

Cooper, Richard N. (1989) "International Cooperation in Public Health as a Prologue to Macroeconomic Cooperation," in Richard N. Cooper, *et al.* (eds) *Can Nations Agree?*, Washington, DC: Brookings Institution Press.

Craig, Campbell (2007) "Hans Morgenthau and the World State Revisited," in Michael C. Williams (ed.) *Realism Reconsidered: The Legacy of Hans Morgenthau in International Relations*, Oxford: Oxford University Press, pp. 196–215.

Culbertson, Ely (1943) *Total Peace: What Makes Wars and How to Organize Peace*, Garden City, NY: Doubleday, Doran & Company, Inc.

Eisenberg, Carol (2008) "Billionaire Koch Plays Politics, but out of Public Eye," *Muckety*, 8 August.

Feinstein, Lee (2005) "Annan's UN Report Seeks to Take into Account UN Interests," 22 March. Online. Available at: www.cfr.org/publication/7953/feinstein.html?breadcrumb=%2Fbios%2F3348%2F%3Fpage%3D2.

Fomerand, J. (2007) "UN–US Relations from the Standpoint of the Organization: What Can the UN Do with an 'Indispensable Nation' and 'Reluctant Sheriff'?," *American Foreign Policy Interests*, 29(4): 267.

Galenson, W. (1981) *The International Labor Organization: An American View*, Madison, WI: University of Wisconsin Press.

Helleiner, E. (2006) "Reinterpreting Bretton Woods: International Development and the Neglected Origins of Bretton Woods," *Development and Change*, 37(5): 943–67.

Holmes, John W. (1988) "Looking Forward and Backwards," keynote speech to the First Annual Meeting of the Academic Council on the UN System, 23 June, published as an occasional paper by the ACUNS Secretariat, Hanover, NH.

Hoover, Herbert and Gibson, Hugh (1943) "The Problems of Lasting Peace," in Henry Seidel Canby (ed.) *Prefaces to Peace*, New York: Simon & Schuster, Doubleday, Reynal & Hitchcock, and Columbia University Press.

Jackson, Robert G.A. (1969) *A Study of the Capacity of the United Nations Development System*, vol. 2, Geneva: United Nations.

Joyce, James Avery (ed.) (1945) *World Organization: Federal or Functional? A Roundtable Discussion*, London: C. A. Watts &Co., Ltd.

Krasner, Stephen D. (2007) "Conversations with History: Stephen D. Krasner," 6 November 2007. Online. Available at: ideo.google.com/videoplay?docid=7645542962499624840&ei=59GySNDiDpDuqwLwsMTqDA&q=Krasner&vt=lf&hl=en.

Lind, Michael (2003) *Made in Texas: George W. Bush and the Southern Takeover of American Politics*, New York: New America Books.

Lyons, Gene M. (1999) *Putting ACUNS Together*, New Haven, CT: Academic Council on the UN System.

Mandelbaum, Michael (2005) *The Case for Goliath: How America Acts as the World's Government in the Twentieth Century*, New York: Public Affairs.

McCormick, Thomas J. (1989) *America's Half Century: United States Foreign Policy in the Cold War*, Baltimore, MD: Johns Hopkins University Press.

Meyers, Steven Lee (2007) "Bush Loyalist Now Sees a White House Dangerously Soft on Iran and North Korea," *The New York Times*, 9 November.

Morgenthau, Hans J. (1966) "Introduction," in D. Mitrany, *A Working Peace System*, Chicago, IL: University of Chicago Press.

Murphy, Craig N. (1994) *International Organization and Industrial Change: Global Governance since 1850*, Cambridge: Polity Press, pp. 163–6.

—— (2006) *UNDP: A Better Way?* Cambridge: Cambridge University Press.

Nichols, Bill (2003) "US View of UN Largely Negative," *USA Today*, 9 September.

Schlesinger, Stephen C. (2003) *Act of Creation: The Founding of the United Nations: A Story of Superpowers, Secret Agents, Wartime Allies and Enemies and Their Quest for a Peaceful World*, Boulder, CO: Westview Press.

Scott, James Brown (1907) *The Reports to the Hague Conferences of 1899 and 1907*, Oxford: Oxford University Press.

Stead, W.T. (1899) *The United States of Europe: On the Eve of the Parliament of Peace*, New York: Doubleday & McClure Co.

Strange, Susan (1997) "An International Political Economy Perspective," in John H. Dunning (ed.) *Governments, Globalization and International Business*, New York: Oxford University Press.

Streit, Clarence K. (1940) *Union Now: The Proposal for an Interdemocracy Federal Union*, New York: Harper & Brothers Publishers.

Touval, Saadia (1982) *The Peace Brokers: Mediators in the Arab-Israeli Conflict, 1948–79*, Princeton, NJ: Princeton University Press.

UN News Centre (2005) "Annan Welcomes France's Airline Ticket Levy to Help Developing Countries,", 27 December 2005. Online. Available at: www.un.org/apps/news/story.asp?NewsID= 17044&Cr=France&Cr1.

Weiss, Thomas G. and Daws, Sam (2007) "World Politics: Continuity and Change since 1945," in Thomas G. Weiss and Sam Daws (eds) *The Oxford Handbook on the United Nations*, Oxford: Oxford University Press.

Wendt, Alexander (2004) "Why a World State is Inevitable: Teleology and the Logic of Anarchy," Civitatis Paper of the Month, No. 4, May. Online. Available at: www.civitatis.org/pdf/wstate.pdf.

Williams, Ian (1992) "Why the Right Loves the UN," *The Nation*, 13 April. Online. Available at: reprinted, www.globalpolicy.org/reform/williams.htm.

Willkie, Wendell L. (1943) *One World*, New York: Simon & Schuster.

Zakaria, Fareed (2008) "What Bush Got Right," *Newsweek*, 18–25 August 2008. Online. Available at: www.newsweek.com/id/151731.

16 Democracy promotion and the New Public Diplomacy

Giles Scott-Smith and Martijn Mos

Introduction

In the wake of 9/11, the United States government set out to clarify the values it stood for in the world. The second section of the 2002 National Security Strategy of the United States, which outlined the aim to 'Champion Aspirations for Human Dignity,' spelled out a series of 'nonnegotiable demands': the rule of law, free speech, freedom of worship, equal justice, and respect for private property. The intention was to direct US actions and resources towards 'expanding liberty' and 'the development of democratic institutions' around the world. This chapter will focus on US public diplomacy efforts to realize this agenda.

Public diplomacy covers an array of government-sponsored activities that aim to influence opinion abroad, thereby creating a more positive, supportive environment within which foreign policies can be conducted. It therefore covers everything from government information programs and news broadcasting to the active role of the private sector in running exchange programs and in cultural diplomacy projects covering the arts. From 1953 to 1999 the main body responsible for this was the United States Information Agency (USIA), which conducted and coordinated its activities with the State Department (Dizard 2004). In 1999, the Foreign Affairs Restructuring Act dissolved USIA and transferred its information and exchange activities to the State Department, whereas broadcasting was placed under the supervision of the independent Broadcasting Board of Governors.

The need to respond rapidly to the shock of 9/11 exposed the fact that public diplomacy had been seriously neglected during the 1990s. As the independent Public Diplomacy Council stated in 2005:

> Buffeted by a decade of budget cuts, hampered by bureaucratic structures that marginalize it and call on its expertise too late in the policy process, public diplomacy as currently constituted is inadequate to perform the urgent national security tasks required of it – to inform, to understand and to influence world publics.
>
> (Public Diplomacy Council 2005: 3)

The emphasis here will be placed on the tensions that have appeared throughout the pursuit of public diplomacy by the United States since 2001. Following the horror of 9/11 there was widespread empathy around the world which could have formed the basis for a US-led international effort to solve problems in a host of policy areas. Instead, concerns over the negative image of the United States abroad and the startling results of opinion polls conducted by the Pew Research Center (particularly in the Middle East) caused an emphasis to be laid on improving the way others understood US values, goals, and actions. This one-way approach sought to deal with the question 'why do they hate us?' not via an engagement with others' concerns, but with an intensified portrayal of why the United States continued to offer the best example to the rest of the world. The declaration of a War on Terror also had major implications, since it not only demanded that all information activities be placed under a national security imperative, but it also increased the role of the Pentagon in media management. The result has been an intensification of efforts to control the message, instead of reflecting on what the message should be and why it was being received by others in certain ways. As a result, the democratizing potential of public diplomacy initiatives, which ideally work towards empowerment and merging interests *with* others as much as projecting the merits of a defined national interest *to* others, has largely been submerged under more limited national security objectives.

The New Public Diplomacy

Public diplomacy was first referred to as a recognizable field of activity in 1965 by Edmund Gullion, a former US Ambassador to the Congo who used the opportunity of opening the Edward R. Murrow Center at Tuft University's Fletcher School of Law and Diplomacy to outline that it entailed:

> the influence of public attitudes on the formation and execution of foreign policies. It encompasses dimensions of international relations beyond traditional diplomacy ... [including] the cultivation by governments of public opinion in other countries; the interaction of private groups and interests in one country with those of another ... (and) the transnational flow of information and ideas.[1]

Up to this point, public diplomacy activities had been referred to either as politically-neutral cultural relations and educational exchange, or as propaganda, which early studies of USIA admitted was essentially the purpose (Dizard 1961). Gullion's definition, on the other hand, highlighted certain aspects that mark out public diplomacy as a unique area of activity. First, the emphasis on the domestic impact of public opinion on the crafting of foreign policy. Second, the essential role of the private sector in building transnational connections, either in collusion with or independent of government. However, the claim that this was 'beyond traditional diplomacy' situated public diplomacy as an addendum to existing channels of inter-state relations. It also assumed, despite its recognition of the role of the private sector, that the nation-state could still make use of public diplomacy as a unitary actor pursuing the national interest abroad.

In recent years there has been increasing interest in the importance of public diplomacy. There are two main strands to this. First, there has been a focus on 'strategic public diplomacy,' a field that draws on political communication and 'the creation, distribution, control, use, processing, and effects of information as a political resource.' Messages are crafted and targeted according to the behavior patterns, cultural norms, and media consumption of a specific audience (Manheim 1994: 7–9). Second, and more extensive in its implications, there is what has become known as New Public Diplomacy, which seeks not just to secure a favorable reception for foreign policies abroad, but also to reflect on how the entire diplomatic machinery of nation-states needs to be overhauled in line with the demands of a changing global political environment. These changes can be outlined in terms of the structure and process of global politics. In terms of structure, the position of the nation-state as an actor within the international system has come under question (Guehenno 2000). Regarded as the preeminent unit in international politics since the Treaty of Westphalia in 1648, it is now operating alongside transnational corporations (TNCs) and non-governmental organizations (NGOs) which, if not partners of an equal stature, are nevertheless increasingly relevant (if not unavoidable) for the successful formulation and implementation of foreign policy. What is more, the level of integration in certain policy fields coupled with the development of supranational organizations has further altered the space within which nation-states operate (Hocking 1999; Melissen 1999; Riordan 2003). As a result foreign policy will 'no longer be the sole province of governments' (Nye 2002: 60).

In terms of processes, the post-Cold War era has witnessed a remarkable shift in the ways that foreign policy and diplomatic activity are now viewed. First, the diversification of media outlets and the diffusion of information and communication technologies have increased the availability of information (to those online and hooked up, at least) and lessened the ability of nation-states to control the news agenda. Other actors, right down to individual citizens, are now able to contribute to and even seize the ways in which news is presented to a global audience. Second, and connected to this, there has been an increasing transparency to political activity in line with the general wave of democratization that occurred following the break-up of the Soviet Union and the end of the Cold War. The decline of foreign policy as the domain of an elite establishment, coupled with the need to legitimize policies in the eyes of the domestic public, has altered the relationship between government and citizen. In this context, strategic public diplomacy aims to carve out a unique place for government communications within the increasingly crowded airwaves. The New Public Diplomacy, on the other hand, aims not so much to take the domestic constituency into account, but also to seek out ways in which it can be utilized to further specific interests of the nation-state as a whole (Brown 2004: 14–19; Hocking 2005: 28–41; Melissen 2005: 3–27). After all, the private sector generally possesses a greater credibility abroad, and through this manages to acquire greater access to regions or constituencies otherwise out of reach of official contact (Leonard 2002).

Strategic public diplomacy is basically an extension of the propaganda and psychological warfare techniques developed during World War II, now applied by governments in peaceful situations. New Public Diplomacy, on the other hand, contrasts with former approaches in three ways: (1) the importance of non-state actors alongside and outside of inter-state relations has increased; (2) the practice of public diplomacy abroad is intimately and necessarily linked to the practice of public affairs at home; and (3) it is not so much geared towards the management of information for the purpose of convincing others to adopt another point of view, but towards an engagement with other constituencies with the aim of establishing a dialogue on the grounds of mutual interest or concern (Melissen 2005: 12–13). The hierarchies of Westphalian state-centric relations are breaking down, and new opportunities – and challenges – are taking their place. The New Public Diplomacy is therefore not so much an addendum to diplomatic practice as the basis for its actual reformulation in the twenty-first century.

The conduct of US public diplomacy following 9/11 has reflected both 'strategic' and 'new' dimensions. Determined to reinstate the primacy and power of democratic values, the emphasis was placed on getting the message out more consistently and at a louder volume. The Defense Department in particular has expanded its public diplomacy activities in a search for greater 'strategic influence' (Gough 2003). The State Department, ostensibly responsible for the public diplomacy effort, has oscillated between talking the new language but operating according to narrow national security demands. Whereas there was a need for a long-term strategy of engagement, instead the public diplomacy that emerged was 'reactive and not the product of forward-looking foreign services caring about relationships with foreign audiences as a new challenge in diplomatic practice' (Melissen 2005: 9). In 2005, the Congressional Research Service conducted a survey of 29 articles and studies on US public diplomacy produced since 2001 in an attempt to highlight where most of the criticisms lay. The results indicated that most concerns centered on the lack of strategic direction, with the State Department unable to make public diplomacy a priority and the White House failing to coordinate between different departments and agencies of government. Further, there was consistent support for an increase in financial investment in human resources, language training, and the forms of public diplomacy that encourage greater dialogue such as exchange programs, information centers, and libraries (CRS 2005). Funding for educational and cultural exchange programs had stagnated through the 1990s, being $242 million in 1993 and still only $245 million in 2003, effectively a decline in real terms (US Advisory Commission 2004: 18). The Council on Foreign Relations published two reports which emphasized the need to move away from a focus on one-way mass communications and invest in methods of engagement that involved fostering debate, dialogue, and taking into account the views of others (Council on Foreign Relations 2002, 2003). Above all, there was general agreement that it had been a mistake to close down USIA, as the result was a fragmented and uncoordinated public diplomacy infrastructure distributed across various locations in the government (Zwiebel 2006).

The State Department: the Under Secretary of State for Public Diplomacy and Public Affairs

The position of Under Secretary was created following the demise of USIA, and on paper seemed to offer the chance to coordinate domestic outreach (public affairs) with public diplomacy abroad, in line with the assumptions of the New Public Diplomacy. The Under Secretary is responsible for three bureaux: Educational and Cultural Affairs, International Information Programs, and Public Affairs. They are assisted in their task by the US Advisory Commission on Public Diplomacy, a bipartisan panel appointed by the President which can make recommendations for improvements.

The first person to hold the post of Under Secretary was Evelyn Lieberman, formerly the Deputy Chief of Staff in the White House and, during 2008, chief operating officer on Hilary Clinton's presidential campaign. Lieberman served during the last phase of the second Clinton administration, and the position only took on real significance after 9/11. Charlotte Beers was sworn in on 2 October 2001, and as a top advertising executive with J. Walter Thompson, Tatham-Lair & Kudner, and Ogilvy & Mather, Beers had a reputation for marketing well-known brands such as Uncle Ben's Rice. With 9/11 raising serious questions about the ways in which the United States was perceived by others, it became Beers' responsibility to improve attitudes towards the United States abroad, with special emphasis on the Middle East. As she stated to the House Foreign Relations Committee a week after being sworn in, she was determined 'to wholeheartedly focus on our number-one priority: fighting the international war on terrorism.'[2]

There were four basic elements that Beers concentrated on: The Messenger, Magnification, Authenticity, and Context.[3] The emphasis on messengers entailed only that all government spokespersons needed to be credible in approach and outlook. Magnification was a term Beers brought from the world of advertising, and in the field of US public diplomacy it referred first to the ability to spread the message in as many languages as possible, and second to the role of each US embassy to expand its formal and informal contacts with local communities. It also involved engaging with media channels which up to that point had been ignored or regarded as hostile to US interests, such as Abu Dhabi TV and Al Jazeera. Third-party authenticity covered the aim to obtain public support for US foreign policies from independent advocates, thereby raising the level of legitimacy for those policies in the eyes of others. As Beers stated, 'There is no question that we are in a time where we desperately need to have other voices speaking for us, and not literally for us, but in their own voice and in their own way.' This was a standard approach from Cold War information campaigns, but Beers' reference to third-party authenticity as 'TV Co-Ops' indicated that its application after 9/11 represented purely a short-term effort to secure as much media exposure as possible.[4] The last factor in Beers' vision of public diplomacy was context, by which she meant providing the facts and conveying emotions, including the need for 'storytelling,' by which she meant highlighting the human element to events in a way that could alter others' perception of the impact of specific policies. A typical example of this approach was the State Department publication *Iraq: From Fear to Freedom*, which was produced in December 2002 and which sought to emphasize the human tragedy faced by the people of Iraq under the regime of Saddam Hussein.[5]

Beers is best known for the Shared Values Initiative (SVI), which was launched in October 2002 and cost $15 million to produce. It was an integrated communication campaign involving public speeches abroad by US diplomats and American Muslims, internet sites and online chat rooms, the magazine *Muslim Life in America*, and newspaper advertisements. At the center of the campaign were five television commercials depicting American Muslims discussing their life in the United States. The commercials, or 'mini-documentaries' as the State Department called them, depicted religious tolerance in the United States and the positive experience of living there for ordinary citizens who were Muslim. The aim was to display a different view to the highly critical assumptions about US interests and values that were then circulating in the Middle East, not least that the USA was in principle hostile to Islam. The SVI series began broadcasting in Indonesia on 29 October 2002. However, hopes for a large-scale campaign were dented by the fact that several states either refused to air the commercials free of charge or, as in the case of Egypt, rejected them outright as no more than propaganda. As a result, the series was discontinued prematurely in December 2002. In June 2003, the US State Department launched an inquiry into the failure of SVI to improve America's image abroad, after an opinion poll conducted by the Pew Research Center for The People & The Press found that negative views of the United States were on the rise in the Middle East.[6] A top-level public diplomacy advisory group determined that while the concept was good, there was a greater need to examine why so many intended recipient countries rejected the campaign, which demonstrated that 'earlier incorporation of host-country expertise' was essential for a successful outcome (Advisory Group on Public Diplomacy for the Arab and Muslim World 2003: 72).

Post-campaign polls conducted in Indonesia did indicate that the basic message had been taken in by the local population, and that it was a mistake to shut it down so soon (Fullerton and Kendrick 2006).

On 3 March 2003, shortly before the invasion of Iraq, Beers unexpectedly announced her resignation from the State Department. Although she cited unspecified 'health reasons,' it was clear from the previous 18 months not only that Beers' application of advertising principles was inadequate for the multi-faceted demands of US public diplomacy, but also that she knew, with the Iraq War looming, that the unpopularity of the USA around the world could only increase. But lessons were drawn from Beers' tenure. She was eventually replaced by Margaret Tutwiler, who assumed the Under Secretary position in October 2003. In contrast to Beers, Tutwiler was someone with a great deal of experience in US politics, both domestic and foreign, having served in top-level positions under both presidents Reagan and H.W. Bush before a stint in the private sector with the Cellular Telecommunications Industry Association (1995–2000).[7] Before taking on the Under Secretary position Tutwiler was US ambassador to Morocco, where she encouraged all her embassy staff to engage with local communities, in particular schools.

Tutwiler brought this firm belief in an interactive approach with her to the State Department, where she emphasized more active listening on the part of the US government – including listening to its diplomats serving on the frontlines – and expanding the discussion of American values and policies to public venues outside of traditional elites in diplomacy and government: 'We only have to look at the activities of US corporations overseas to see the value of being present and engaged in neighborhoods that we in government have for too long neglected.'[8] For Tutwiler, in stark contrast to Beers, the problems associated with 'branding' a country and selling its values abroad were complex. As she told the Senate Foreign Relations Committee during her confirmation hearing, 'there is not one magic bullet, magic program or magic solution.'[9] Tutwiler concentrated on programs to build long-term relationships abroad, to this end securing an increase in funding for educational and youth exchanges and starting the Partnerships for Learning Undergraduate Studies Program (PLUS) which opened up the possibility for an American college education for younger people abroad who displayed academic excellence and leadership potential.[10]

Tutwiler, like Beers, was another victim of the collapse of US standing during the lead-up and follow-through of the Iraq War. It was no coincidence that Tutwiler's sudden announcement to leave the State Department for a job covering communications for the New York Stock Exchange in April 2004 coincided with the first brutal images of abused Iraqi prisoners at Abu Ghraib being released worldwide.[11]

The Broadcasting Board of Governors (BBG)

The Broadcasting Board of Governors (BBG) was created in 1999 as an independent body with the responsibility to oversee broadcasting operations such as the Voice of America (VoA), Radio Free Europe/Radio Liberty (RFE/RL), Radio Marti, and Radio Free Asia. In 2002 Congress granted an extra $245 million for a rapid upgrade of broadcasting capability in the Near East. The first result of this was Radio Sawa (Radio Together), established in March 2002 as a 24-hour Arabic entertainment and current affairs radio station aimed at a youthful audience (65 per cent of the population in the region is below the age of 25). Radio Farda, broadcasting similarly in Farsi and aimed at Iran, was created jointly by the VoA and RFE/RL. Al-Hurra (The Free One), an Arabic satellite TV station, followed in early 2004. Both Sawa and Al-Hurra, which operated according to the Cold War models of Radio Free Europe, Radio Liberty, and Radio Free Asia (all of which are still operating) are funded by the BBG but run by the independent Middle East Broadcasting Networks Inc. A key individual behind both stations, and a member of the BBG itself, is Los Angeles media mogul Norman Pattiz, founder of the largest US radio conglomerate Westwood One. Al-Hurra was intended to directly challenge the prominence of Al-Jazeera, the satellite news channel based in Qatar, and the Saudi Arabian Al-Arabiya. Since 2006 Al-Hurra is also broadcast to Arabic-speaking audiences in Europe. However, their status as independent networks was undermined by their inability to air criticism of US policies, making them unable to build credibility by airing self-reflection and self-criticism. Once again, the urge to control the message and remove dissent has undermined a public diplomacy initiative. Both Sawa and Al-Hurra may gather audiences keen to sample American popular culture, but this is totally separate from being able to convince them that the US role in the Near East – particularly with regards to its relation with Israel – is beneficial for all. The overall negative impact of US foreign policy has undermined the credibility of its message, however it may be packaged. Both stations have also been funded at the expense of the Voice of America, a broadcaster that had precisely built up such credibility over several decades, and which lost its Arabic broadcasting capability as a result (Miles 2005: 382–8).

The Defense Department and strategic influence

On 20 September 2001, President Bush declared to a joint session of Congress that the war on terror against Al Qaeda and all terrorist organizations had begun. With military operations soon to begin in Afghanistan, it was clear that the Pentagon would occupy the driving role, including in the field of communications. Yet as one influential report stated in 2003, the result is that:

> the role the Defense Department plays in public diplomacy is neither broadly recognized nor well coordinated ... While the State Department is considered the lead agency ... we are concerned that the Defense Department, with resources that dwarf those of all other agencies of government, is not fully integrated into the public diplomacy architecture.
>
> (Advisory Group on Public Diplomacy for the Arab and Muslim World 2003: 68)

The Pentagon's wish to control information and media affairs in support of the war on terror is based on its aim to secure 'strategic influence' and 'influence opinions, attitudes, and behaviour of foreign groups in ways that will promote US national objectives' (Gough 2003: 1). However, the methods to achieve this have crossed into explicit propaganda and psychological warfare operations. In October 2001, the Defense Department set up the Office of Strategic Influence (OSI), which had the task of conducting covert disinformation and deception operations, including planting false news items with disguised origins in the media abroad. In February 2002, the *New York Times* observed that it was OSI's intention to have these fabricated news reports picked up by US news media and distributed in the United States itself, as a means to bolster domestic support for US actions overseas. Following the leak Rumsfeld was forced to shut down the organization, but the office's operations were effectively passed to another unit called the Information Operations Task Force (IOTF), and the goals did not change (Bamford 2005). In October 2003, the Defense Department issued the Information Operations Roadmap, which called for the formation of a strategic psychological operations unit and increased budgetary support for these activities. This was further backed up by the National Defense Strategy of March 2005, which included within the US military's dossier the intention to help 'change Muslim misperceptions of the United States and the West,' and to project the message that the war on terror 'is not a war against Islam' (The White House 2005).

A notable feature of the Pentagon's search for strategic influence since 2001 has been its use of the private sector. In October 2001, a contract worth $16 million was awarded to John Rendon, leader of the public relations firm the Rendon Group and a well-known practitioner of 'perception management.' Rendon had received several large-scale contracts since the Gulf War in 1991, and had been closely involved with, first, the CIA and then the Pentagon in undermining Saddam Hussein's regime and running the dissident Iraqi National Congress of Ahmed Chalabi. In 2001, Rendon was given the task of reversing the negative image of the United States abroad by tracking the global news cycle on a 24-hour basis and responding instantly to significant breaking news items. The Group effectively ran an Information War Room in the Pentagon's IOTF, and its principal target was the Qatar-based satellite channel Al-Jazeera, which the Pentagon considered its chief adversary in the war on terror's information campaign. Rendon's task stretched to working together with US allies (Saudi Arabia, Turkey, Egypt, Indonesia, Pakistan, and Uzbekistan) 'in developing and delivering specific messages to the local population, combatants, front-line states, the media and the international community' in support of US objectives (Bamford 2005). The implications of these kinds of activities for US public diplomacy as a whole are severe, since once again the need to sustain credibility over time has been replaced by the short-term demand to manipulate the news.

In November 2007, Robert Gates, the successor to Donald Rumsfeld as Secretary of Defense, gave a speech at Kansas State University during which he spoke of the need 'to make the case for strengthening our capacity to use "soft" power and for better integrating it with "hard" power.' Declaring that the civilian tools of government needed a serious upgrade, Gates continued: 'Public relations was invented in the United States, yet we are miserable at communicating to the rest of the world what we are about as a society and a culture, about freedom and democracy, about our policies and out goals.'[12] To illustrate his point, he exclaimed that the State Department's foreign affairs budget of $36 billion was less than what the Pentagon spent on health care. Meanwhile Gates created a new position, the Deputy Assistant Secretary of Defense for Support to Public Diplomacy. With Gates staying on as Defense Secretary under President Obama, it is clear that the Pentagon's influence over public diplomacy and information programs will continue.

Transformational diplomacy

That democracy promotion is a centerpiece of US foreign policy under the presidency of George W. Bush was once more emphasized in his second Inaugural Address, where he insisted that it is 'the policy of the United States to seek and support the growth of democratic movements and institutions in every nation and culture with the ultimate goal of ending tyranny in our world.' The aim was to 'help others find their own voice,' a cause towards which the United States would offer every assistance.[13]

Building on this mandate, in January 2006, Secretary of State Condoleeza Rice outlined her vision for the future outlook of the State Department, termed Transformational Diplomacy, in an address at Georgetown University's School of Foreign Service: 'To work with our many partners around the world to build and sustain democratic, well-governed states that will respond to the needs of their people – and conduct themselves responsibly in the international system.'[14]

Rice aimed to counter the criticism of the previous few years by situating the State Department as the central coordinator of US government information programs. To this end, it required revamping the Department 'to answer a new historic calling' around five themes.[15] First, *Global Repositioning* required a shift of resources and personnel from traditional allies (Europe, Japan) to new ideological battlegrounds in Asia and the Near East (Indonesia, Malaysia, Egypt, India). Second, *Regional Focus* aimed to concentrate activities in Regional Public Diplomacy Centers that look beyond the limitations of nation-states and bilateral relations, the most important being the Regional Presence Center in Dubai which is directed at countering Iranian influence in the region. Third, *Localization* sought to spread the US diplomatic presence beyond capital cities by means of American Presence and Virtual Presence Posts.[16] Fourth, *Transformational Diplomacy* required that 'diplomats must be diverse, well-rounded, agile, and able to carry out multiple tasks' working together with local communities. Lastly, it called for close *Coordination* with other agencies, in particular via the State Department's Office of Reconstruction and Stabilization, established in 2004 to ensure sufficient inter-departmental planning for post-conflict situations. With Iraq and Afghanistan in mind, it also called for a more prominent role for political advisors in coordination with military operations.

Transformational Diplomacy therefore attempted to position the State Department as a pivotal player combining diplomatic affairs, economic reconstruction and military operations within a broad strategy to promote democratic institutions abroad. Under this rubric, the second Bush administration took up a new worldview whereby nation-building, the strengthening of the rule of law and the creation of a strong and proactive civil society took on pre-eminence. As the Director of Policy Planning at the State Department and one of the leading architects behind the redesigned notion of diplomacy, Stephen Krasner, elucidated, 'transformational diplomacy is essentially about supporting changes within states, not relations among them' (CGD 2006). It was no longer the distribution of power between states, but the nature of their regimes that mattered most. As one commentator has noted, this signified 'a shift from classical realism to neo-conservatism' in the basic outlook of the State Department (Henrikson 2006: 34).

Under Secretary of State Karen Hughes

In September 2005, Rice gained a new Under Secretary to replace Tutwiler: Karen Hughes. Hughes had a long background working with Bush, having been his director of communications when he was Governor of Texas and staying in close contact thereafter before rejoining the President to assist in his re-election campaign in August 2004. Shortly after being appointed, Hughes spoke in Washington, DC, about her intentions, and her initial statements – the need for a long-term strategy, the need to listen as much as to speak, and the need to 'foster a sense of common interests and common values between Americans and the people of different countries, cultures and faiths' – seemed to bode well for a much-needed new direction in US public diplomacy.[17] The broad goals were as follows: Support the promotion of freedom and hope, isolate extremists, and strengthen shared values and common interests between Americans and the rest of the world. Hughes went on to talk of the four Es: Engage, Exchange, Educate and Empower. Engagement meant not only working with other partners in and outside the USA, but also to upgrade the State Department's media capacity with a Rapid Response Unit 'to monitor media and help us more aggressively respond to rumors, inaccuracies, and hate speech.' Exchange recognized that of all the forms of public diplomacy, exchange programs were consistently identified as the most effective means to build lasting cross-border understanding and relationships. Education focused on the need for Americans to learn other languages, and for others to learn English. Finally, Empowerment referred to the need to utilize to a greater extent the resources of US citizens and the private sector, since in many situations 'a government official may not be the most effective or the most credible voice.'[18] A citizen ambassador program, particularly geared for American Muslims to go abroad as national advocates, was to be one result of this. All four of the E's were presented as forms of two-way communication – the United States would learn as much as it would tell.

In short, Hughes gave the strong impression that she was going to re-energize public diplomacy efforts, both institutionally (within the State Department as a whole) and procedurally (in terms of applying a New Public Diplomacy approach). But Hughes was also very much an administration insider, as demonstrated by her role in bodies such as the White House Iraq Group (or White House Information Group – WHIG), which was established in August 2002 under Karl Rove and had the task of convincing the US public of the need to neutralize the threat of Saddam Hussein's Iraq. Her determination to advocate US interests 'very aggressively' also did not bode well. Hughes did secure more funding for public diplomacy, with the State Department's allocation for these activities rising from $519 million in 2004 to $629 million in 2006 (GAO 2006: 5). Participants on State Department-sponsored exchange programs rose from 27,000 to 39,000 in the same period.[19] But she never wavered in defending all aspects of US foreign policy, including the detention center at Guantánamo Bay.[20] Her approach did not work towards establishing dialogue with others but towards highlighting, once again with as much media coverage as possible, the merits of United States society and its policies, thereby undermining the two-way communication she seemed to promise when she arrived at the State Department.[21]

Hughes did work towards solving the lack of governmental coordination in public diplomacy, but this only further emphasized her wish to determine what the message was that was being sent out. In 2002, at the suggestion of Hughes, the Bush White House created the Office of Global Communications to coordinate strategic communications overseas in the aftermath of the Afghan campaign. This was supplemented in the same year by the Strategic Communication Policy Coordination Committee, run by the National Security Council and the State Department, with the aim of ensuring 'that all agencies work together to develop and disseminate America's message across the globe' (US Advisory Commission on Public Diplomacy 2004: 9). Yet this effort stalled, largely due to inter-agency inertia. In response to repeated criticisms that the

State Department had failed to produce a clear strategy to both direct its own programs and to coordinate them with other departments and agencies (GAO 2006: 2), Hughes led the way in formulating a solution. Following on from Rice's announcement of Transformational Diplomacy, in April 2006 President Bush created the Policy Coordination Committee on Public Diplomacy and Strategic Communications, to be led by Hughes. In December 2006, this body issued the US National Strategy for Public Diplomacy and Strategic Communication, which stated that all public diplomacy activities should be carried out in support of national security objectives and fundamental values such as human rights and the 'struggle for freedom and democracy' (Policy Coordination Committee on Public Diplomacy and Strategic Communications 2006: 2). Faced with intense criticism abroad, the Bush administration therefore raised public diplomacy to being an issue of national security, in doing so undermining the possibility for open dialogue with others and dissenting opinion among its own officials. Announcing her resignation in late 2007, Hughes said that she had succeeded in 'transforming public diplomacy and making it a national security priority central to everything we do in government.'[22] This was indeed an achievement, but not one that made use of the merits of two-way exchange, empowerment, and democratic legitimacy as outlined in the New Public Diplomacy. Hughes and Rendon were effectively the overt and covert sides to the same coin of controlling information and image in the interests of US national security.[23]

USAID and democracy promotion

The sharpened emphasis on democracy promotion within transformational diplomacy also implied a reorientation of the United States Agency for International Development (USAID). The logic of transformational diplomacy was transposed into a notion of transformational development. That the adjective of transformational implies a politicization of development aid became clear in the agency's budget and program overview for the 2007 fiscal year, which stated the intention to tie 'higher aid levels to countries that have made progress in building effective democracies, promoting economic freedom and investing in their own peoples.'[24]

This means that progress in the field of development is not measured by traditional indicators such as literacy, nutrition and access to clean drinking water, but by 'political will and commitment to promote economic freedom, rule justly, and make sound investments in people.'[25]

In order to effectively carry out this strategy, the Secretary of State created a new position in 2006, namely that of Director of US Foreign Assistance (DFA). The position of DFA entails a rank equivalent to Deputy Secretary of State together with being USAID Administrator, 'ensuring that foreign assistance is used as effectively as possible to meet broad foreign policy objectives.'[26] As a result there has been a 'semi-fusion' of USAID with the State Department (Vaïsse 2007: 38). A typology has been crafted to distinguish between rebuilding countries that are engaging in post-conflict reconstruction; developing countries that are characterized by a low GDP but that do not meet the requirements for transformational development; and transforming countries that do display at least the prerequisite hallmarks of good governance (ibid.: 37). States that belong to this third category are eligible for funds from the Millennium Challenge Account (MCA). When announcing the plans for this initiative in Mexico in March 2002, George W. Bush remarked that 'greater contributions from developed nations must be linked to greater responsibility from developing nations,' requiring that the latter must meet performance indicators such as 'governing justly' (corruption, rule of law), 'investing in people' (immunization rates, primary education completion rates) and 'promoting economic freedom' (inflation, budget deficit, national trade policies).[27] The MCA started functioning in 2004, and although overall US development assistance did increase, MCA effectively took funds away from USAID, and by setting highly political performance indicators many countries that are in dire need of foreign assistance are sidestepped. For example, the second Bush administration has invested, per capita, nearly fifty times as much on Egyptian citizens as it has on inhabitants from Bangladesh (ibid.: 34).

USAID could provide the basis for a New Public Diplomacy strategy that combines the talents and charitable energy of the private sector with a government-run development assistance program (Keilson 2006). Instead, it has had to contend with a continuing decline in funds (since the early 1990s), subordination to the newly-created MCA, and a wholesale politicization of its operations more in line with Strategic Public Diplomacy thinking.[28]

Future prospects?

Since 2001, the pattern in US public diplomacy has been clear. The language of New Public Diplomacy has been used, but Strategic Public Diplomacy has determined the goals and the methods. Established agencies – VoA, USAID – have been bypassed and underfunded while new creations – Radio Sawa, Al-Hurra, MCA – have been created and led by uncritical advocates of the Bush administrations. Transformational Diplomacy represented a significant move towards clarifying the State Department's mission and coordinating role, but increased resources to match the demands of this large-scale reformulation have not come with it. Meanwhile the emphasis remained on short-term image and information management, particularly in the autonomous (and often covert) operations of the Pentagon. As one source succinctly puts it, 'if it is true that public opinion in Arab and Muslim countries responds more to policies than to public diplomacy, it is clear that successful public diplomacy will not be able to change minds dramatically in the presence of strong opposition to policy' (Advisory Group on Public Diplomacy for the Arab and Muslim World 2003: 66).

The way ahead will be determined by the next administration under President Obama, but already significant statements have been made to try and map out what this might be. In November 2007, the independent Center for Strategic International Studies (CSIS) produced the report 'A Smarter, More Secure America,' which recognizes the need to bolster and maintain credible international organizations, respect international legal norms, and work with others towards solving common global problems (CSIS 2007). Equally significant was the Princeton Project on National Security that produced 'Forging a World of Liberty under Law' in September 2006, an extensive document that called for, among other things, a Concert of Democracies 'to institutionalise and ratify the "democratic peace"' (Princeton Project for National Security 2006: 7). Both studies, which gathered together a bipartisan cross-section of some of the best US thinkers on foreign affairs, could lay the basis for frameworks of cooperation that are 'interest-based rather than threat-based' (ibid.: 6), and therefore open up opportunities for a genuine application of the New Public Diplomacy concept. But it is worth recalling that Obama's political philosopher of choice, Reinhold Niebuhr, argued from a Christian Realist position that the use of power had to be justified in a world where evil was omnipresent and inevitable. Such self-awareness and self-restraint will be necessary as Obama looks to forge a new foreign policy approach away from the crusade for democracy of the Bush years.

Notes

1 Murrow Center brochure. This and other definitions are available online at: http://www.publicdiplomacy.org/1.htm (accessed 29 May 2008).
2 Charlotte Beers (2001), 'Statement at Hearing: Public Diplomacy,' 10 October 2001, House Foreign Affairs Committee. Online. Available at:
3 Charlotte Beers (2002) 'Public Diplomacy after 9/11,' 18 December, National Press Club.
4 One example of third-party authenticity was the way in which Beers and the State Department in early 2003 persuaded Brookings Institution scholar Ken Pollack to undertake a series of digital video conferences and visits to countries such as France, Austria, Finland, Germany, Hungary and South Africa to talk about the pros and cons of invading Iraq. Pollack's (2003) book *The Threatening Storm* had critically stated the case for invading Iraq, and his reasonable 'third voice' was considered a useful addition to the US government's efforts to sell the war.
5 The document is available online. Available at: http://usinfo.state.gov/products/pubs/iraq/ (accessed 30 May 2008).
6 The report is online. Available at: http://people-press.org/reports/display.php3?ReportID=185 (accessed 24 April 2008).
7 Tutwiler served under President Reagan as Deputy Assistant to the President for Political Affairs (1981–5) and Assistant Secretary for Public Affairs and Public Liaison with the Treasury (1985–9). She went on to serve as Assistant Secretary of State (March 1989–August 1992) and Special Adviser for Communications (August 1992–January 1993) for President George H.W. Bush. She was briefly, between January and June 2001, also President George W. Bush's Special Adviser for Communications.
8 Tutwiler (2004).
9 Tutwiler (2003).
10 PLUS is still running, although as of May 2008 there were only 175 students from Africa, the Middle East, and South Asia who were studying via PLUS in the United States. Online. Available at: http://exchanges.state.gov/education/p4l/ (accessed 29 May 2008).
11 Snow (2004).
12 Speech online, available at: http://www.defenselink.mil/speeches/speech.aspx?speechid+1199 (accessed 2 June 2008).
13 White House (2005b) 'President Sworn in for Second Term,' 20 January 2005, Press Release.
14 Rice (2006).
15 Department of State (2006) 'Transformational Diplomacy,' Fact Sheet, 18 January 2006.
16 In Korea, an internet community was created through the establishment of *Café USA* in which Korean citizens can debate in the Korean language with US officials on consular affairs, political and security issues, US–Korea relations and American history. See the US Embassy's website at http://seoul.usembassy.gov/cafeusa.html (accessed 2 June 2008).
17 Karen Hughes, speech at Loy Henderson Auditorium, 8 September 2005.
18 Ibid.
19 McKenna (2007).
20 'US Envoy Defends Guantanamo Conditions,' *USA Today*, 22 February 2006. Online. Available at: http://www.usatoday.com/news/world/2006-02-20-hughes-guantanamo_x.htm (accessed 2 June 2008).
21 Brown (2007).
22 'Key Bush Image Advisor to Leave,' BBC News, 31 October 2007. Online. Available at: http://news.bbc.co.uk/1/hi/world/americas/7071638.stm (accessed 2 June 2008).
23 In December 2007, President Bush nominated the chair of the BBG, American Enterprise Institute fellow James Glassman, as Hughes' successor.

24 Summary of FT 2007 Budget and Program Overview. Online. Available at: http://www.usaid.
   gov/policy/budget/cbj2007/summary.html (accessed 3 June 2008).
25 Ibid.
26 Director of US Foreign Assistance. Online. Available at: http://www.state.gov/f/ (accessed 3
   June 2008).
27 The Millennium Challenge Account. Online. Available at: http://www.whitehouse.gov/infocus/
   developingnations/millennium.html (accessed 3 June 2008)
28 USAID's allocation declined from $12.6 million in 2004 to $9.1 million in 2006. Summary of
   FT 2007 Budget and Program Overview. Online. Available at: http://www.usaid.gov/policy/
   budget/cbj2007/summary.html (accessed 3 June 2008).

References

Advisory Group on Public Diplomacy for the Arab and Muslim World (2003) *Changing Minds,
   Winning Peace*, Washington, DC: US Government Printer.
Bamford, J. (2005) 'The Rendon Group,' *Rolling Stone*, 988. Online. Available at: http://www.
   rollingstone.com/politics/story/8798997/the_man_who_sold_the_war
Beers, C. (2001) 'Statement at Hearing: Public Diplomacy,' 10 October 2001, House Foreign
   Affairs Committee. Online. Available at: http://www.state.gov/r/us/5473.htm (accessed 30
   May 2008).
—— (2002) 'Public Diplomacy after 9/11,' 18 December, National Press Club. Online. Available
   at: http://www.state.gov/r/us/16269.htm (accessed 24 April 2008).
Brown, J. (2007) 'Karen Hughes and Her "Diplomacy of Deeds",' 9 April. Online. Available at:
   http://www.commondreams.org/archive/2007/04/09/411/ (accessed 24 April 2008).
Brown, R. (2004) 'Information Technology and the Transformation of Diplomacy,' *Knowledge,
   Technology, & Policy*, 18: 14–29.
CGD (Center for Global Development) (2006) 'Transformational Diplomacy.' Online. Available
   at: http://www.cgdev.org/doc/event%20docs/Krasner%20Transcript.pdf.
Council on Foreign Relations (2002) *Public Diplomacy: A Strategy for Reform*, Washington,
   DC: CFR Independent Task Force.
—— (2003) *Finding America's Voice: A Strategy for Reinvigorating Public Diplomacy*.
   Washington, DC: CFR Independent Task Force.
CRS (2005) *Public Diplomacy: A Review of Past Recommendations*, Congressional Research
   Service, September, Washington, DC: Library of Congress.
CSIS (Center for Strategic International Studies) (2007) 'A Smarter, More Secure America,'
   Commission on Smart Power. Online. Available at: http://www.csis.org/component/option,
   com_csis_pubs/task,view/id,4156/type,1/ (accessed 2 June 2008).
Cull, N.J. (2008) *The Cold War and the United States Information Agency: American Propaganda
   and Public Diplomacy 1945–1989*, Cambridge: Cambridge University Press.
Department of State (2006) 'Transformational Diplomacy,' Fact Sheet, 18 January. Online.
   Available at: http://www.state.gov/r/pa/prs/ps/2006/59339.htm (accessed 2 June 2008).
Dizard, W. (1961) *The Strategy of Truth: The Story of the US Information Service*, Washington,
   DC: Public Affairs Press.
—— (2004) *Inventing Public Diplomacy: The Story of the US Information Agency*, Boulder, CO:
   Lynne Rienner.
Fullerton, J. and Kendrick, A. (2006) *Advertising's War on Terrorism: The Story of the US State
   Department's Shared Values Initiative*, Spokane, WA: Marquette Books.
GAO (Government Accountability Office) (2006) 'US Public Diplomacy: State Department
   Efforts Lack Certain Communication Elements and Face Persistent Challenges,' Washington,
   DC: GAO.
Gough, S. (2003) 'The Evolution of Strategic Influence, USAWC Strategy Research Project.'
   Online. Available at: http:www.fas.org/irp/eprint/gough.pdf.

Guehenno, J-M. (2000) *The Decline of the Nation-State*, Minneapolis: University of Minnesota Press.

Henrikson, A. (2006) *What Can Public Diplomacy Achieve?*, Discussion Papers in Diplomacy, Clingendael: Netherlands Institute of International Relations.

Hocking, J. (ed.) (1999) *Foreign Ministries: Change and Adaptation*, London: Macmillan.

—— (2005) 'Rethinking the "New" Public Diplomacy,' in J. Melissen (ed.) *The New Public Diplomacy: Soft Power in International Relations*, London: Macmillan.

Hughes, K. (2005) Speech at Loy Henderson Auditorium, 8 September. Online. Available at: http://www.state.gov/secretary/rm/2005/52748.htm (accessed 29 May 2008).

Keilson, J. (2006) 'Opportunities for Public Diplomacy Programs in USAID and the Peace Corps,' in W. Kiehl (ed.) *America's Dialogue with the World*, Washington, DC: Public Diplomacy Council.

Leonard, M. (2002) *Public Diplomacy*, London: Foreign Policy Centre.

Manheim, J. (1994) *Strategic Public Diplomacy and American Foreign Policy*, New York: Oxford University Press.

McKenna, T. (2007) 'Hughes Tackles a Shaky Image,' 23 July, *PR Week*. Online. Available at: http://www.prweek.com/us/news/article/671821/Hughes-tackles-shaky-image/ (accessed 24 July 2007).

Melissen, J. (ed.) (1999) *Innovation in Diplomatic Practice*, London: Macmillan.

—— (2005) 'The New Public Diplomacy: Between Theory and Practice,' in J. Melissen (ed.) *The New Public Diplomacy: Soft Power in International Relations*, London: Macmillan.

Miles, H. (2005) *Al-Jazeera: How Arab TV News Changed the World*, London: Abacus.

Nye, J. (2002) 'The Information Revolution and American Soft Power,' *Asia-Pacific Review*, 9: 60–76.

Policy Coordination Committee on Public Diplomacy and Strategic Communications (2006) *US National Strategy for Public Diplomacy and Strategic Communication*, Washington, DC.

Pollack, K. (2003) *The Threatening Storm*, New York: Random House.

Princeton Project on National Security (2006) 'Forging a World of Liberty under Law,' G. John Ikenberry and Anne-Marie Slaughter (co-directors).

Public Diplomacy Council (2005) *A Call for Action on Public Diplomacy*, Washington, DC: author.

Rice, C. (2006) 'Transformational Diplomacy,' 18 January. Online. Available at: http://www.state.gov/secretary/rm/2006/59306.htm (accessed 2 June 2008).

Riordan, S. (2003) *The New Diplomacy*, Cambridge: Polity Press.

Snow, N. (2004) 'US Public Diplomacy: A Tale of Two who Jumped Ship at State,' *Foreign Policy in Focus*, 27 May. Online. Available at: http://www.fpif.org/papers/0405taleoftwo_body.html#_ftn1 (accessed 24 April 2008).

Tutwiler, M. (2003) 'Testimony before the Senate Foreign Relations Committee,' 29 October. Online. Available at: http://www.state.gov/r/us/27372.htm (accessed 29 May 2008).

—— (2004) 'Public Diplomacy Activities and Programs,' 10 February, testimony before the House Committee on Government Reform, Subcommittee on National Security, Emerging Threats and International Relations. Online. Available at: http://www.state.gov/r/us/2004/29251.htm (accessed 30 May 2008).

US Advisory Commission on Public Diplomacy (2004) 'Report.' Online. Available at: http://state.gov/document/organization/36625.pdf.

Vaïsse, J. (2007) 'Transformational Diplomacy,' *Chaillot Papers*, 103, EU Institute for Security Studies.

The White House (2005a) 'National Defense Strategy of the United States.' Online. Available at: http://www.globalsecurity.org/military/library/policy/dod/nds-usa_mar2005.htm.

—— (2005b) 'President Sworn in for Second Term,' 20 January 2005, White House Press Release. Online. Available at: http://www.whitehouse.gov/news/releases/2005/01/20050120–21.html (accessed 2 June 2008).

Zwiebel, M. (2006) 'Why We Need to Reestablish USIA,' *Military Review*, 86: 26–35.

Further reading

Bogart, L. (1976) *Premises for Propaganda: The United States Information Agency's Operating Assumptions in the Cold War*, New York: Free Press.

Elder, R. (1968) *The Information Machine: The United States Information Agency and American Foreign Policy*, Syracuse, NY: Syracuse University Press.

Henderson, J. (1969) *The United States Information Agency*, Westport, CT: Praeger.

Lord, C. (2006) *Losing Hearts and Minds? Public Diplomacy and Strategic Influence in the Age of Terror*, Westport, CT: Praeger.

Snow, N. and Taylor, P. (eds) (2008) *The Routledge Handbook of Public Diplomacy*, London: Routledge.

Snyder, A. (1995) *Warriors of Disinformation*, New York: Arcade.

Websites

Pew Research Center's Global Attitudes Project: http://pewglobal.org/

Under Secretary of State for Public Diplomacy and Public Affairs: http://www.state.gov/r/

17 Illusions of empire and the spectre of decline

Nicholas Kitchen and Michael Cox

We had, we were told reached the end of history (Fukuyama 1992). Liberalism had triumphed over its last ideological competitor and the world would coalesce around the values and form of government epitomised in the last remaining superpower, the United States, a 'Rome on the Potomac' that would rule a benevolent empire (Kagan 1998). Yet today, in the aftermath of Iraq, with China and Russia resurgent, the unipolar moment appears to have been just that: a historical blip, an interregnum between the bipolarity of the Cold War and a new international structure in which the United States, no longer the indispensable nation, is a normal country once again. The American Empire is in decline.

America's victory in the Cold War had seemingly closed the book on the 'Kennedy thesis', which stated that as inevitably as the British and Habsburg empires before it, the United States had risen and was now in decline (Kennedy 1988). Kennedy's was hardly an original thesis, resting as it did on a realist understanding of international relations in which the international system created basic structural incentives for power to be balanced and hegemons reined in. Indeed, narratives of American decline had previously risen to prominence in the aftermath of the Vietnam War, when the military defeat in South-East Asia had combined with rising national debt and the emergence of a more interdependent global economy to provoke calls for America to manage rather than resist the process of its inexorable decline (Hoffmann 1978). Of course, in Ronald Reagan, the declinists found a President whose polarising deficit-based policies seemed certain to overstretch the United States still further, hence the influence of Kennedy's book when it was published in 1987 in the run-up to a crucial presidential election – manna from heaven for the opposition Democratic Party.

Yet for all the furore that the Kennedy thesis generated, it was not academic debate but events that put notions of American decline to bed. The unexpected end of the Cold War and the subsequent collapse of the Soviet Union demonstrated that the United States had not been the one that was overstretched, and in the 1990s the talk was not of decline but of another American century. Victory in the Gulf War kicked the Vietnam syndrome, Japan's economic miracle proved a mirage and the United States bailed out an impotent and divided Europe on its own borders in Yugoslavia. In the new world order America was totally dominant militarily, boasted a massive and robust economy and at the same time maintained unsurpassed cultural and ideological appeal. Most Americans were loath to admit it, but this was an empire in all but name.

There were of course those prepared to embrace the notion of the American Empire, arguing that the end of the Cold War had left America in a dominant position, and from that position America needed to not only maintain but extend its superiority. The fact of American dominance was indisputable: as early as the 1980s the United States was seen to retain 'on all indicators' a degree of dominance that Britain had never achieved in the nineteenth century (Russett 1985), and the collapse of the USSR in 1991 had removed the only other near-superpower – and crucially the only other ideological competitor to the United States – from the scene. The United States accounted for around one quarter of world GDP throughout the 1990s and remained the most technologically advanced major economy with expenditures on research and development nearly equalling the rest of the G-7 combined (Wohlforth 1999: 17). This economic and technological dominance allowed the United States to sustain military expenditures that meant it had command of the global commons as no other nation had done before, underwriting world trade, travel and global telecommunications (Posen 2003).

Maintaining this imperial geopolitical position would guarantee American security, because no potential adversary could hope to get close enough to the power of the United States in order to challenge it. As Colin Powell told the Senate Armed Services committee, 'If you look like you can kick someone's butt, more often than not, it will not be necessary.' Others, particularly on the 'neoconservative' wing of the Republican Party, were prepared to go farther, to argue that not only was an imperial grand strategy right for America's own security, it was also a good thing for the world. American values of individual liberty were universal and emancipatory, and America's noble project to spread norms of democratic political organisation and open market economics would bring both prosperity and peace, fulfilling America's destiny (Muravchik 1991).

Indeed, such was America's greatness and righteousness that any constraints on the exercise of American power in pursuit of that destiny were to be cast aside. Instruments of multilateralism constrain the strongest most, and so as long as America must coexist with untrustworthy and tyrannical regimes for whom 'moral suasion is a farce', multilateral agreements to which America would bind herself entail a loss of power to those regimes (Krauthammer 2004). Treaties constrain 'good guys' who will adhere to them; 'bad guys' will either not sign, cheat or openly violate the agreements. On this basis, American neo-imperialists came to reject any multilateral policy which might result in the weakening of the relative power of the United States (Bolton 2000).

The neo-imperialists' arguments rested on a number of key ideas. The key one is that a unipolar international structure could be a stable one. Rejecting realism's assertions that overwhelming power repels and causes other states to balance against it (Waltz 1991: 669), American neo-imperialism viewed the strategies of second-order states as inconsequential, since the scale of the power disjunction meant their choices could only range from enthusiastic bandwaggoning to studious avoidance of direct enmity. Added to this, the United States' peculiar advantages of geography, and in particular, its enduring alliances to the north and south, reinforce the likely longevity of American unipolarity (Wohlforth 1999: 23–37).

Crucially, the neo-imperialists rejected notions that American power would be considered benign through 'self-binding', a process which sanitises power through restraint, multilateralism and the promotion of joint gains (Kupchan 1998). Rather, there was an explicit assumption that the United States would be seen as benign because, quite simply, the United States *is* benign – a truth that rests on distinctively American ideas about the special nature of their own nation and the universality of ideas of liberty. American power was justified in the eyes of one prominent commentator because America's self-interest was so enlightened that it came 'dangerously close to resembling generosity' (Kagan 1998: 28). For the proponents of American primacy then, the world had nothing to fear from American dominance, and felt assured that 'most of the world's major powers ... prefer America's benevolent hegemony to the alternatives' (Kristol and Kagan 1996: 21). The American empire had been invited; therefore its leadership would be welcomed (Lundestad 1986).

The story from here is of course well known. Provided with what appeared to be a new organising principle for grand strategy by the attacks of 9/11, the American Empire moved into full swing, invading first Afghanistan and Iraq and singling out Iran and North Korea alongside Saddam Hussein to construct that notorious triumvirate, the 'axis of evil'. Global solidarity in the immediate months after 9/11 was swiftly lost amidst the perceived illegitimacy of the Iraq invasion. Although 'shock and awe' and the breathtaking speed of the American advance to Baghdad appeared to underline the total dominance of the American empire, the insurgency soon drew US forces deep into an irregular conflict and undermined attempts to rebuild. An unwelcome occupier, as the United States expended yet more blood and treasure in an increasingly difficult conflict the decline argument surfaced once more. With America's military power apparently ineffective and her soft power squandered, economic and political rivals were rising and the American Empire's days were numbered after less than two decades.

In the summer of 2008, a conjunction of events served to vividly highlight the decline of American power. As authoritarian China wowed the world with an opening ceremony to the Beijing Olympics that was as a spectacular demonstration of Chinese national greatness and economic success, an emboldened Russia marched its troops into Georgia, a democracy and a NATO candidate, destroying several years' worth of American military assistance in the process. The United States could only stand and watch as these two new giants announced themselves to the world, and it appeared that American values and interests were now fair game in a world that is no longer unipolar but non-polar (Haass 2008).

What are we to make of this rapid shift between ideas of empire and protestations of decline? Both concepts are bound by our understandings of power on the one hand and resistance on the other. How we measure power and the significance we attach to resistance are therefore central questions in the debate surrounding the global status of the United States – is it an empire, overwhelming in its power and merely irritated by bouts of asymmetric opposition, or is resistance to American power a genuine challenge that renders nonsensical continued talk of American imperium?

The argument that America is in decline rests on two not unrelated propositions. First, that foreign policy failures, most notably the Iraq conflict, have eroded America's position in the world, both by revealing the impotence of American power and by eroding its legitimacy. Second, other powers are rising to challenge the dominant position of the United States: primarily the European Union, China and Russia.

If the history of empire teaches us anything it is that *hubris* leads to defeat (Snyder 1991; Kupchan 1994). After 9/11, the United States benefited from near universal international sympathy, and most saw the Afghanistan campaign as a necessary and justified response to the attacks (Colombani 2001). Yet the rush to wage a war of choice to remove Saddam Hussein from power in Iraq smacked of a worrying militarism at the heart of United States foreign policy that alienated allies, enraged publics and squandered that goodwill (Bacevich 2005). The wars to which America committed itself under the banner of the Global War on Terror turned out to be far less straightforward than anticipated. The 'spectacular' failure to impose order and stabilise Iraq in particular had been brought on by the ideological arrogance of an empire flush with notions of both its own power and righteousness (Dodge 2005).

Perhaps more worryingly than the apparent ineffectiveness of American military power is that many of the means by which the United States pursued its global war on terror have undermined the moral authority that America once held over potential great power rivals. It is difficult to lecture China on human rights when the United States presides over Guantánamo and Abu Ghraib, and Russian action against Chechen 'terrorists' looks acceptable alongside American assaults on Fallujah. American preference for anti-terrorist governments over democratic ones leaves it with little claim to be the beacon of liberal values in the world, and in so doing may have relinquished its authority to lead (Buzan 2008).

Nowhere was that loss of legitimacy more noticeable than in Europe, where anti-American sentiment had been growing with every unilateral action of the Bush administration. Public sentiment translated into policy as it seldom had as the peace-niks of 'Old Europe' made a public show of opposing American action in the theatre of the United Nations. The tensions in the transatlantic alliance were by 2003 more important than ever – no longer a US dependent, the European Union had become the biggest single market on the planet with a GDP higher than that of the United States, with its own foreign and security policy and way of war. The promise of membership was proving to be a more effective power than any element of geopolitics – as one writer confidently put it, in the new European century, the European way of doing things would become the world's (Leonard 2005).

The lessons of the American experience in Iraq, and to a lesser extent Afghanistan, are lessons about the utility of military power. Not only does overwhelming military power inevitably generate anxiety and resistance, the use of that power both brings with it a loss of authority and the generation of forms of resistance which military power finds very difficult to counter. Asymmetric warfare – as any warfare the United States is engaged in must necessarily be – exploits the twin vulnerabilities of democratic powers by encouraging mission creep while at the same time forcing that mission to face the threat of casualties (Freedman 2006: 49–61). In particular, indigenous insurgents have a profound advantage over foreign forces in that they need not 'win' as such – all they need do is to prolong the conflict and sap the great power's stomach for the fight (Layne 2006).

Of course, when it comes to fighting wars, non-democracies are made of sterner stuff than their liberal counterparts, blessed as they are with the absence of an electoral cycle. Hence Russia has been able to conduct its campaign in Chechnya – as an ally of the United States in the broader war on terror – with greater ruthlessness and determination than the US has mustered in Iraq. Emboldened by its military successes and having grown rich on the back of rising oil prices, Russia is resurgent. After contracting in the 1990s, Russian growth has averaged nearly 7 per cent since 2000. But it is the nature of Russian export growth that underpins its revival as a great power, in that much of Europe is now dependent on Russia for supplies of natural gas. Energy accounts for over 65 per cent of all EU imports from Russia, and the Kremlin has not been averse to viewing that dependence as a strategic asset, adroitly using it to prevent a common EU policy towards Russia. Russia is therefore the best example of emerging 'petro-authoritarian' states, basing its assertive nationalism on the security provided by its strategic exports of oil and gas (Friedman 2006). Record oil prices (ironically in part fuelled by the uncertainty brought on by American policies in the Middle East) only serve to strengthen those assets; it is surely no coincidence that Russia felt able to push the West as far as it has in Georgia when oil prices oscillated around the $120/barrel mark.

For the declinists, the conflict sparked by Mikheil Saakashvili's miscalculations in South Ossettia is a vivid example of American impotence. With its European allies split and the United States both unwilling and realistically unable to take military action in defense of Georgian territorial integrity one commentator complained that the United States had turned in its global sheriff badge (Rosett 2008). Yet the idea that America would ever have been willing or able to put its military power down on the borders of a still-nuclear Russia to defeat Russian interests is absurd. Indeed, it may be argued that it was by overreaching itself by attempting to exercise power in former Soviet space that the United States got itself into this mess (Greenway 2008). Decline must be a relative concept, in which a power advantage over other states ebbs away over time; it is not the distance from omnipotence. Temporary overstretch therefore need not precipitate decline, as Hadrian well knew.

On the other hand, overstretch may run deeper than the travails of the American military. Kennedy's central point was that in the long run there exists a very clear connection between a state's relative economic rise and fall and its growth and decline as a military power, which leads us from Russia, which despite its growth and natural resources ranks only eleventh globally in terms of GDP, to the economic rise of China, which has been little short of meteoric. Since the implementation of market reforms in the 1970s, its economy has quadrupled, and as the world's manufacturing centre it consumes roughly a third of the global supply of iron, coal and steel (Ikenberry 2008). China's growth through the 1990s averaged 10.6 per cent, barely slowing to 9.6 per cent since in the twenty-first century, so that GDP now stands at over $7 trillion. Trade surpluses during this period have allowed China to accumulate over $1 trillion of foreign currency reserves, mainly invested in US Treasury bonds, a level of control over the US national debt and its currency that has led the prospect of liquidation of Chinese dollar holdings to be talked of as a 'nuclear option' (Evans-Pritchard 2007).

China's economic strength was highlighted by the Beijing Olympics, where an estimated budget of $44 billion was lavished on a carefully controlled and choreographed games designed to reinforce China's burgeoning soft power (Beech 2008). The success of Chinese athletes and of the games themselves have increased China's prestige, and so the likelihood that other states will aspire to follow its example (Nye 2004). Already the so-called Beijing consensus offers an alternative development model, particularly in Africa and the Middle East, where Chinese respect for sovereignty and rhetoric of non-interference is beginning to trump Washington's model of economic openness and political liberalisation (Thompson 2005; Springborg 2008).

We should, however, be cautious not to over-estimate the impact of Chinese growth, since the US economy remains strong. It remains the largest national economy in the world, as well as being ranked by the World Economic Forum as the world's most competitive economy, with productivity growth over the last decade a full percentage point higher than the European average. The United States is dominant in higher education and emerging technologies and retains the dynamism of immigration (Zakaria 2008). Furthermore, China does not appear to be immune from the current economic crisis, with notions that emerging markets might 'decouple' from a US-led recession looking increasing far-fetched (Bennett 2008). So although even the most pessimistic expect China's growth to remain well ahead of that of the United States, China is still a long way from becoming the most powerful economic actor, and its fortunes remain bound up with those of the United States.

The sheer size of the American economy also allows it to sustain simply massive military spending, which totalled $547 billion in 2007. The defence budget accounts for only around 4 per cent of GDP, but this is a staggering 45 per cent of all military spending worldwide, a military dominance that is unprecedented in world history. Despite having increased military expenditures by 59 per cent in real terms since 2001, the burden of military spending is less than it was during previous peak spending years in the post-World War II period (Kennedy 2008).

Militarily, China continues to invest, increasing its military spending threefold over the past decade (Stålenheim *et al.* 2008). It now accounts for 5 per cent of world military spending, which at just 2.1 per cent of GDP can be increased still further. Yet China has not focused solely on expanding its coercive capabilities. China's growing power has brought with it real political influence, particularly in its relationship with ASEAN, the Association of Southeast Asian Nations, which caught the United States unaware and at a stroke put American dominance in East Asia in question (Mahbubani 2008). Indeed, while America's focus has been on the Middle East since 2001, some analysts have noted how its inattentiveness in Asia has hastened the arrival of the Asian Century, centred around the military and economic power of China, India, Japan and South Korea (Kaplan 2007).

However, it is not just in Eurasia where American dominance is increasingly in question. The war on terror and the issues of China and Russia have led the United States to take its eye off the ball in Latin America, perhaps assuming that the Monroe Doctrine was a perpetual condition. Venezuela's hostile ideological petro-diplomacy reflects anti-American sentiment in the region and broader disillusionment with democratic politics, a situation that is allowing China to expand its interests in Latin America (Hakim 2006). Within the region itself, while Brazil and Mexico's growth has yet to really take off, they are expected to be the world's fourth and fifth largest economies by 2050 (Wilson and Stupnytska 2007).

Given all these measures, America's position relative to the rest of the world is clearly not as dominant as it was in the early 1990s. Yet capabilities and alignments tell us only part of the story. The real issue is not simply how much power you seem to have, but how much influence and freedom of action that power gives you.

Both neo-imperial notions of American dominance and the recent discussions of decline assume that power is intrinsic to capabilities, that those resources of power that we can measure translate directly into power *per se*. During the Cold War zero-sum relationships abounded within the framework of a diametrically opposed global bipolarity. In military capabilities, economic strength and ideological success, capabilities did essentially translate into power, because one side's gain was necessarily the other's loss. However, this strong relationship between capabilities and power was an empirical one, not a logical one. No less a profound – if too often overlooked – thinker on international relations as Raymond Aron understood that political power is not absolute, that it is fundamentally a human relationship in which men apply power to their fellow creatures, and that therefore our measures of power are approximate and the factors that bestow power change (Aron 1966: 47–53).

In the post-Cold War world the aims of actors are more diffuse and the relationships between them less clearly defined. Released from the necessity to see all of international politics through the prism of the global conflict, actors may act for security, for power itself – 'the intoxication of ruling' – for glory, for ideas (ibid.: 73–6). That crucial human relationship of power and resistance no longer has embedded in it the mechanics of bipolar structure, which automatically conferred upon the actions of great powers the role of conqueror or legitimate sovereign. In the post-Cold War world, great powers seeking to apply their power to their fellow men need to generate their own legitimacy, having lost the animating greater struggle through which they could contextualise and justify themselves.

It appears then that both the neo-imperialists and the declinists miss the point. In both being wedded to Cold War notions of power, the neo-imperialists wrongly assume that America's military and economic dominance can translate into effective policy, whereas the declinists assume that the failure of those policies and the rise of others means that America is in decline.

The reality is that what power is and the ways in which states are able to use it have changed greatly in the past twenty years. The world has become flatter – not in the sense that Friedman considered globalised economics to be taking place on a level playing field but in the sense that states are less able to 'put their power down' and so the balance of power itself matters less. The United States has found that military hardware cannot be relied on to simply crush resistance, particularly in a world where global communications serve the needs of resistance far more effectively than they serve governments. Since nuclear weapons have effectively rendered great power war obsolete, asymmetry is now the dominant mode of military conflict, eroding not only the usefulness of military power but also the legitimacy of its use, in that modern militaries pitted against civilians and irregulars swiftly becomes seen as bullying. In economics, the universal acceptance of free market capitalism as the organising principle of globalisation has created a level of interdependence that renders trade competition counterproductive and creates significant barriers to the use of economic power, even raising the possibility of mutually assured economic destruction. These new social imperatives which flatten out traditional power disparities have rendered the notion of compulsion virtually obsolete. States and populations no longer regard the exercise of military force as a means of defending or promoting national interests. The tools of power that the imperial narratives of the 1990s focused on are less effective than we thought, but that truth is not limited to the United States.

A second dynamic that is at work in this debate is that the promising illusions of neo-imperialism bring with them the spectre of decline. To the extent that the United States has been unable to succeed as the empire it was thought to be, we perceive American power to be in decline. The reality, of course, is that America was never as powerful as the neo-imperialists would have had us believe, nor is its power now so eroded, something that we can understand when we consider the unique historical nature of the American Empire.

After 1945, America had embedded much of its national power in the western order, which after the collapse of the rival communist system became the global order. This order had been based on economic openness and cooperative management through liberal democratic institutions (Ikenberry 1996). The American Empire that emerged after the collapse of the Soviet Union was therefore, in spite of its overwhelming military dominance, one that was based on structural power and the creation of international norms rather than the coercive use of national power. In a sense, the American Empire was one in which the unipolar power had prevented itself from acting imperially solely for its own interests, because to do so was to undermine the very system that sustained it. Instead, American imperial power could be used to sustain the system itself, something that it did largely with the consent of other states, a sanction that ranged from enthusiastic bandwagoning to acceptance of a *fait accompli*. Where states made attempts to undermine or revise the system the use of American power was justified not by the protection of US interests but by the maintenance of the public good of international order. That states accepted that the United States was constrained in this way explains the failure of others to engage in military build-ups to challenge American hegemony. Thus the American national interest, as the dominant power, was to exercise that power cautiously and only in pursuit of the interests of the international system, since by doing so the United States could ease others' perceptions of threat and prevent the emergence of aspiring great powers.

Of course, the disconnectedness of power and capabilities and the maintenance of American power through its exercise in pursuit of systemic rather than national interests are logics that apply differently in peacetime from how they do in wartime, as evidenced by the zero-sum relationships of the Cold War. Yet for all the talk of global war in the aftermath of 9/11, and the profound way in which those events continue to animate American politics, the notion of a war on terror has not created a new global war paradigm which justifies the accumulation and use of national power. So when the United States was perceived over Iraq to be acting in pursuit of its own interests rather than the interests of international stability, it forfeited the acquiescence to its power that had sustained it, and released the resistance that had been calmed.

So where next for American foreign policy in such world? In its dying days the Bush Administration appears to have been recanting its imperial ways and advocating a return to a more limited, realist conception of the national interest (Rice 2008). Certainly America seems likely to be haunted by Iraq for some time, and with the need to reinvigorate the economy at home in the wake of the credit crunch, there is unlikely to be much willingness to see American power as the answer to many of the world's problems. Having said that, those in Europe who hope for a full-scale reversal of US foreign policy are certain to be disappointed. Bush's foreign policy is not so far out of step with American history as many believe, and the foreign policy narrative in the United States continues to be constructed around the events of 9/11.

The challenge for the United States is to re-establish its legitimacy as the sustainer of its own system. That will require a foreign policy that relies more on alliances, and we have already seen an effort to reengage European elites, although at the popular level much more needs to be done as anti-Americanism is more enduring than many believe (Cox 2008). In this, and in a broader effort to unify Western policy towards Russia in particular, the United States retains many of the advantages of empire. Its liberal political values remain by far the most animating ideas on the world stage – one cannot imagine a candidate to lead the Chinese Communist Party being met by a crowd of 200,000 in Berlin. The international system remains the American system, and there are no realistic challengers to it, with even the autocracies of Russia and China now fully engaged with and constrained by global capitalism. Whether you term it structural power or hegemonic power, the basic elements of the international system are set up to favour the means and ends of the United States (Strange 1988; Mead 2004: 25). Fundamentally, nothing has emerged to replace the reliance upon American leadership in the major issues of international relations. Whether that leadership can once more be accepted rather than resisted is the challenge that the new incumbent of the White House will face.

References

Aron, R. (1966) *Peace and War: A Theory of International Relations*, London: Weidenfeld and Nicolson.

Bacevich, A.J. (2005) *The New American Militarism: How Americans Are Seduced by War*, New York: Oxford University Press.

Beech, H. (2008) 'The Lessons of the Beijing Olympics', *Time*.

Bennett, T. (2008) 'Is China's Miracle Economy Heading for a Fall?', *Money Week*, 396.

Bolton, J.R. (2000) 'Should We Take Global Governance Seriously?', *Chicago Journal of International Law*, 1: 205–23.

Buzan, B. (2008) 'A Leader Without Followers? The United States in World Politics after Bush', *International Politics*, 45: 554–70.

Colombani, J.-M. (2001) 'We Are All Americans', *Le Monde*, 10 September.

Cox, M. (2008) 'Europe's Enduring Anti-Americanism', *Current History*, 107: 231–5.

Dodge, T. (2005) 'Iraqi Transitions: From Regime Change to State Collapse', *Third World Quarterly*, 26.

Evans-Pritchard, A. (2007) 'China Threatens "Nuclear Option" of Dollar Sales', *The Telegraph*, 10 August.

Freedman, L. (2006) 'The Transformation of Strategic Affairs', *Aldephi Papers*, 379.

Friedman, T.L. (2006) 'The First Law of Petropolitics', *Foreign Policy*, May/June.

Fukuyama, F. (1992) *The End of History and the Last Man*, London: Hamish Hamilton.

Greenway, H.D.S. (2008) 'America Botches Georgia', *International Herald Tribune*, 19 August.

Haass, R. (2008) 'U.S. Foreign Policy in a Nonpolar World', *Foreign Affairs*, 87: 44–56.

Hakim, P. (2006) 'Is Washington Losing Latin America?' *Foreign Affairs*, January/February.

Hoffmann, S.H. (1978) *Primacy or World Order: American Foreign Policy since the Cold War*, New York: McGraw-Hill.

Ikenberry, G. J. (1996) 'The Myth of Postwar Chaos', *Foreign Affairs*, 75: 79–91.

—— (2008) 'The Rise of China and the Future of the West: Can the Liberal System Survive?', *Foreign Affairs*, January/February.

Kagan, R. (1998) 'The Benevolent Empire', *Foreign Policy*, 111: 24–35.

Kaplan, R.D. (2007) 'Lost at Sea', *New York Times*, 21 September.

Kennedy, P.M. (1988) *The Rise and Fall of the Great Powers: Economic Change and Military Conflict from 1500 to 2000*, London: Unwin Hyman.

—— (2008) 'The Power Game', *LSE Magazine*, 20.

Krauthammer, C. (2004) 'Democratic Realism: An American Foreign Policy for a Unipolar World', 2004 Irving Kristol Lecture. American Enterprise Institute.

Kristol, W. and Kagan, R. (1996) 'Toward a Neo-Reaganite Foreign Policy', *Foreign Affairs*, 75: 18–32.

Kupchan, C.A. (1994) *The Vulnerability of Empire*, Ithaca, NY: Cornell University Press.

—— (1998) 'After Pax Americana: Benign Power, Regional Integration, and the Sources of a Stable Multipolarity', *International Security*, 23: 40–79.

Layne, C. (2006) 'Impotent Power? If America Is the World's Only Superpower, Why Can't It Seem to Get Anything Done?', *The National Interest*, 85.

Leonard, M. (2005) 'Ascent of Europe', *Prospect*.

Lundestad, G. (1986) 'Empire by Invitation? The United States and Western Europe, 1945–52', *Journal of Peace Research*, 23: 263–77.

Mahbubani, K. (2008) 'Welcome to the Asian Century', *Current History*, 107: 195–200.

Mead, W.R. (2004) *Power, Terror, Peace, and War: America's Grand Strategy in a World at Risk*, New York: Knopf.

Muravchik, J. (1991) *Exporting Democracy: Fulfilling America's Destiny*, Washington, DC: American Enterprise Institute for Public Policy Research.

Nye, J.S. (2008) 'The Olympics and Chinese Soft Power', *The Huffington Post*, 24 August.

Posen, B. (2003) 'Command of the Commons: The Military Foundation of U.S. Hegemony', *International Security*, 28: 5–46.

Rice, C. (2008) 'Rethinking the National Interest: American Realism for a New World', *Foreign Affairs*, 87.

Rosett, C. (2008) 'Georgia and the American Cowboy', *National Review*. Online.

Russett, B. (1985) 'The Mysterious Case of Vanishing Hegemony; or, Is Mark Twain Really Dead?' *International Organization*, 39: 207–31.

Snyder, J.L. (1991) *Myths of Empire: Domestic Politics and International Ambition*, Ithaca, NY: Cornell University Press.

Springborg, R. (2008) 'From Washington to Beijing: In Search of a Development Model', in *The Middle East in London*, Dec. 2007–Jan. 2008: 3–4.

Stålenheim, P., Perdomo, C. and Sköns, E. (2008) 'Military Expenditure', in *Sipri Yearbook 2008*, Oxford: Oxford University Press.

Strange, S. (1988) 'The Future of the American Empire', *Journal of International Affairs*, 42.

Thompson, D. (2005) 'China's Soft Power in Africa: From the "Beijing Consensus" to Health Diplomacy', *China Brief*, 5.

Waltz, K. (1991) 'America as a Model for the World? A Foreign Policy Perspective', *PS: Political Science and Politics*, 24: 667–70.

Wilson, D. and Stupnytska, A. (2007) 'The N-11: More Than an Acronym', *Global Economics Paper*, 153, New York: Goldman Sachs.

Wohlforth, W.C. (1999) 'The Stability of a Unipolar World', *International Security*, 24: 5–41.

Zakaria, F. (2008) 'The Future of American Power: How America Can Survive the Rise of the Rest', *Foreign Affairs*, May/June.

18 Internationally recognized core labor standards under the George W. Bush Administration

Christopher Candland[1]

This chapter examines the direction that the administration of George W. Bush (2001–9) has taken regarding the long-standing US commitment to the promotion of internationally recognized core labor standards (hereafter, core labor standards). US headlines and public discussions since September 2001 have been dominated by the war in Iraq, the "war on terror," and other "national security" issues. While media and public attention has focused on the Administration's initiatives to promote the security of the state, the Bush Administration has quietly undermined the ability of the US government to protect the security of US workers. The Administration has negotiated "free trade" agreements with three times as many governments as have all previous US administrations combined.[2] Each of these agreements includes a chapter on labor, but effectively strips the US government of its ability to enforce the internationally recognized core labor standards.

The chapter focuses on promotion of core labor standards through two US government activities: trade agreements, negotiated by the US Trade Representative (USTR) and enacted by the US Congress, and labor diplomacy, engaged in by the US Department of State. Specifically, the chapter considers the impact of the Trade Act of 2002 on US promotion of core labor standards and examines the Administration's use of the federal Advisory Committee on Labor Diplomacy, the central body for the coordination of US labor diplomacy activities. The study also considers the place of core labor standards in the US administration of Iraq after 2003.

The chapter finds that the George W. Bush Administration, with the support of key pro-trade Democrats, weakened the ability of the US government to protect core labor standards at home and to promote core labor standards abroad.[3] Under previous administrations, trade sanctions (or threat of sanctions) had been used unilaterally and inequitably but also effectively. Trade agreements negotiated under the Bush Administration include language on labor but discard effective enforcement mechanisms. Additionally, the Bush Administration has blocked the work of the Department of State in advancing core labor standards.

Core labor standards

Since the middle of the nineteenth century, and with greater clarity since the founding of the International Labor Organization (ILO) at the Paris Peace Conference in 1919, governments, typically prompted by workers' representatives, have advocated for basic and uniform standards for terms of employment and conditions of work. The business, labor, and governmental representatives that are members of the ILO have negotiated more than 180 conventions. Eight of these conventions are now internationally recognized to constitute five core labor standards[4] (Table 18.1).

The foundation of internationally recognized core labor standards is freedom from forced labor. The principle that no human should be made to work against his or her will (i.e., that forced labor is inhumane) is the basis of the other internationally recognized core labor standards – freedom to associate, freedom to bargain collectively for terms of employment and conditions of work, freedom from discrimination in employment and at work, and freedom from child labor.

These internationally recognized labor standards are no more than fundamental human rights at the workplace and in employment relations. That is, they are based on the right to control one's own body, the right to associate freely, and the right of equal treatment under the law. The standard that has received the most recent public attention relates to freedom from child labor. That standard belongs to a later generation of ILO activity than the other fundamental labor standards. It also appears to be based on a different principle, the notion that the innocence of childhood should be protected. However, as children are not as physically or psychologically as well equipped as adults to defend (or know) their own interests, freedom from child labor is based on the same principle as freedom from forced labor (i.e., the freedom of will).

The ILO's 1998 Declaration on Fundamental Rights at Work incorporates all five of these internationally recognized core labor standards. The Declaration commits all member states of the ILO to recognize and promote these standards, whether or not governments have ratified the specific conventions that define these standards.[5] Critics of the inclusion of internationally recognized core labor standards in trade agreements occasionally claim that such standards include a mandatory universal minimum wage, which would be prejudicial to employment in low income countries. Accordingly, it is worth noting that there is no ILO core labor standard for a global minimum wage.

Trade agreements

In most economies, including in the US economy, most workers serve or produce for the domestic market. Why, then, is there such attention to labor standards in trade agreements? One reason is that standards can be transferred through a demonstration effect. A change of standards in one sector can have an effect on another sector even if there is no economic connection between the two sectors. Further, standards are inherent in all economic behavior. Standards are found in environmental practices, intellectual property protection, levels of hygiene and sanitation, methods for dispute settlement, and anywhere else that there are measures and norms for quality and behavior. Accordingly, every US trade agreement contains several chapters, each specifying the standards that will be followed in each area (e.g., how inputs define a good's

Table 18.1 The core labor standards

Standards	ILO Conventions	Basis
1 Freedom from Forced Labor	29 (1930) and 105 (1957)	Freedom of Will
2 Freedom to Form Unions	87 (1948) and 98 (1949)	Freedom of Association
3 Freedom to Bargain Collectively	98 (1949)	Freedom of Association
4 Freedom from Discrimination	100 (1951) and 111 (1958)	Equality of Individuals
5 Freedom from Child Labor	138 (1973) and 182 (1999)	Freedom of Will

country of origin). Whether trade agreements explicitly address specific standards or not, they do affect standards because an exchange of goods and services is also a negotiation of the terms under which such goods and services are produced and provided. Trade is not merely the exchange of goods and services; trade is also the normalization of the standards – environmental, hygienic, labor, and other – under which these goods and services are produced and provided.

There is a long history of US "aggressive unilateralism" in protecting labor standards domestically and in improving core labor standards internationally, especially in the years immediately following World War I and then the years immediately following World War II.[6] In the past two decades, internationally recognized core labor standards have been promoted through five US trade laws. These are the Generalized System of Preferences Renewal Act of 1984; the Overseas Private Investment Corporation Renewal Act of 1985; the Caribbean Basin Economic Recovery Act of 1986; the Omnibus Trade and Competitiveness Act of 1988, and the Trade Act of 2002.

Standards that are enforced through trade sanction or through the threat of trade sanction are coercive, unilateral, and applied unevenly and unfairly. They are understandably not widely supported by governments that might be targets of these US laws.[7] The pursuit of core labor standards through trade agreements, accordingly, has been criticized as aggressively unilateral and thus contrary to principles of international law. According to Philip Alston,

> The form in which the standards are stated is so bald and inadequate as to have the effect of providing a *carte blanche* to the relevant U.S. government agencies, thereby enabling them to opt for whatever standards they choose to set in any given situation.
>
> (Alston 1993: 7–8)

As labor rights provisions of US trade law require a finding by the executive branch, US trade law on labor standards is likely to be used for foreign policy objectives rather than principled promotion of core labor standards. Indeed, the first countries to lose US. Generalized System of Preference status, in 1987, for alleged neglect of core labor standards were Paraguay, Nicaragua, and Romania. These were not the countries with the world's worst records on labor standards at the time. They were rather countries that were targeted by the Reagan Administration for foreign policy reasons. More recently, banana plantations in Guatemala, where core labor standards are higher than in neighboring Ecuador, were threatened in 2002 with Generalized System of Preference trade sanctions by Bush's then USTR, Robert Zoellick.

At the same time, trade sanctions and the threat of sanctions are often effective. When, for example, the United Mine Workers of America and the State of Alabama pressured the US Government to ban the import of South African coal in 1974 as it was produced "by indentured labour under penal sanction," the Government of South Africa "repealed several penal provisions from its labour legislation" (Charnovitz 1987: 570). More recently, governments in Guatemala, India, Indonesia, Pakistan, and Sri Lanka have answered US allegations of core labor standard violations by passing new labor legislation, improving existing labor legislation, or increasing inspection and enforcement.[8] Even the implicit threat of loss of US market access is effective. It was in part in response to the visit to India by then US Commerce Secretary Ron Brown that India's National Commission on Child Labor was established. Senator Harkin's Child Labor Deterrence and Child Labor Free Consumer Information Bills have not been passed into law. Nevertheless, these bills have helped to remove hundreds of thousands of children from factory work.

The manner in which labor standard violations findings are made, rather than the attachment of labor standards to US trade law, introduces the danger that the law will be used as a weapon of foreign policy by the executive branch rather than as instruments for the principled promotion of core labor standards. Like other human rights provisions of US law, the legal mechanisms for promoting international standards are activated by elected politicians and unelected officials.

The "aggressive unilateralism" of governments in net import-oriented industrialized countries is neither consensual nor equitable. However, it does encourage governments in export-oriented, industrializing countries to improve core labor standards. Government officials in industrializing countries that are likely targets sometimes protest that their values are different from those of the United States.[9] Nevertheless, while targeted governments also strengthen their labor laws.

Core labor standards in Bush Administration trade agreements

The promotion of core labor standards in trade agreements is not as much a partisan issue as is often portrayed by partisans. Some Republicans have been supportive of effective mechanisms for promoting core labor standards. Some Democrats have been opposed to such mechanisms. The Omnibus Trade Act of 1983, which provides organized labor with more leverage on core labor standards than any other piece of multilateral US trade legislation, was signed into law by then President Reagan, a Republican. The New Trade Policy Template Act of 2007, discussed below, which weakens the enforcement mechanisms for protecting and promoting core labor standards, was advocated by the House Democrat leadership.

The George W. Bush Administration was not expected to take initiatives to promote core labor standards. The Bush Administration was outspoken against such "restrictions," backing the US Chamber of Commerce, which vowed to have the standards established in the United States–Jordan Free Trade Agreement removed. Nevertheless, neither the Bush White House nor Republican Senators amended the United States–Jordan Free Trade Agreement. Approved in September 2001, unanimously, it is the first US trade agreement to include core labor standards in the text of the agreement.[10] The Agreement was negotiated under the second Clinton Administration. "In the wake of the 11 September attacks," quoting Hong Kong's *Business Alert*, "the US ... moved this bill forward to demonstrate support for a key Middle Eastern ally."[11] It is the United States' second bilateral free trade agreement. The first free trade agreement was with Israel.

The Trade Act of 2002 was passed by one vote in the US House of Representatives on December 6, 2001, and by the US Senate on May 23, 2002. The Trade Act of 2002 gave the President Trade Promotion Authority, an authority lent by the Congress to the President in ways that the authors of the US Constitution had apparently not contemplated.[12] Under the Trade Promotion Authority, provided by the Trade Act of 2002, the Congress limits its authority to voting on negotiated treaties in whole, without amendment.

Included in the Trade Act are "overall trade negotiating objectives," negotiating guidelines for the USTR. These objectives include to "promote respect for worker rights and the rights of children consistent with core labor standards of the ILO" and to "seek provisions in trade agreements under which parties to those agreements strive to ensure that they do not weaken or reduce the protections afforded in domestic ... labor laws as an encouragement for trade."[13] However, the dispute settlement and enforcement mechanisms are so weak that they have yet to be used.

Under the Trade Act of 2002, each of the free trade agreements negotiated by the Bush Administration requires that the Administration report on the impact of these agreements on labor standards in the United States and in the foreign country with which these free trade agreements are negotiated. Further, the Trade Act of 2002 requires the Administration to verify to Congress that the governments enjoying these free trade agreements do not lower their labor standards in an attempt to improve their trade advantage. The Trade Act also requires the administration to produce reports on labor trends in the United States and in the countries with which the US government negotiates free trade agreements. The Act requires the President to produce three reports on: (1) labor rights in the countries of governments with which the USTR negotiates any agreement; (2) the impact that any agreement will have on US employment and US labor markets, produced "sufficiently early in the negotiating process to inform the development of negotiating positions;" and (3) foreign law on child labor of the government with which the USTR is negotiating.[14] This reporting was demanded by Congressional Democrats for their support of the Trade Act. The Administration failed to produce these reports early enough in the negotiating process for the Congress to consider them. Moreover, the reports that were produced were not meaningful. They were compilations of existing law without any consideration of the adequacy of these laws or attention to whether these laws are being followed. For violations of labor standards under the Trade Act are defined narrowly, only as a weakening of existing law to gain a trade advantage. The adequacy and implementation of the law are not relevant under the Trade Act. The USTR's own advisory committee on labor reported that

> the agreements [negotiated under the Trade Act] actually step backwards from existing labor rights provisions in the U.S. ... only one single labor rights obligation – the obligation for a country to enforce its own labor laws – is actually enforceable ... All of the other obligations contained in the labor chapters, many of which are drawn from Congressional negotiating objectives, are explicitly not covered by the dispute settlement system and thus completely unenforceable.
> (Labor Advisory Committee for Trade Negotiations
> and Trade Policy 2003: 5–6)

The Trade Act 2002 and its 2005 renewal seriously weakened the ability of the United States government to promote core labor standards. Members of the Democratic Party and their staff have been complicit in the Administration's weakening of core labor standards. Indeed, it was the proposal of Democratic Party staff that penalties be lowered from sanctions to fines, to be held in escrow while the dispute is resolved. The US government had not initiated a dispute with any of the fourteen trade partners with which the George W. Bush administration has signed a free trade agreement, despite violations of core labor standards in many of these countries. Indeed, the

Administration has negotiated an agreement with the government of Columbia, which is alleged to have been involved in more assassinations of trade union leaders than all other governments combined (ICFTU 2006: 110–18). The Bush Administration tied passage of the Troubled Assets Relief Program Act to passage of the Columbia–United States Free Trade Agreement.

US labor diplomacy

Trade agreements are not the only place that the US government attempts to promote core labor standards. "Labor diplomacy" is a phrase coined by officials in the Department of State to refer to US foreign policy goals, such as the promotion of democratic polities and market economies, that can be advanced by promoting independent unions and core labor standards. The US government has been involved in labor diplomacy for decades. The labor attaché program was initiated in 1943 (Friszman 1965). The Department of State, through its Bureau of Democracy, Human Rights, and Labor, and the Department of Labor, through its Bureau of International Labor Affairs, have a long-standing cooperative relationship in the field of international labor affairs. Fifty foreign-service officers hold labor portfolios.

For most of US labor diplomacy's history, the work of US unions overseas suited the professed foreign policy aims of the US government. Both the executive and legislative branch had authority over labor diplomacy activities. The executive branch, however, improved its purchase on US unions in the early 1960s to the late 1980s. The character of US labor diplomacy changed because of John Sweeney's election in 1995 as President of the American Federation of Labor-Congress of Industrial Organizations (AFL-CIO). The AFL-CIO no longer took its position on international issues from the US government. The AFL-CIO's International Affairs Department and its regional Free Labor Institutes – African-American Labor Center, the American Institute for Free Labor Development, the Asian-American Free Labor Institute, and the Free Trade Union Institute (for Europe) – were reorganized as American Centers for International Labor Solidarity.

Hundreds of advisory committees serve the federal government. More than 40,000 individuals have volunteered for this work, a remarkable feature of US public affairs. These committees may be established by the President, the Secretary or director of a federal department or agency, or the Congress. The Federal Advisory Committee Act of 1972 specifies procedures for advisory committees. The Act requires that all committees operate in the public. Meetings must be open to the public and announced in the Federal Registry at least 15 days in advance. The General Services Administration monitors advisory committee activities.

Members of these committees provide a valuable public service. They are not paid for their work. They volunteer their time and expertise because they believe that their advice might positively influence government policy. The bureaus to which advisory committees report typically hold these committees in high regard, seeing these advisory committees as critical both to the formulation and legitimacy of these policies. The secretary or director of a department or agency to which a federal advisory committee advises might ask the committee to suggest policy initiatives, to make propose policy, or to recommend administrative or staffing changes.

More than a dozen advisory committees serve the Department of State. The first of these was the Advisory Commission on Public Diplomacy, established by the US

Congress in 1948. More recently appointed advisory committees include the Advisory Committee on Democracy Promotion and the Advisory Committee on Transformational Diplomacy, each established by Secretary Rice in 2006. Not surprisingly, the creation of advisory committees and the work to which they are tasked reflect the priorities of the administration or Congress under which they are appointed.

Secretary of State Madeline Albright created the Advisory Committee on Labor Diplomacy in May 1999 to advise the US President and the Secretary of State on international labor affairs. The Committee's creation was in large part the attempt of the Clinton Administration to repair relations with organized labor after President Clinton's promotion of the North American Free Trade Agreement over the objections of organized labor. (See Stigliani 2000: 181–3.) The Committee is a group of "prominent persons with expertise in the area of international labor policy and labor diplomacy" (ACLD 1999). Secretary Albright chose Thomas Donahue to chair the Committee. Donahue was a President and long-time Treasurer of the AFL-CIO. Other members of the committee include Linda Chavez-Thompson, Executive Vice President of the AFL-CIO; Frank Doyle, former Executive President of the General Electric Company; Anthony Freeman, then the Director of the International Labor Organization's Washington, D.C. Office; John Joyce, President of the International Union of Bricklayers and Allied Craftworkers; William Lucy, Secretary-Treasurer of the American Federation of State, County and Municipal Employees; Ray Marshall, former Secretary of Labor and Professor of Economic and Public Policy at the University of Texas, Austin; and John Sweeney, President of the AFL-CIO.

The Committee delivered its first report to President Clinton and Secretary Albright in 2000. The report, "A World of Decent Work: Labor Diplomacy for the New Century" (ACLD 2003), argued that independent unions and workers' rights are a necessary foundation for the promotion of democracy worldwide, a professed US foreign policy goal. It also made a number of policy and staffing recommendations to the President and Secretary of State, many of which were implemented.

Secretary of State Colin Powell, who succeeded Secretary Albright, was supportive of the work of the Advisory Committee and renewed its charter in 2001. The Committee delivered its second report to President Bush and Secretary Powell in December 2001. The report, "Labor Diplomacy: In the Service of Democracy and Security" (ACLD 2001), made the argument that independent unions and workers' rights would advance democracy and thereby promote security. It also made a number of recommendations to the President and Secretary of State, some of which were adopted and implemented.

The Committee prepared a third report, as requested by Secretary Powell, "A Labor Diplomacy Strategy for the Muslim World" (ACLD 2004). A final draft of the report was to be issued and discussed by the committee in April 2004. The public was notified and invited to participate through the Federal Registry, in accordance with the Federal Advisory Committee Act of 1972. The report suggested ways that US government overseas work and international policy could improve adherence to law and improve US and foreign labor trends. The main concerns of the report were promoting freedom of association, generating employment, empowering women workers, and protecting migrant workers.

The draft report included analysis of trends in employment, unemployment, and underemployment; schooling, literacy, and education; observance and monitoring of core labor standards; and other issues of significance to US labor diplomacy in 83 countries. Sources for the report included Labor officers' cables for the workers' rights sections of the Department of State's annual *Country Reports on Human Rights Practices*; responses by labor officers to specific requests for information; conversations with labor officers; and the annual reports of the International Confederation of Free Trade Unions on *Violations of Trade Union Rights*. The Committee also solicited and considered comments from government intelligence analysts and academics. Two work days before the Committee was scheduled to release a draft of its third report which had been announced publicly, as required under public access laws, the White House informed the Committee that it would not be permitted to meet until a review of the credentials of members was conducted. The White House did not conduct a review or make further contact with the Committee.

The White House seems to have treated other federal advisory committees similarly. As the James Hoffa, the President of the International Brotherhood of Teamsters, wrote to President Bush upon his resignation from another advisory Committee, the Advisory Committee on Transformational Diplomacy (ACTPN):

> Initially, I viewed my participation in ACTPN as an opportunity to contribute, on behalf of the labor community, to the formation of United States trade policy. Since my appointment to ACTPN in April of 2003, the Teamsters Union has provided you and the U.S. Trade Representative (USTR) with input on a number of free trade agreements, including CAFTA [The Central American Free Trade Agreement]. However, our advice consistently has been ignored.
>
> (Hoffa 2004)

Disregard for international law was a noteworthy feature of US foreign policy under former President George W. Bush. The experience of the Federal Advisory Committee on Labor Diplomacy suggests that the administration has a similar disregard for domestic law, in this case, the Federal Advisory Committee Act of 1972. The George W. Bush Administration showed disdain not only for those professionals who accepted the government's request that they work, voluntarily, on a federal advisory committee, but also for members of their own cabinet who dared to solicit advice from these professionals.

Disagreeing with the findings of a federal advisory committee is within the right of any administration. Preventing a federal advisory committee from performing its duties, however, is a violation of the law. Although it is difficult to know another's motivations, it is possible that the Committee was permitted to perform its duties until the eve of the release of its 2004 report as a way to penalize then Secretary Powell for having reappointed the committee and supported its work.

A revitalized labor imperialism?

Much of the press on the Advisory Committee on Labor Diplomacy accuses the Committee of being an agent of Bush foreign policy. According to Lee Siu Hin:

> Behind the scenes the AFL-CIO [has] a very close relationship with certain high-ranking members of the US diplomatic and intelligence communities and has directly supported neo-liberal/neo-con policies since World War II, regardless of who has been in the White House. One such beneficiary of behind the scenes AFL-CIO

support is the Advisory Committee on Labor Diplomacy, a little-known agency of the State Department. It was created in May 1999, during the Clinton era, and has become very active since the Bush II presidency.

(Lee 2005)

The Committee has been active since (and before) the administration of George W. Bush. However, it is wrong to argue on that basis alone, as does Lee, that the George W. Bush White House supported this activity.

Kim Scipes claims that union leaders' participation on the Committee indicates "the return of labor imperialism at the highest levels of the federation." Scipes claims that "there are good reasons to believe that under AFL-CIO President John Sweeney, labor's foreign policy has reverted back to 'traditional' labor imperialism" (Scipes 2005). The experience of the Committee, however, contradicts Scipes' claim. The theory that Sweeney's AFL-CIO is engaged in a revitalized "labor imperialism" cannot explain why the White House did not permit the Committee to deliver its third report.

The union representatives on the Committee maintained a healthy suspicion of the Administration. The support of Secretary Powell, the first US Secretary of State to have been a union member, persuaded some committee members that they might be able to influence positively a government that was otherwise hostile to labor rights. The involvement of the AFL-CIO represents the AFL-CIO leadership's attempt to work with the Administration, not its willingness to be controlled by it. The wisdom of the decision to advise an Administration famously unresponsive to public opinion can be questioned. However, that decision does not constitute a revival of AFL-CIO "labor imperialism."

US labor diplomacy and the occupation of Iraq

In spring 2003, the Department of State asked members and staff to the Advisory Committee on Labor Diplomacy to speak to the fifty labor officers attending the annual Labor Officers' Conference on the relevance of "labor diplomacy" to "Iraq and other countries in crisis." Committee members and staff noted that internationally core recognized labor standards in Iraq deserved attention in the late 1970s when Iraq was an ally of the United States and the government of Iraq was involved in enforced disappearances of labor activists and labor organizers. Committee members and staff underscored that employment of Iraqis should be a priority. They also noted that the observance of core labor standards by the Coalition Provisional Authority would be key to successful reconstruction in Iraq.[15]

In spring 2003, after US Operation Shock and Awe in Iraq, the White House solicited federal government employees to work in or on Iraq. The White House asked staff from across the federal government to staff the US occupation of Iraq. US officials worked as shadow secretaries (as acting chiefs, not in the UK sense of opposition) in Bremer's Coalition Provisional Authority, especially the Iraqi Ministry of Social Welfare and Labor. That Ministry was headed by an Iraqi but run by the Assistant USTR for Labor and by the Deputy Assistant Secretary of State Department's Bureau for Democracy, Human Rights, and Labor.[16] The Advisory Committee recommended to these officials that they advocate promoting employment and union rights, including the right to organize, as British officials were doing in the Basra sector. The Committee noted that the British forces in their theatre, had decided to allow

Iraqis in public sector enterprises, especially oil, to unionize. The British reasoned that it would be easier to manage public sector enterprises if there were worker representatives with whom to negotiate. Instead of following the Committee's advice, the US authorities prohibited Iraqi public sector workers from forming unions. Today, trade union leaders are kidnapped and assassinated. Only one federation is legally recognized in Iraq. Trade union finances are controlled by the state.[17] These are not products of the new Iraqi government. These are intended legacies of the Coalition Provisional Authority.

The greatest need of the Iraqis after "the end of major hostilities" was employment. The Advisory Committee and the ILO estimated unemployment in Iraq at near 80 per cent of the economically active population. The Committee advised those involved in the reconstruction efforts in Washington DC and in Baghdad to make employment of Iraqis a priority. Instead of heeding that advice, Halliburton, the no-bid, cost-plus and only US contractor in Iraq, imported workers from South and Southeast Asia. Most of the "third country nationals" were imported from the Philippines, India, Pakistan, Sri Lanka, and Nepal. John Owens, General Foreman of the US Embassy project helped to build five other US embassies. After resigning from the US embassy project in Baghdad in protest, Owens reported that "I've never seen a project more fucked up. Every US labor law was broken" (Phinney 2006).

Halliburton, through its then subsidy, Kellogg, Brown, and Root (KBR), and sub-contractors to KBR, illegally trafficked workers. Workers were told that they were being flown to Kuwait to work there but were flown instead to Baghdad. Contractors confiscated workers' passports. Workers were forced to work overtime without pay. Conditions of work were dangerous. The US contractors routinely violated core labor standards – freedom from discrimination at work, freedom from forced labor, freedom to form unions, and freedom to bargain collectively. These abuses were documented by major US newspapers, including the *Los Angeles Times* and the *New York Times* (e.g., Cha 2004; Rohde 2004).

The future of US support for core labor standards

Before George W. Bush occupied the White House, the United States had two free trade agreements – with Israel and Jordan – and one regional free trade agreement – the North American Free Trade Agreement. Seven and one half years later, the government of the United States has concluded free trade agreements with governments in an additional fifteen countries. The Bush Administration negotiated bilateral agreements with Singapore, Australia, Chile, Bahrain, Morocco, Peru, Columbia, Panama, and South Korea (in order of signing of agreements).[18] The Administration has notified the US Congress, as required by the Trade Act of 2002, to negotiate free trade agreements with the governments of Malaysia, Thailand and the United Arab Emirates. The Administration negotiated a regional agreement with Central America (Costa Rica, Ecuador, El Salvador, Guatemala and Nicaragua) and the Dominican Republic.[19] The Administration attempted to negotiate a free trade agreement with the Southern Africa Customs Union (Botswana, Lesotho, Namibia and South Africa).[20] Governments of the Southern Africa Customs Union, however, withdrew from the negotiations in April 2006 because the US government insisted on including its standard template of chapters, covering agriculture, expropriation, intellectual property, investment, sanitation, services, taxation, telecommunications and other issues, rather than agreeing to negotiate an agreement covering only trade.

The passage of the Central American Free Trade Agreement (CAFTA), in July 2005, made a farce of democratic procedures of government. After the vote had been concluded with the defeat of the CAFTA, the House reopened the vote. One Republican claims that he voted against passage, though his vote was counted in favor. Had his vote been recorded as he wanted, the Agreement, passed by a single vote, would have been defeated a second time. Nancy Pelosi, Democratic Party Leader, referred to the manner in which the CAFTA was passed as an "abuse of power, an unethical way of passing legislation" (*Democracy Now* 2005).

On May 10, 2007, a month before the President's Trade Promotion Authority was to expire, Congressional leaders and the President agreed to a New Trade Policy Template. The Template professedly provides for improved labor in future trade agreements, including those then being negotiated with Colombia, Peru, Panama and South Korea. The promoters of the Template touted their agreement as bipartisan, despite opposition to the Template from most Democrats. The support of the Template by staff of the key pro-trade Democrats in the House Committee on Ways and Means, however, permits the Administration to continue to weaken economic and social standards abroad and in the United States. In response to the weaknesses of the Template, other members of Congress, on June 4, 2008, proposed the Trade Reform, Accountability, Development, and Employment (TRADE) Act.

The New Trade Policy Template of 2007 is ambiguous, seemingly intentionally. The Template appears to restore the US government's concern with core labor standards evident prior to the Trade Act of 2002. However, the Template incorporates the weak disputes settlement and enforcement of the Trade Act. For example, a violation of labor standards, according to the Trade Act, and according to the Template, must involve a consistent pattern of abuse and have a demonstrable positive effect on a foreign government's trade with or investment in the United States. A single abuse, no matter how serious, is not grounds for a dispute. Further, a consistent pattern of abuses is not sufficient grounds for a dispute. Abuses must be designed to advantage a foreign government's investment in and trade with the United States. The Organization for Economic Cooperation and Development's influential study on the issue finds that economies with low regard for core labor standards do not constitute a trade advantage[21] (OECD 1996). The Office of the USTR, in its press release on the Template, assures US exporters that the Template will not be enforced (United States Trade Representative's Office 2007). It reassures US exporters that only governments, not businesses or unions, are authorized to initiate disputes and clarifies that no decisions on a dispute are binding. A government found in violation of a labor standard, the USTR clarifies, may choose to ignore any proposed settlement.

Non-governmental organizations in high and low income countries have fundamental differences over whether trade can and should be used as a vehicle for improvement of core labor standards.[22] The inter-governmental organizations that might enforce observance of core labor standards, the World Bank and the World Trade Organization (WTO), have taken the position that labor standards – unlike other standards – are not trade related. Thus, the chief vehicle for the advance of core labor standards is likely to remain the conventional mechanism whereby domestic constituencies, such as organized labor and labor rights groups, petition their elected representatives and use national legislation to investigate and threaten to impose trade penalties.

Organized labor in the United States has a clear interest in protecting the labor conditions and terms of employment of its membership against the threat of imports produced by workers laboring under lower standards. Organized labor in the United States is often accused of being protectionist. The protection of labor standards, however, is a form of protectionism of which unions may be rightly accused. There is another, less obvious, US constituency for the promotion of core labor standards.

Many US corporations also have an interest in seeing core labor standards promoted internationally. US corporations that respect core labor standards can have trouble competing with foreign corporations that do not. Foreign governments in the countries in which US corporations subcontract for labor and supplies are more likely to monitor, regulate, and target foreign, including US, corporations. The popularity of President Clinton's US Apparel Partnership Initiative with US textile manufacturers suggests that there is a high road to international competitiveness for US corporations even in labor-intensive industries.

In January 1999, the governments of the United States and Cambodia entered into the US–Cambodia Bilateral Textile Agreement. It is the first trade agreement to provide expanded market access as the basis of enforcement of core labor standards. The Agreement has eliminated child labor and forced labor from Cambodian factories that produce textile and apparel for the US market. Further, the Agreement has improved enforcement of other core labor standards, improved labor–management relations, helped to attract investment and create employment, created an effective role for the ILO in monitoring labor standards, strengthened the rule of law, and broadened US public support for trade expansion.

Before the Agreement, the Nike Corporation withdrew its contracts from Cambodian subcontractors when it faced allegations that one of its suppliers used child laborers. Nike has returned to Cambodia because the presence of the ILO ensures that core labor standards are enforced. "Made in Cambodia," Nike's Vice President for Corporate Responsibility Compliance Dusty Kidd argues, might become a label that US clothing firms rely upon to preserve their brand integrity.[23] US corporations, such as Nike, are strong supporters of the Agreement precisely because it includes the ILO, which works with the government of Cambodia to license for export only those factories that adhere to core labor standards.

Greater international economic interdependence is seemingly inevitable. If core labor standards are promoted internationally, it is likely that they will be promoted in the conventional way, not by inter-governmental organizations, such as the World Bank or WTO, not by trans-national alliances of non-governmental organizations, but by unilateral governmental responses to workers' demands that their governments take the high road to greater international economic interdependence. Whether that is possible, of course, depends on whether workers and their representatives have legal mechanisms to demand that foreign corporations not be allowed to run the low road through their country.[24]

Notes

1 The author teaches political science at Wellesley College, MA. As an International Affairs Fellow of the Council on Foreign Relations, he worked as a trade specialist in the US House of Representatives, Subcommittee on Trade, in 2002, and as the senior advisor to the US Department of State's federal Advisory Committee on Labor Diplomacy, from 2003 to 2004. Perspectives presented here are solely those of the author and may not be attributed to the House Subcommittee on Trade, to the Committee on Labor Diplomacy, or to any members or staff of either Committee.

2 As explained below, these agreements are not well described as "free trade" agreements are not free; they impose a single set of rules, entailing compromise and cost; further, they are not merely about trade; they establish rules in non-traded sectors as well.

3 This chapter does not make the case for incorporating labor standards in trade agreements. For economic arguments for incorporating labor standards in trade agreements, see Marshall (2005), Palley (2004), and Polaski (2003).

4 Some distinguish between the right to form trade unions and the right to bargain collectively. By such rekoning there are five internationally recognized core labor standards. Others combine the right to form trade unions and the right to bargain collectively as a single standard and thereby identify four standards. US trade law distinguishes between the right to form trade unions and the right to bargain collectively, omits the freedom from discrimination in employment or at the workplace, and adds a standard related to "acceptable conditions of work with respect to minimum wages, hours, and health and safety." See US House of Representatives, Committee on Ways and Means (2001: 318).

5 The government of the United States is a signatory to only two of the eight ILO Conventions that define the five core core labor standards. However, the government of the United States was an "enthusiastic supporter" of the 1998 ILO Fundamental Declaration. See Marshall (2005: 6).

6 Alston borrows the phrase "aggressive unilateralism" from Jagdish Bhagwati and Hugh Patrick's discussion of Section 301 of the Omnibus Trade Act of 1988. Alston argues that it applies as well to the labor standards provisions of US trade laws. See Alston (1993); Bhagwati and Patrick (1990). On the vagaries of US support for human rights, including human rights at the workplace, see Sikkink (2005).

7 Much of the debate between advocates and opponents of the inclusion of core labor standards in trade agreements has focused on whether such standards distort economic outcomes and serve merely to protect the economic advantage of advanced capitalist economies. Accordingly, much of the debate on the inclusion of core labor standards in trade agreements misses the central issue, namely who decides who is sanctioned for alleged violations of core labor standards.

8 The International Labor Rights Fund petitioned the Office of the US Trade Representative to review labor problems in Guatemala, India, Indonesia, Pakistan, and Sri Lanka. The Office of the US Trade Representative authorized a review. The governments of these countries, in response, amended the offending parts of their labor law.

9 Marshall, in response to the allegation that core labor standards are based on US rather than international values, notes that the ILO Conventions that define core labor standards have been developed by governments, business associations, and labor associations over generations, often without the support of the US representatives at the ILO. See Marshall (2005: 15).

10 The North American Free Trade Agreement includes core labor rights language in side agreements.

11 See Business Alert (2001).

12 Article 1, Section 8 of the US Constitution establishes that "The Congress shall have power ... to regulate commerce with foreign nations." Nowhere in the US Constitution is the Congress given the authority to cede its trade authority to the President.

13 See United States House of Representatives, Subcommittee on Trade (2002).

14 Ibid.

15 The government of Iraq has ratified each of the eight core ILO Conventions, with the exception of Convention 87 on the Freedom of Association and Right to Form Unions.

16 The engagement of the Assistant US Trade Representative for Labor in Iraq might help to explain why the Administration failed to produce the reports required under the Trade Act of 2002.

17 See ICFTU (2007: 357–60).

18 Negotiations with the government of Chile preceded negotiations with the governments of Singapore and Australia. The US Trade Representative slowed its negotiations with the government of Chile as punishment for not supporting the Bush Administration's invasion of Iraq and advanced its negotiations with the governments of Singapore and Australia as a reward for supporting the invasion.

19 The government of the Dominican Republic, the largest trading partner of the United States in the Caribbean, persuaded the US Trade Representative that it should be included in the Central American Free Trade Agreement so as not to be disadvantaged by the market access of the Central American signatories.

20 Former US Trade Representative (now World Bank President) Robert Zoellick referred to his strategy of negotiating multiple bilateral trade agreements, rather than focusing on a global trade agreement, as "competitive liberalization." Critics of this approach argued that a patchwork of bilateral and regional free trade agreements would make more difficult the establishment of an open global trade regime.
21 For similar findings, see Hasnat (2002).
22 On the debate between trade unionists from high-income and low-income over the place of core labor standards in trade agreements, see Candland (1996).
23 Interview with author, November 22, 2002.
24 For details on the argument that the major force for the promotion of core labor standards internationally is the "partnership" of US labor and US corporations working "unilaterally" through the US government, see Candland (2004).

References

ACLD (Advisory Committee on Labor Diplomacy) (1999) "Charter," Washington, DC: US Department of State, May. Online. Available at: http://www.state.gov/g/drl/rls/10045.htm.
—— (2001) "Labor Diplomacy: In the Service of Democracy and Security," Report of the Advisory Committee on Labor Diplomacy to the Secretary of State and the President of the United States," (first report) (December 31) Washington, DC: US Department of State. Online. Available at: http://www.state.gov/g/drl/rls/10043.htm.
—— (2003) "A World of Decent Work: Labor Diplomacy for the New Century. Report of the Advisory Committee on Labor Diplomacy to the Secretary of State and the President of the United States," (second report) (October 10) Washington, DC: US Department of State. Online. Available at: http://www.state.gov/www/global/human_rights/labor/acld_report/acld_toc.html.
—— (2004) "A Labor Diplomacy Strategy for the Muslim World," Report of the Advisory Committee on Labor Diplomacy to the Secretary of State and the President of the United States," (third report) (December) Washington, D.C.: U.S. Department of State.
Alston, Philip (1993) "Labor Rights Provisions in US Trade Law," *Human Rights Quarterly*, 15(1): 1–35.
Bhagwati, Jagdish and Patrick, Hugh (eds) (1990) *Aggressive Unilateralism: America's 301 Trade Policy and the World Trading System*, Ann Arbor, MI: University of Michigan Press.
Business Alert (2001) "Jordan FTA Becomes Law," *Business Alert-US*, 20 (8 October). Online. Available at: http://info.hktdc.com/alert/us0120e.htm.
Candland, Christopher (1996) "Reviewing the Options and Issues: Situating the Debate," *New Political Economy*, 1(2): 260–4.
—— (2004) "How Are International Labor Standards Advanced?," paper presented at the Council on Foreign Relations, October 24. Online. Available at: http://www.candland.info/ILSadvanced.pdf.
Cha, Ariana Eunjung (2004) "Underclass of Workers Created in Iraq: Many Foreign Laborers Receive Inferior Pay, Food and Shelter," *Washington Post*, July 1, A1. Online. Available at: http://www.washingtonpost.com/wp-dyn/articles/A19228–2004Jun30.html.
Charnovitz, Steven (1987) "The Influence of International Labour Standards on the World Trading Regime: A Historical Overview," *International Labour Review*, 126(5). Online. Available at: http://www.geocities.com/charnovitz/ILO.htm.
Democracy Now (2005) "CAFTA Voting Irregularities," July 29. Online. Available at: http://www.democracynow.org/2005/7/29/cafta_voting_irregularities.
Fiszman, Joseph R. (1965) "The Development of Administrative Roles: The Labor Attaché Program of the U. S. Foreign Service," *Public Administration Review*, 25(3): 203–12.
Hasnat, Baban (2002) "The Impact of Core Labor Standards on Exports," *International Business Review*, 11(5): 563–75.
Hoffa, James (2004) "Statement on Resigning from the President's Advisory Committee on Trade Policy and Negotiations," Press Release, Washington, DC: AFL-CIO, June 24 Online. Available at: http://www.globalexchange.org/campaigns/cafta/2105.html.pf.

Human Rights Watch (2007) "The 2007 US Trade Policy Template: Opportunities and Risks for Workers' Rights," Backgrounder, 2, (June). New York: Human Rights Watch. Online. Available at: http://hrw.org/backgrounder/usa/trade0607/index.htm.

ICFTU (International Confederation of Free Trade Unions) (2006) *Annual Survey of Violations of Trade Union Rights 2006*, Brussels: ICFTU. Online. Available at: http://www.icftu.org/www/pdf/survey06/Survey06-EN.pdf.

Labor Advisory Committee for Trade Negotiations and Trade Policy (2003) "The U.S.-Chile Free Trade Agreement," Washington, DC: Labor Advisory Committee for Trade Negotiations and Trade Policy, February 23.

Lee, Siu Hin (2005) "Labor's China Syndrome: AFL-CIO, Solidarity Center, NED, and the Neo-cons – An Unholy Alliance," *Z Magazine*, July/August. Online. Available at: http://www.thirdworldtraveler.com/Labor/Labor_China_NED.html.

Marshall, Ray (2005) "Labor Standards, Human Capital, and Economic Development," Working Paper 271, Washington, DC: Economic Policy Institute, February. Online. Available at: http://www.epi.org/content.cfm/wp271.

McWilliams, Edward (2001) "There's Still a Place for Labor Diplomacy," *Foreign Service Journal*, Washington DC: American Foreign Service Association July/August. Online. Available at: http://www.afsa.org/fsj/julaug/mcwilliamsjulaug01.cfm.

OECD (Organization for Economic Cooperation and Development) (1996) *Trade Employment and Labor Standards: A Study of Core Workers' Rights and International Trade*, Paris: Organization for Economic Cooperation and Development. Online. Available at: http://www.oecd.org/LongAbstract/0,3425,en_2649_201185_1894458_1_1_1_37401,00.html.

Palley, Thomas (2004) "The Economic Case for International Labor Standards," *Cambridge Journal of Economics*, 28(1): 21–36.

Phinney, David (2006) "A U.S. Fortress Rises in Baghdad: Asian Workers Trafficked to Build World's Largest Embassy," Oakland: Corporation Watch. Online. Available at: http://www.corpwatch.org/article.php?id=14173.

Polaski, Sandra (2003) "Trade and Labor Standards: A Strategy for Developing Countries," Washington, DC: Carnegie Endowment for International Peace. Online. Available at: http://www.carnegieendowment.org/pdf/files/Polaski_Trade_English.pdf.

Rohde, David (2004) "Iraq: Indian Contract Workers in Iraq Complain of Exploitation," *New York Times*, May 7. Online. Available at: http://www.nytimes.com/2004/05/07/international/asia/07INDI.html?ex=1218168000&en=c2adaa58620a2c9a&ei=5070.

Scipes, Kim (2005) "Labor Imperialism Redux? The AFL-CIO's Foreign Policy since 1995," *Monthly Review*. Online. Available at: http://www.monthlyreview.org/0505scipes.htm.

Sikkink, Kathryn (2005) "Mixed Signals: The United States and International Human Rights Law," paper presented at the annual meeting of the International Studies Association, Honolulu, March 5. Online. Available at: http://www.allacademic.com/meta/p70301_index.html.

Stigliani, Nicholas A. (2000) "Labor Diplomacy: A Revitalized Aspect of U.S. Foreign Policy in the Era of Globalization," *International Studies Perspectives*, 1(2): 177–94.

—— (2001) "Recasting Labor Diplomacy: Rejoinder to Wilkinson *et al.*," *International Studies Perspectives*, 2(2): 212–19.

United States House of Representatives, Committee on Ways and Means (2001) *Overview and Compilation of U.S. Trade Statutes*, Washington, DC: US Government Printing Office.

United States House of Representatives, Subcommittee on Trade (2002) "Trade Act of 2002," in *Compendium of U.S. Trade Statutes*, Washington, DC: House of Representatives.

United States Trade Representative's Office (2007) *Bipartisan Agreement on Trade Policy: Labor*, May 11. Online. Available at: http://www.ustr.gov/assets/Document_Library/Fact_Sheets/2007/asset_upload_file627_11284.pdf.

Wilkinson, Rorden, Haworth, Nigel and Hughes, Steve (2001) "Recasting Labor Diplomacy: A Comment on Stigliani," *International Studies Perspectives*, 2(2): 207–12.

Index